JAM '10

SETONA MIZUSHIRO

After School Nightmare is a manga that is jam-packed with all my favorite elements. It's got cute stuff. Cruel stuff. Dark stuff embedded in blackness. Round, sparkly, transparent things. Sincerely erotic stuff, vague boundaries, fluttering skirts and long silky hair. Feathers! Keys! Moons! Somehow, I've actually been able to include everything I wanted, so I'm in bliss.

ABOUT THE MANGA-KA

Setona Mizushiro's first real dabble in the world of creating manga was in 1985 when she participated in the publication of a dojinshi (amateur manga). She remained active in the dojinshi world until she debuted in April of 1993 with her short single *Fuyu ga Owarou Toshiteita* (Winter Was Ending) that ran in Shogakukan's *Puchi Comic* magazine. Mizushiro-sensei is well-known for her series *X-Day* in which she exhibits an outstanding ability to delve into psychological issues of every nature. Besides manga, Mizushiro-sensei has an affinity for chocolate, her two cats (Jam and Nene), and round sparkly objects.

SEP

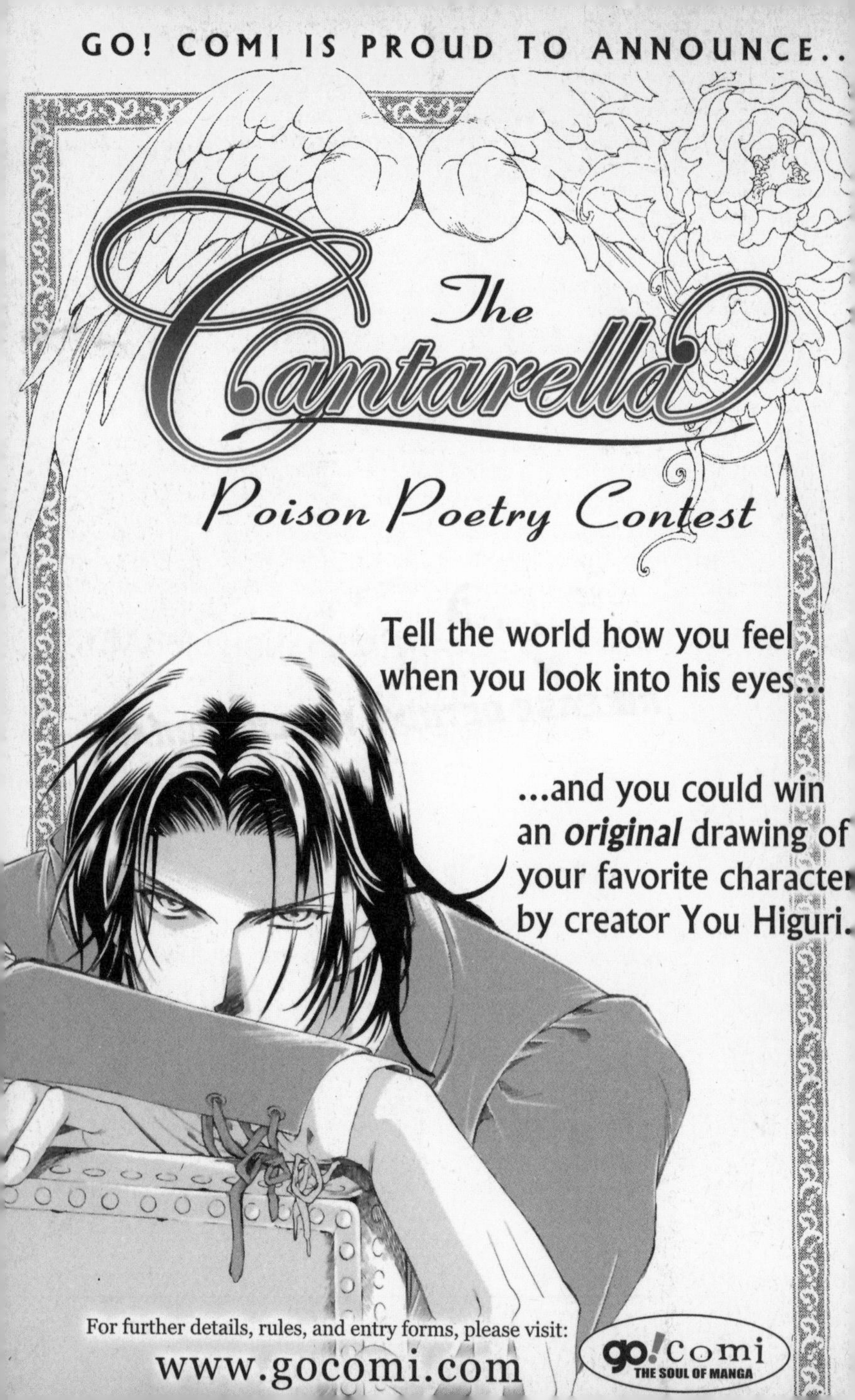
GO! COMI IS PROUD TO ANNOUNCE..
The Cantarella
Poison Poetry Contest
Tell the world how you feel when you look into his eyes...
...and you could win an *original* drawing of your favorite character by creator You Higuri.
For further details, rules, and entry forms, please visit:
www.gocomi.com
go!comi
THE SOUL OF MANGA

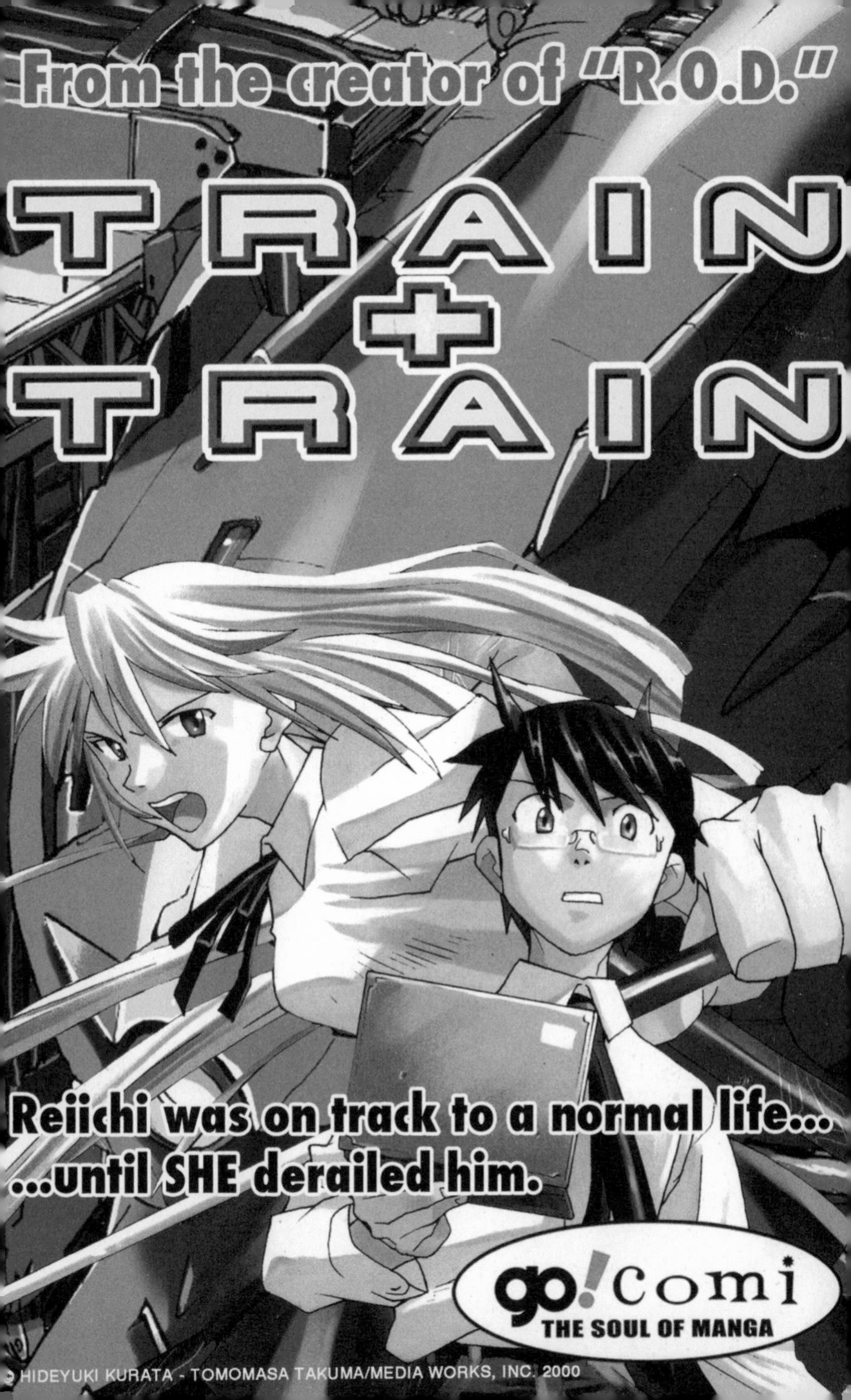
From the creator of "R.O.D."
TRAIN + TRAIN
Reiichi was on track to a normal life...
...until SHE derailed him.
go!comi
THE SOUL OF MANGA
© HIDEYUKI KURATA - TOMOMASA TAKUMA/MEDIA WORKS, INC. 2000

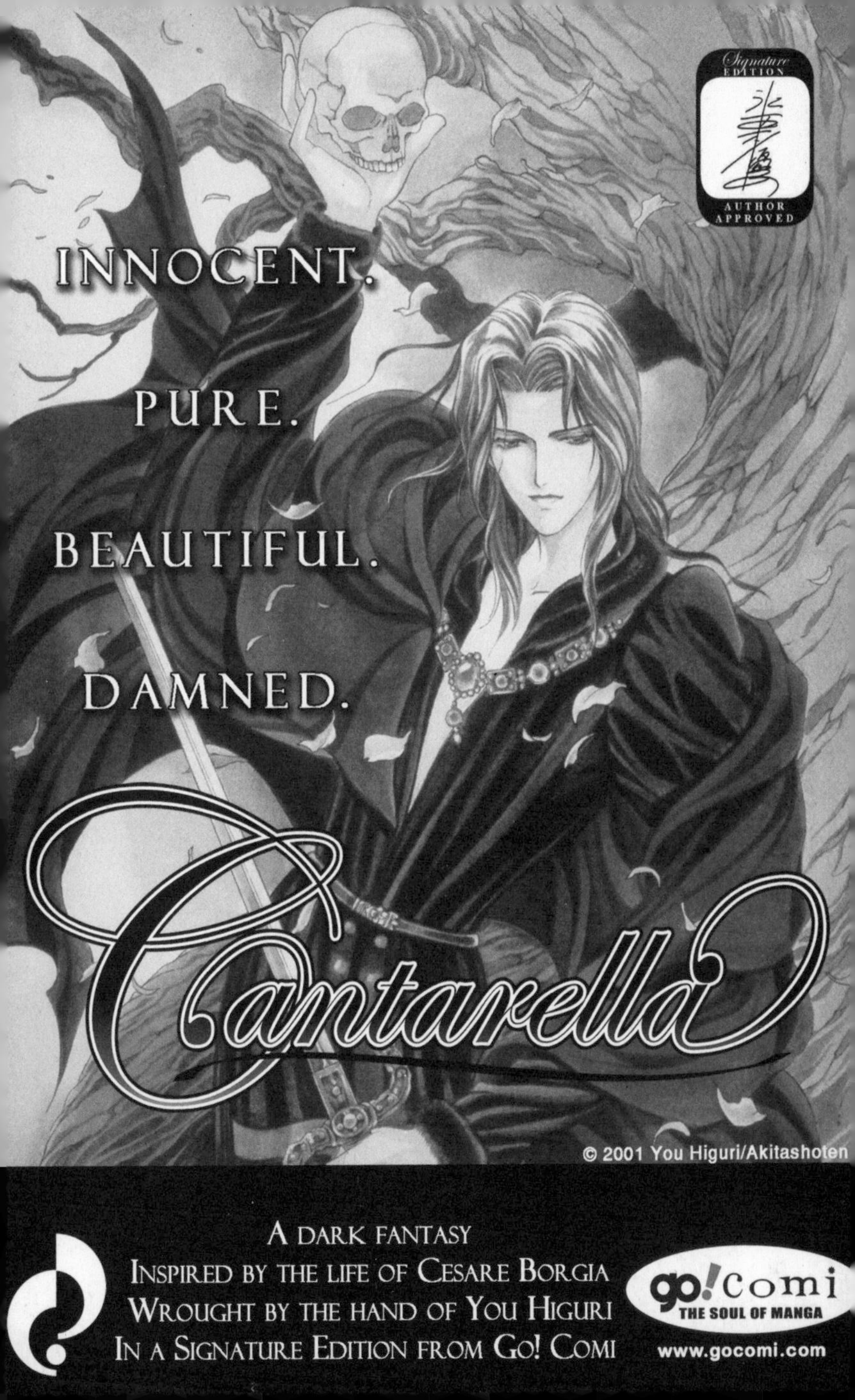
Signature EDITION
AUTHOR APPROVED
INNOCENT.
PURE.
BEAUTIFUL.
DAMNED.
Cantarella
© 2001 You Higuri/Akitashoten
A DARK FANTASY
INSPIRED BY THE LIFE OF CESARE BORGIA
WROUGHT BY THE HAND OF YOU HIGURI
IN A SIGNATURE EDITION FROM GO! COMI
go!comi
THE SOUL OF MANGA
www.gocomi.com

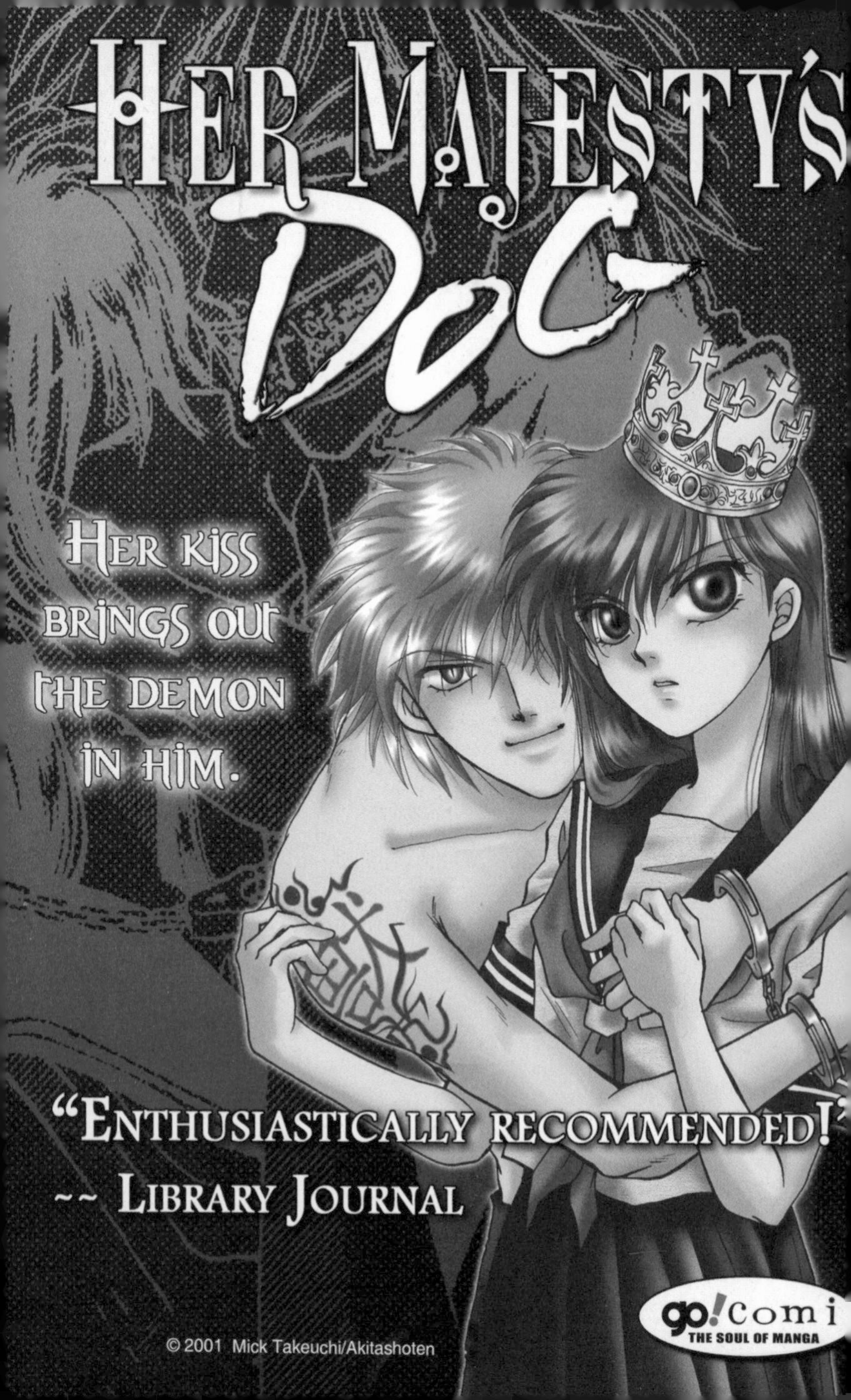
HER MAJESTY'S DOG
HER KISS BRINGS OUT THE DEMON IN HIM.
"ENTHUSIASTICALLY RECOMMENDED!"
~~ LIBRARY JOURNAL
go!comi
THE SOUL OF MANGA
© 2001 Mick Takeuchi/Akitashoten

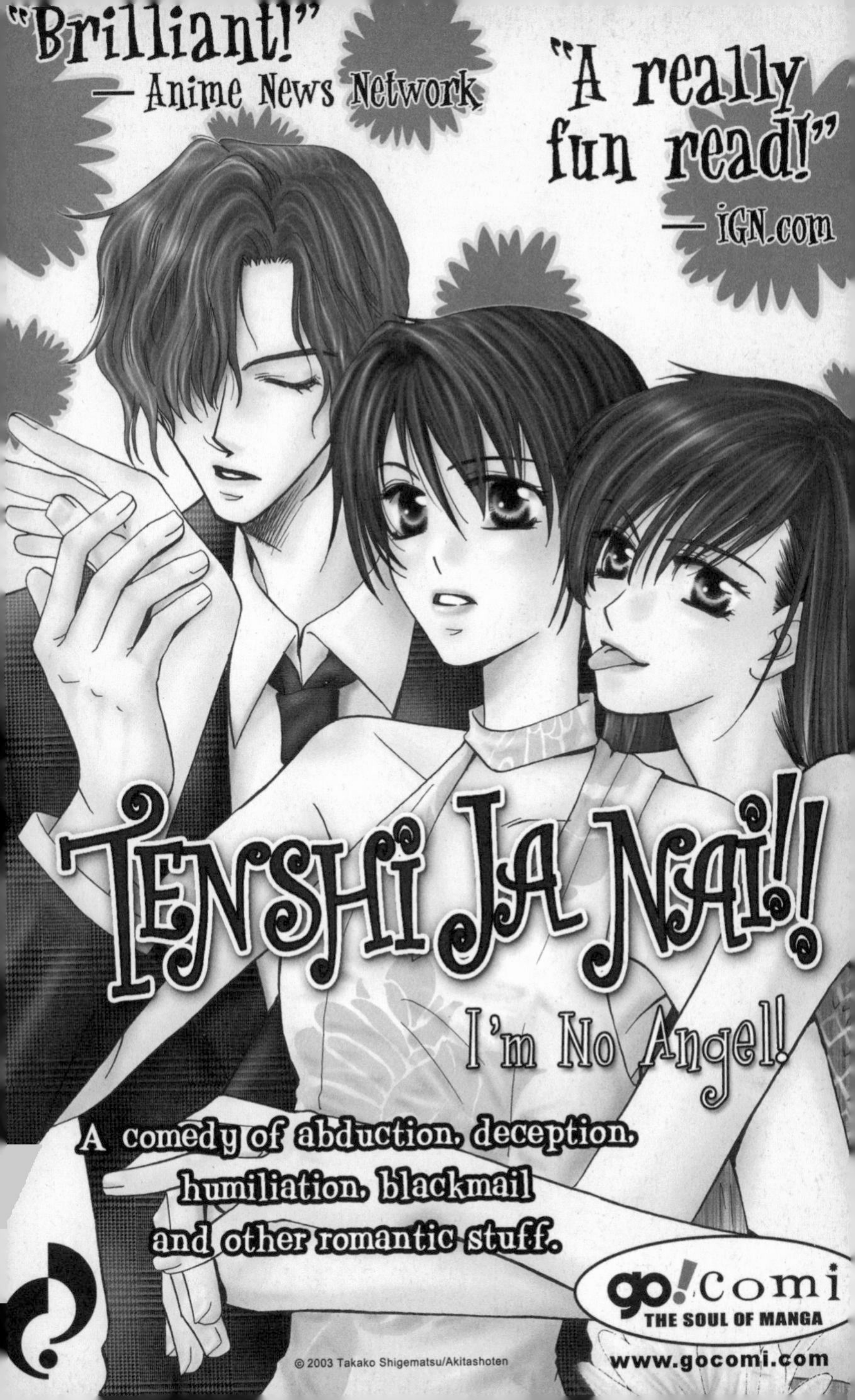
"Brilliant!"
— Anime News Network
"A really fun read!"
— IGN.com
TENSHI JA NAI!!
I'm No Angel!
A comedy of abduction, deception, humiliation, blackmail and other romantic stuff.
go!comi
THE SOUL OF MANGA
© 2003 Takako Shigematsu/Akitashoten
www.gocomi.com

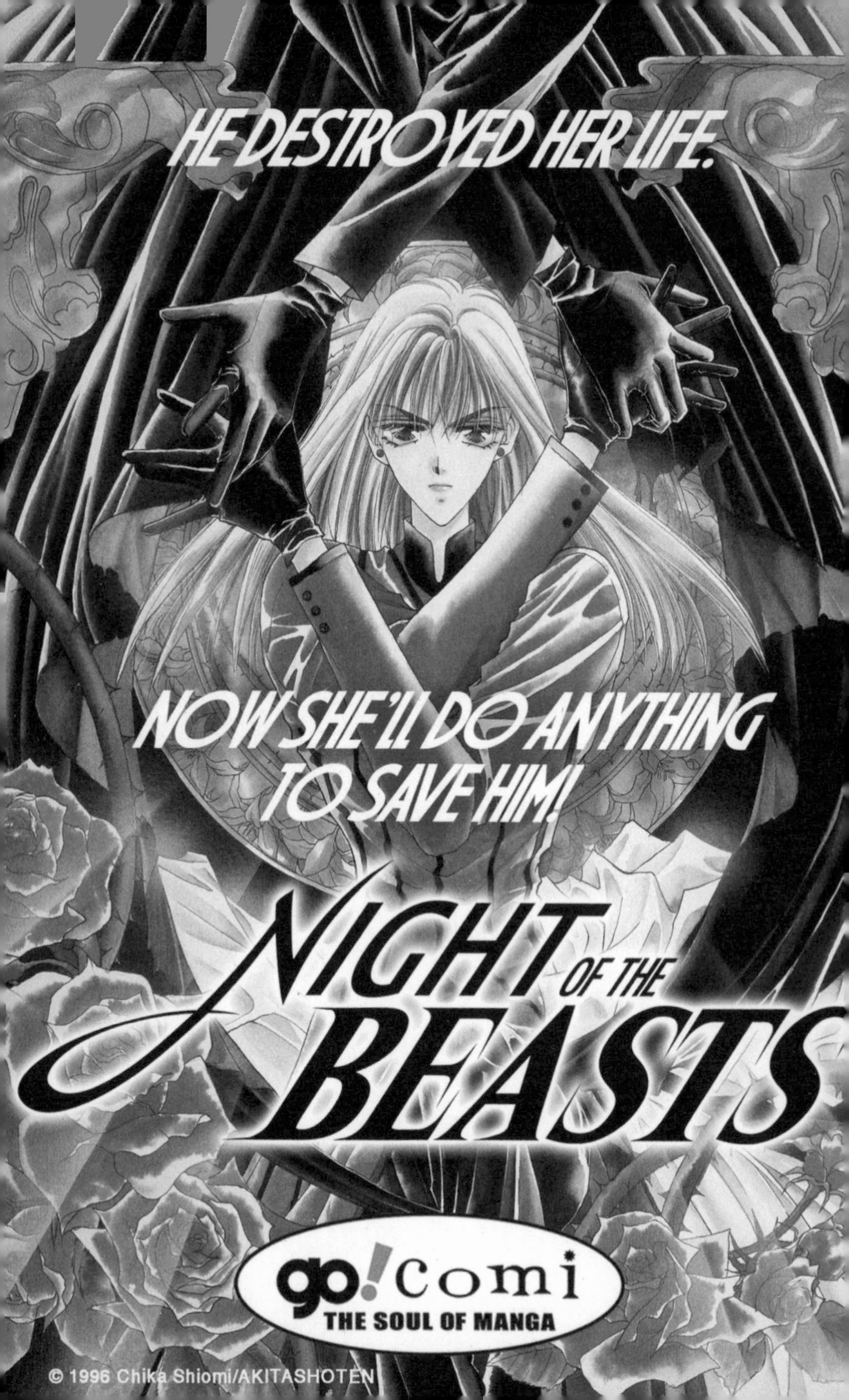
HE DESTROYED HER LIFE.
NOW SHE'LL DO ANYTHING TO SAVE HIM!
NIGHT OF THE BEASTS
go!comi
THE SOUL OF MANGA
© 1996 Chika Shiomi/AKITASHOTEN

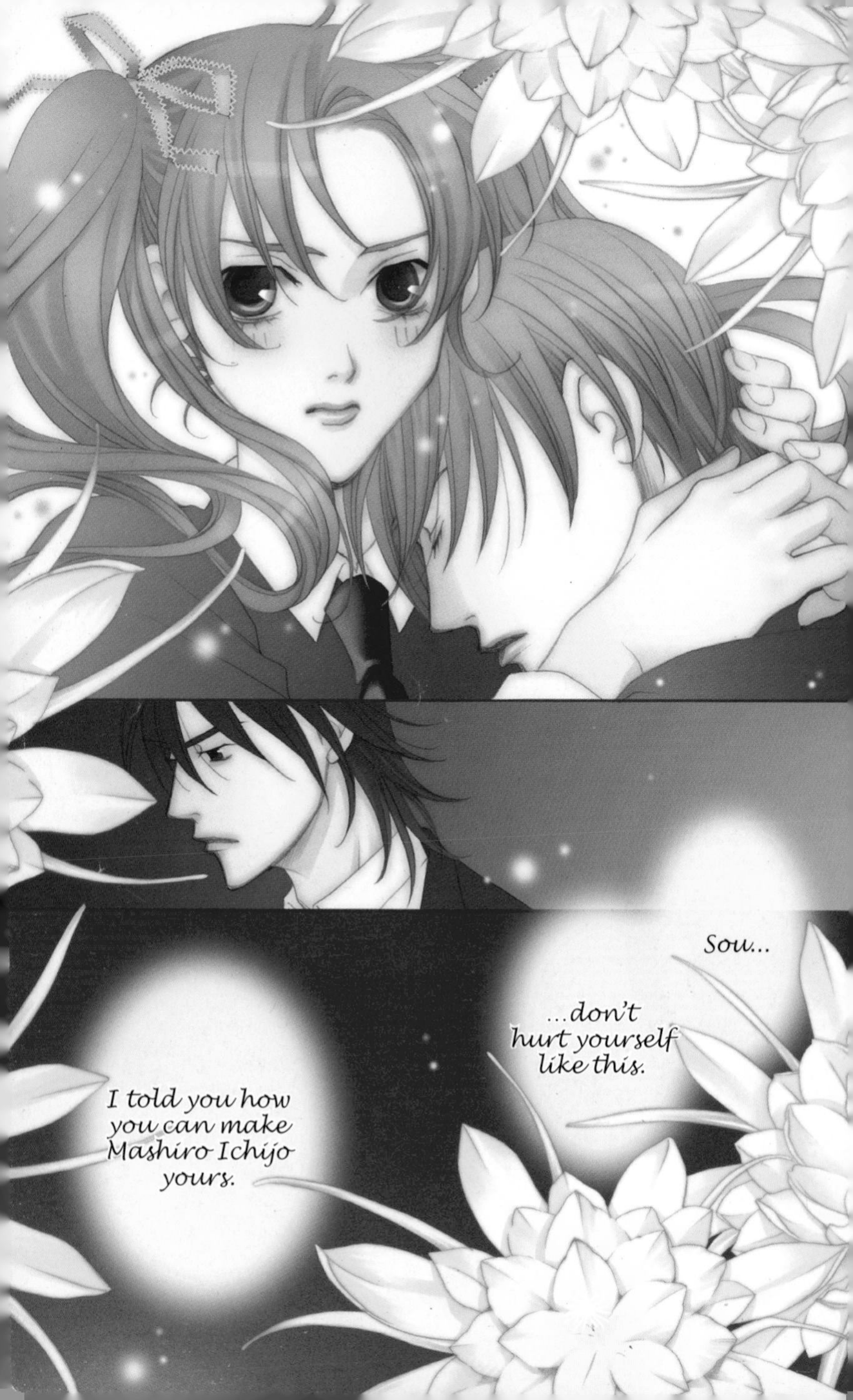
Sou...
...don't hurt yourself like this.
I told you how you can make Mashiro Ichijo yours.

AFTER SCHOOL NIGHTMARE Chapter 5

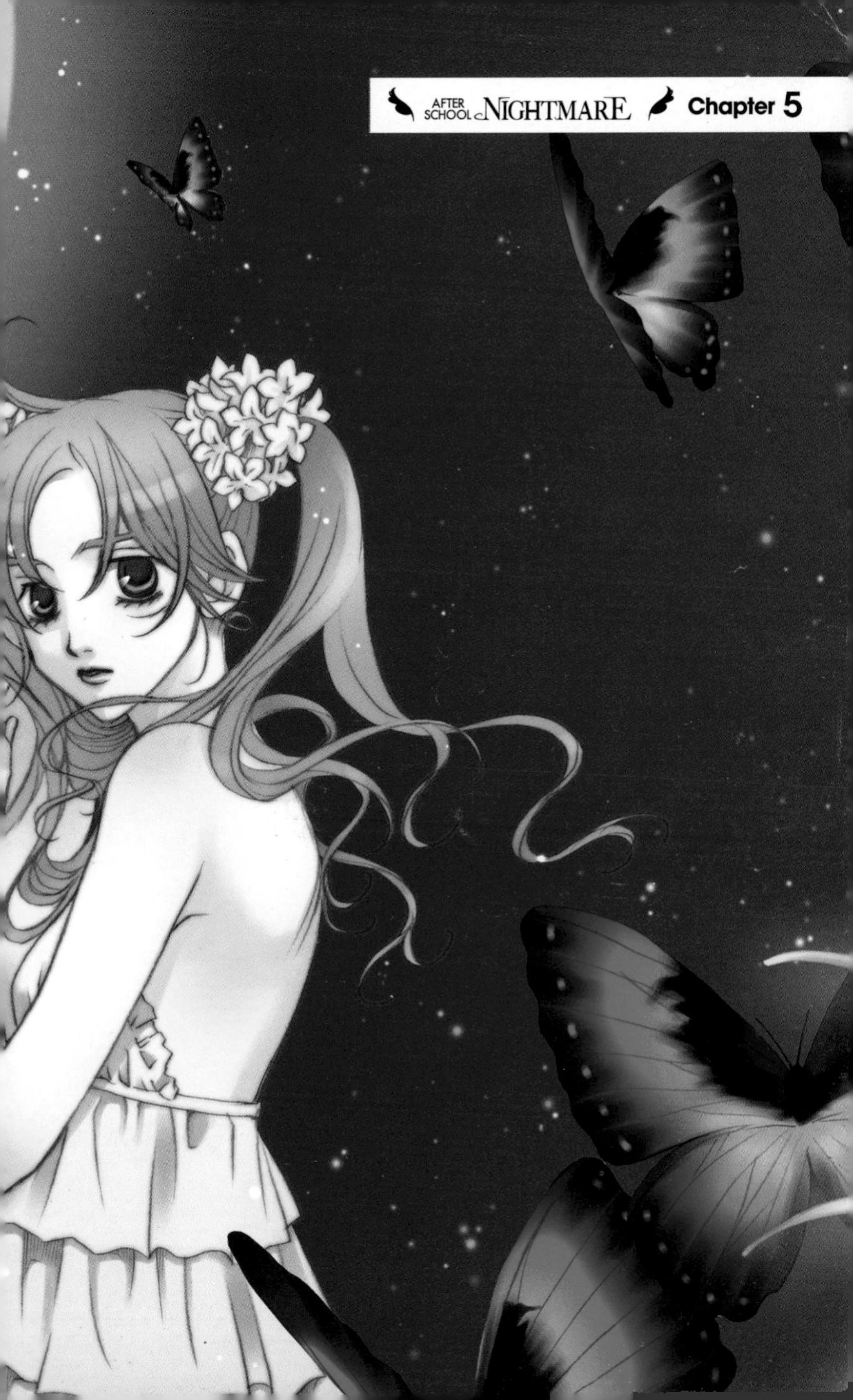

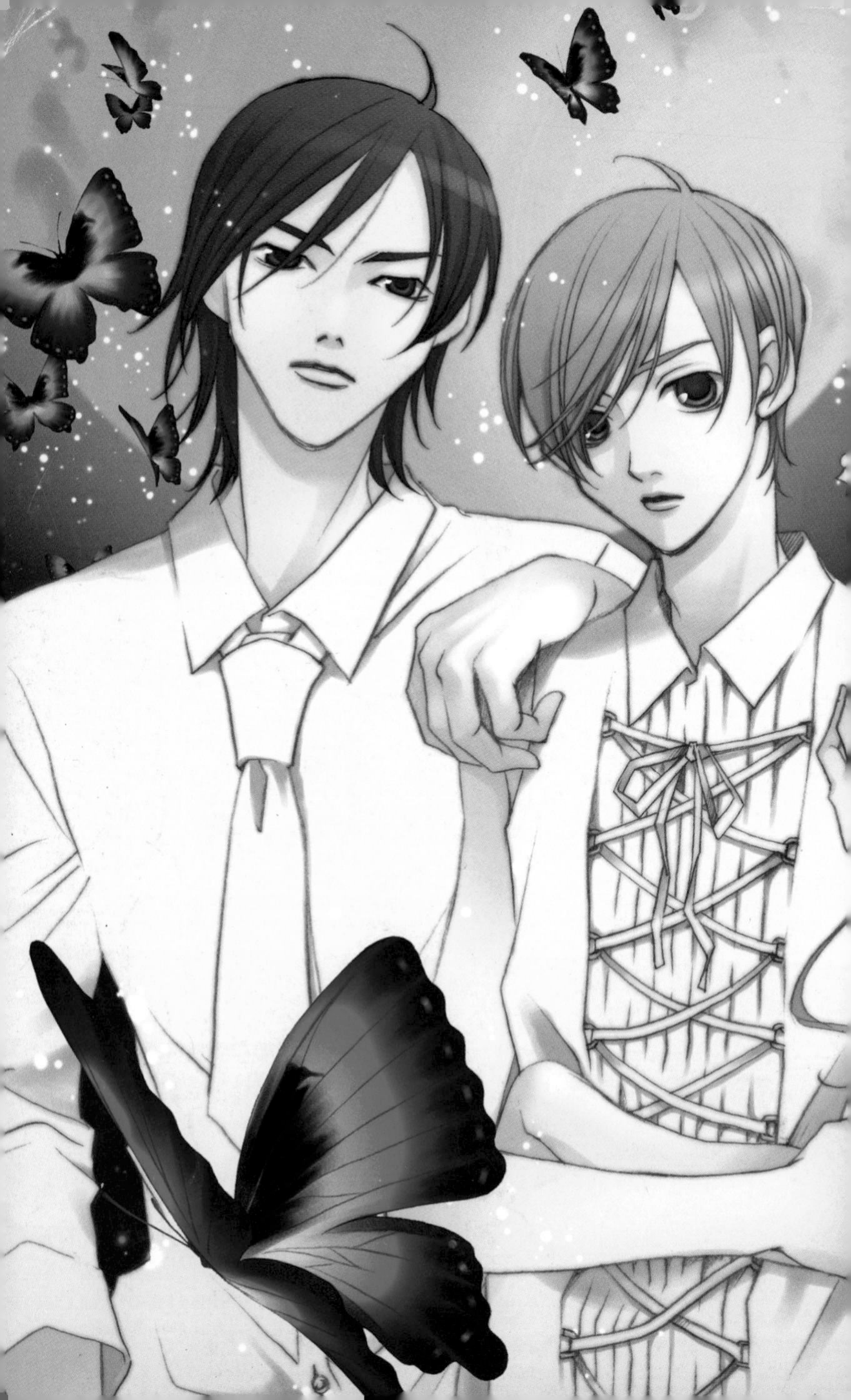

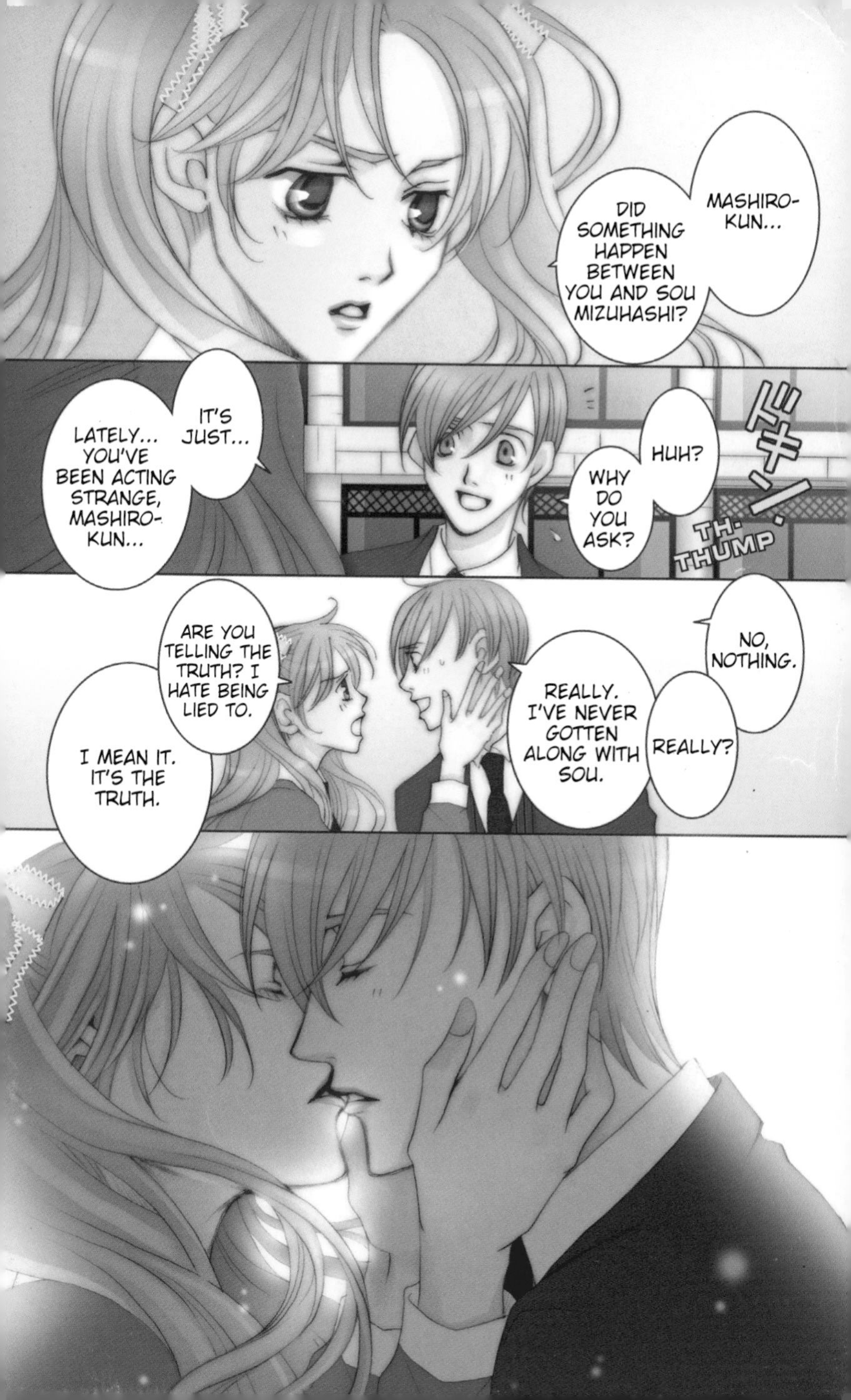
MASHIRO-KUN...
DID SOMETHING HAPPEN BETWEEN YOU AND SOU MIZUHASHI?
TH-THUMP
HUH?
WHY DO YOU ASK?
IT'S JUST...
LATELY... YOU'VE BEEN ACTING STRANGE, MASHIRO-KUN...
NO, NOTHING.
REALLY?
REALLY. I'VE NEVER GOTTEN ALONG WITH SOU.
ARE YOU TELLING THE TRUTH? I HATE BEING LIED TO.
I MEAN IT. IT'S THE TRUTH.

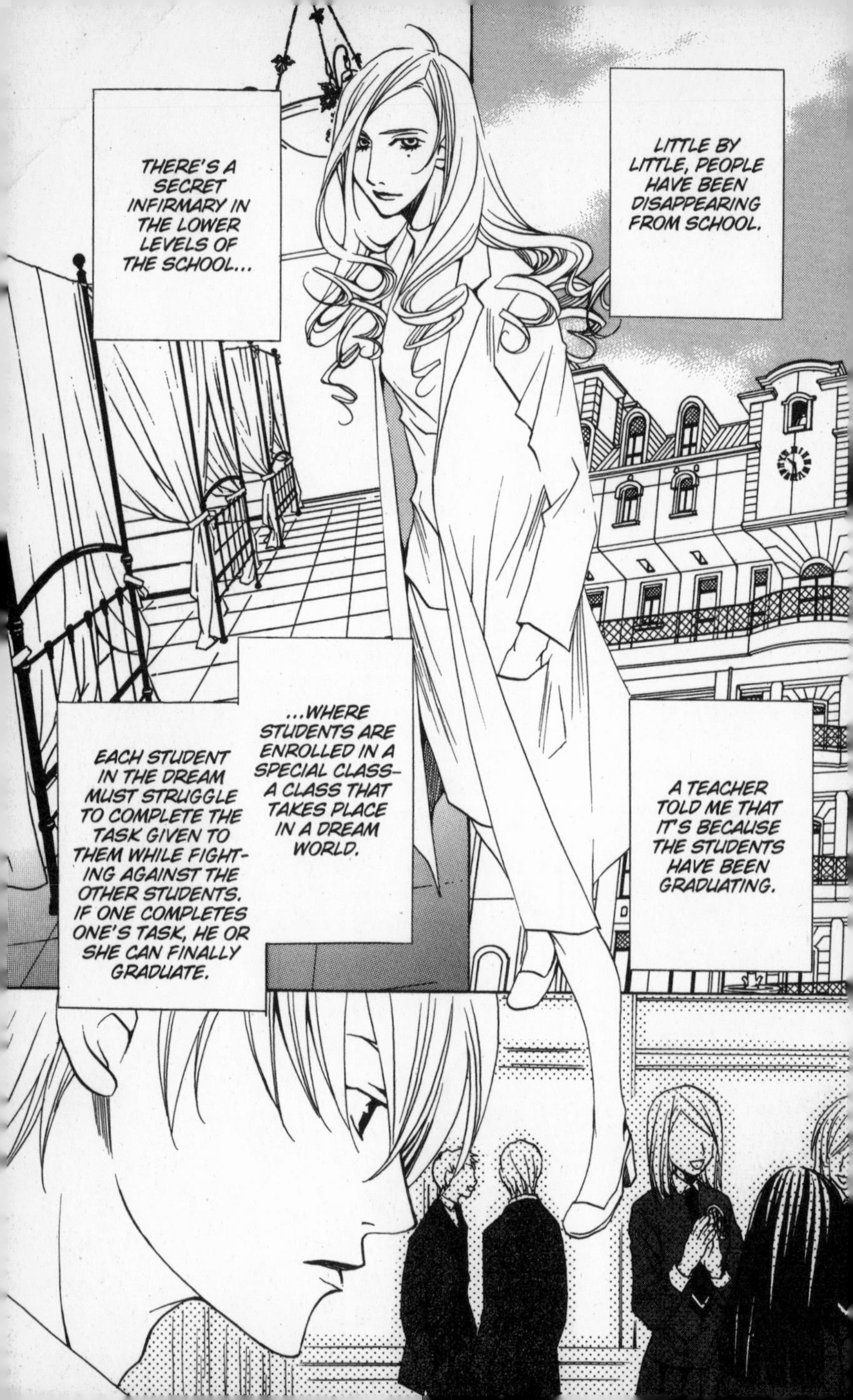
LITTLE BY LITTLE, PEOPLE HAVE BEEN DISAPPEARING FROM SCHOOL.
THERE'S A SECRET INFIRMARY IN THE LOWER LEVELS OF THE SCHOOL...
A TEACHER TOLD ME THAT IT'S BECAUSE THE STUDENTS HAVE BEEN GRADUATING.
...WHERE STUDENTS ARE ENROLLED IN A SPECIAL CLASS– A CLASS THAT TAKES PLACE IN A DREAM WORLD.
EACH STUDENT IN THE DREAM MUST STRUGGLE TO COMPLETE THE TASK GIVEN TO THEM WHILE FIGHTING AGAINST THE OTHER STUDENTS. IF ONE COMPLETES ONE'S TASK, HE OR SHE CAN FINALLY GRADUATE.

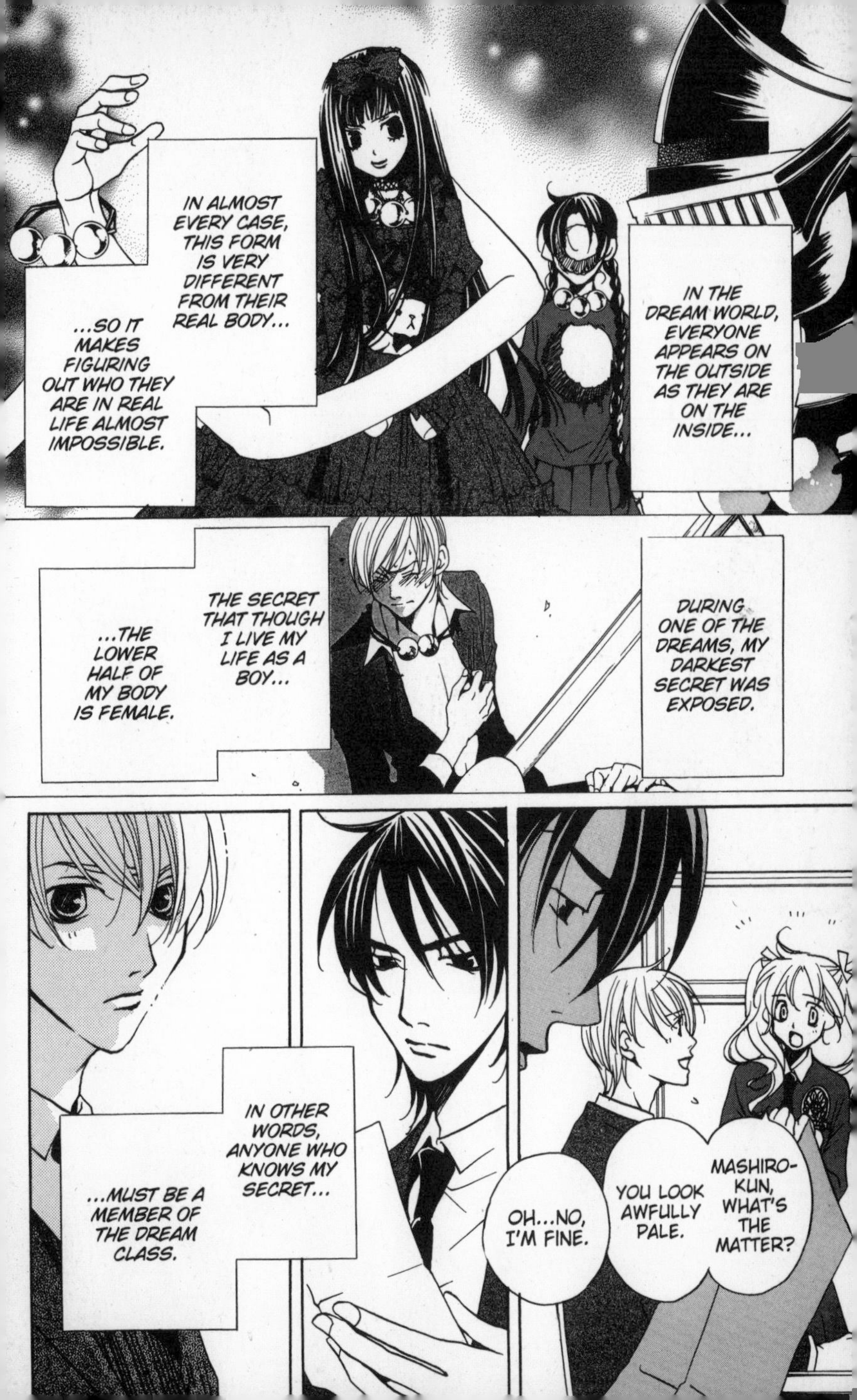
IN THE DREAM WORLD, EVERYONE APPEARS ON THE OUTSIDE AS THEY ARE ON THE INSIDE...
IN ALMOST EVERY CASE, THIS FORM IS VERY DIFFERENT FROM THEIR REAL BODY...
...SO IT MAKES FIGURING OUT WHO THEY ARE IN REAL LIFE ALMOST IMPOSSIBLE.
DURING ONE OF THE DREAMS, MY DARKEST SECRET WAS EXPOSED.
THE SECRET THAT THOUGH I LIVE MY LIFE AS A BOY...
...THE LOWER HALF OF MY BODY IS FEMALE.
MASHIRO-KUN, WHAT'S THE MATTER?
YOU LOOK AWFULLY PALE.
OH...NO, I'M FINE.
IN OTHER WORDS, ANYONE WHO KNOWS MY SECRET...
...MUST BE A MEMBER OF THE DREAM CLASS.

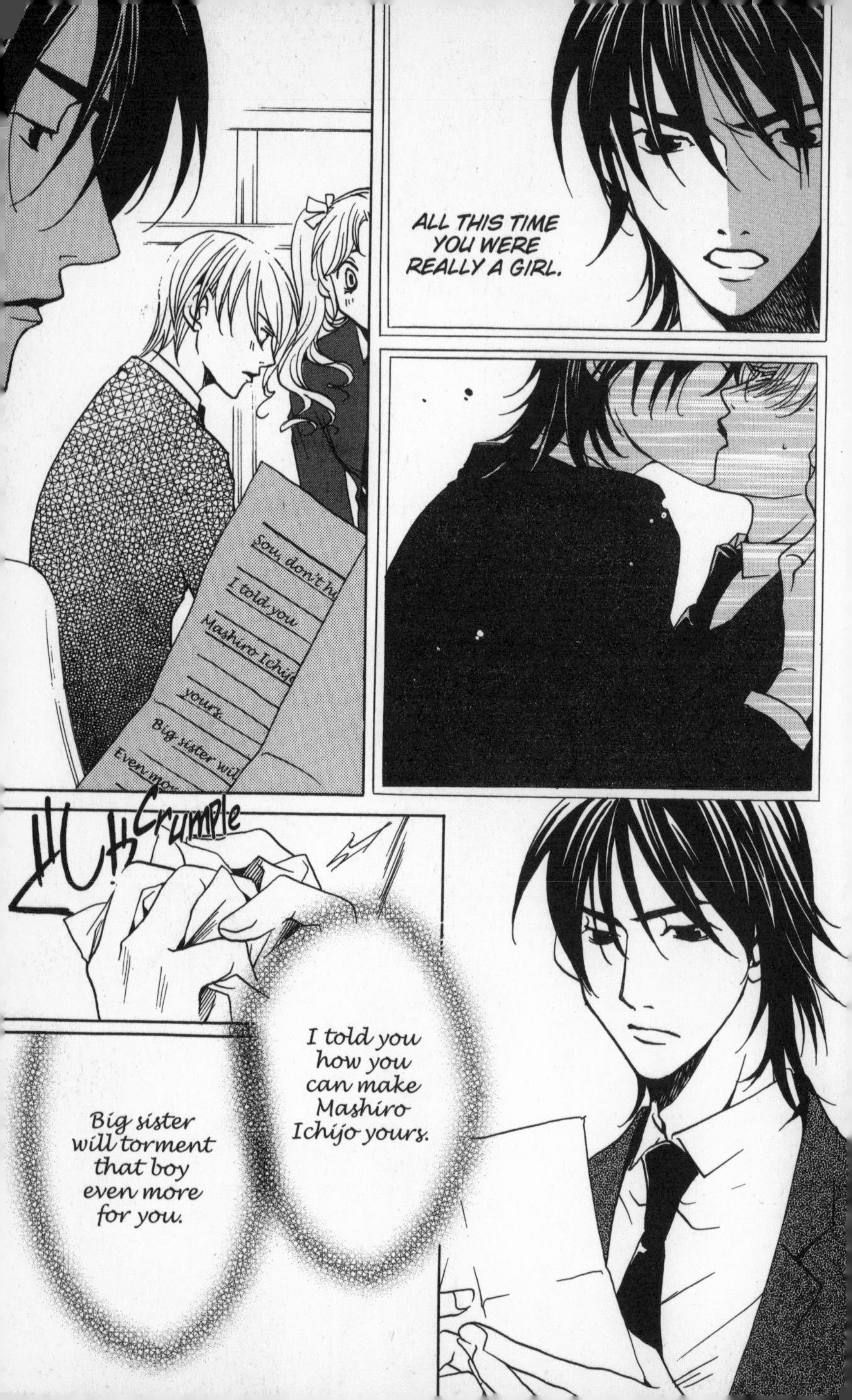
ALL THIS TIME YOU WERE REALLY A GIRL.
I told you
yours.
Crumple
I told you how you can make Mashiro Ichijo yours.
Big sister will torment that boy even more for you.

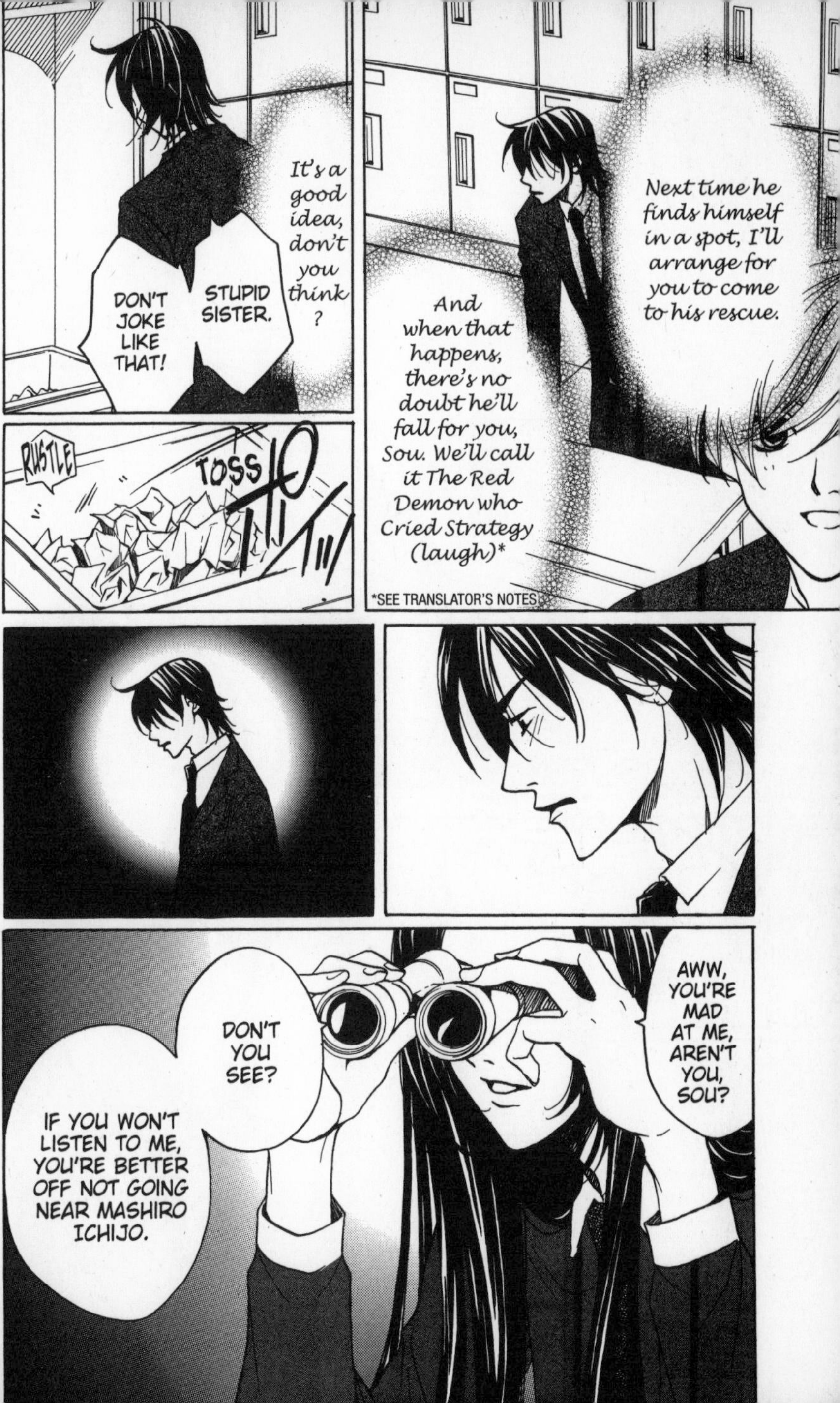
Next time he finds himself in a spot, I'll arrange for you to come to his rescue.
And when that happens, there's no doubt he'll fall for you, Sou. We'll call it The Red Demon who Cried Strategy (laugh)*
*SEE TRANSLATOR'S NOTES
It's a good idea, don't you think?
STUPID SISTER.
DON'T JOKE LIKE THAT!
TOSS
RUSTLE
AWW, YOU'RE MAD AT ME, AREN'T YOU, SOU?
DON'T YOU SEE?
IF YOU WON'T LISTEN TO ME, YOU'RE BETTER OFF NOT GOING NEAR MASHIRO ICHIJO.

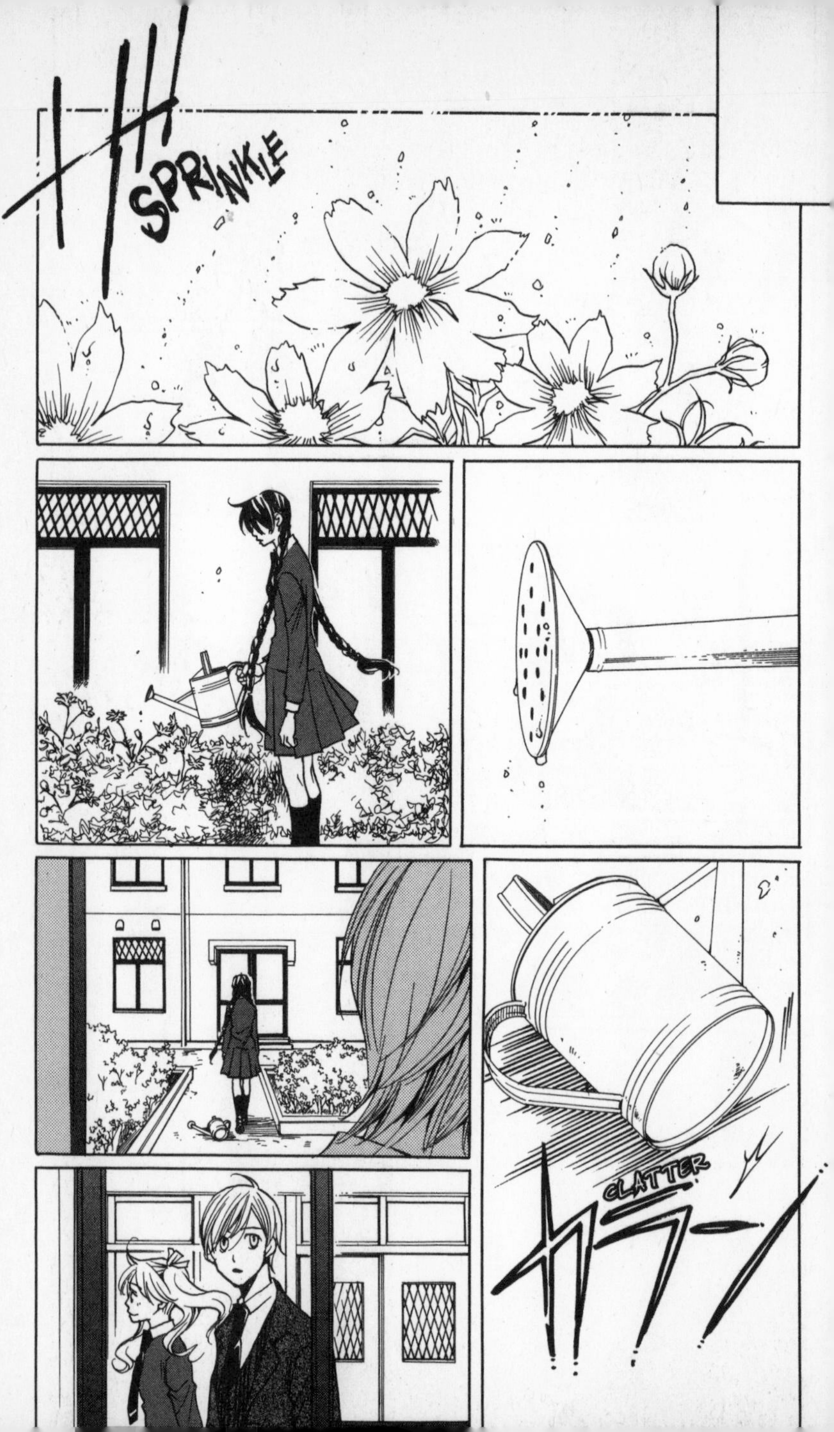
SPRINKLE
CLATTER

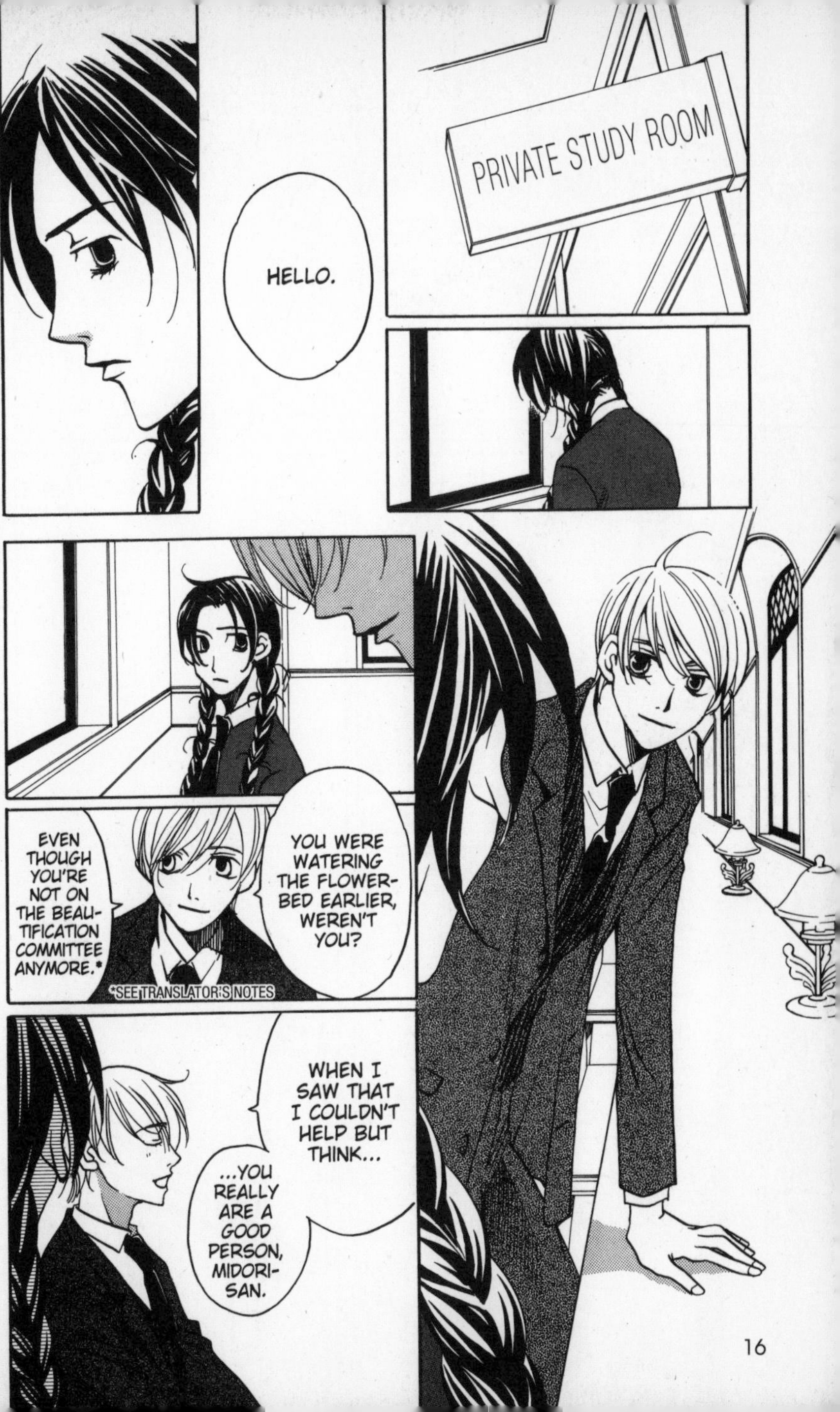
PRIVATE STUDY ROOM
HELLO.
YOU WERE WATERING THE FLOWER-BED EARLIER, WEREN'T YOU?
EVEN THOUGH YOU'RE NOT ON THE BEAU-TIFICATION COMMITTEE ANYMORE.*
*SEE TRANSLATOR'S NOTES
WHEN I SAW THAT I COULDN'T HELP BUT THINK...
...YOU REALLY ARE A GOOD PERSON, MIDORI-SAN.

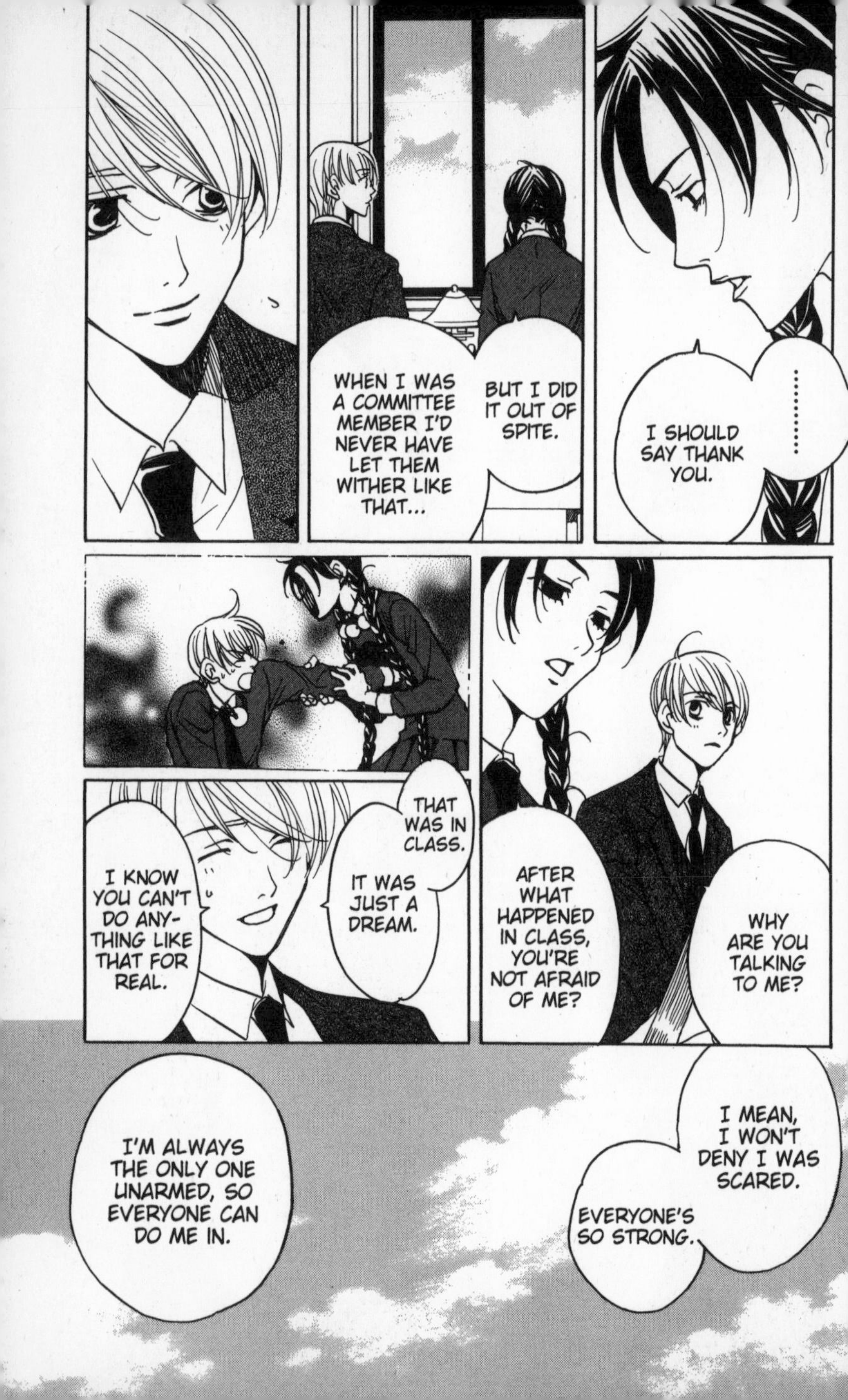
……
I SHOULD SAY THANK YOU.
BUT I DID IT OUT OF SPITE.
WHEN I WAS A COMMITTEE MEMBER I'D NEVER HAVE LET THEM WITHER LIKE THAT...
AFTER WHAT HAPPENED IN CLASS, YOU'RE NOT AFRAID OF ME?
WHY ARE YOU TALKING TO ME?
THAT WAS IN CLASS.
IT WAS JUST A DREAM.
I KNOW YOU CAN'T DO ANY-THING LIKE THAT FOR REAL.
I MEAN, I WON'T DENY I WAS SCARED.
EVERYONE'S SO STRONG.
I'M ALWAYS THE ONLY ONE UNARMED, SO EVERYONE CAN DO ME IN.

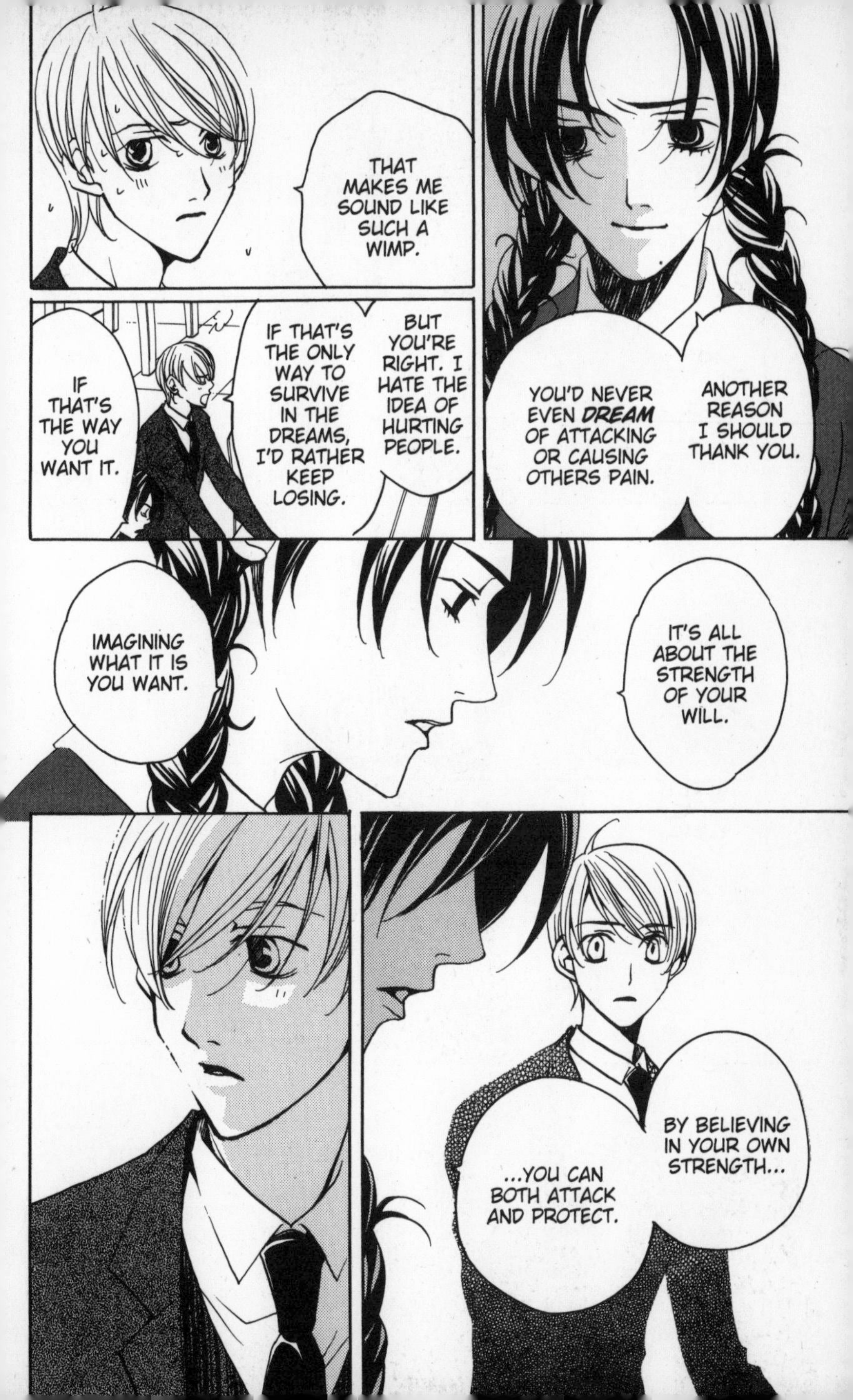
ANOTHER REASON I SHOULD THANK YOU.
YOU'D NEVER EVEN *DREAM* OF ATTACKING OR CAUSING OTHERS PAIN.
THAT MAKES ME SOUND LIKE SUCH A WIMP.
BUT YOU'RE RIGHT. I HATE THE IDEA OF HURTING PEOPLE.
IF THAT'S THE ONLY WAY TO SURVIVE IN THE DREAMS, I'D RATHER KEEP LOSING.
IF THAT'S THE WAY YOU WANT IT.
IT'S ALL ABOUT THE STRENGTH OF YOUR WILL.
IMAGINING WHAT IT IS YOU WANT.
BY BELIEVING IN YOUR OWN STRENGTH...
...YOU CAN BOTH ATTACK AND PROTECT.

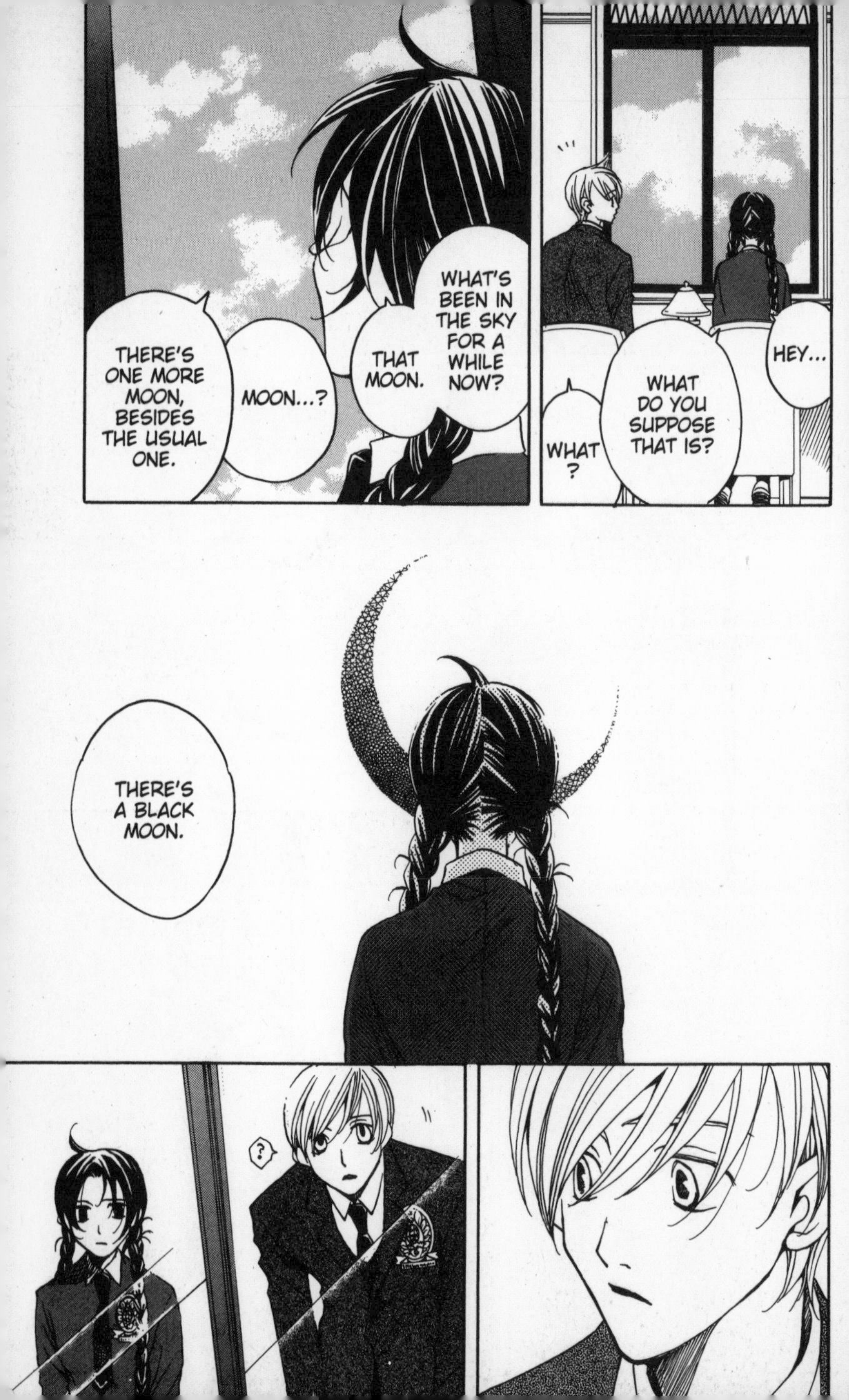
HEY...
WHAT DO YOU SUPPOSE THAT IS?
WHAT?
WHAT'S BEEN IN THE SKY FOR A WHILE NOW?
THAT MOON.
MOON...?
THERE'S ONE MORE MOON, BESIDES THE USUAL ONE.
THERE'S A BLACK MOON.
?

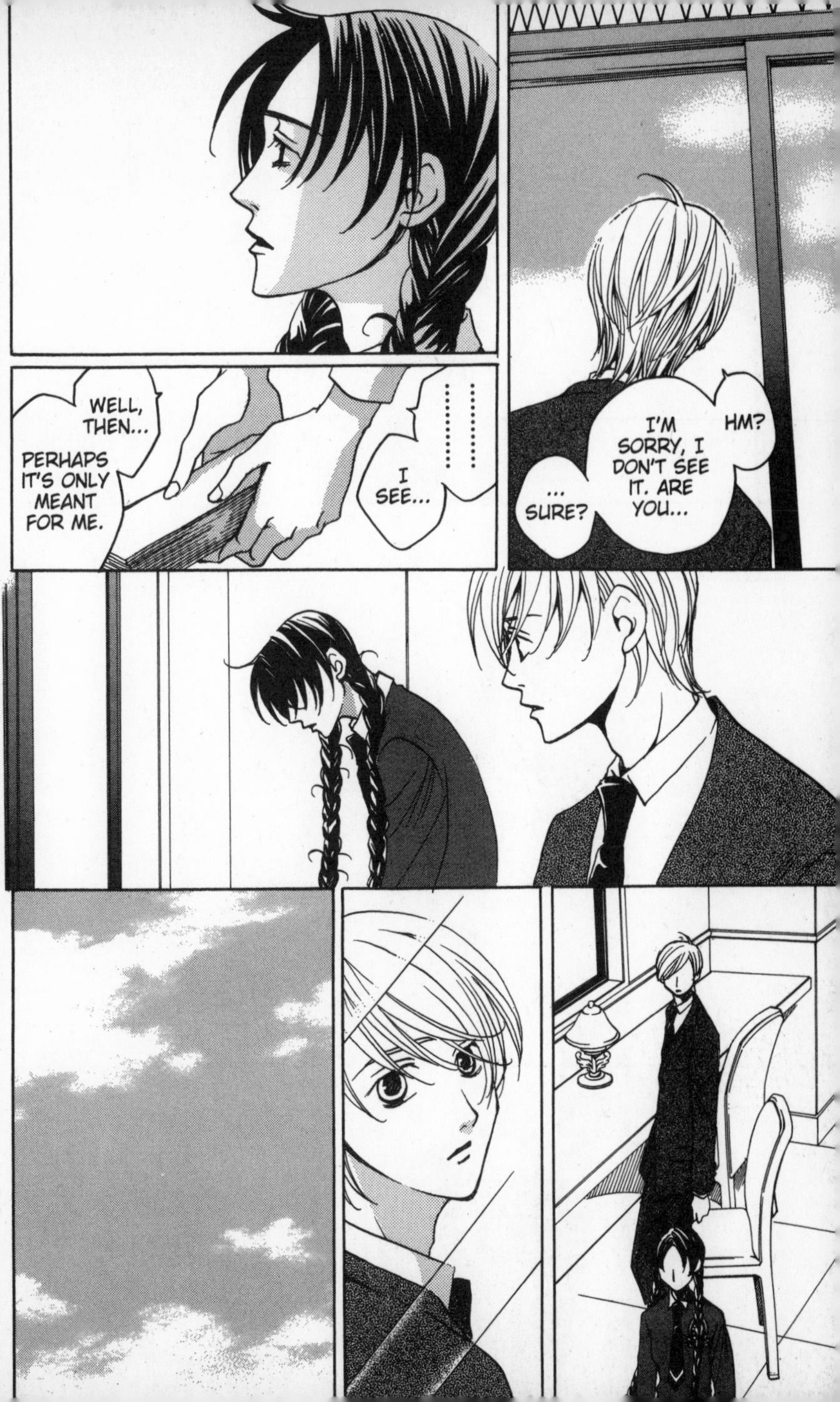
HM?
I'M SORRY, I DON'T SEE IT. ARE YOU...
... SURE?
......
......
I SEE...
WELL, THEN...
PERHAPS IT'S ONLY MEANT FOR ME.

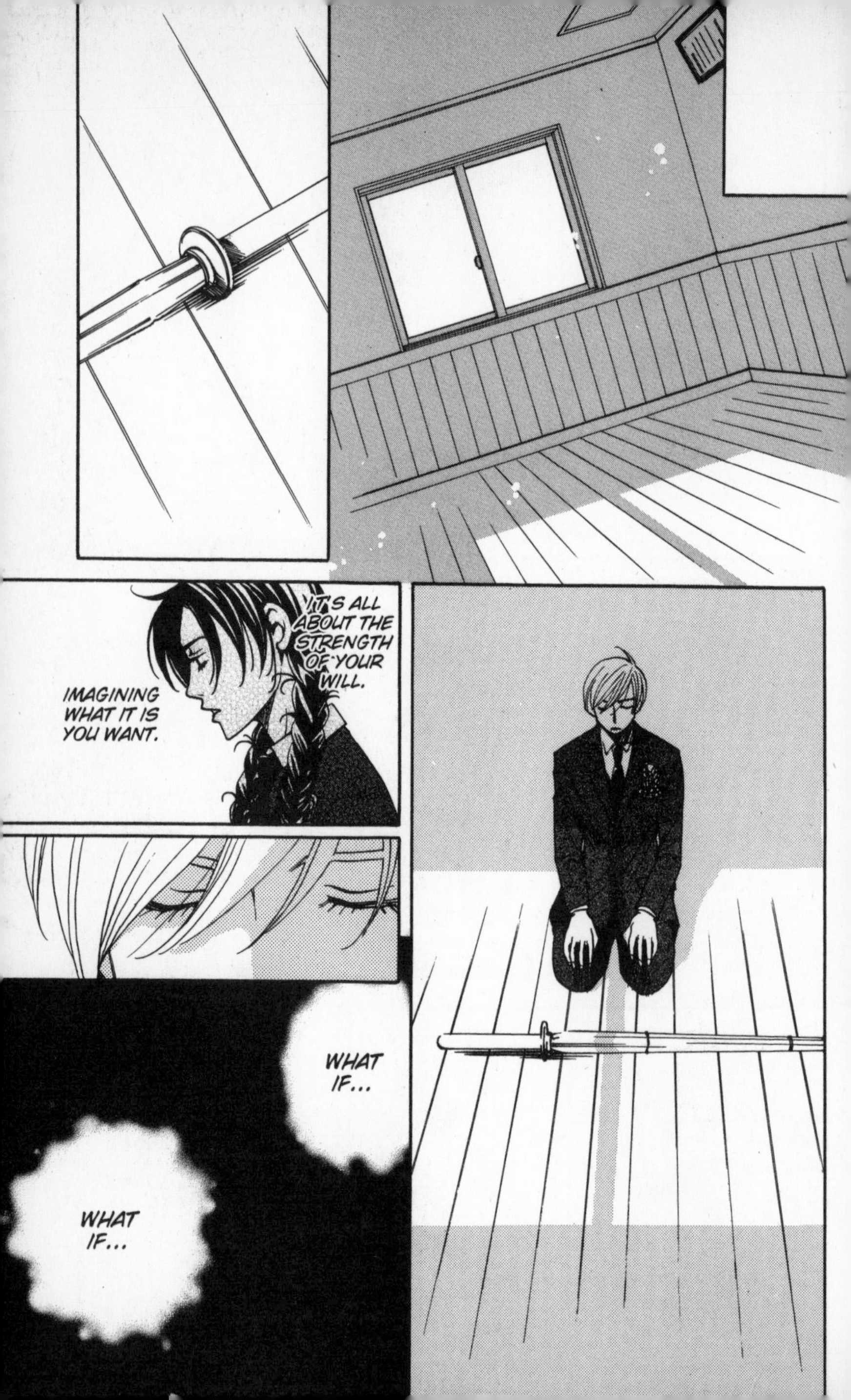
IT'S ALL ABOUT THE STRENGTH OF YOUR WILL.
IMAGINING WHAT IT IS YOU WANT.
WHAT IF...
WHAT IF...

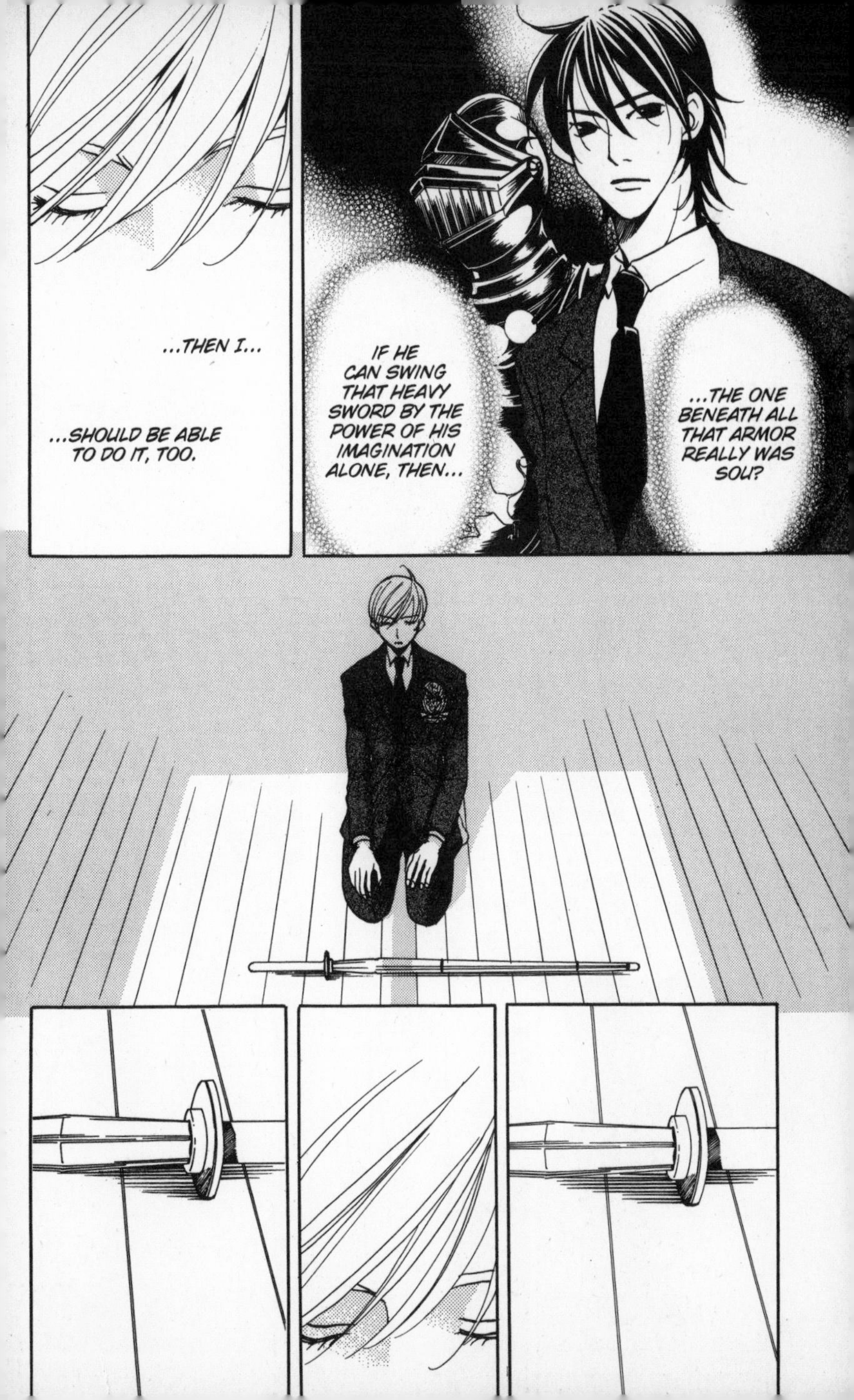
...THE ONE BENEATH ALL THAT ARMOR REALLY WAS SOU?
IF HE CAN SWING THAT HEAVY SWORD BY THE POWER OF HIS IMAGINATION ALONE, THEN...
...THEN I...
...SHOULD BE ABLE TO DO IT, TOO.

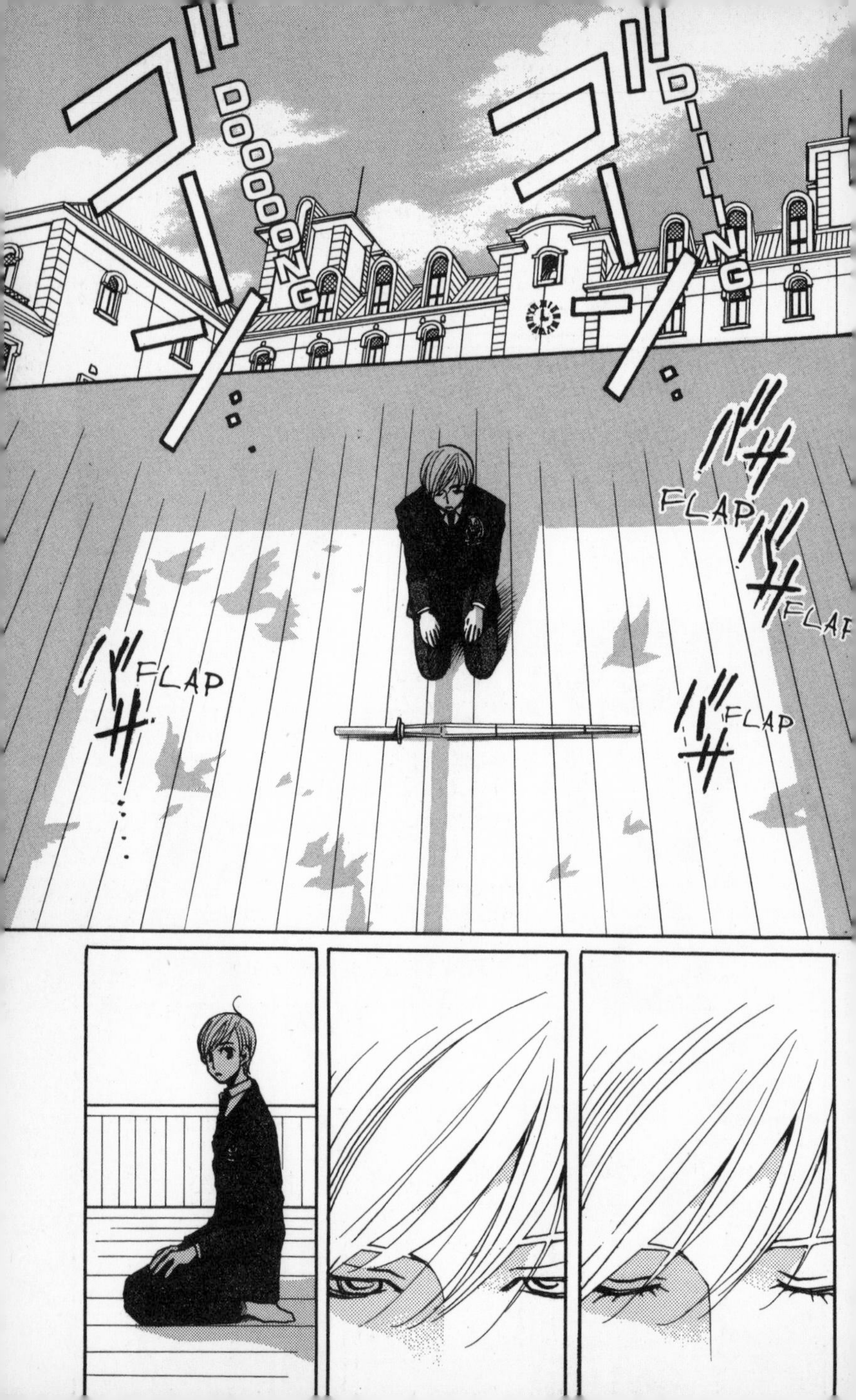
DI---NG
DOOOOONG
FLAP
FLAP
FLAP
FLAP

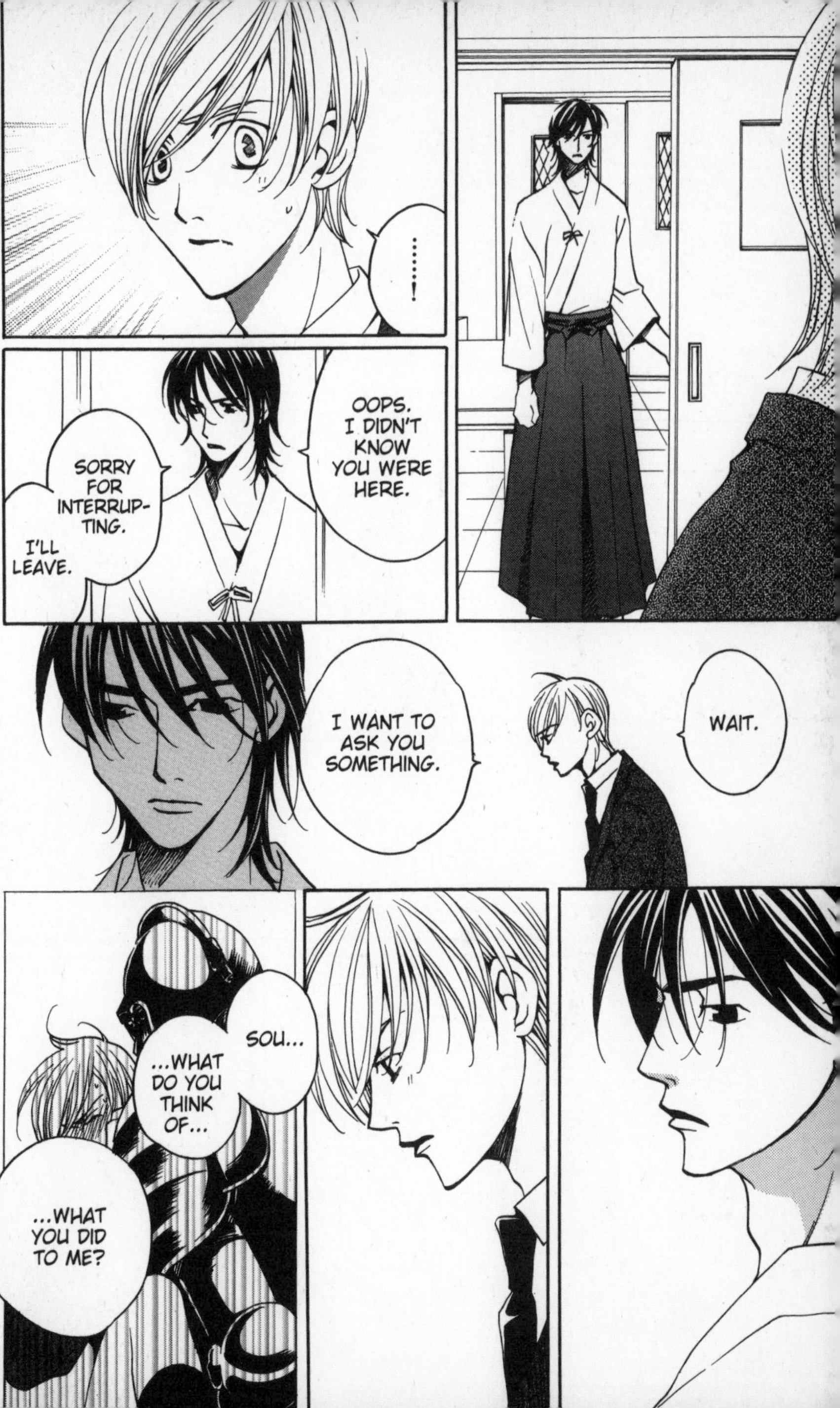
......!
OOPS. I DIDN'T KNOW YOU WERE HERE.
SORRY FOR INTERRUP-TING.
I'LL LEAVE.
WAIT.
I WANT TO ASK YOU SOMETHING.
SOU...
...WHAT DO YOU THINK OF...
...WHAT YOU DID TO ME?

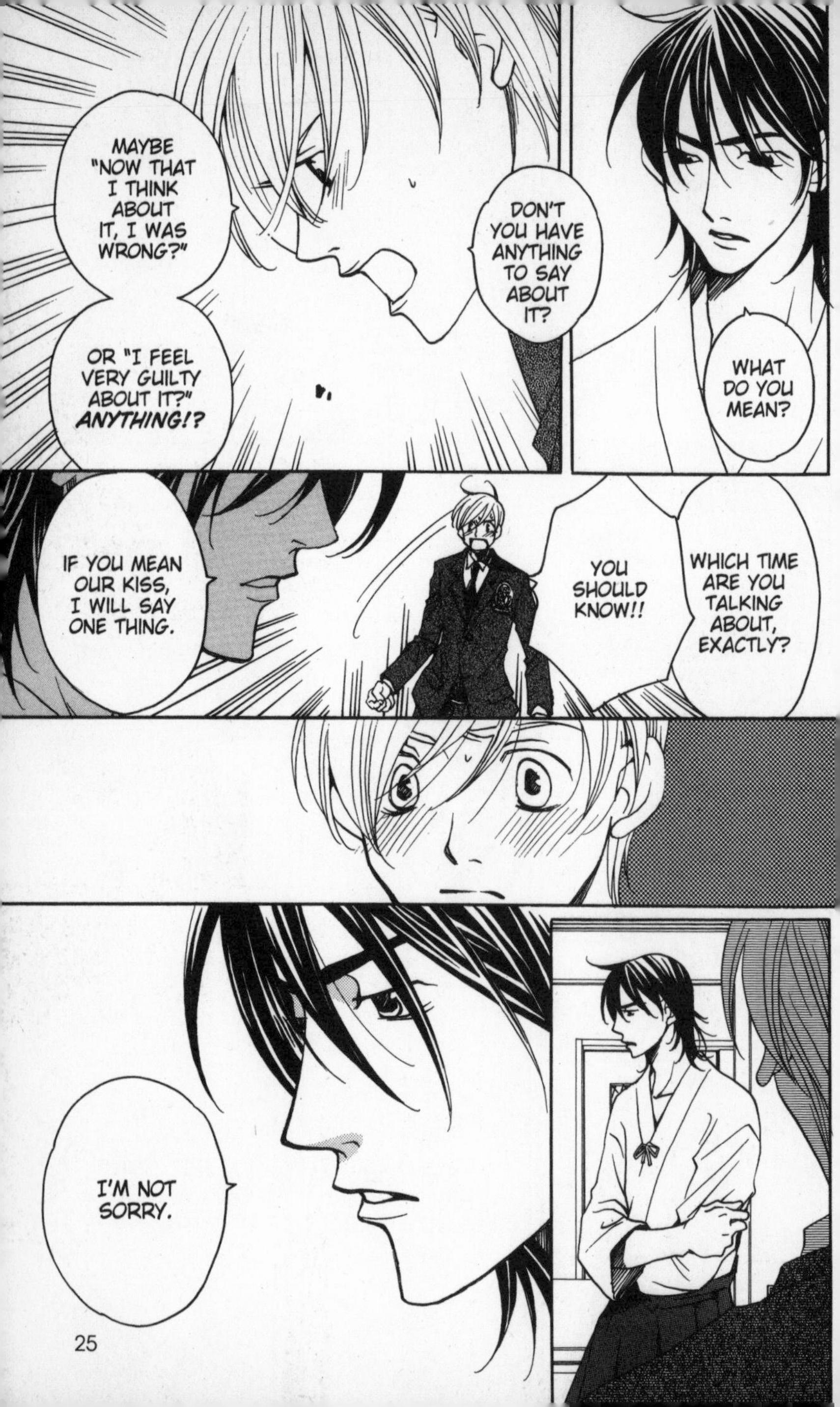
DON'T YOU HAVE ANYTHING TO SAY ABOUT IT?
WHAT DO YOU MEAN?
MAYBE "NOW THAT I THINK ABOUT IT, I WAS WRONG?"
OR "I FEEL VERY GUILTY ABOUT IT?" ANYTHING!?
WHICH TIME ARE YOU TALKING ABOUT, EXACTLY?
YOU SHOULD KNOW!!
IF YOU MEAN OUR KISS, I WILL SAY ONE THING.
I'M NOT SORRY.

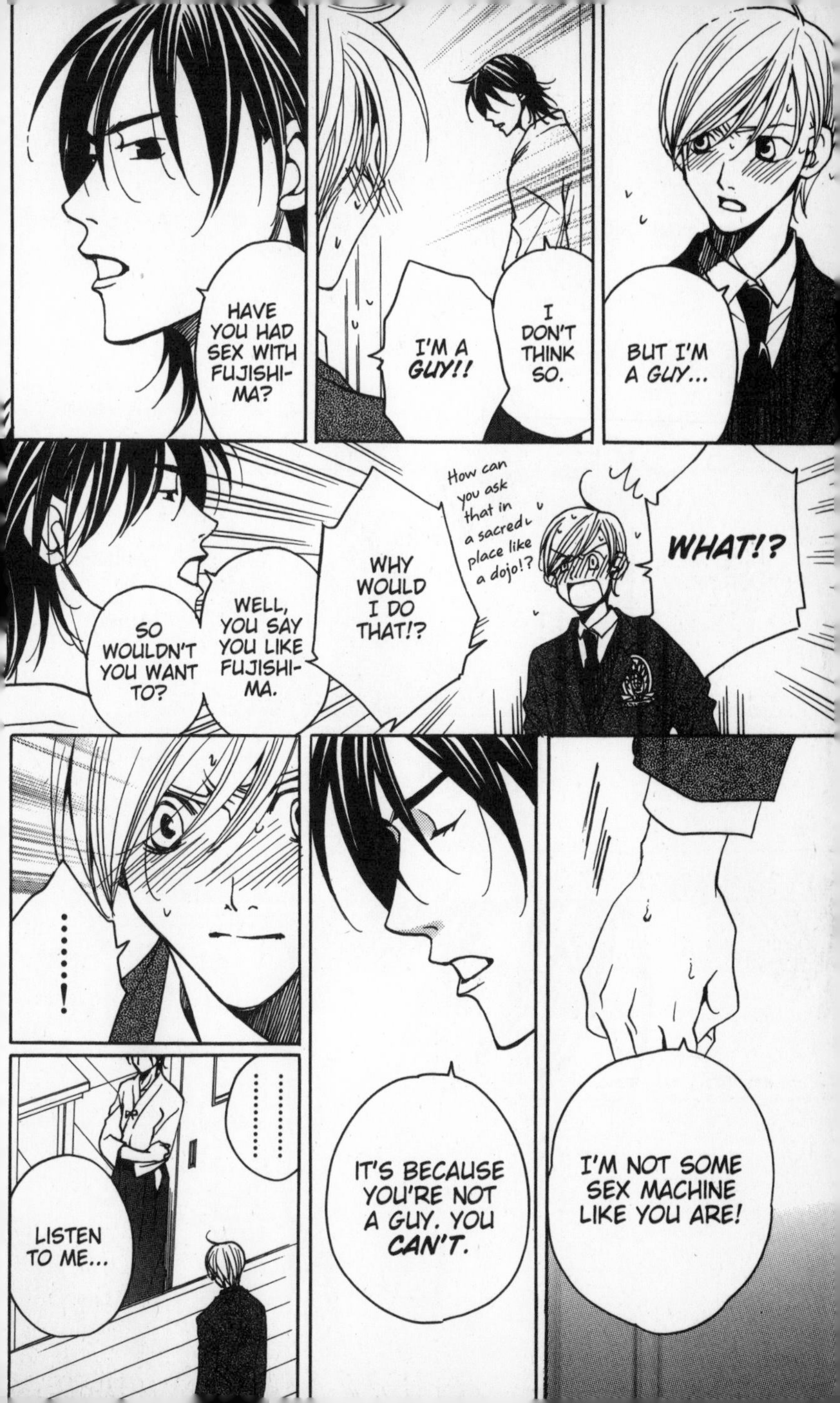
BUT I'M A GUY...
I DON'T THINK SO.
I'M A *GUY!!*
HAVE YOU HAD SEX WITH FUJISHIMA?
WHAT!?
How can you ask that in a sacred place like a dojo!?
WHY WOULD I DO THAT!?
WELL, YOU SAY YOU LIKE FUJISHIMA.
SO WOULDN'T YOU WANT TO?
I'M NOT SOME SEX MACHINE LIKE YOU ARE!
IT'S BECAUSE YOU'RE NOT A GUY. YOU *CAN'T*.
......!
......
LISTEN TO ME...

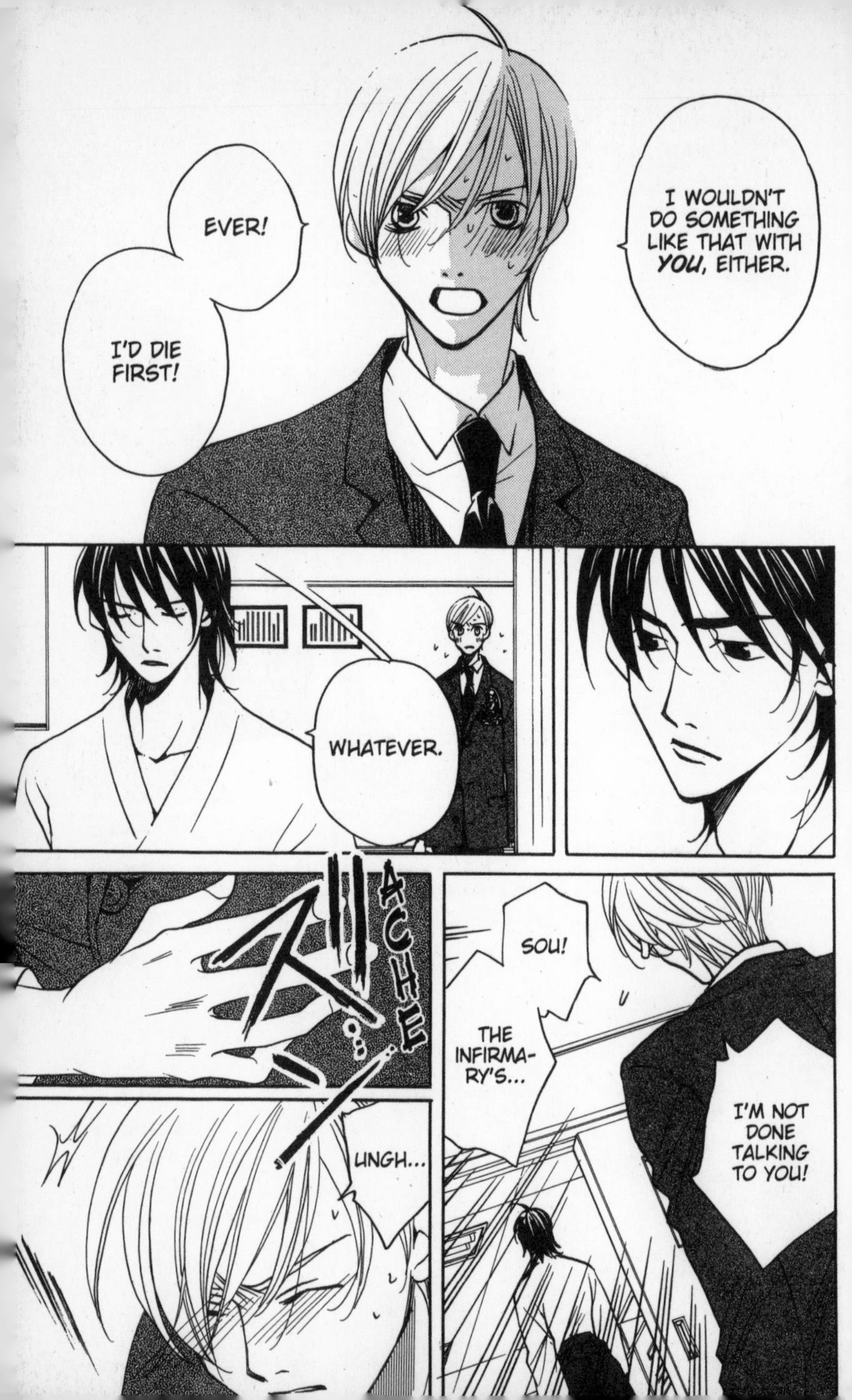
I WOULDN'T DO SOMETHING LIKE THAT WITH *YOU*, EITHER.
EVER!
I'D DIE FIRST!
WHATEVER.
SOU!
I'M NOT DONE TALKING TO YOU!
THE INFIRMA-RY'S...
ACHE
UNGH...

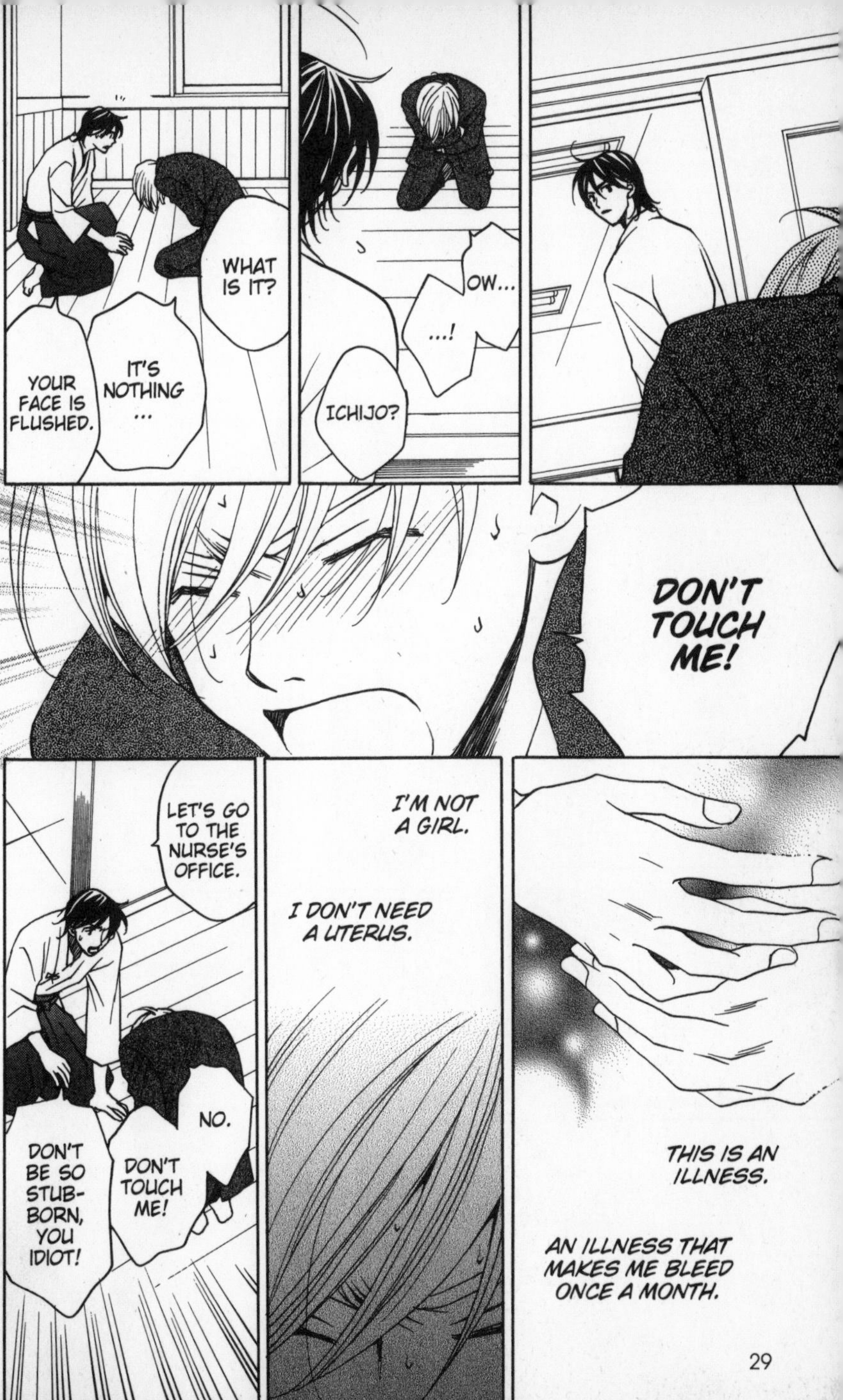
OW...
...!
ICHIJO?
WHAT IS IT?
IT'S NOTHING ...
YOUR FACE IS FLUSHED.
DON'T TOUCH ME!
THIS IS AN ILLNESS.
AN ILLNESS THAT MAKES ME BLEED ONCE A MONTH.
I'M NOT A GIRL.
I DON'T NEED A UTERUS.
LET'S GO TO THE NURSE'S OFFICE.
NO.
DON'T TOUCH ME!
DON'T BE SO STUB-BORN, YOU IDIOT!

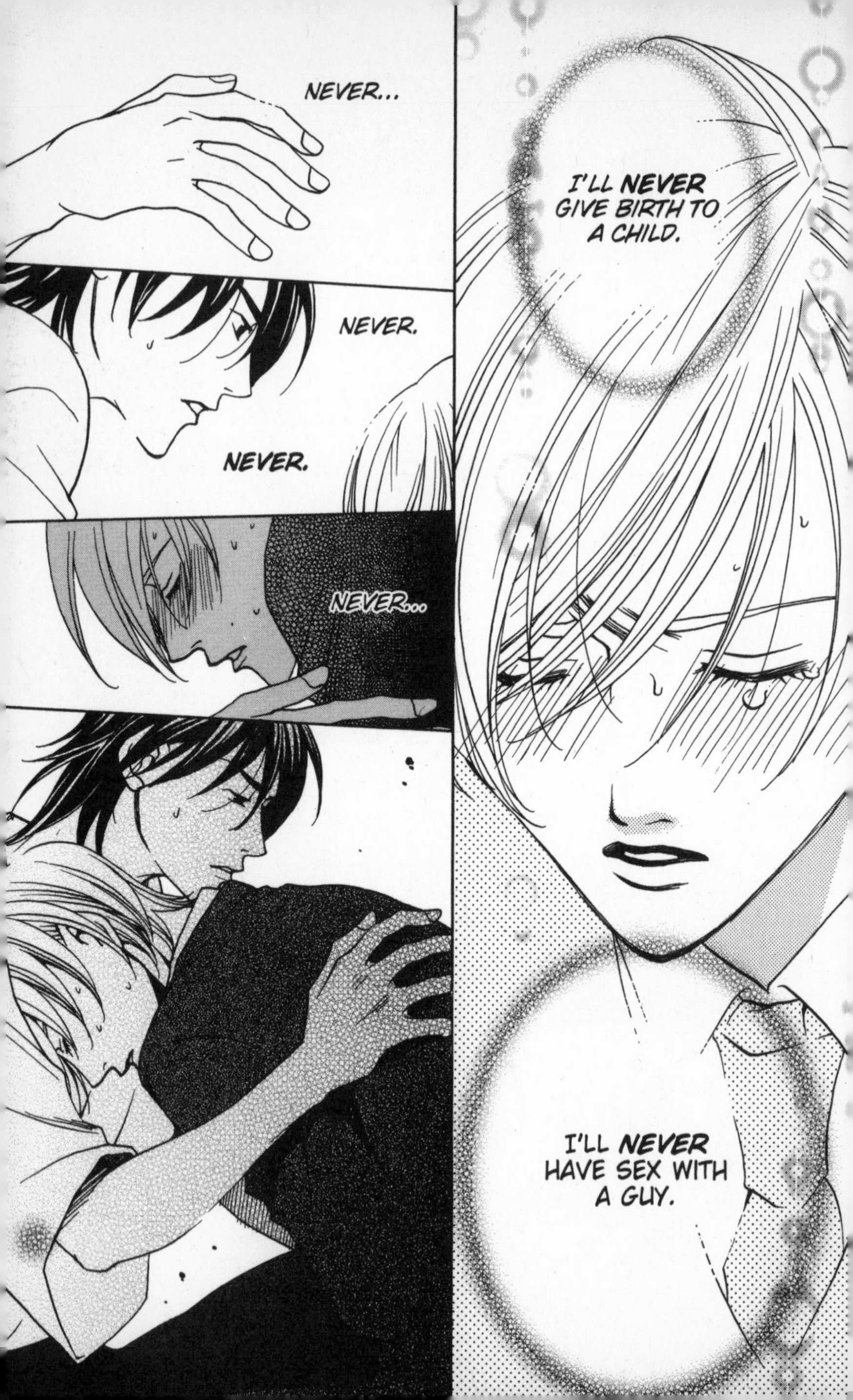
I'LL **NEVER** GIVE BIRTH TO A CHILD.
I'LL **NEVER** HAVE SEX WITH A GUY.
NEVER...
NEVER.
NEVER.
NEVER...

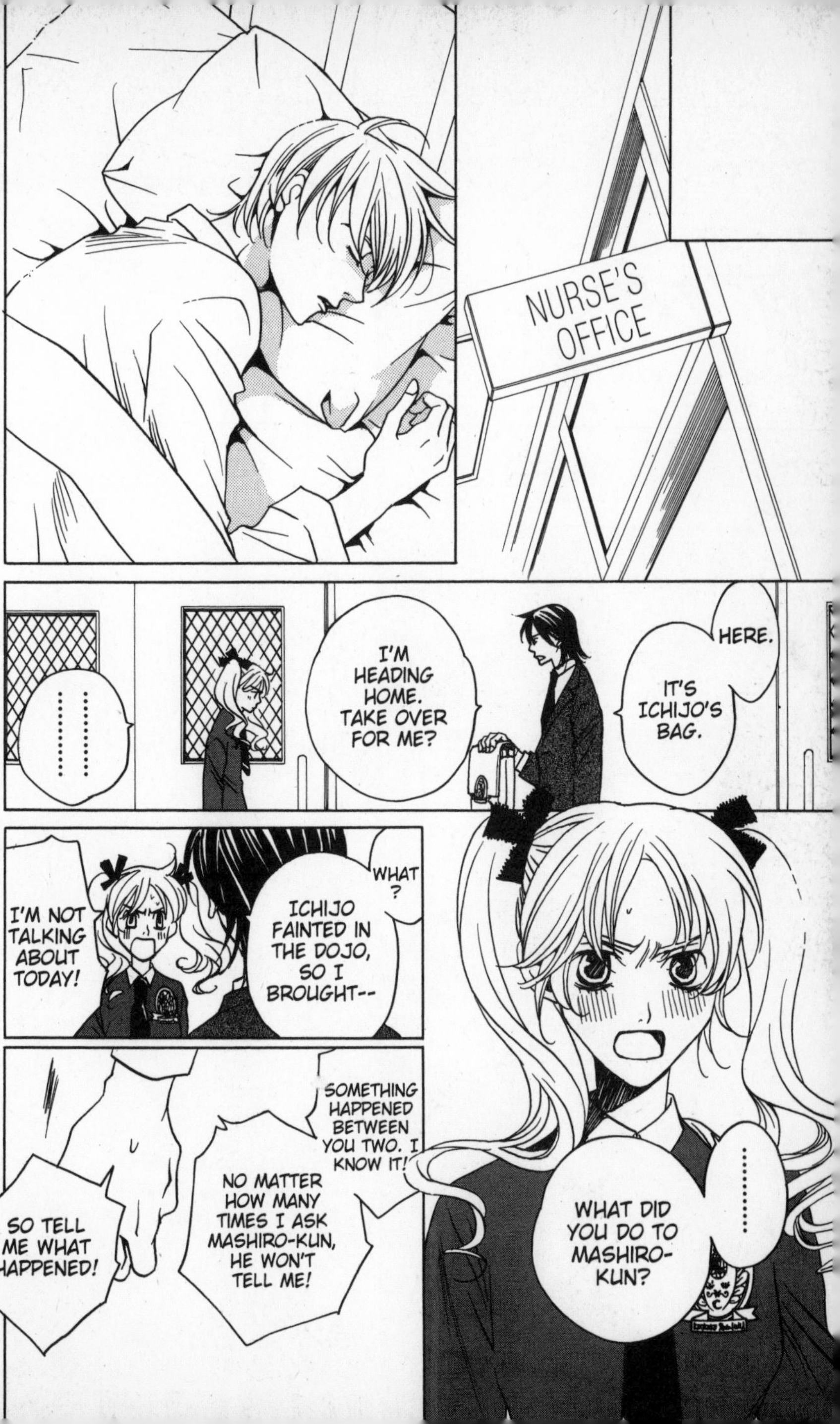
NURSE'S OFFICE
HERE.
IT'S ICHIJO'S BAG.
I'M HEADING HOME. TAKE OVER FOR ME?
......
......
WHAT DID YOU DO TO MASHIRO-KUN?
WHAT?
ICHIJO FAINTED IN THE DOJO, SO I BROUGHT--
I'M NOT TALKING ABOUT TODAY!
SOMETHING HAPPENED BETWEEN YOU TWO. I KNOW IT!
NO MATTER HOW MANY TIMES I ASK MASHIRO-KUN, HE WON'T TELL ME!
SO TELL ME WHAT HAPPENED!

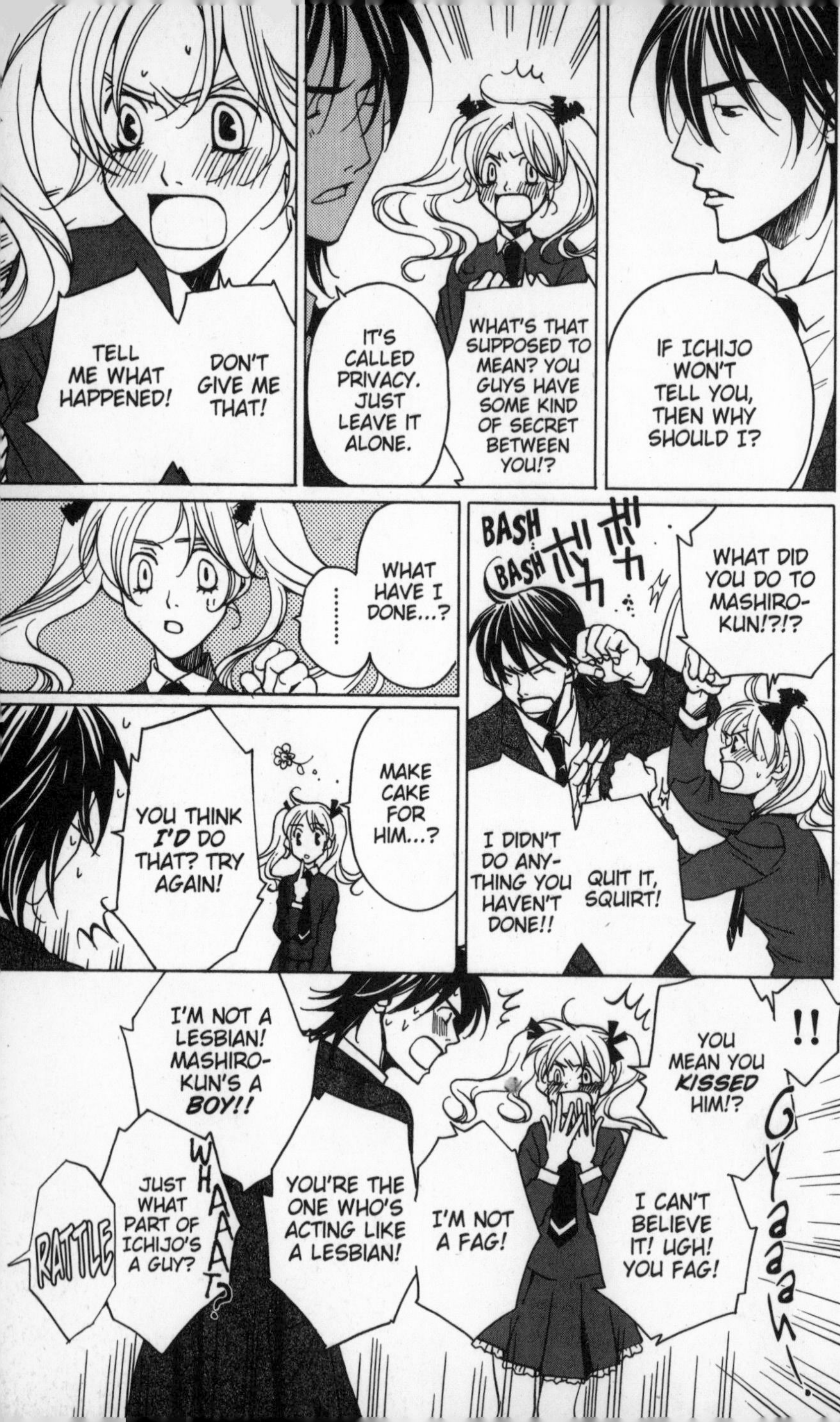
IF ICHIJO WON'T TELL YOU, THEN WHY SHOULD I?
WHAT'S THAT SUPPOSED TO MEAN? YOU GUYS HAVE SOME KIND OF SECRET BETWEEN YOU!?
IT'S CALLED PRIVACY. JUST LEAVE IT ALONE.
DON'T GIVE ME THAT!
TELL ME WHAT HAPPENED!
WHAT DID YOU DO TO MASHIRO-KUN!?!?
ボカ ボカ
BASH BASH
QUIT IT, SQUIRT!
I DIDN'T DO ANYTHING YOU HAVEN'T DONE!!
WHAT HAVE I DONE...?
....
MAKE CAKE FOR HIM...?
YOU THINK ***I'D*** DO THAT? TRY AGAIN!
!!
YOU MEAN YOU ***KISSED*** HIM!?
Gyaaaah!
I CAN'T BELIEVE IT! UGH! YOU FAG!
I'M NOT A LESBIAN! MASHIRO-KUN'S A ***BOY!!***
I'M NOT A FAG!
YOU'RE THE ONE WHO'S ACTING LIKE A LESBIAN!
WHAAAT?
JUST WHAT PART OF ICHIJO'S A GUY?
RATTLE

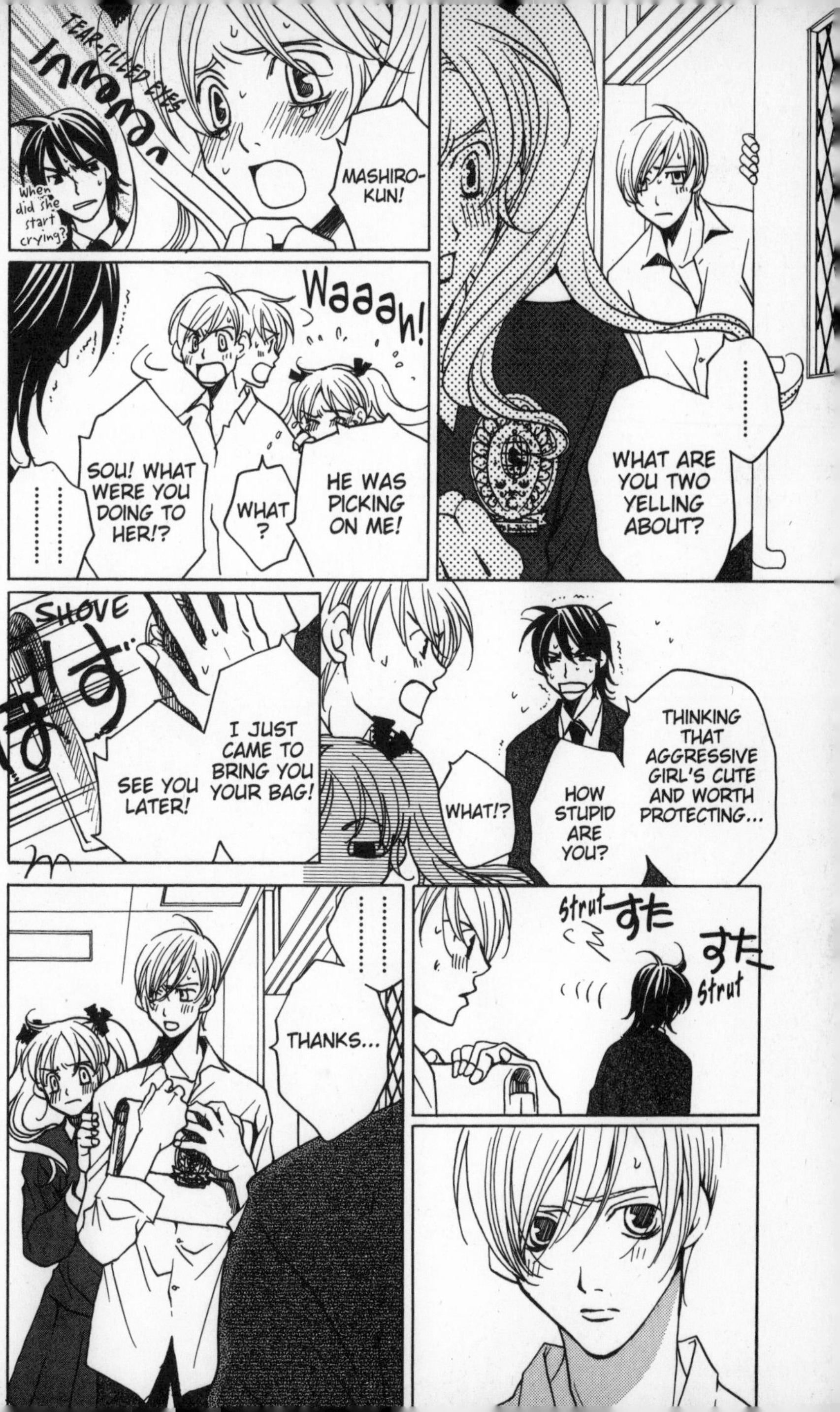
......
WHAT ARE YOU TWO YELLING ABOUT?
TEAR-FILLED EYES
MASHIRO-KUN!
When did she start crying?
Waaaah!
HE WAS PICKING ON ME!
WHAT?
SOU! WHAT WERE YOU DOING TO HER!?
......
THINKING THAT AGGRESSIVE GIRL'S CUTE AND WORTH PROTECTING...
HOW STUPID ARE YOU?
WHAT!?
I JUST CAME TO BRING YOU YOUR BAG!
SEE YOU LATER!
SHOVE
Strut すた
すた Strut
......
THANKS...

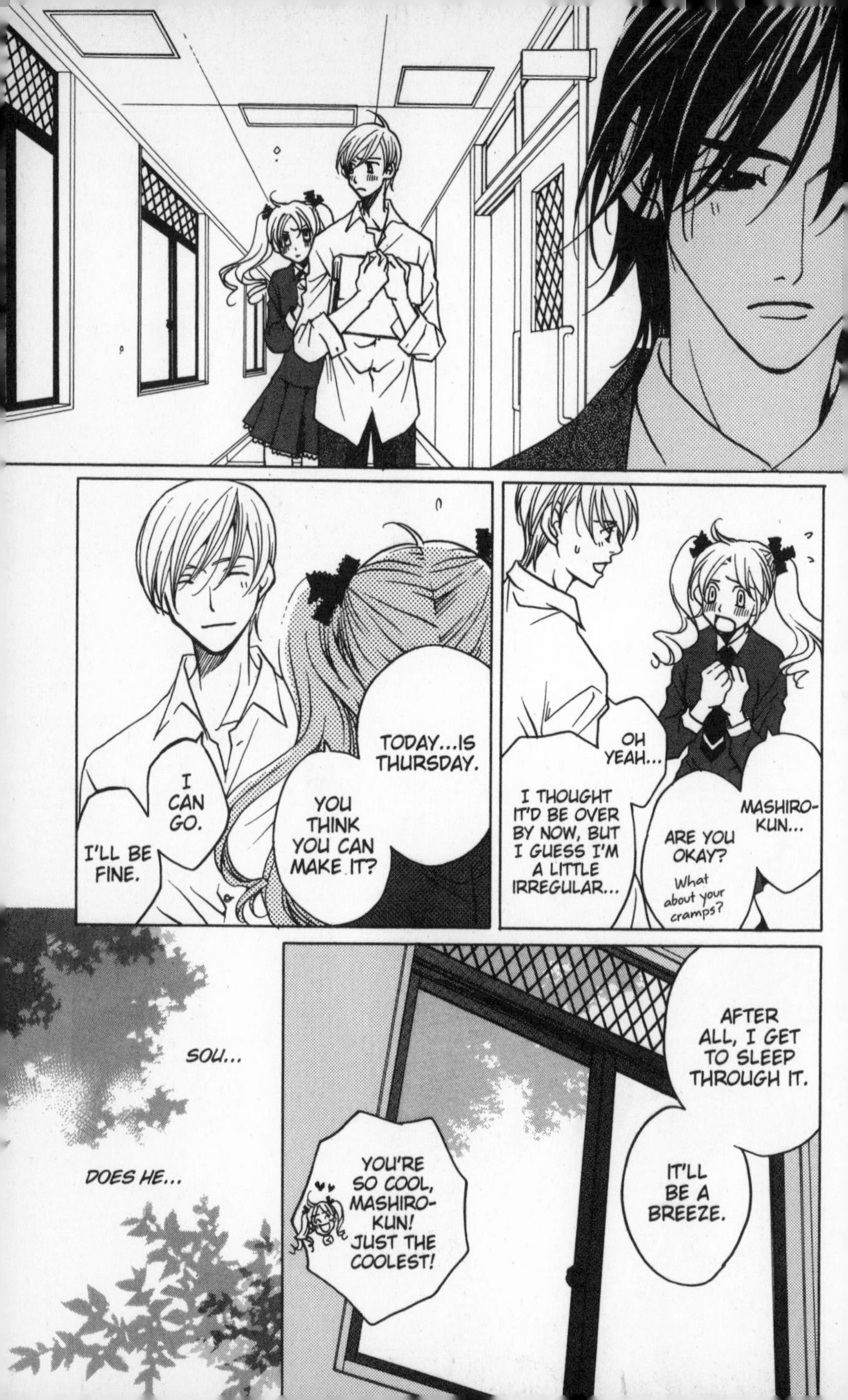
MASHIRO-KUN...
ARE YOU OKAY?
What about your cramps?
OH YEAH...
I THOUGHT IT'D BE OVER BY NOW, BUT I GUESS I'M A LITTLE IRREGULAR...
TODAY...IS THURSDAY.
YOU THINK YOU CAN MAKE IT?
I CAN GO.
I'LL BE FINE.
AFTER ALL, I GET TO SLEEP THROUGH IT.
IT'LL BE A BREEZE.
YOU'RE SO COOL, MASHIRO-KUN! JUST THE COOLEST!
SOU...
DOES HE...

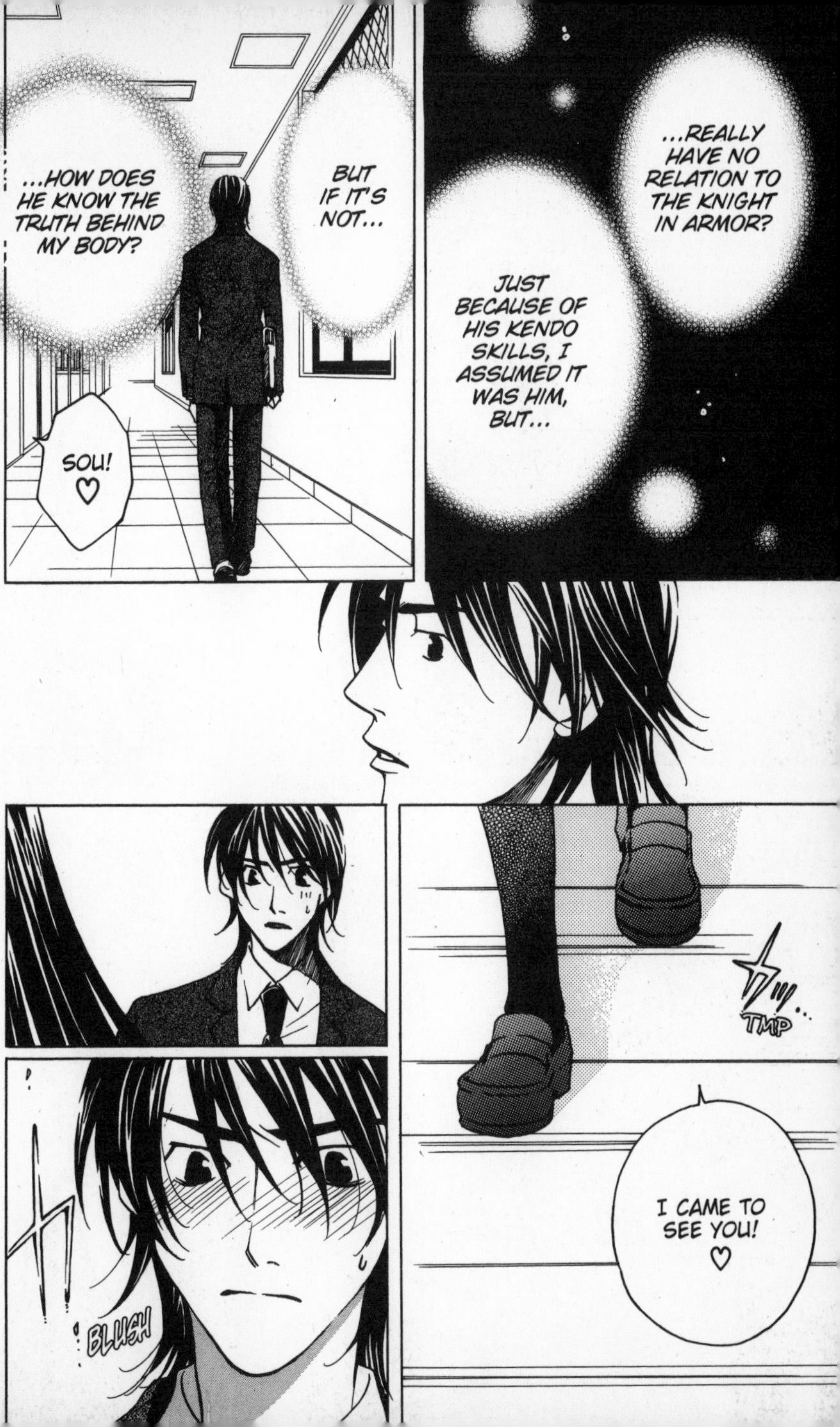
...REALLY HAVE NO RELATION TO THE KNIGHT IN ARMOR?
JUST BECAUSE OF HIS KENDO SKILLS, I ASSUMED IT WAS HIM, BUT...
BUT IF IT'S NOT...
...HOW DOES HE KNOW THE TRUTH BEHIND MY BODY?
SOU! ♡
TMP
I CAME TO SEE YOU! ♡
BLUSH

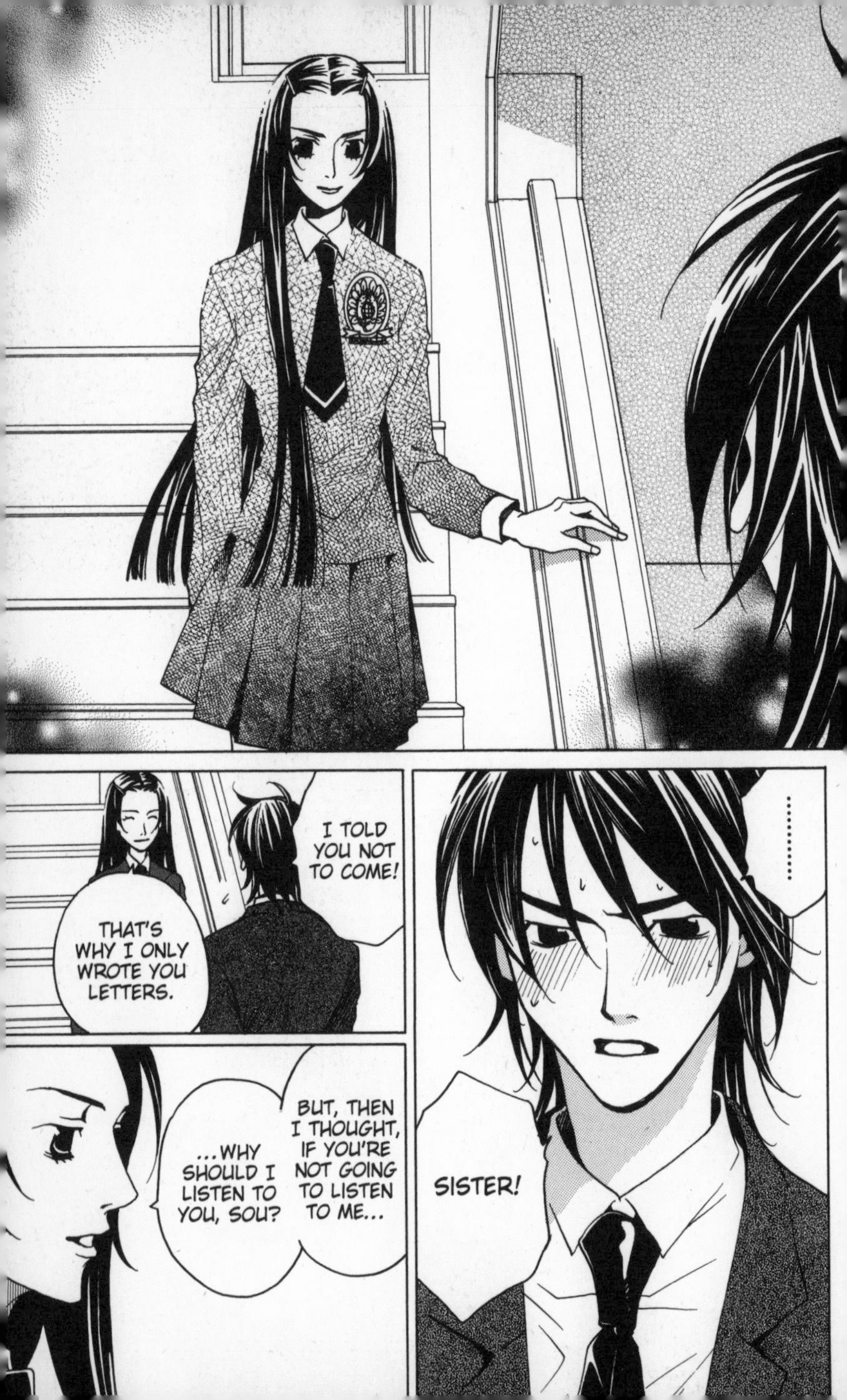
....
SISTER!
I TOLD YOU NOT TO COME!
THAT'S WHY I ONLY WROTE YOU LETTERS.
BUT, THEN I THOUGHT, IF YOU'RE NOT GOING TO LISTEN TO ME...
...WHY SHOULD I LISTEN TO YOU, SOU?

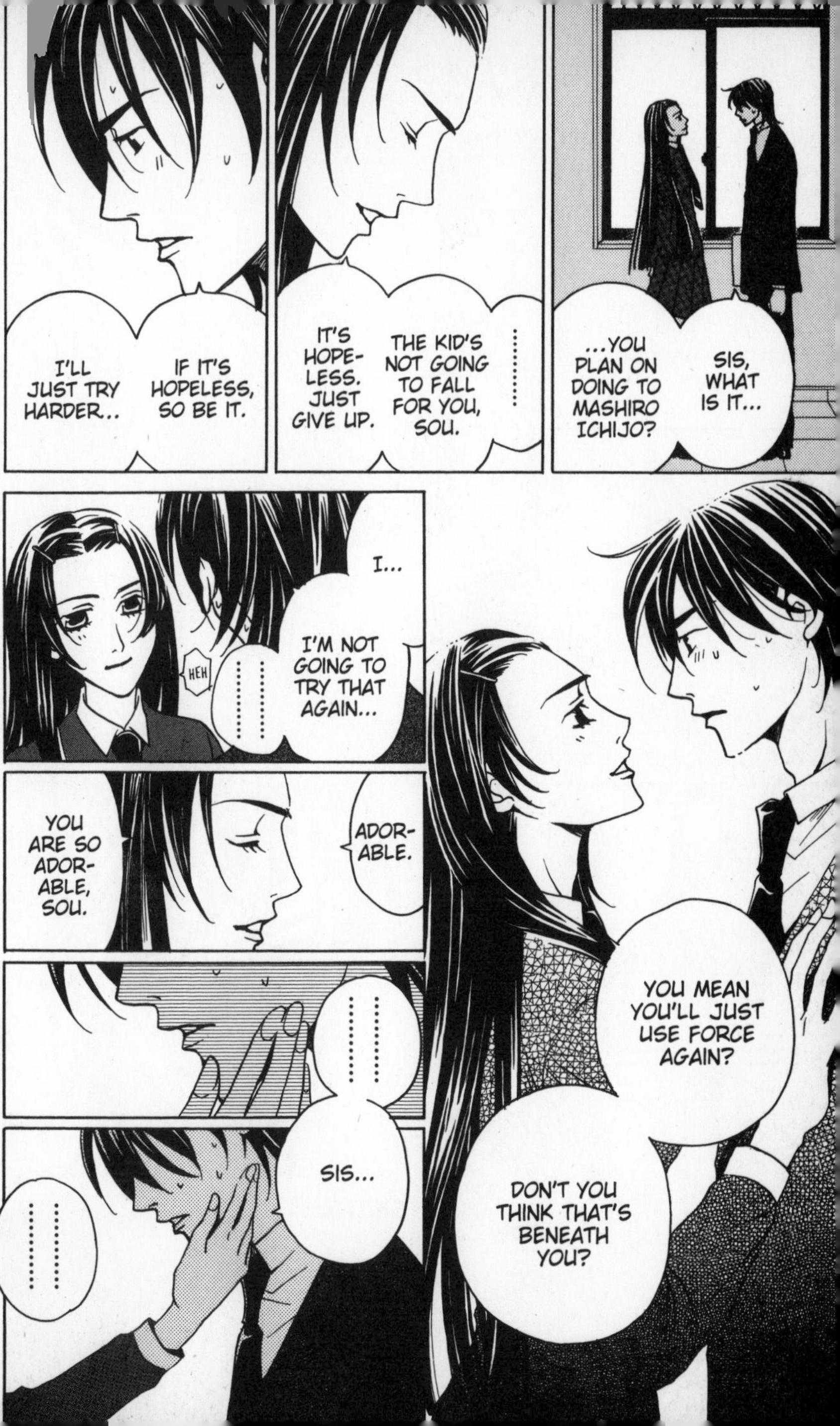
SIS, WHAT IS IT...
...YOU PLAN ON DOING TO MASHIRO ICHIJO?
......
THE KID'S NOT GOING TO FALL FOR YOU, SOU.
IT'S HOPE-LESS. JUST GIVE UP.
IF IT'S HOPELESS, SO BE IT.
I'LL JUST TRY HARDER...
YOU MEAN YOU'LL JUST USE FORCE AGAIN?
DON'T YOU THINK THAT'S BENEATH YOU?
I...
I'M NOT GOING TO TRY THAT AGAIN...
......
HEH
ADOR-ABLE.
YOU ARE SO ADOR-ABLE, SOU.
......
SIS...
......

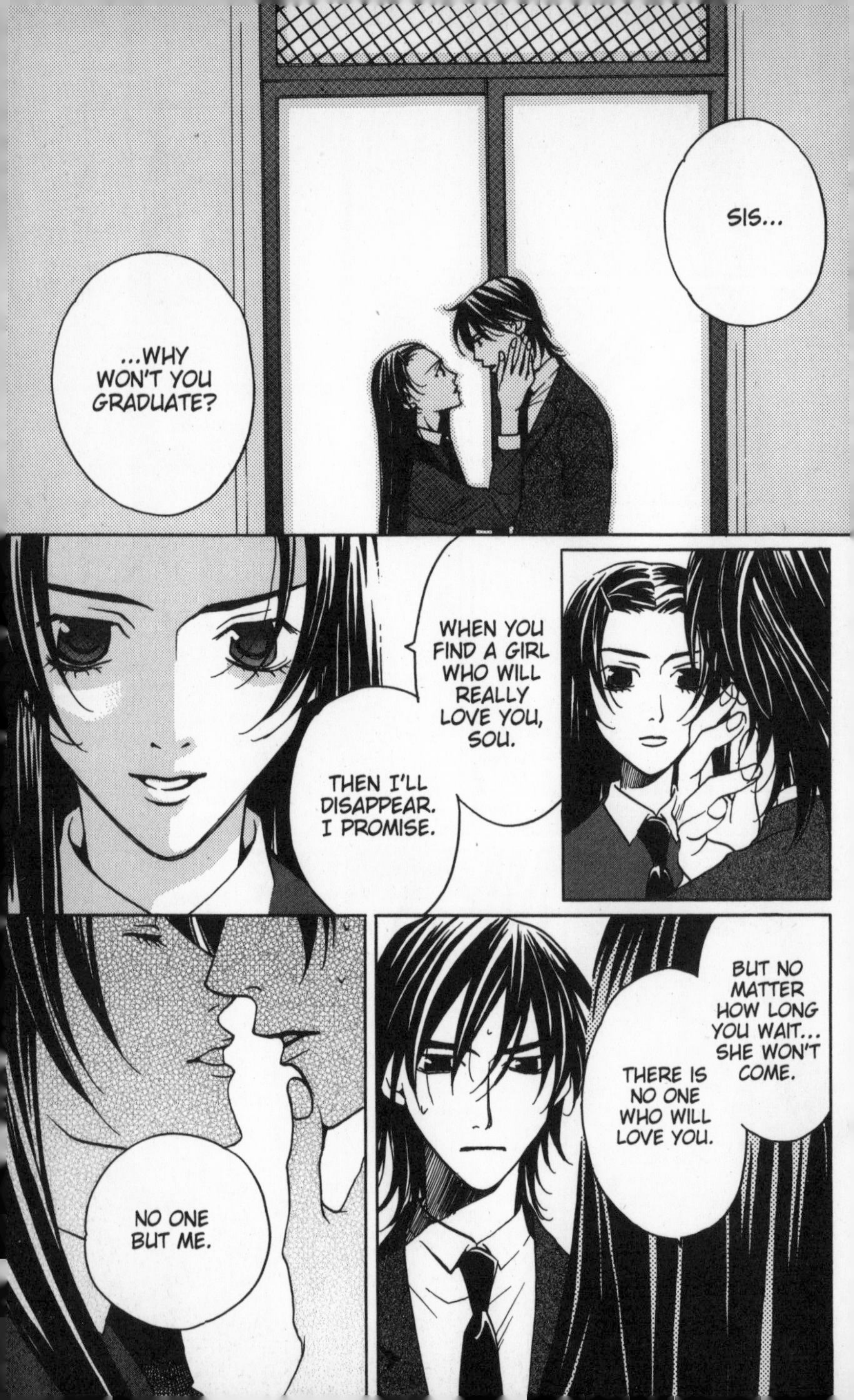
SIS...
...WHY WON'T YOU GRADUATE?
WHEN YOU FIND A GIRL WHO WILL REALLY LOVE YOU, SOU.
THEN I'LL DISAPPEAR. I PROMISE.
BUT NO MATTER HOW LONG YOU WAIT... SHE WON'T COME.
THERE IS NO ONE WHO WILL LOVE YOU.
NO ONE BUT ME.

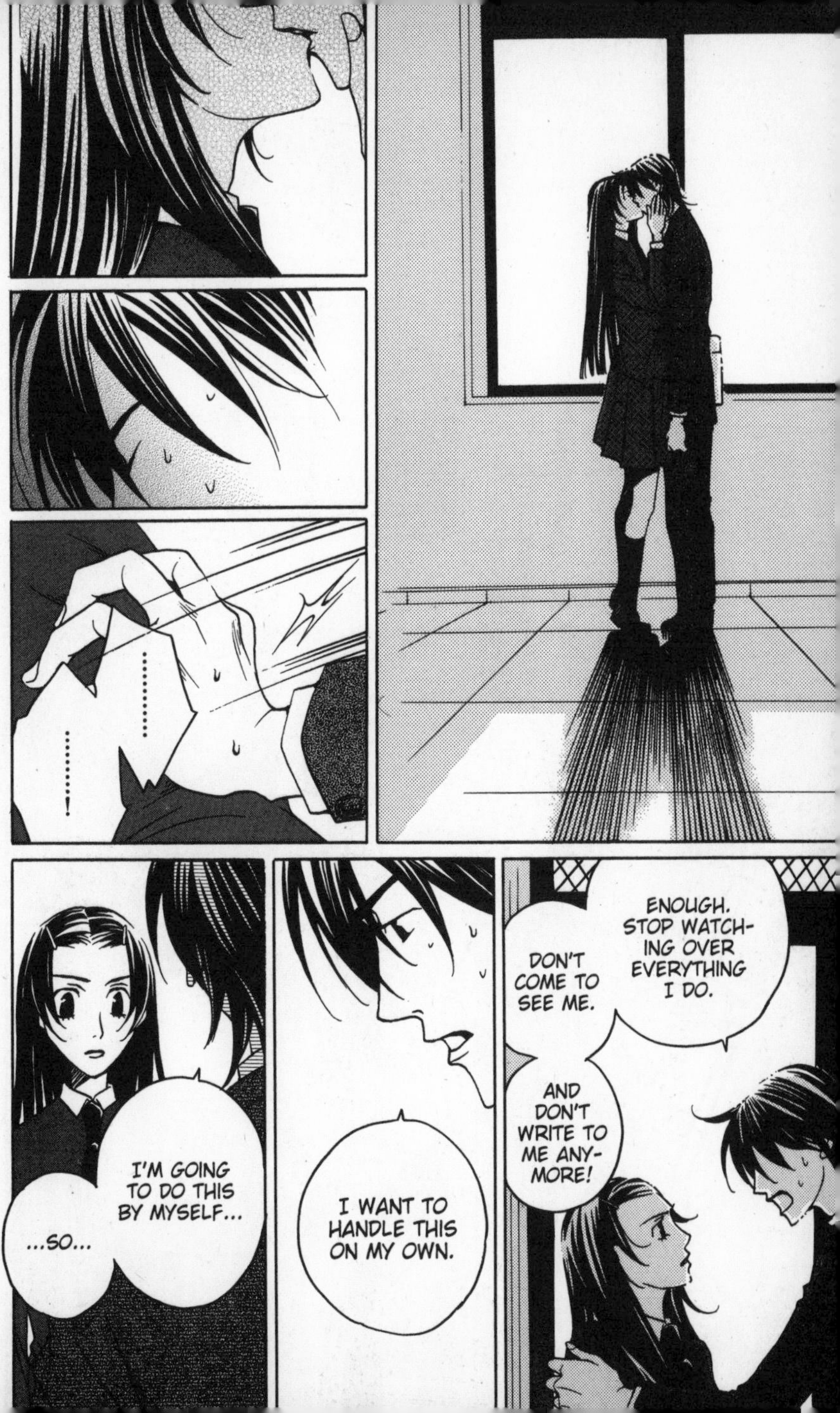

......
......!
ENOUGH. STOP WATCHING OVER EVERYTHING I DO.
DON'T COME TO SEE ME.
AND DON'T WRITE TO ME ANYMORE!
I WANT TO HANDLE THIS ON MY OWN.
I'M GOING TO DO THIS BY MYSELF...
...SO...

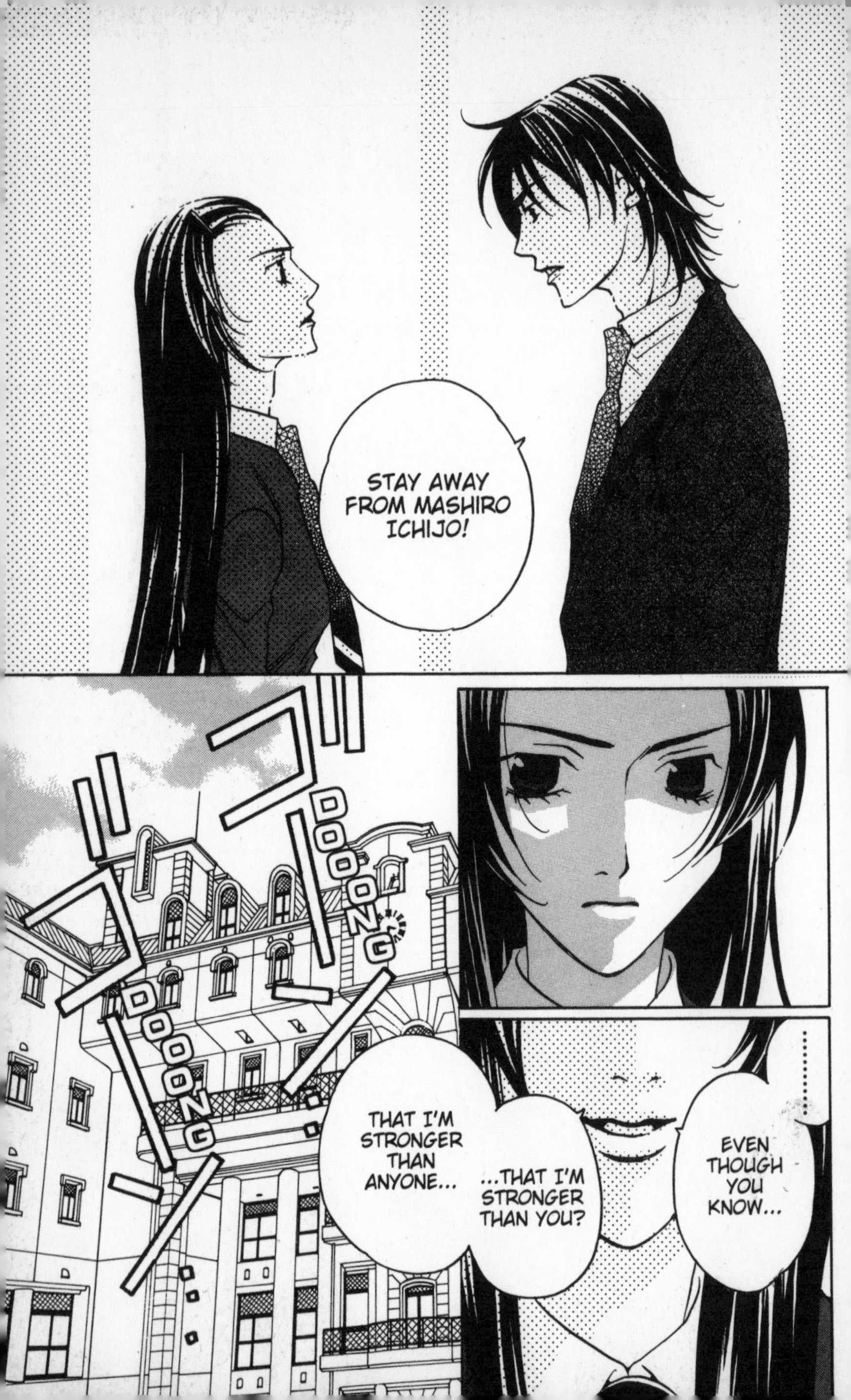
STAY AWAY FROM MASHIRO ICHIJO!
......
EVEN THOUGH YOU KNOW...
...THAT I'M STRONGER THAN YOU?
THAT I'M STRONGER THAN ANYONE...
DOOONG
DOOONG

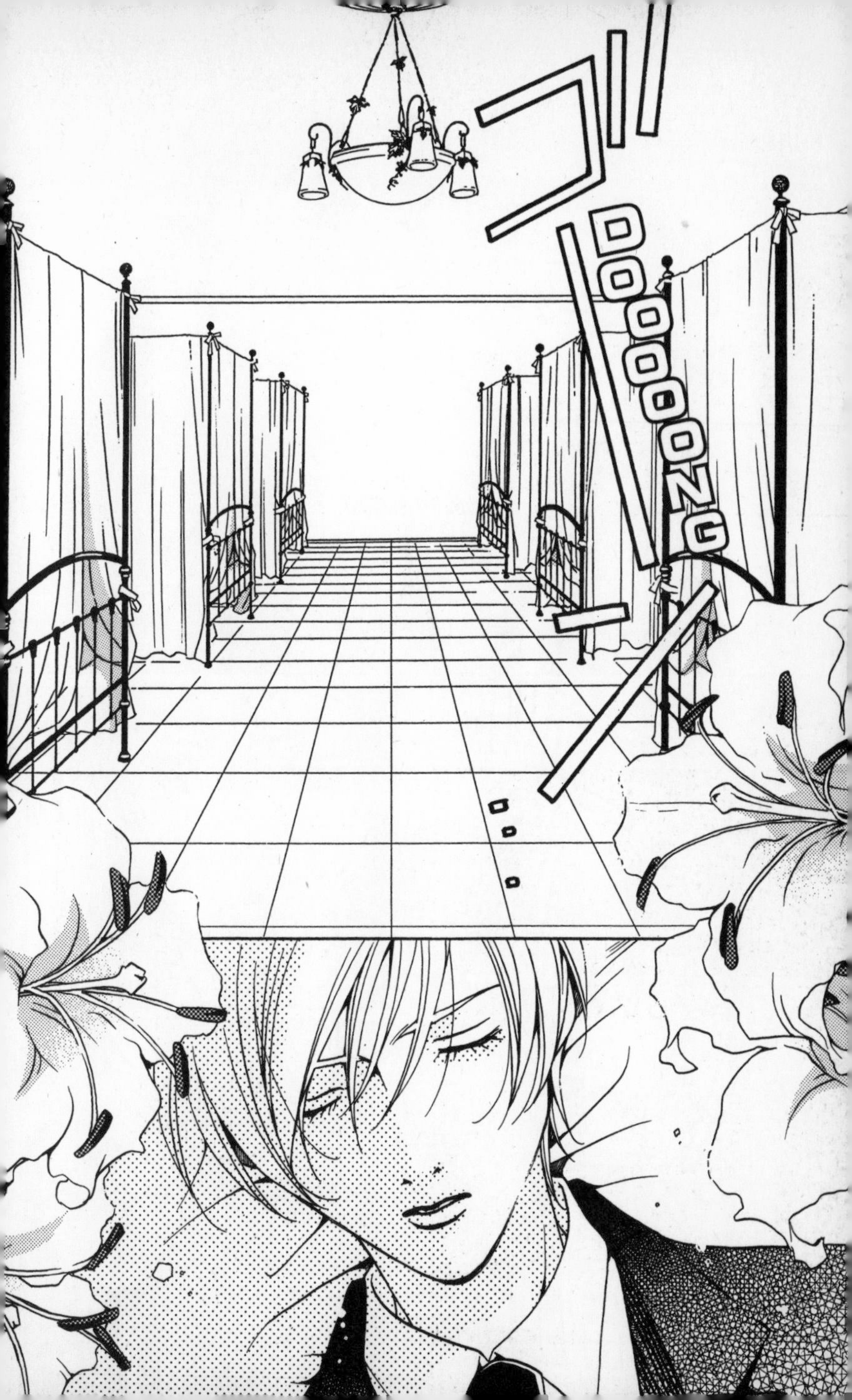
ゴ
DOOOOONG
...

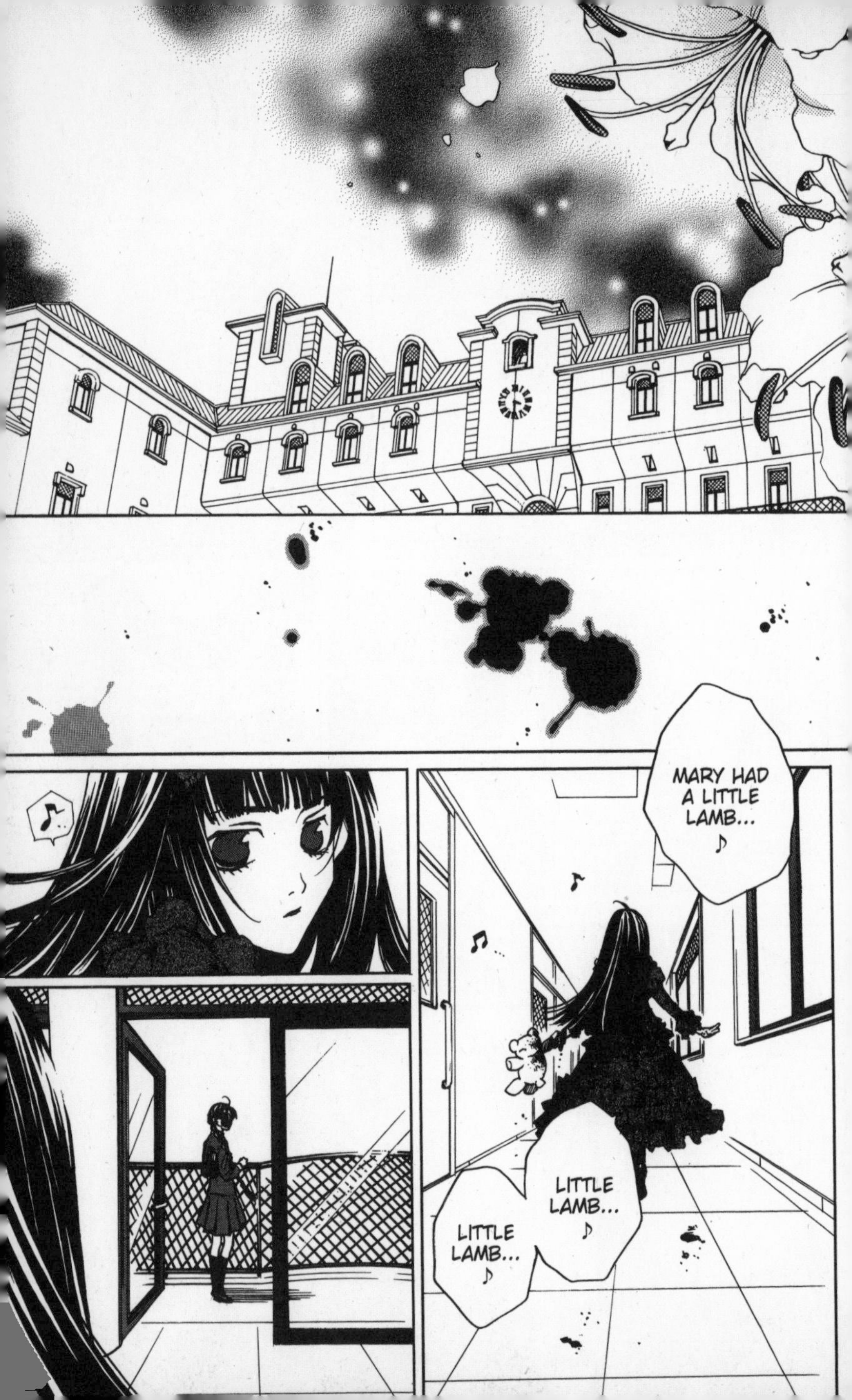
MARY HAD A LITTLE LAMB... ♪
♪
♪...
LITTLE LAMB... ♪
LITTLE LAMB... ♪
♪...

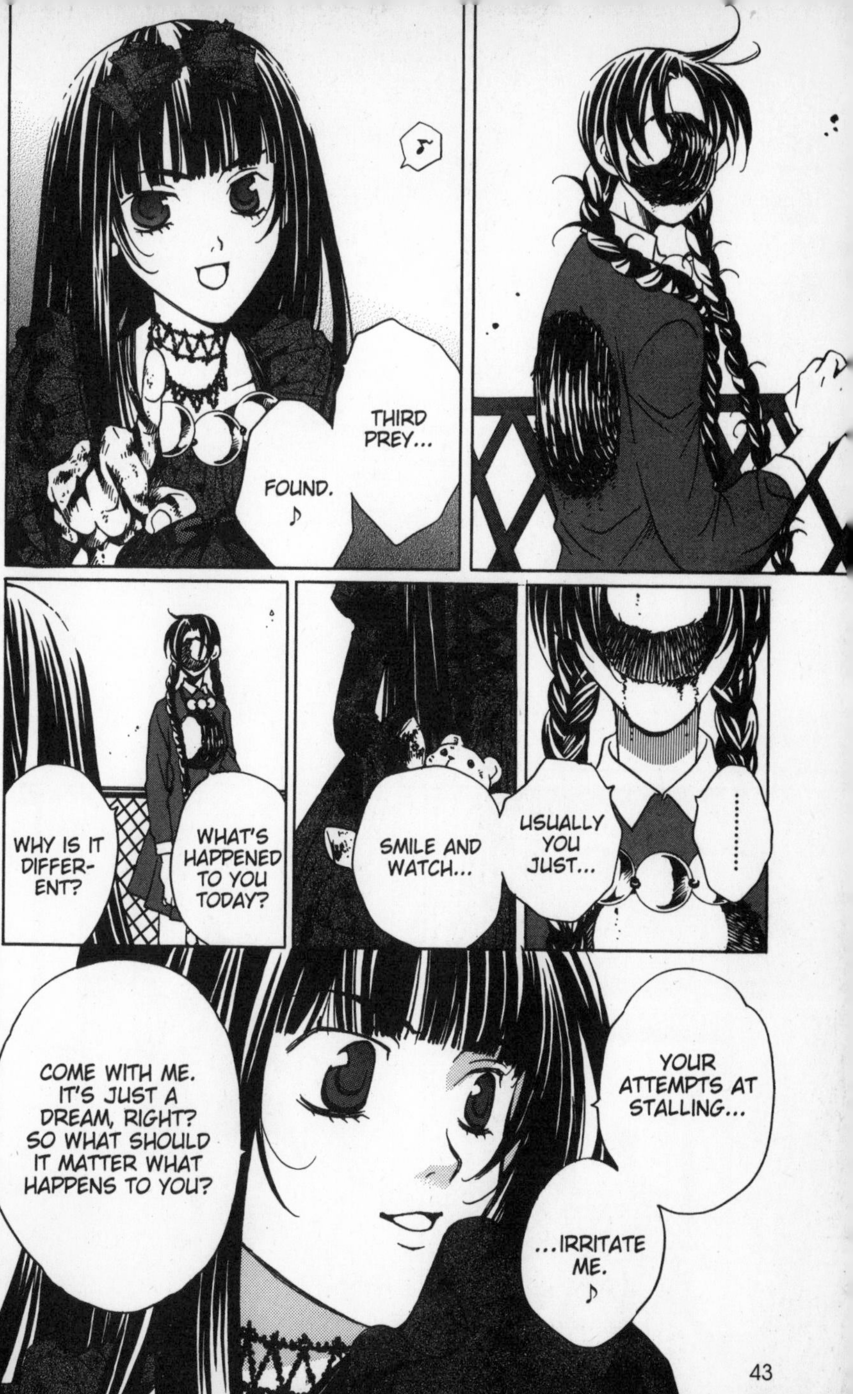
♪
THIRD PREY...
FOUND. ♪
......
USUALLY YOU JUST...
SMILE AND WATCH...
WHAT'S HAPPENED TO YOU TODAY?
WHY IS IT DIFFER-ENT?
YOUR ATTEMPTS AT STALLING...
...IRRITATE ME. ♪
COME WITH ME. IT'S JUST A DREAM, RIGHT? SO WHAT SHOULD IT MATTER WHAT HAPPENS TO YOU?

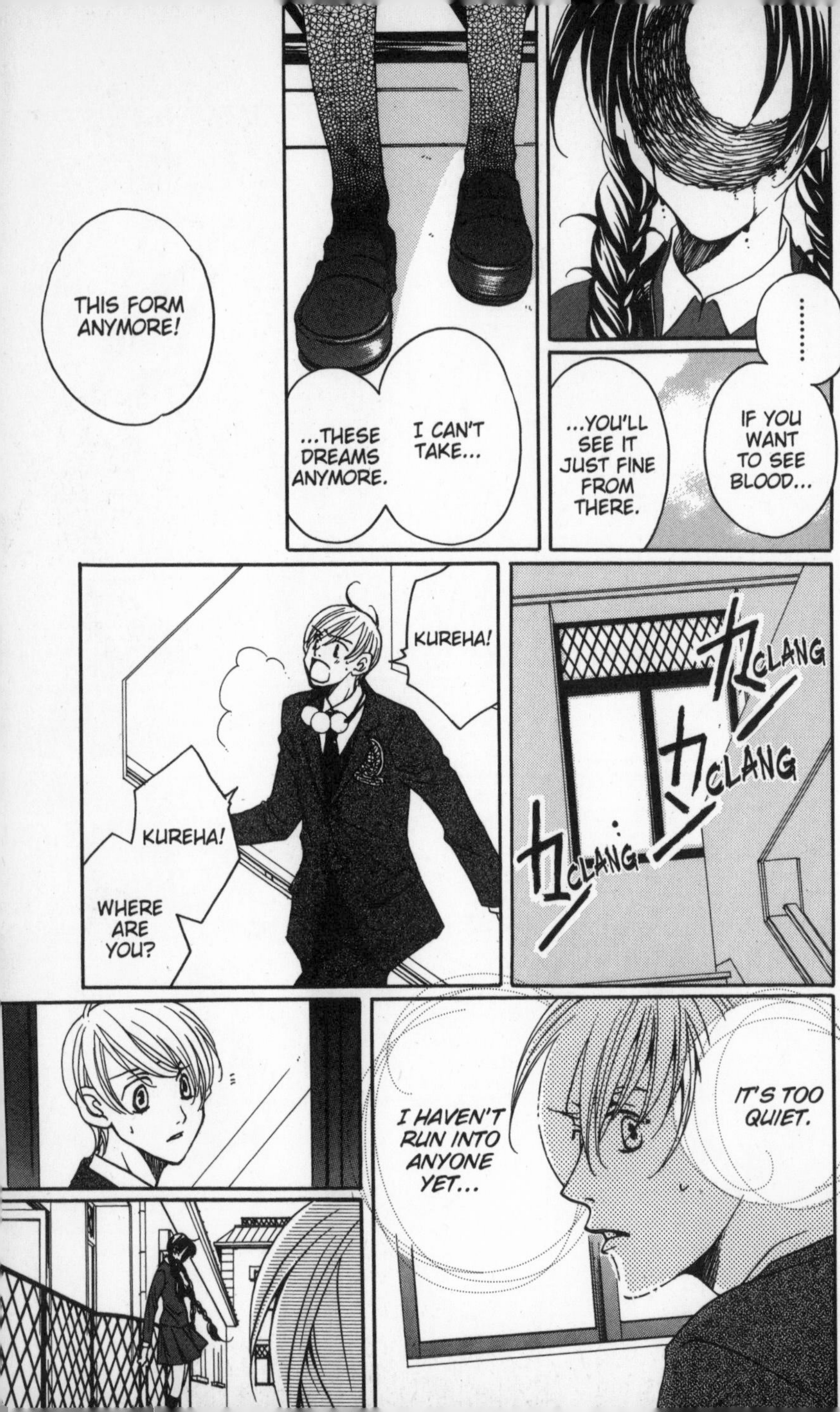
……
IF YOU WANT TO SEE BLOOD...
...YOU'LL SEE IT JUST FINE FROM THERE.
I CAN'T TAKE...
...THESE DREAMS ANYMORE.
THIS FORM ANYMORE!
CLANG
CLANG
CLANG
KUREHA!
KUREHA!
WHERE ARE YOU?
IT'S TOO QUIET.
I HAVEN'T RUN INTO ANYONE YET...

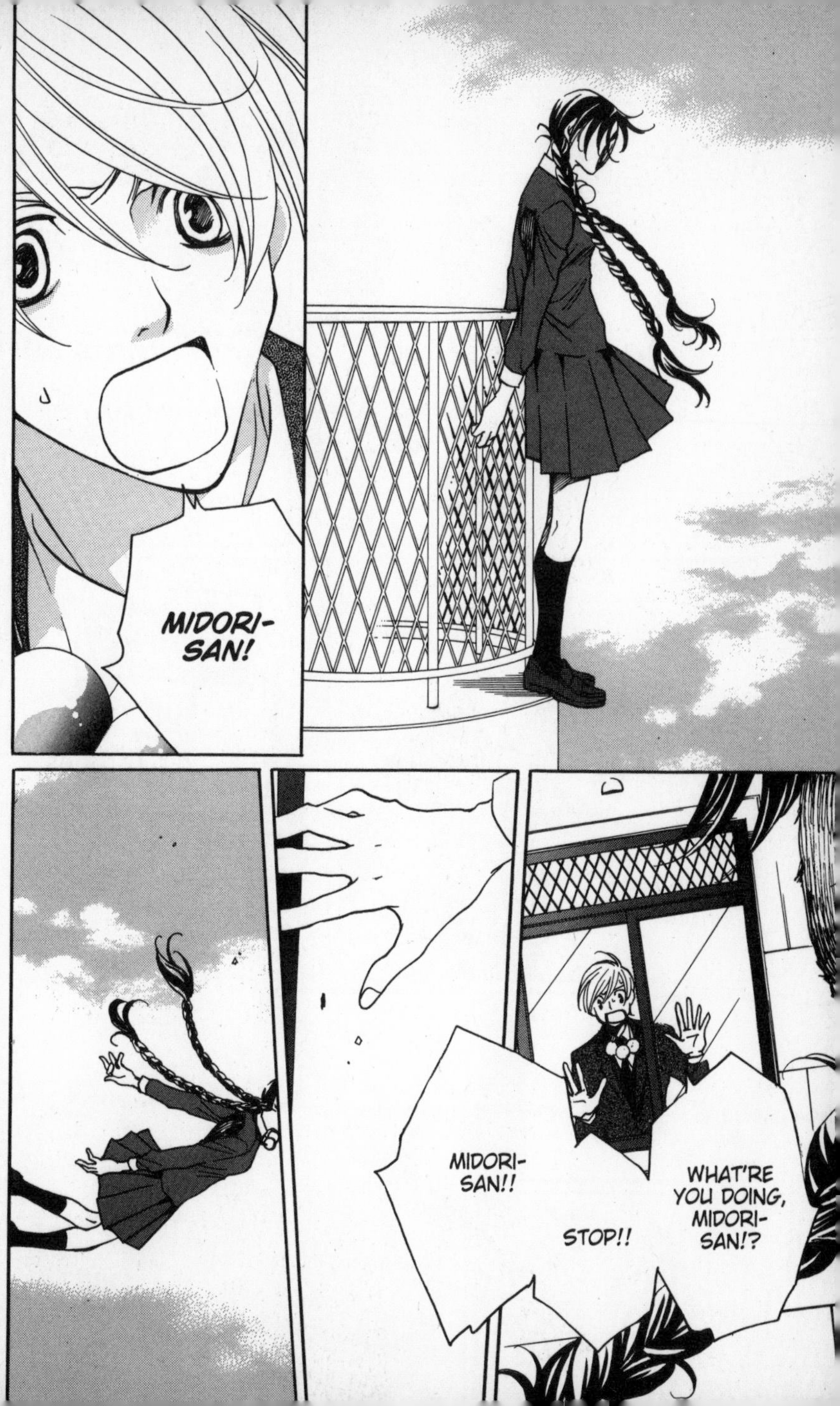
MIDORI-SAN!
WHAT'RE YOU DOING, MIDORI-SAN!?
STOP!!
MIDORI-SAN!!

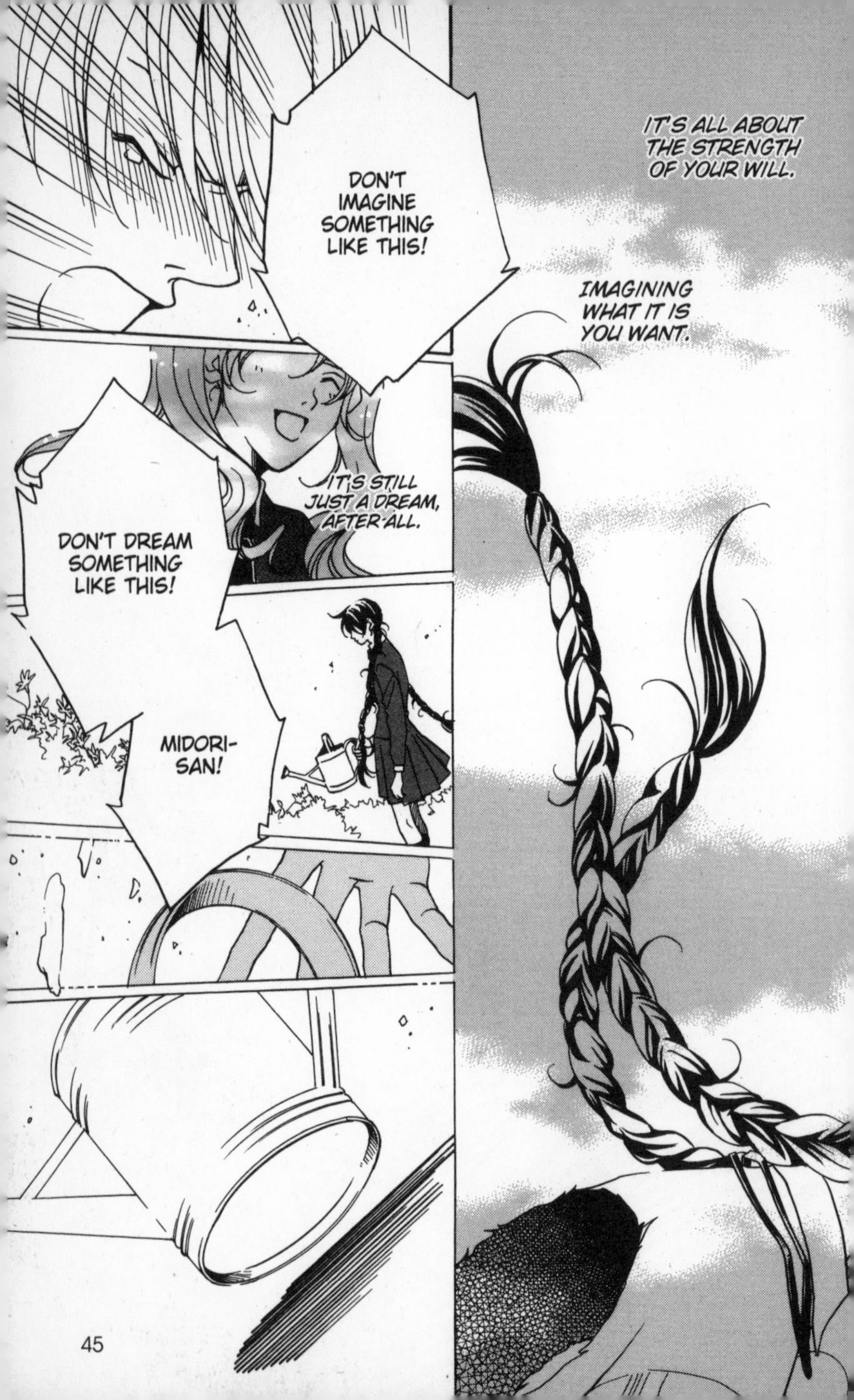
IT'S ALL ABOUT THE STRENGTH OF YOUR WILL.
IMAGINING WHAT IT IS YOU WANT.
DON'T IMAGINE SOMETHING LIKE THIS!
IT'S STILL JUST A DREAM, AFTER ALL.
DON'T DREAM SOMETHING LIKE THIS!
MIDORI-SAN!

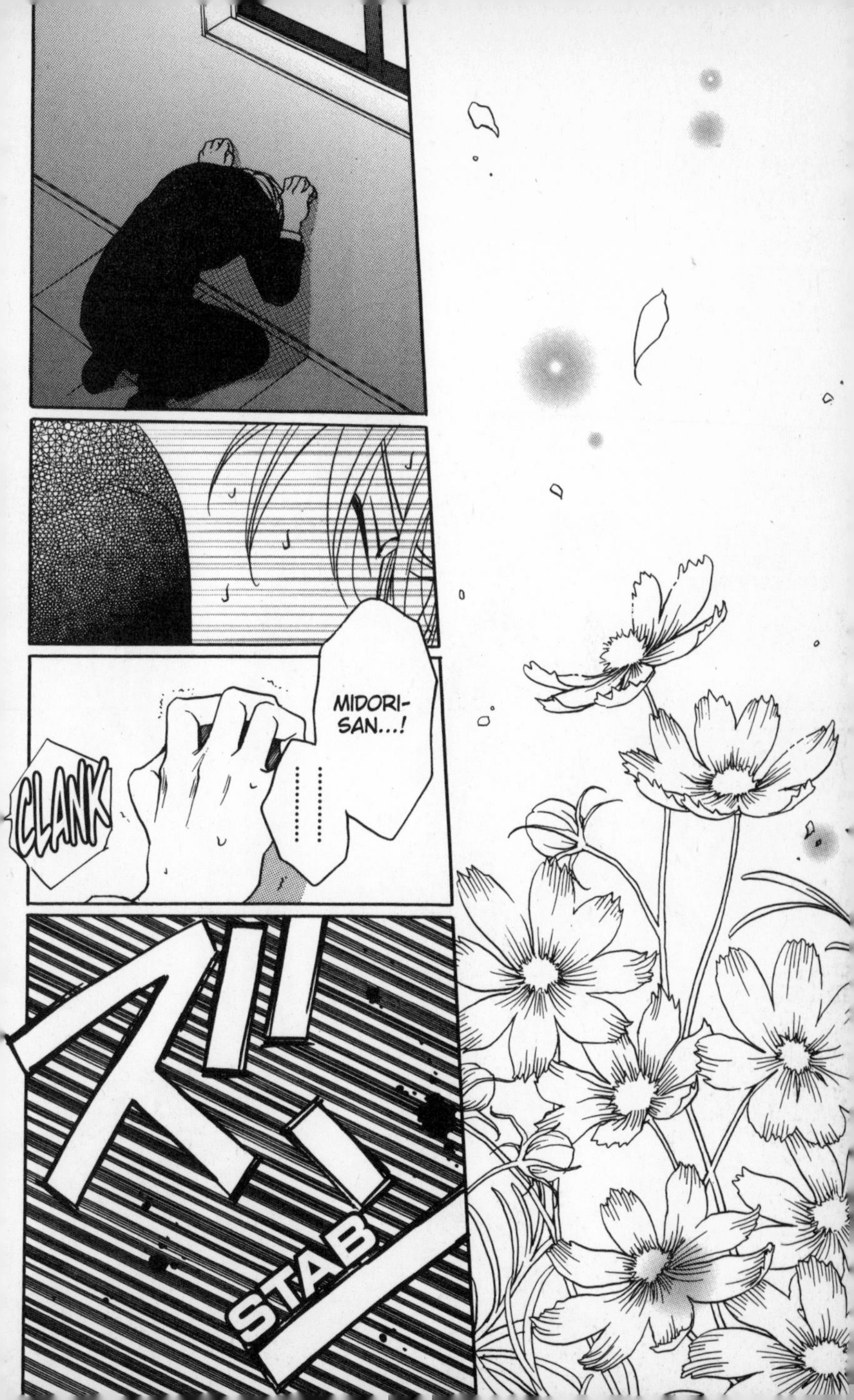
MIDORI-SAN...!
......
CLANK
STAB

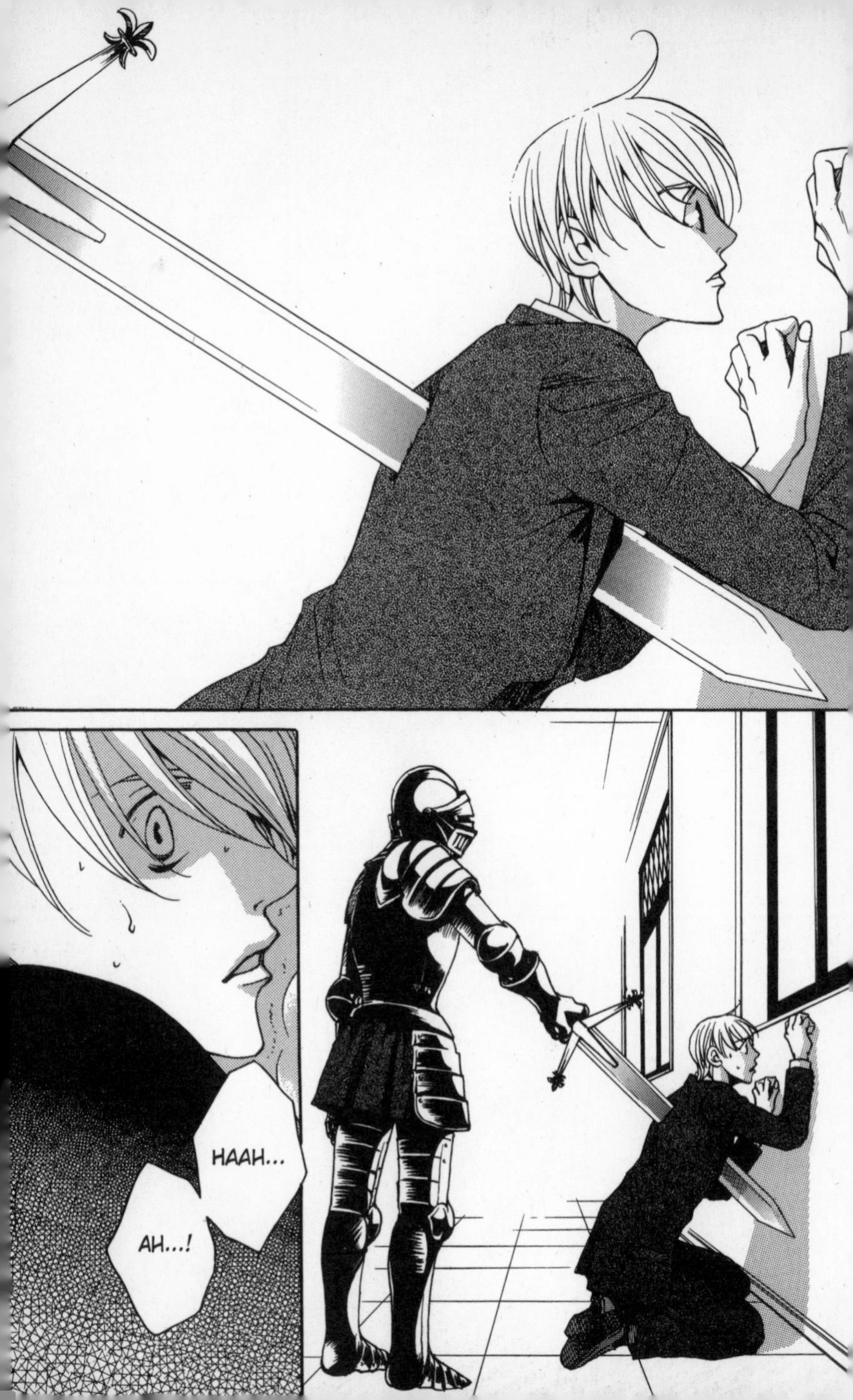
HAAH...
AH...!

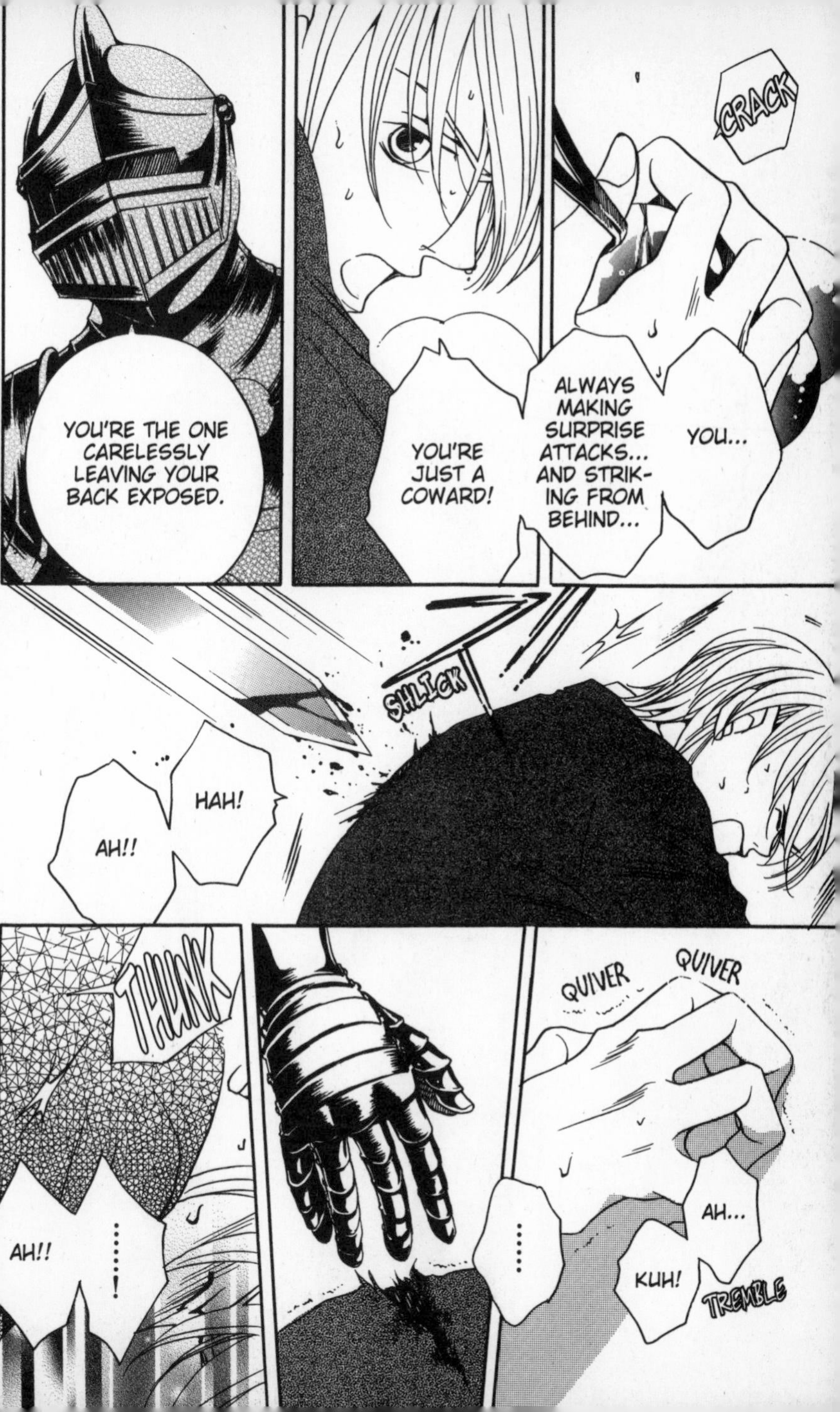
CRACK
YOU...
ALWAYS MAKING SURPRISE ATTACKS... AND STRIKING FROM BEHIND...
YOU'RE JUST A COWARD!
YOU'RE THE ONE CARELESSLY LEAVING YOUR BACK EXPOSED.
SHLICK
HAH!
AH!!
QUIVER
QUIVER
AH...
KUH!
TREMBLE
......
THUNK
......!
AH!!

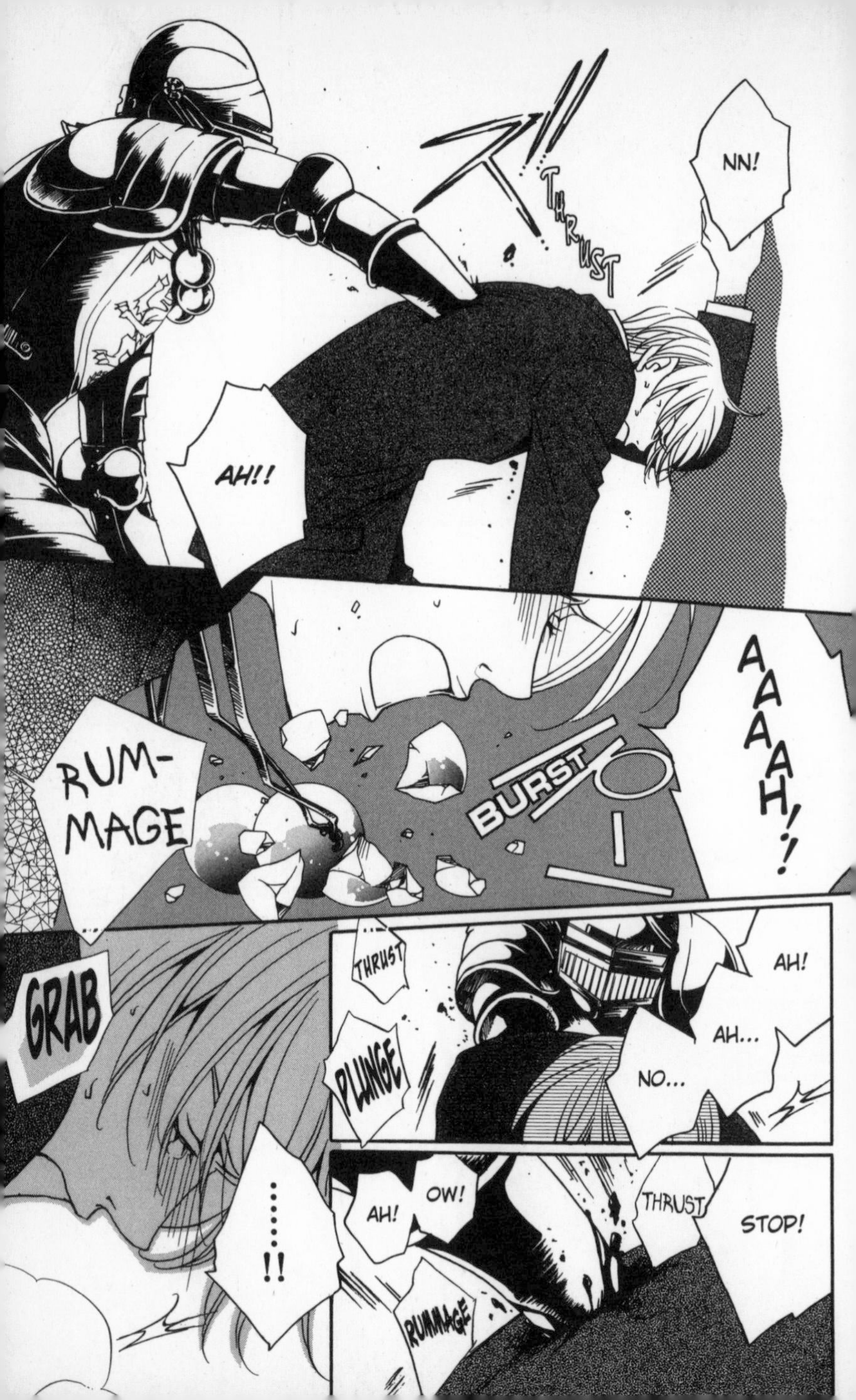
NN!
THRUST
AH!!
AAAAH!!
BURST
RUM-
MAGE
AH!
AH...
NO...
THRUST
PLUNGE
STOP!
THRUST
OW!
AH!
RUMMAGE
GRAB
......!!

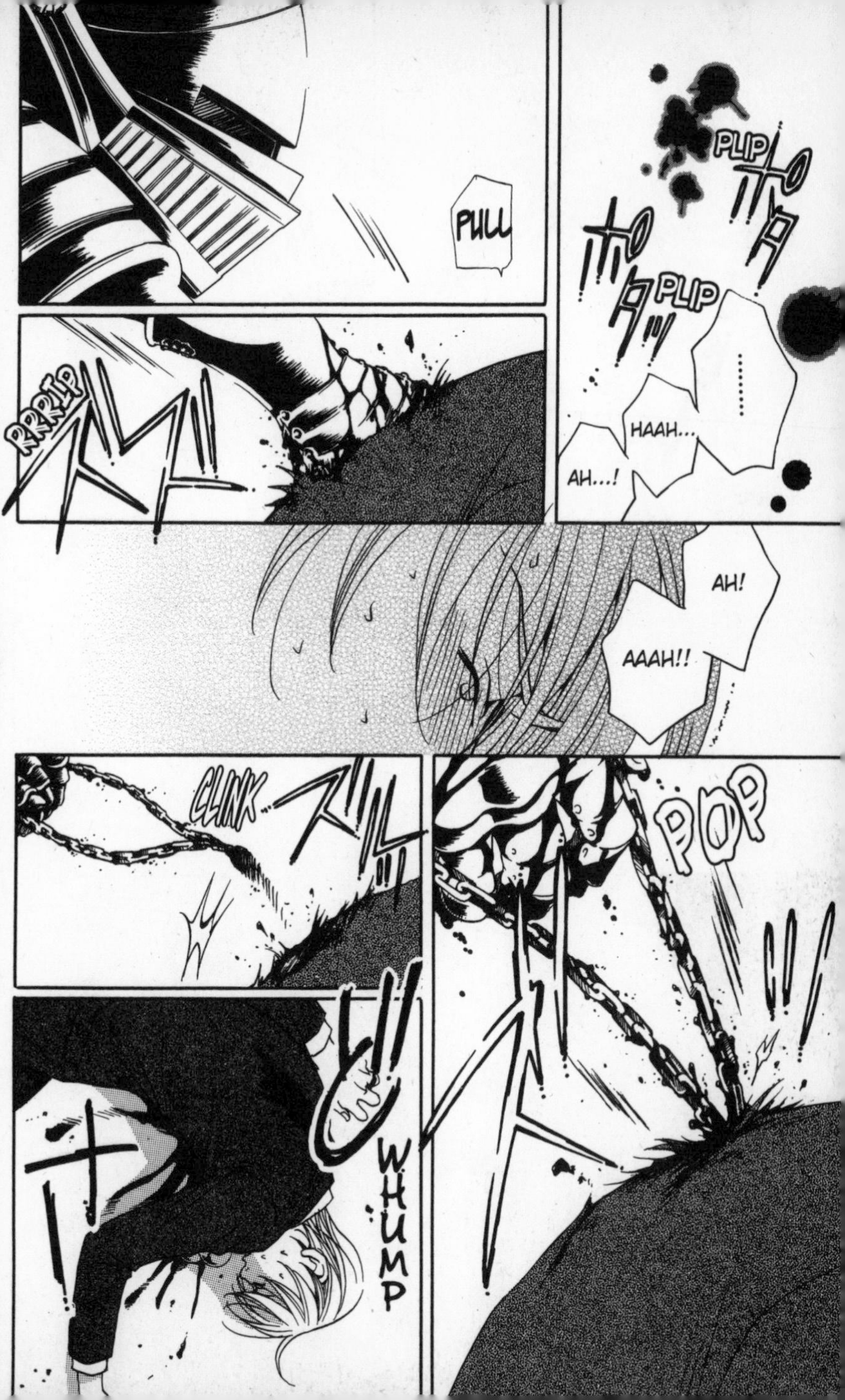
PLIP
PLIP
......
HAAH...
AH...!
PULL
RRRIP
AH!
AAAH!!
POP
CLINK
WHUMP

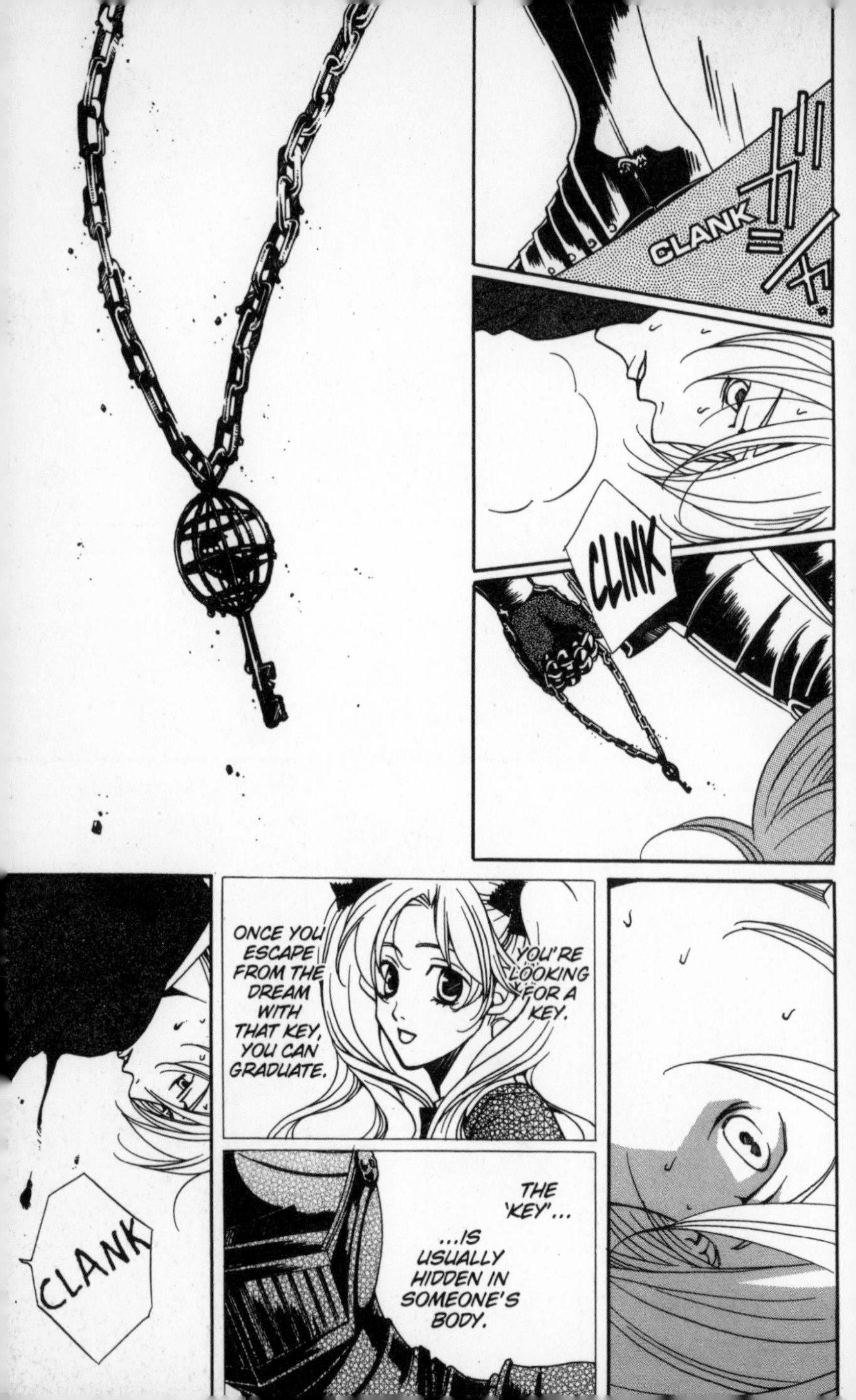
CLANK
CLINK
YOU'RE LOOKING FOR A KEY.
ONCE YOU ESCAPE FROM THE DREAM WITH THAT KEY, YOU CAN GRADUATE.
THE 'KEY'...
...IS USUALLY HIDDEN IN SOMEONE'S BODY.
CLANK

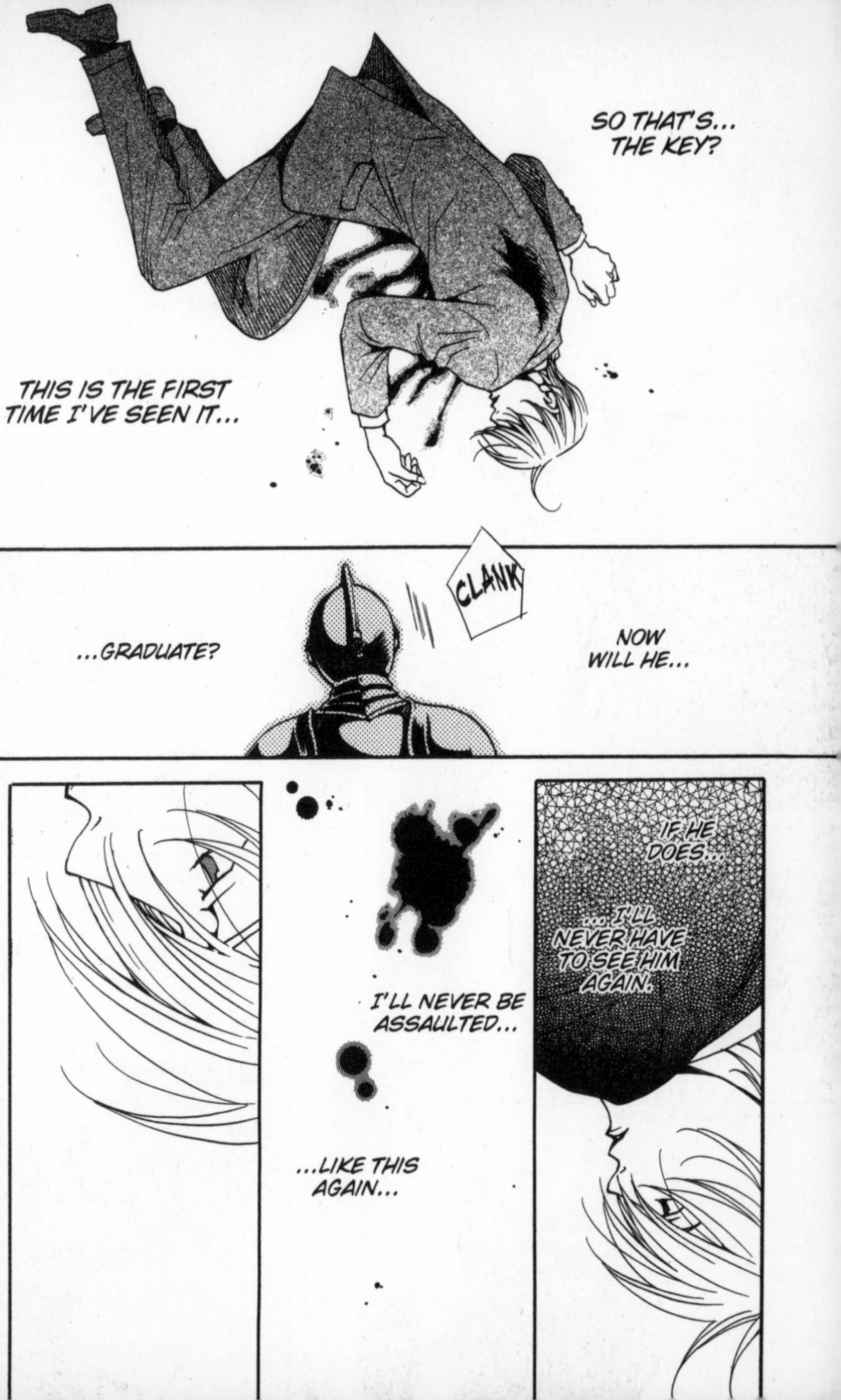
SO THAT'S... THE KEY?
THIS IS THE FIRST TIME I'VE SEEN IT...
CLANK
NOW WILL HE...
...GRADUATE?
IF HE DOES...
...I'LL NEVER HAVE TO SEE HIM AGAIN.
I'LL NEVER BE ASSAULTED...
...LIKE THIS AGAIN...

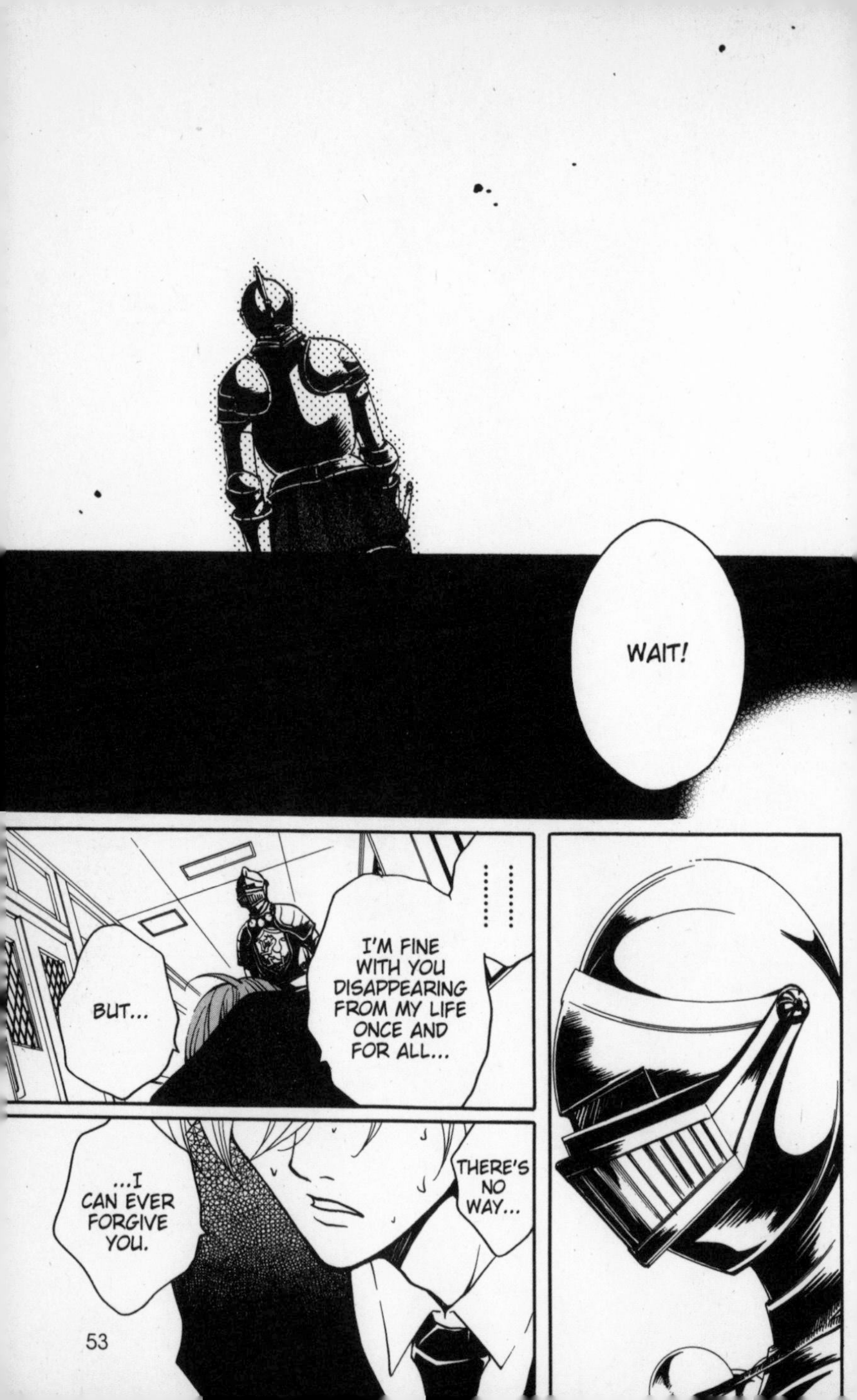
WAIT!
......
I'M FINE WITH YOU DISAPPEARING FROM MY LIFE ONCE AND FOR ALL...
BUT...
THERE'S NO WAY...
...I CAN EVER FORGIVE YOU.

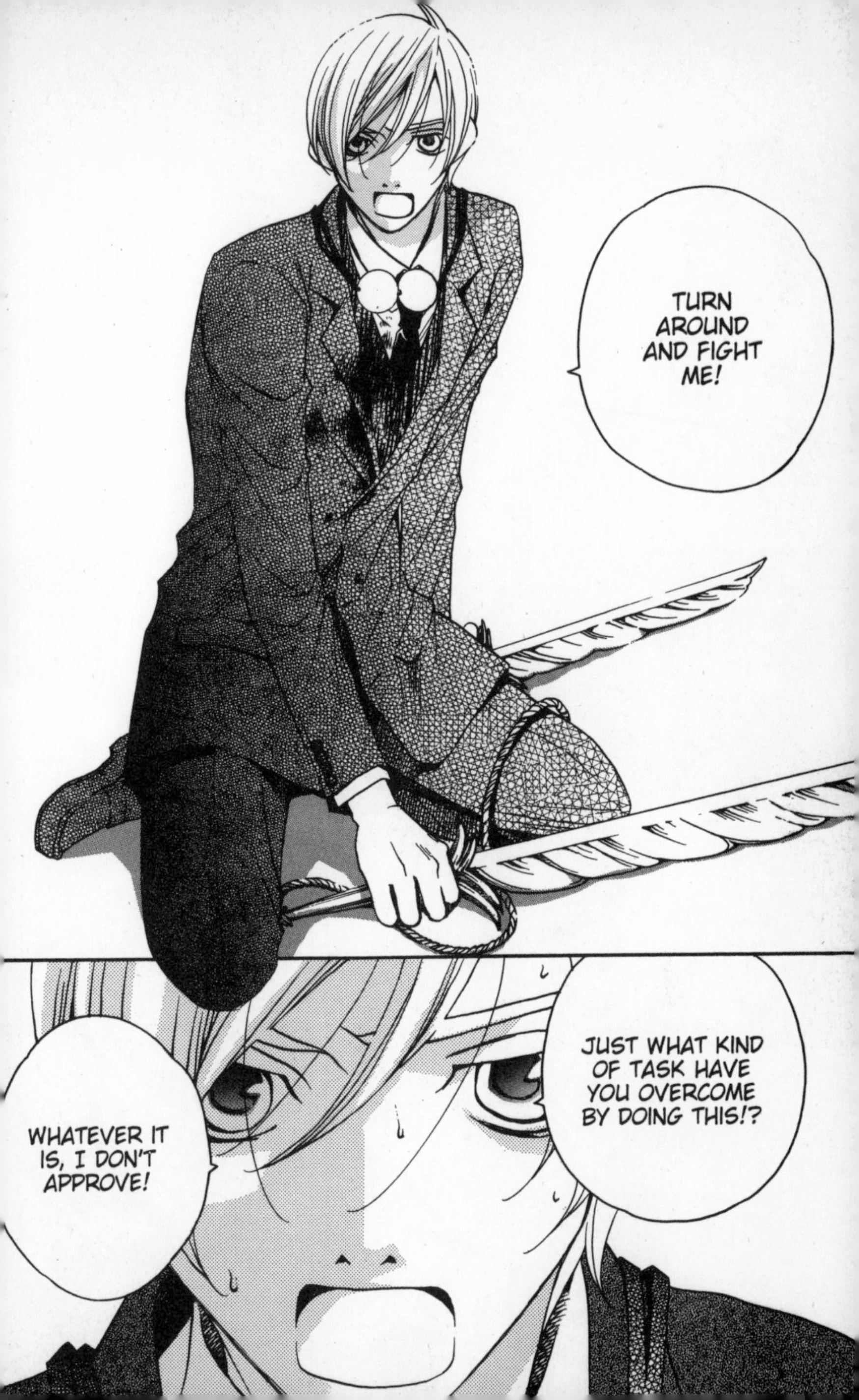
TURN AROUND AND FIGHT ME!
JUST WHAT KIND OF TASK HAVE YOU OVERCOME BY DOING THIS!?
WHATEVER IT IS, I DON'T APPROVE!

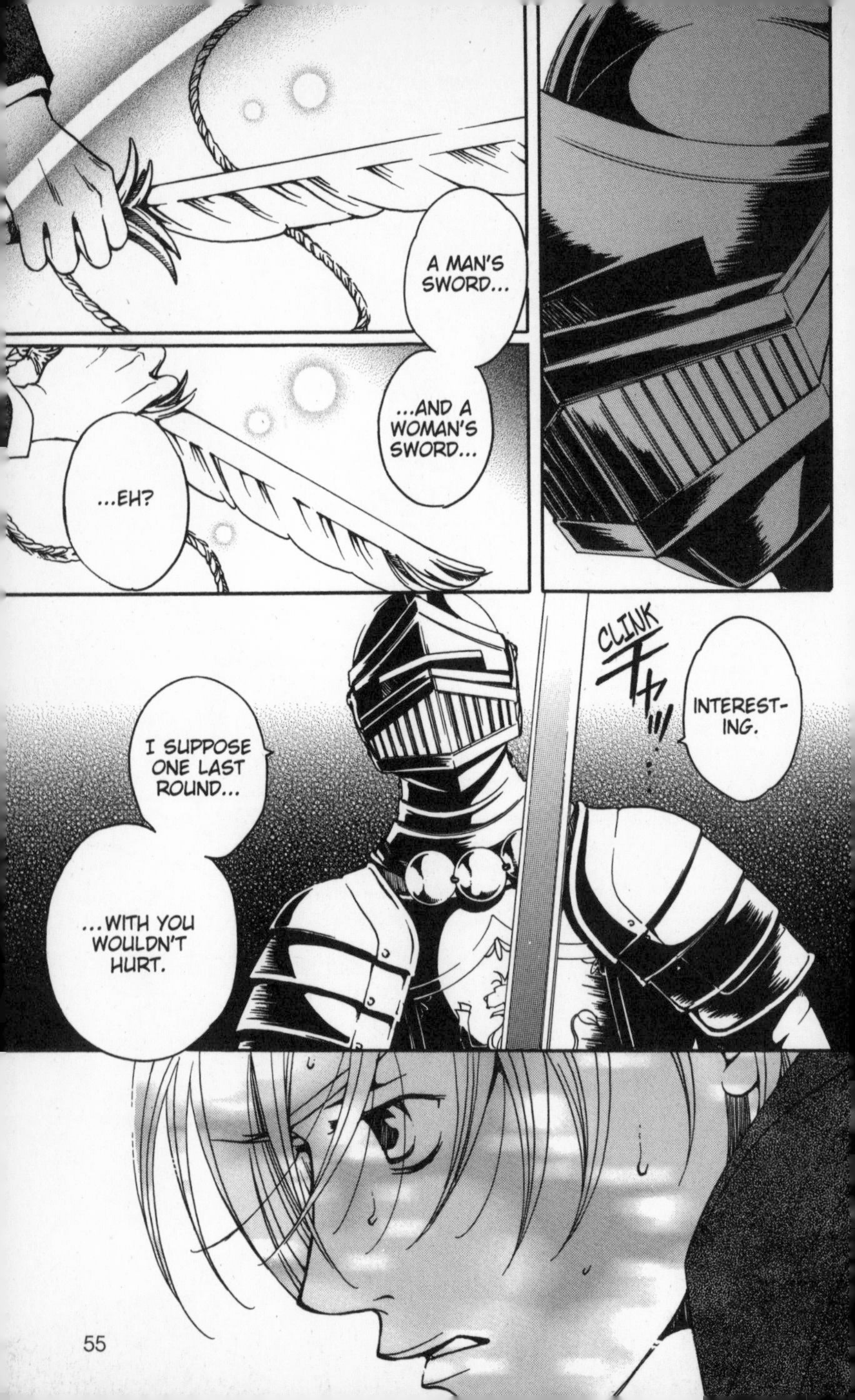
A MAN'S SWORD...
...AND A WOMAN'S SWORD...
...EH?
CLINK
INTEREST-ING.
I SUPPOSE ONE LAST ROUND...
...WITH YOU WOULDN'T HURT.

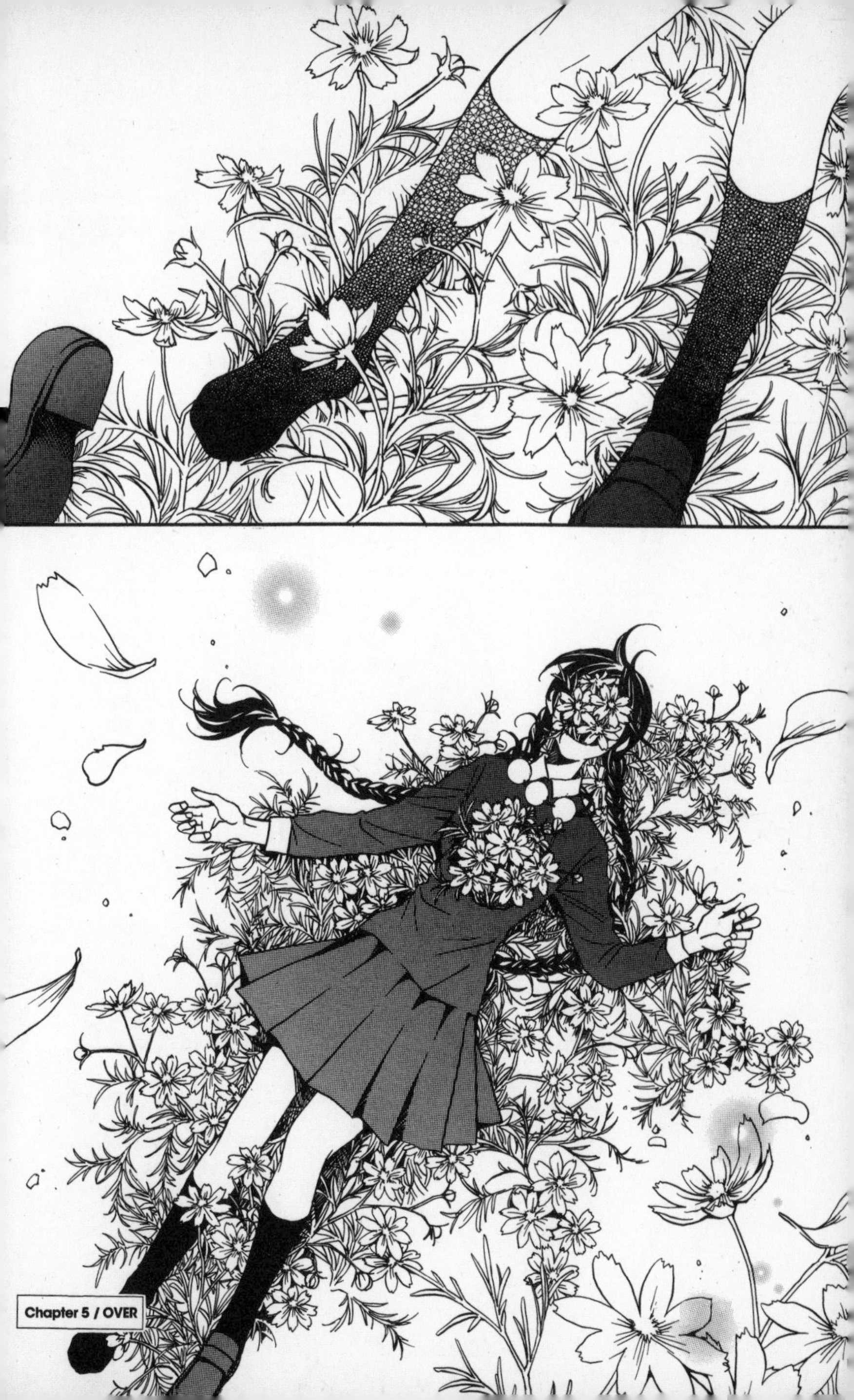
Chapter 5 / OVER

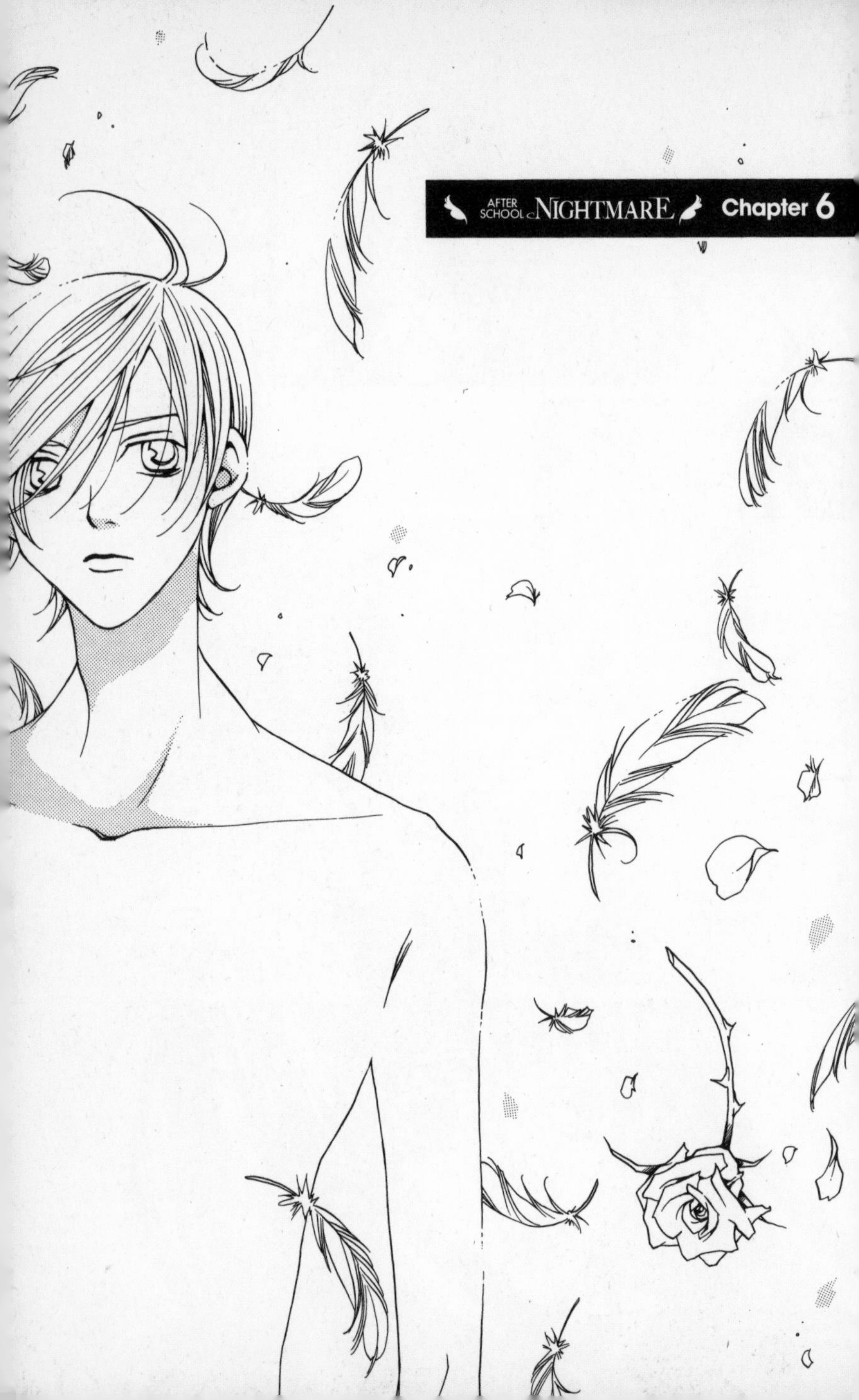
AFTER SCHOOL NIGHTMARE
Chapter 6

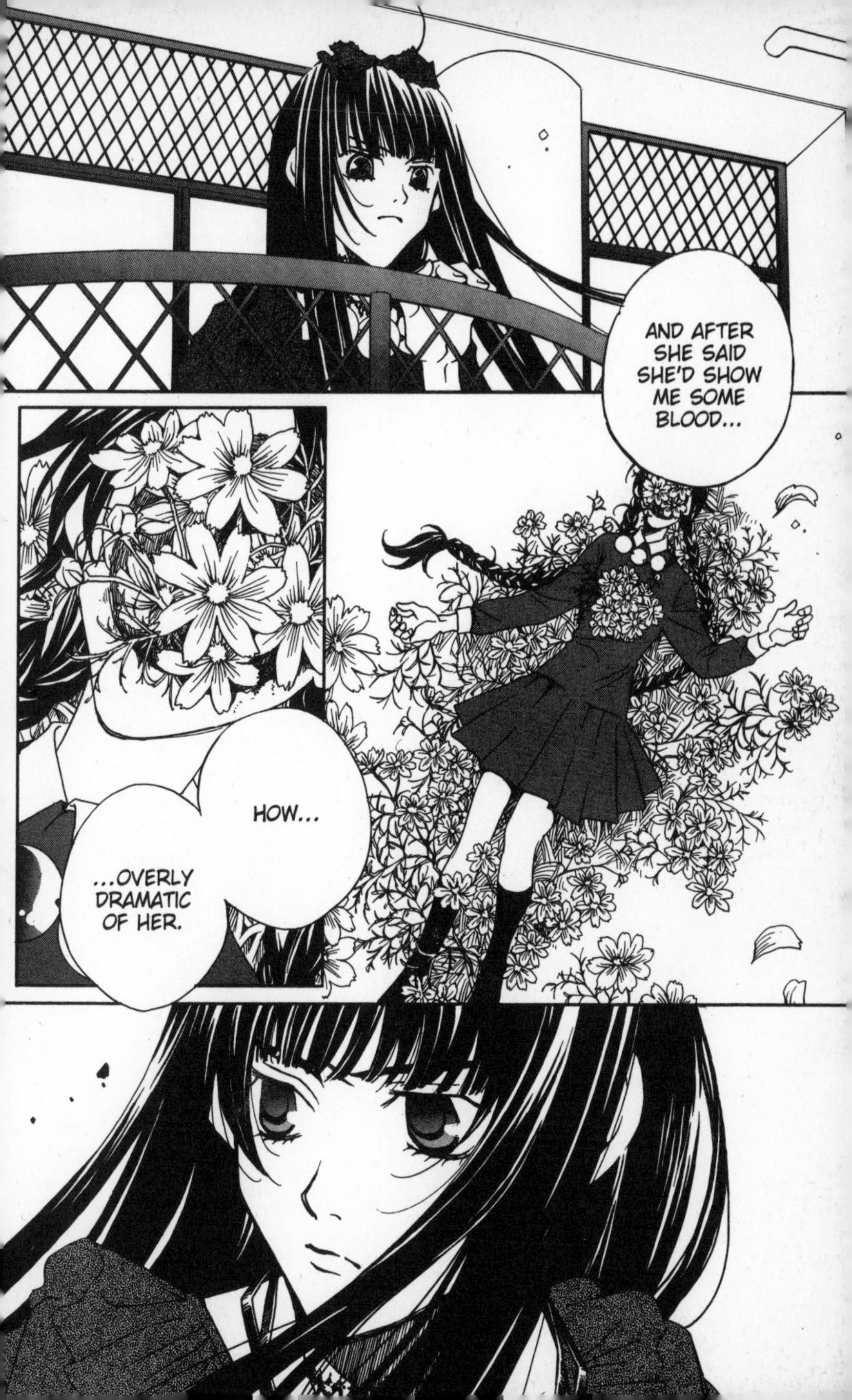
AND AFTER SHE SAID SHE'D SHOW ME SOME BLOOD...
HOW...
...OVERLY DRAMATIC OF HER.

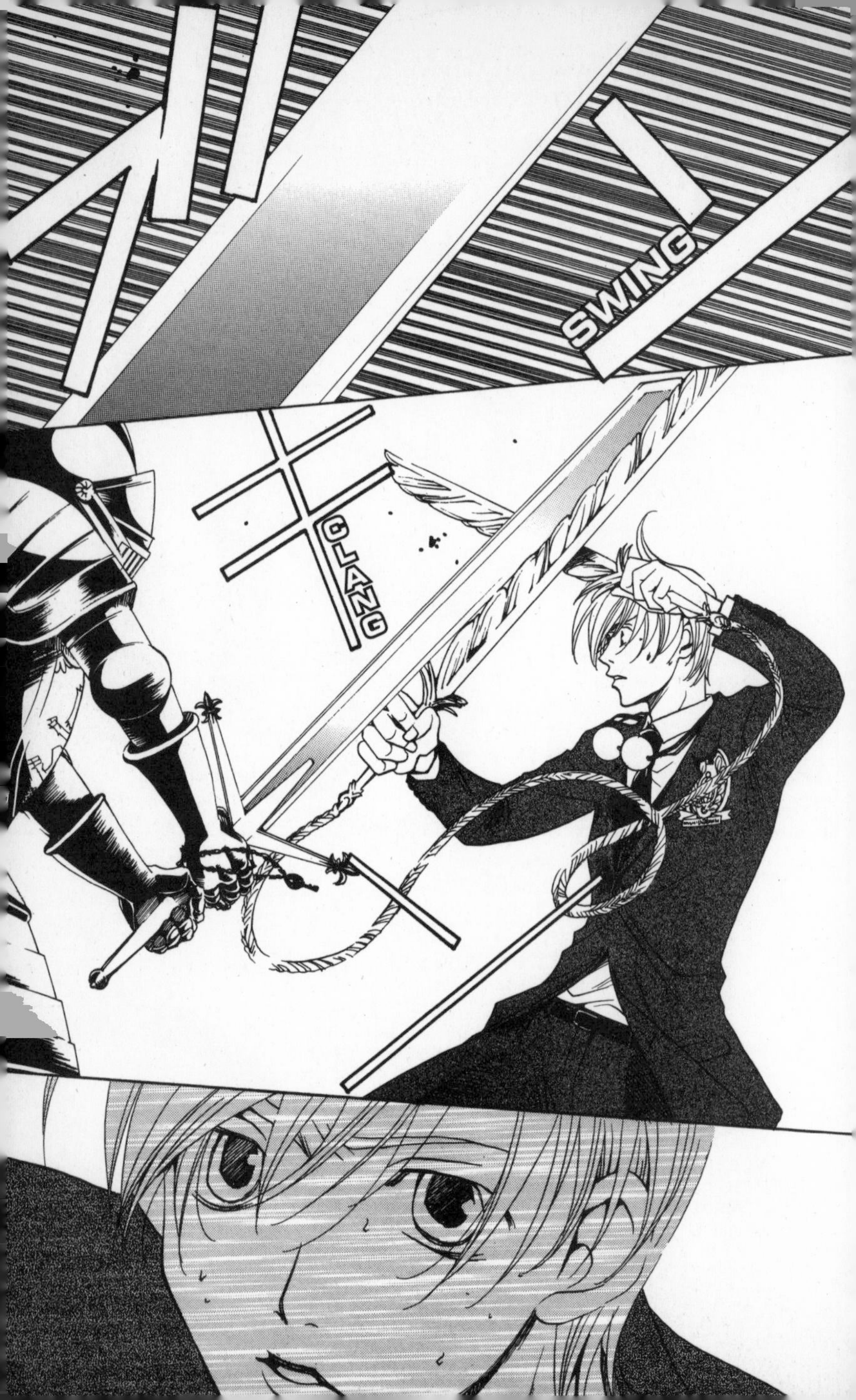
SWING
CLANG

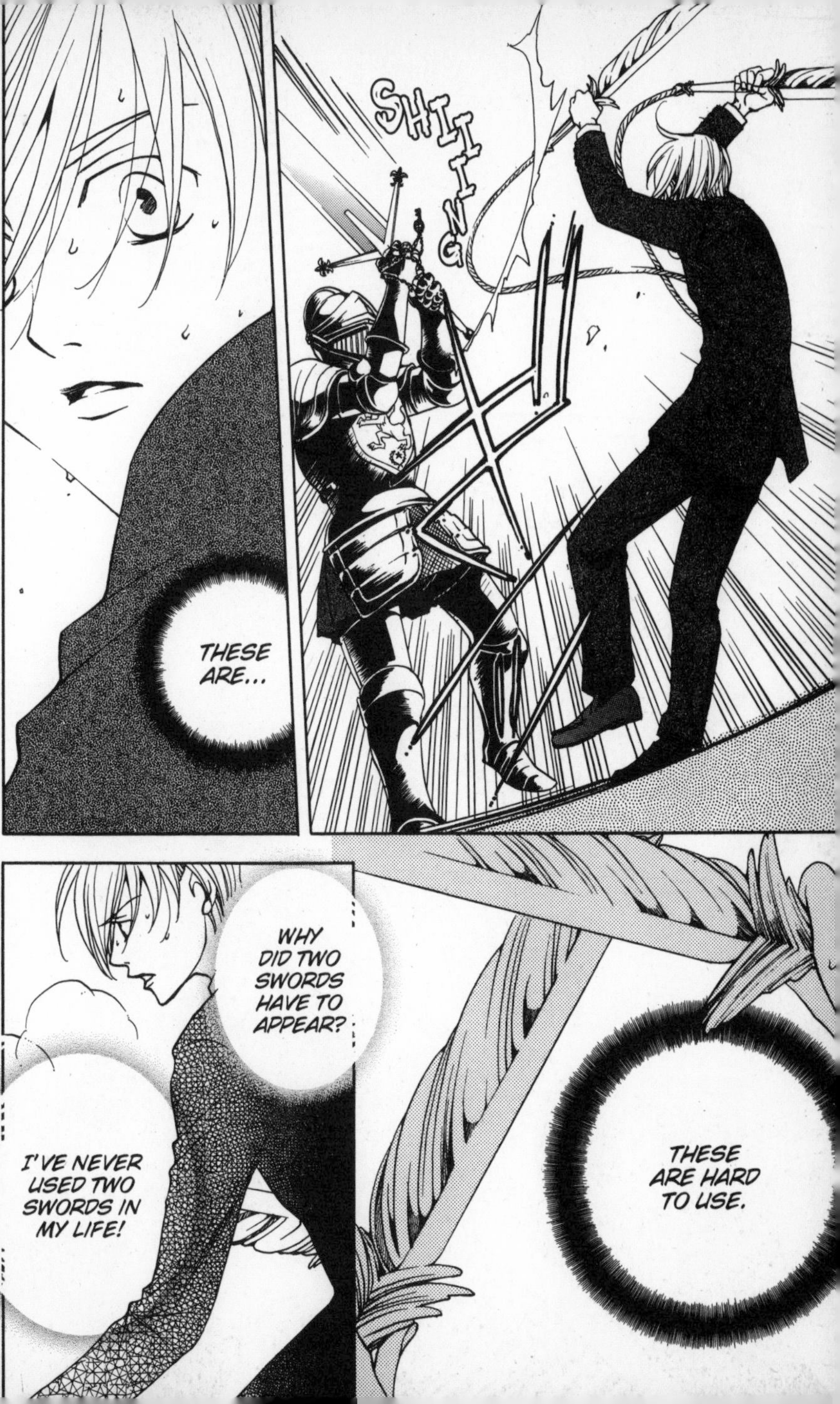
SHIIING
THESE ARE...
THESE ARE HARD TO USE.
WHY DID TWO SWORDS HAVE TO APPEAR?
I'VE NEVER USED TWO SWORDS IN MY LIFE!

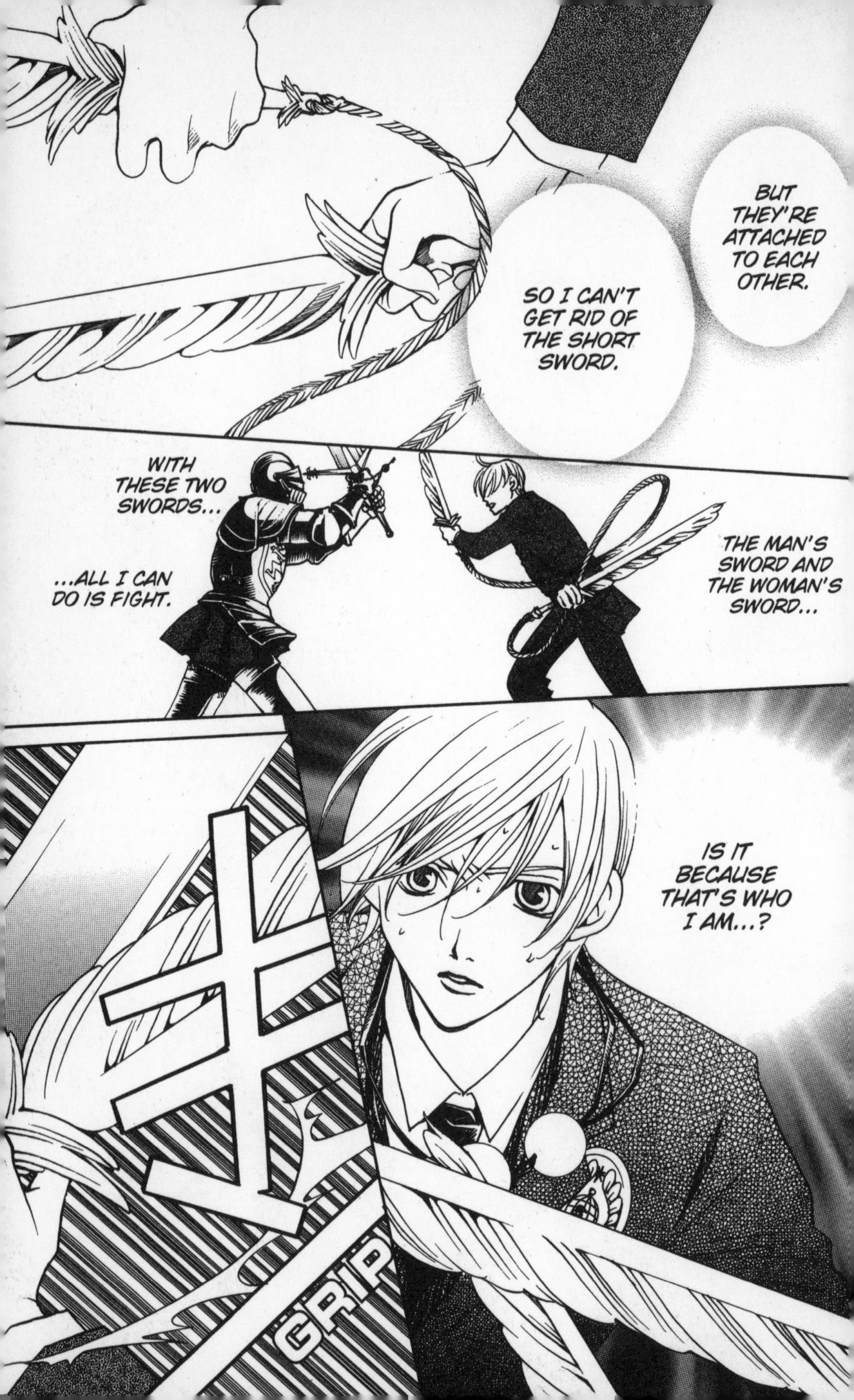
BUT THEY'RE ATTACHED TO EACH OTHER.
SO I CAN'T GET RID OF THE SHORT SWORD.
THE MAN'S SWORD AND THE WOMAN'S SWORD...
WITH THESE TWO SWORDS...
...ALL I CAN DO IS FIGHT.
IS IT BECAUSE THAT'S WHO I AM...?
GRIP

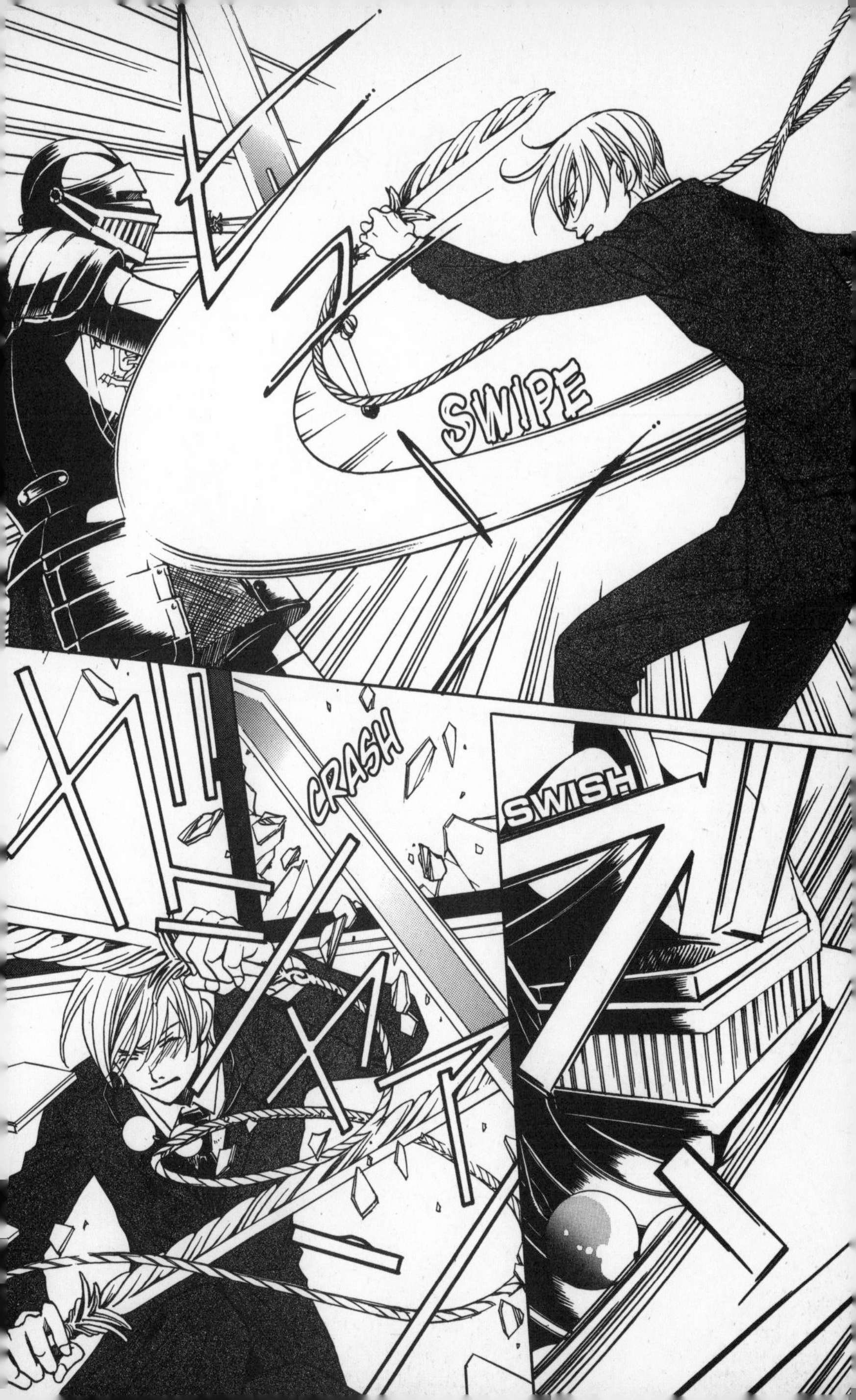
SWIPE
SWISH
CRASH

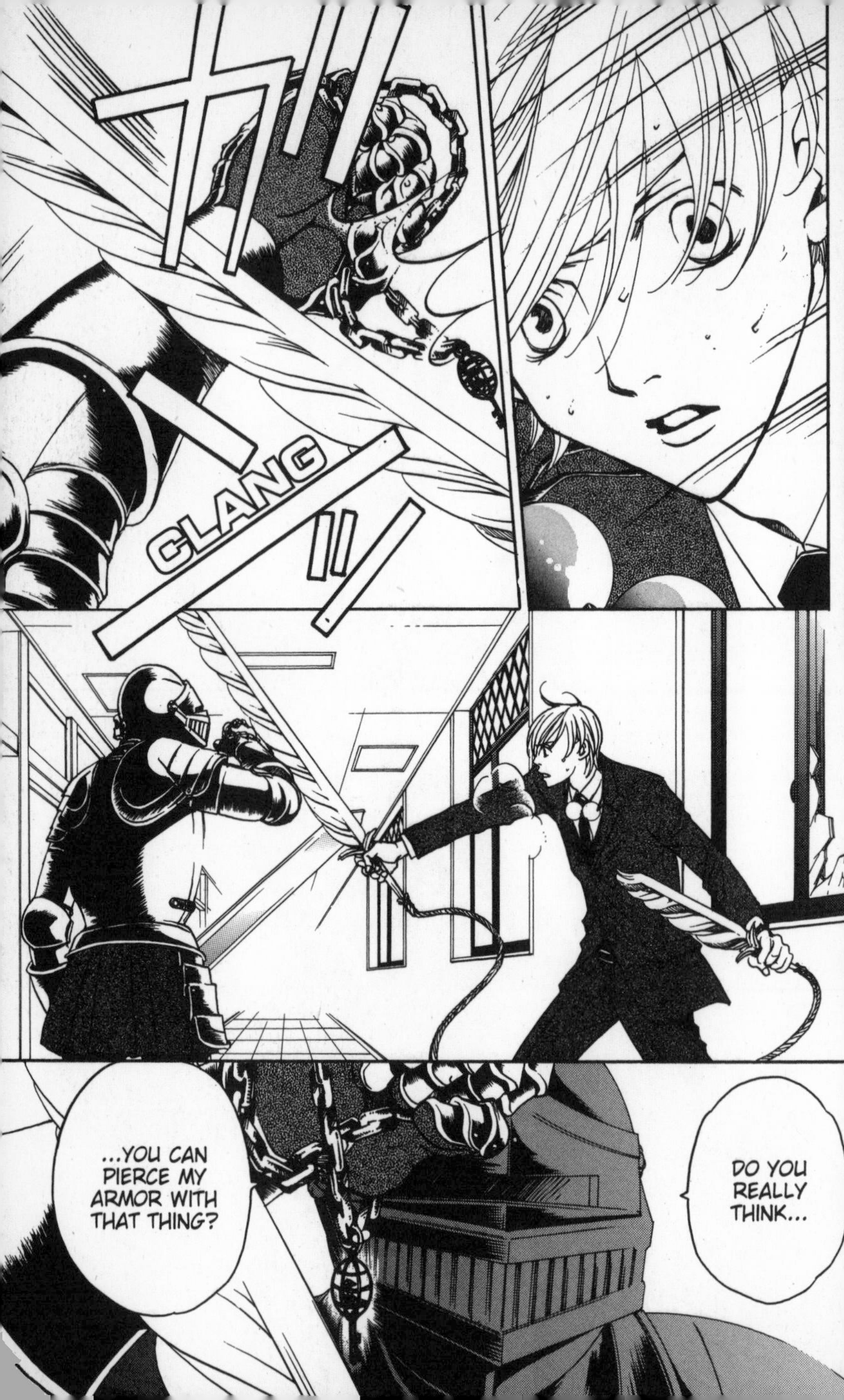
CLANG
DO YOU REALLY THINK...
...YOU CAN PIERCE MY ARMOR WITH THAT THING?

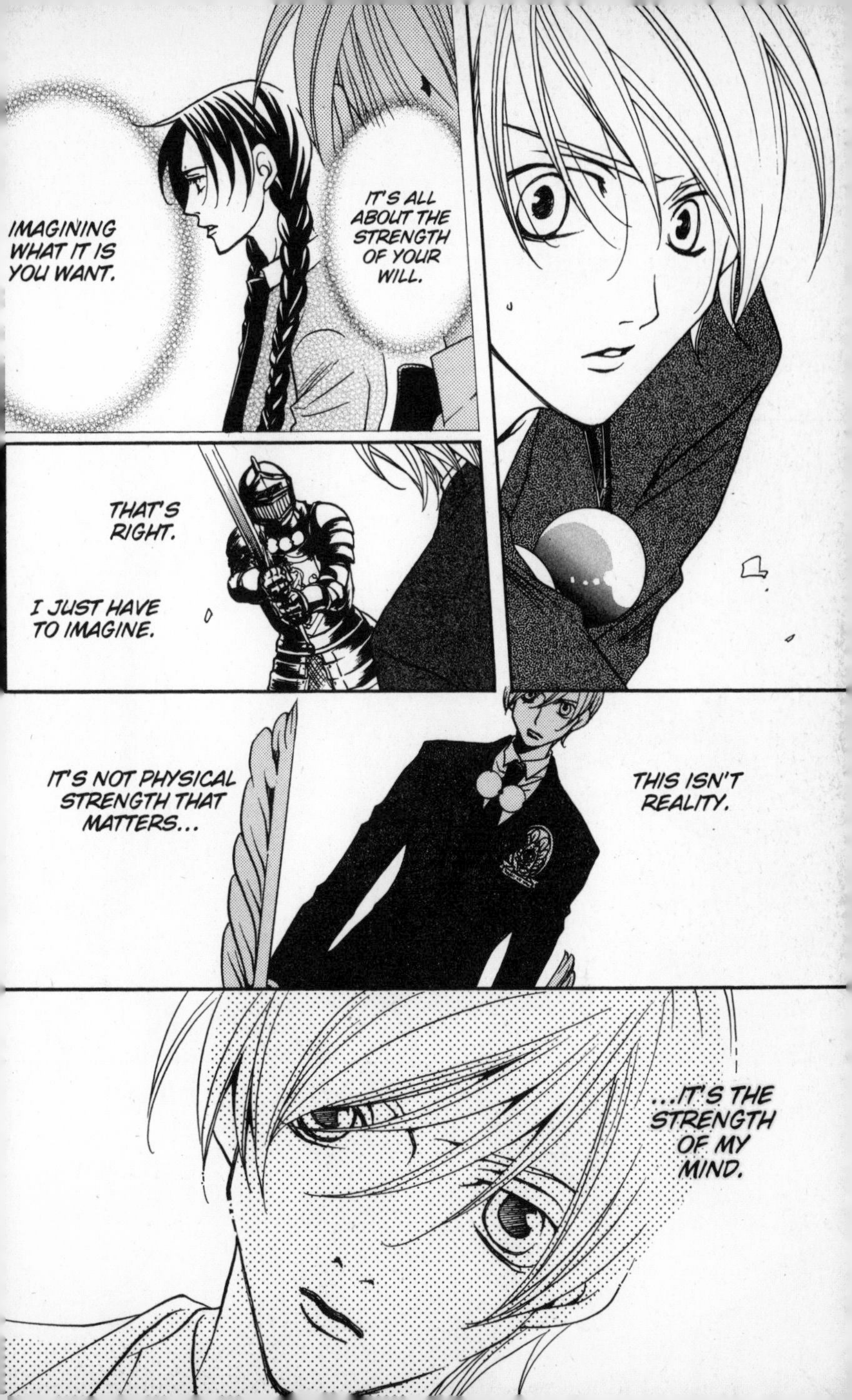
IT'S ALL ABOUT THE STRENGTH OF YOUR WILL.
IMAGINING WHAT IT IS YOU WANT.
THAT'S RIGHT.
I JUST HAVE TO IMAGINE.
THIS ISN'T REALITY.
IT'S NOT PHYSICAL STRENGTH THAT MATTERS...
...IT'S THE STRENGTH OF MY MIND.

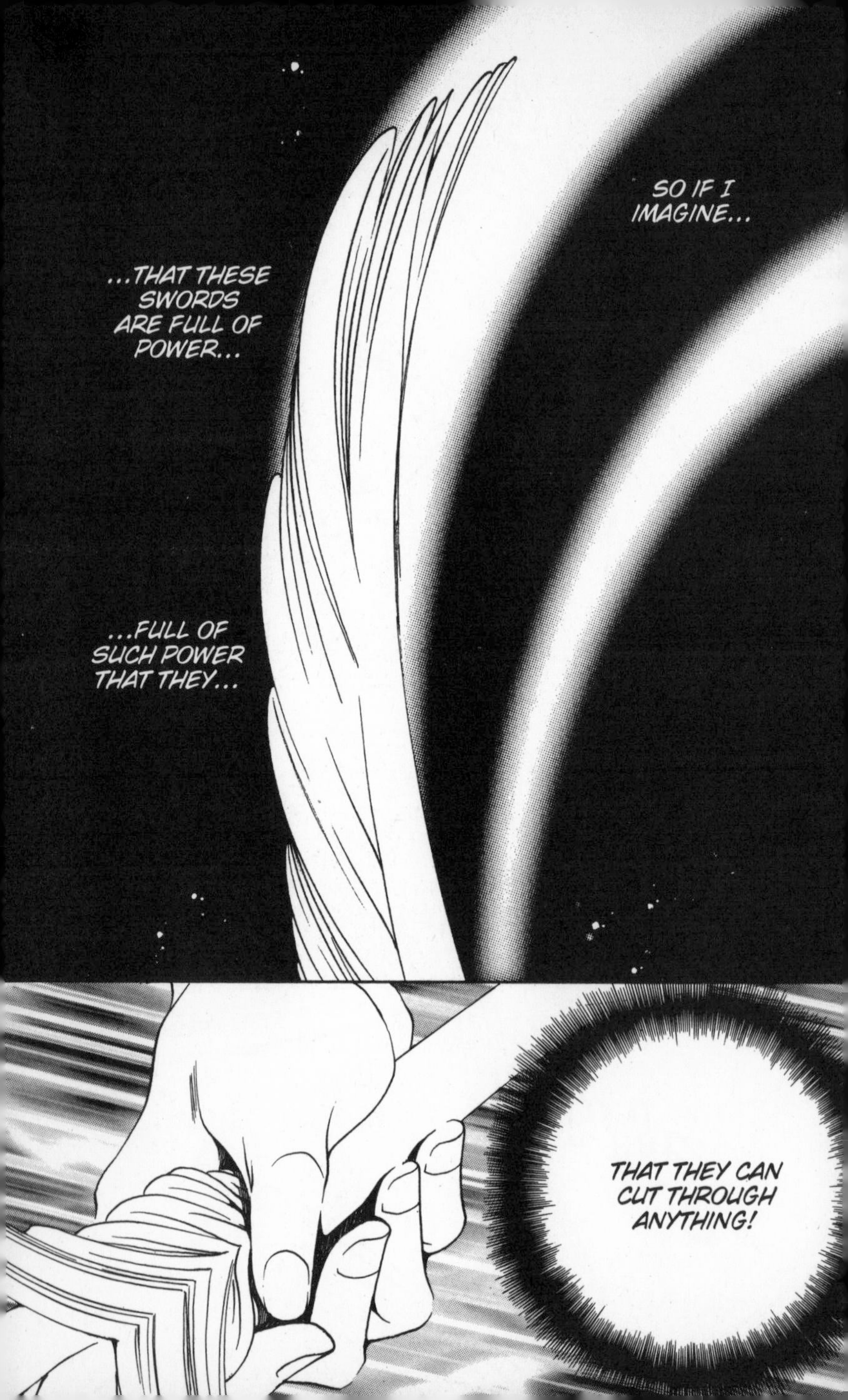
SO IF I IMAGINE...
...THAT THESE SWORDS ARE FULL OF POWER...
...FULL OF SUCH POWER THAT THEY...
THAT THEY CAN CUT THROUGH ANYTHING!

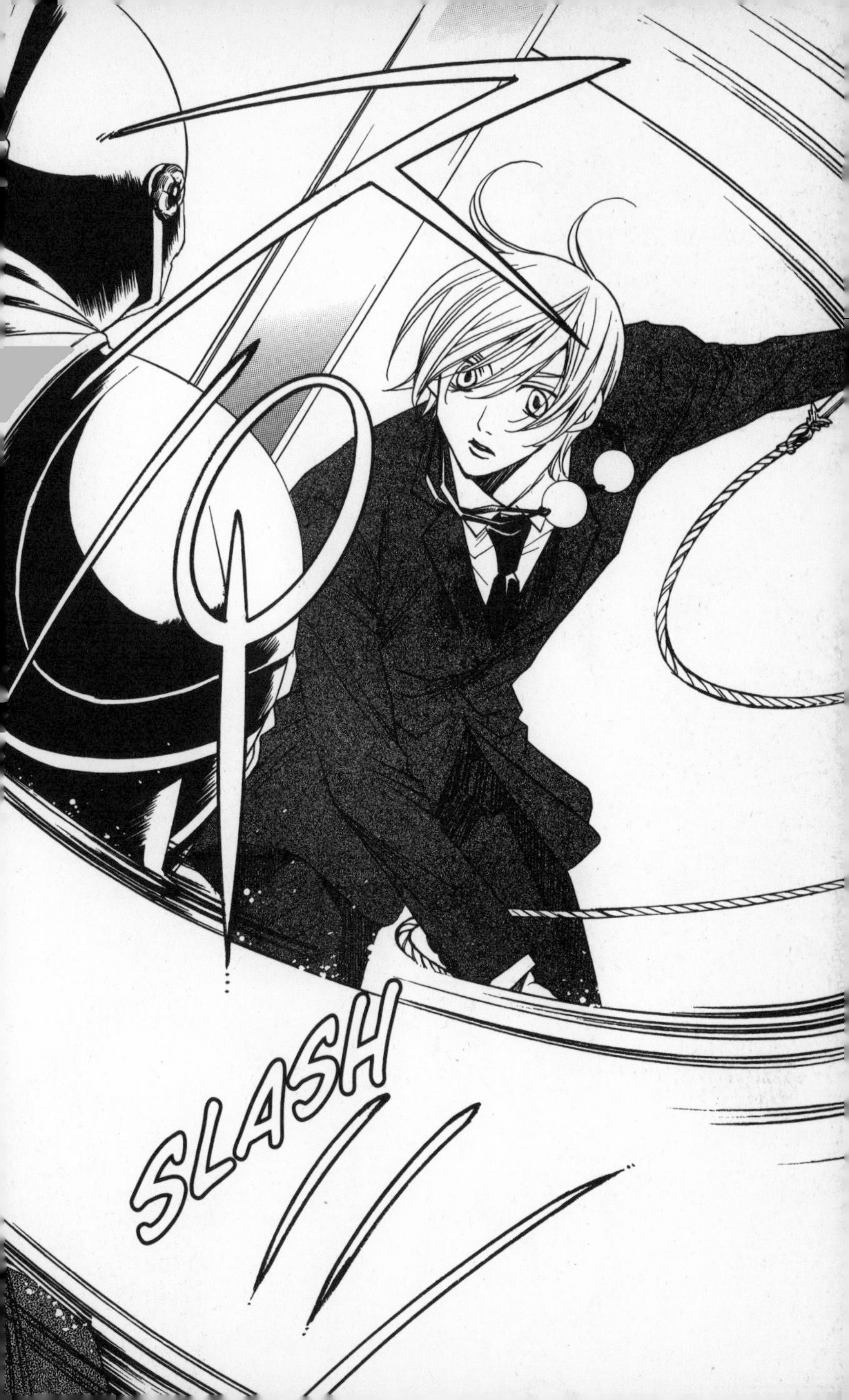
SLASH

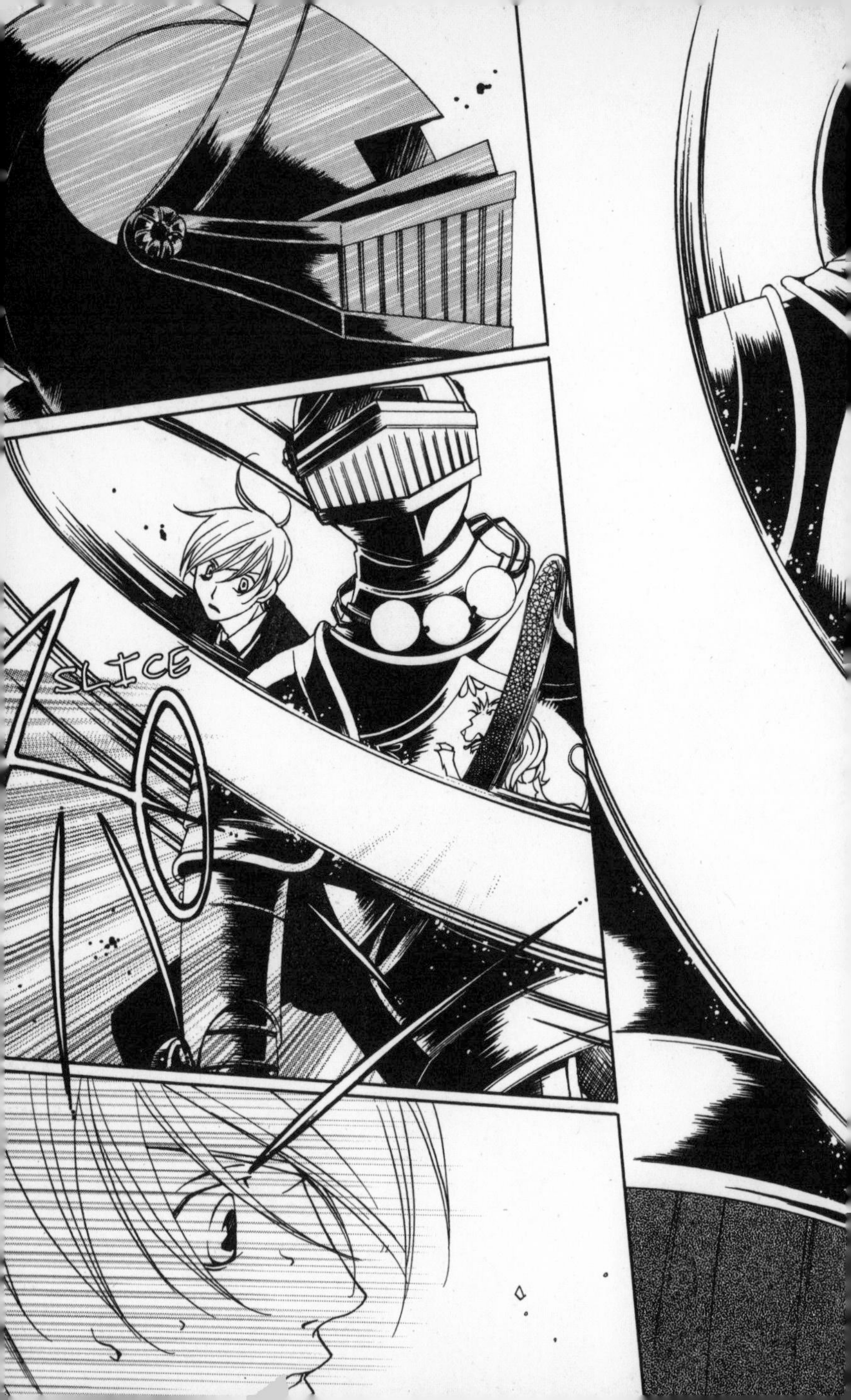
SLICE

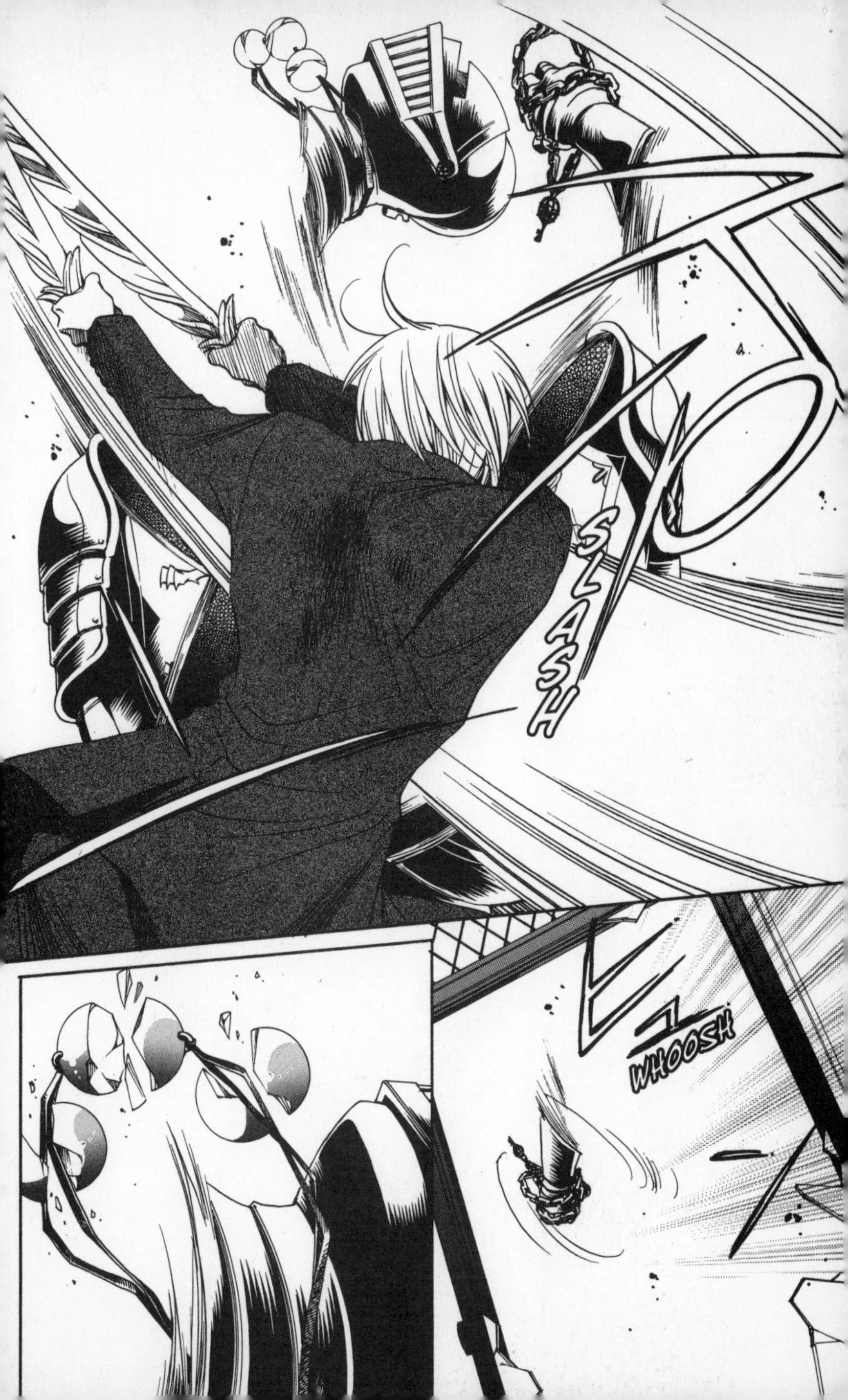
SLASH
WHOOSH

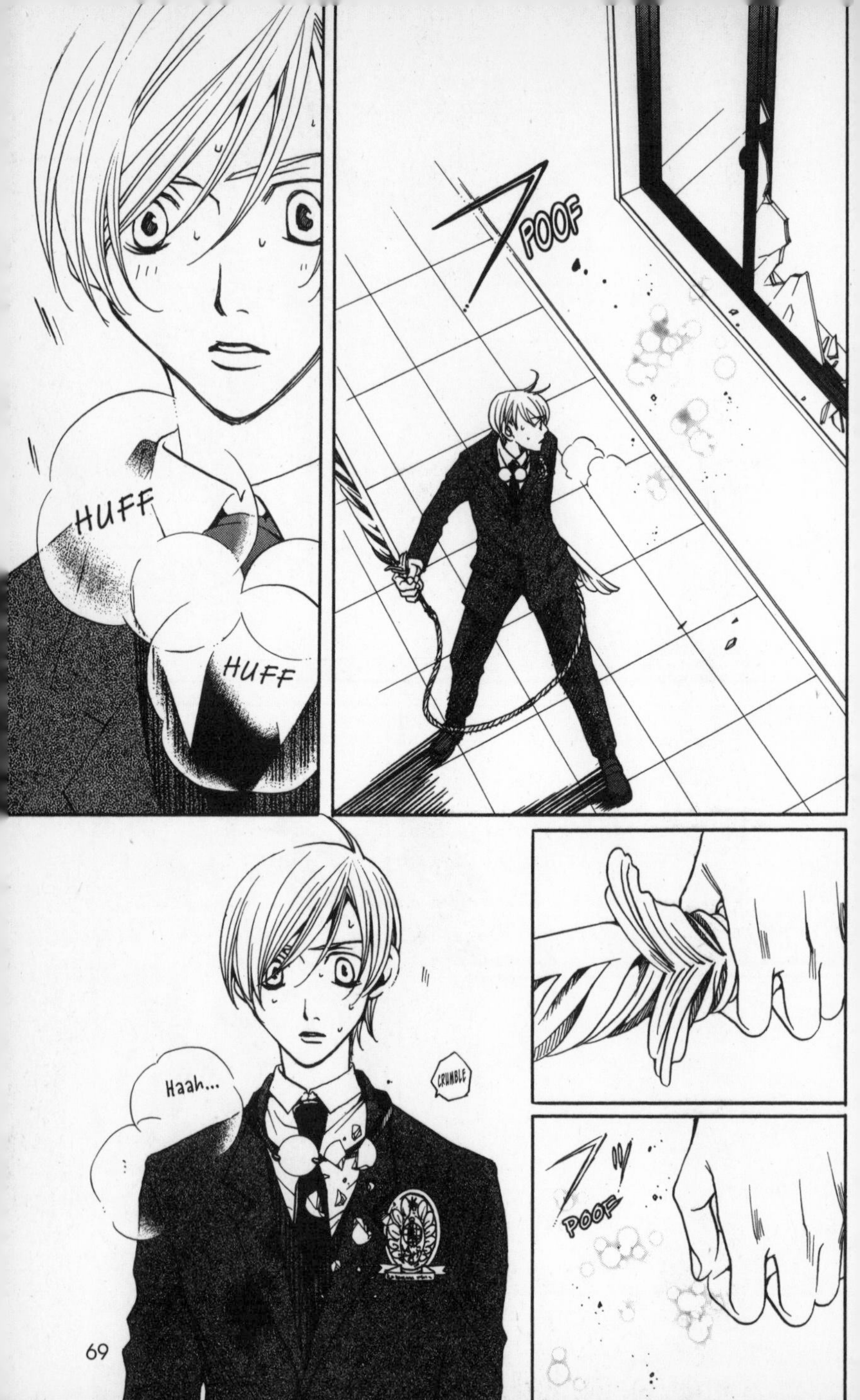
POOF
HUFF
HUFF
POOF
CRUMBLE
Haah...

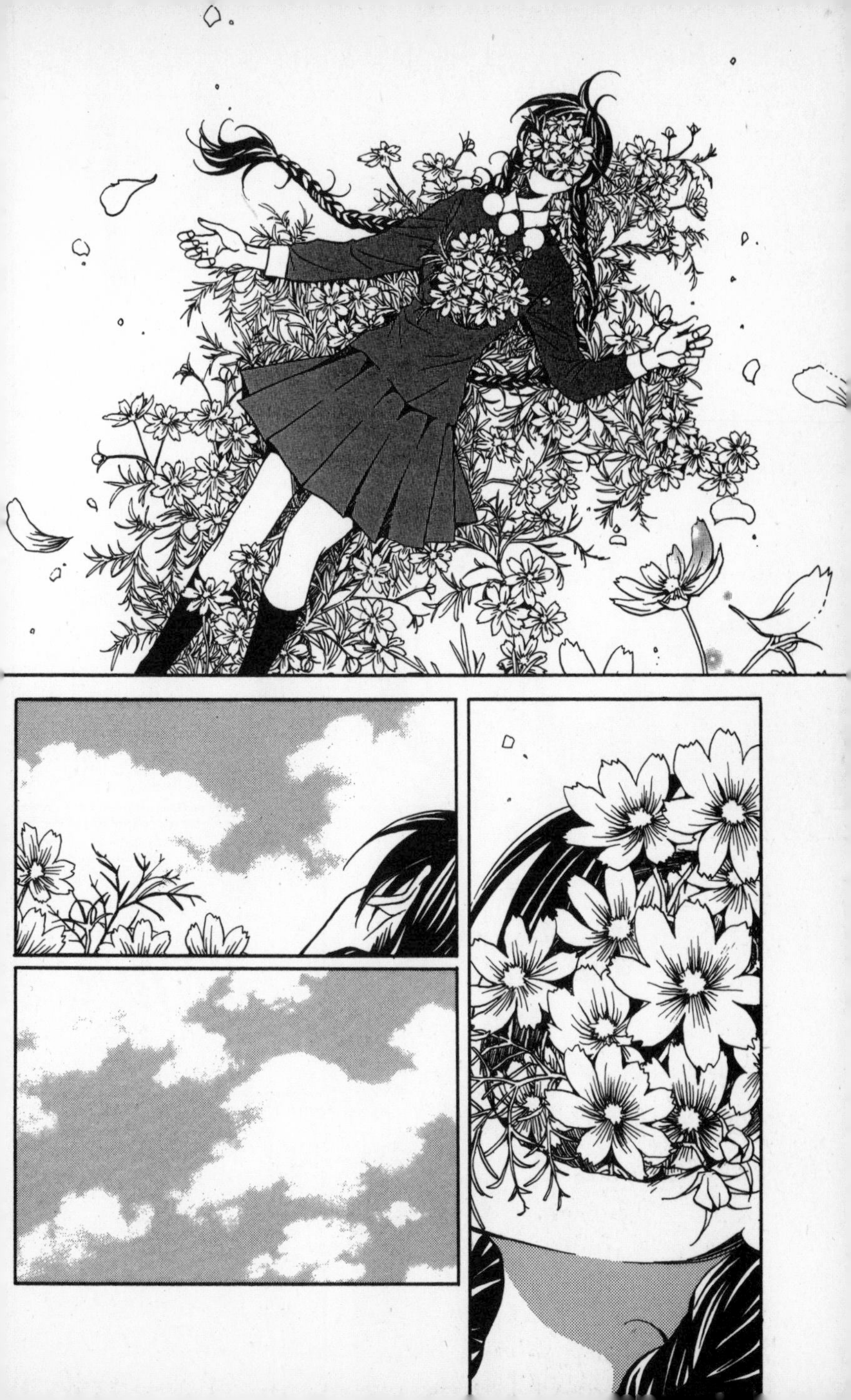

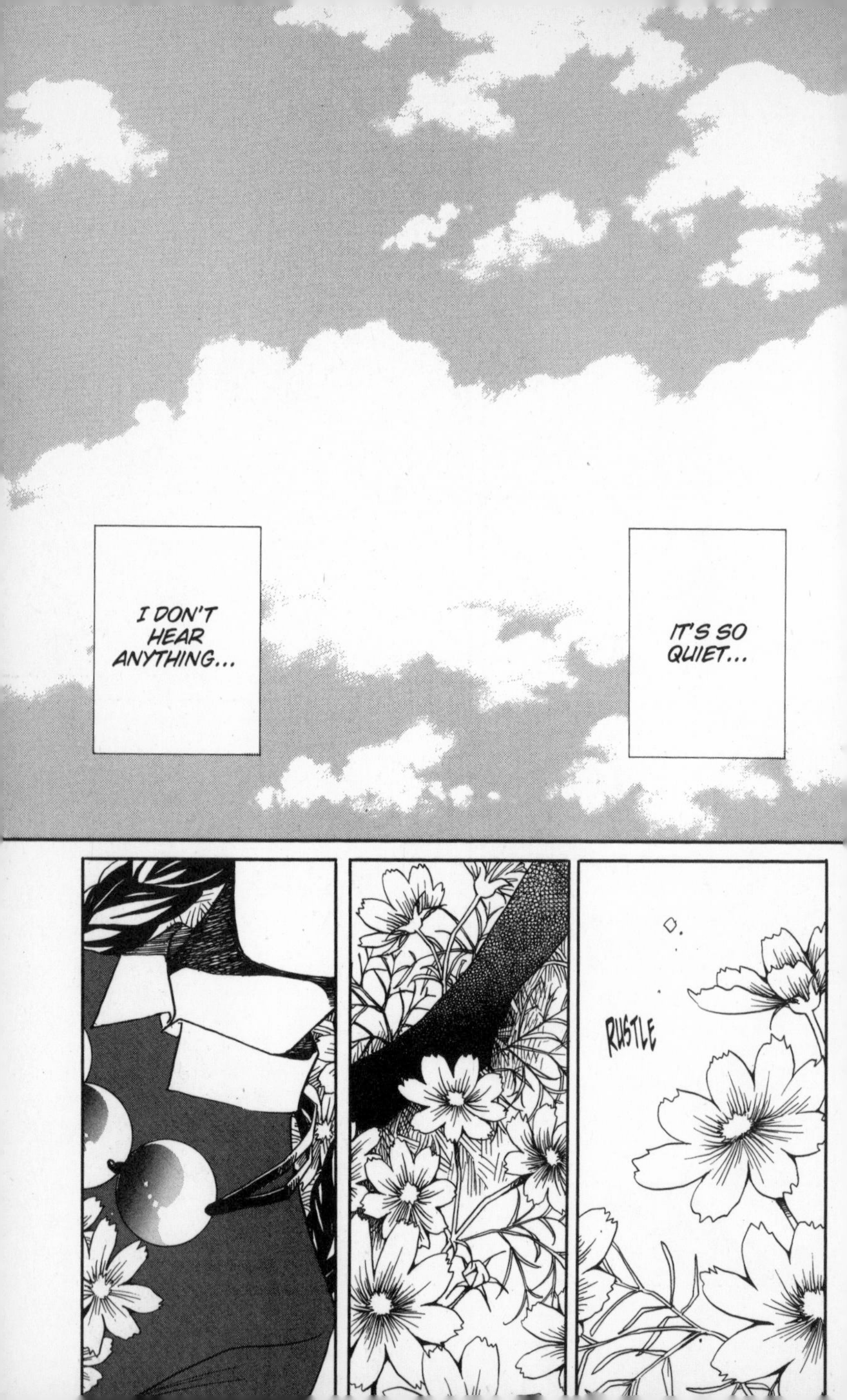
IT'S SO QUIET...
I DON'T HEAR ANYTHING...
RUSTLE

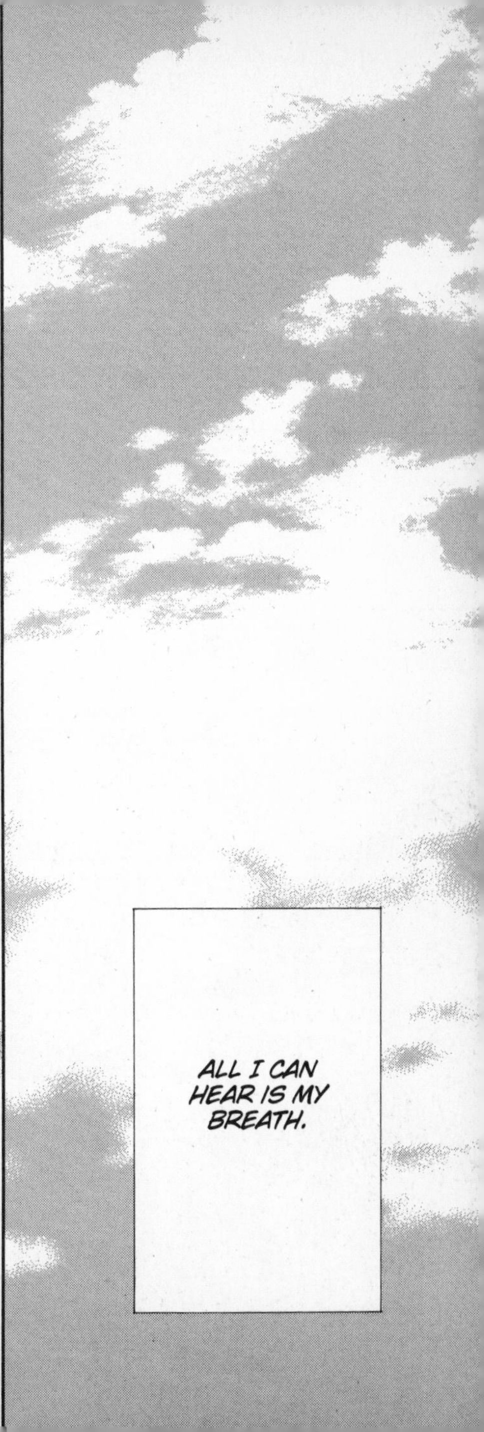
ALL I CAN HEAR IS MY BREATH.

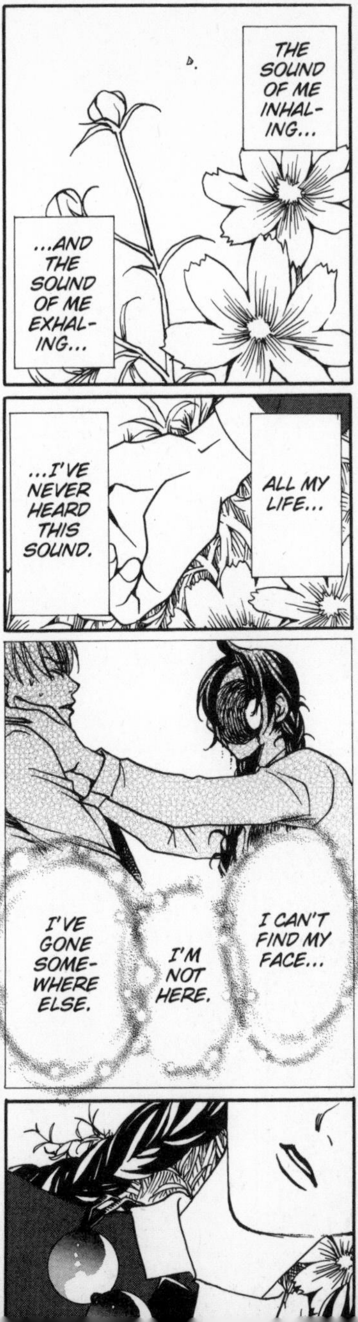
THE SOUND OF ME INHALING...
...AND THE SOUND OF ME EXHALING...
ALL MY LIFE...
...I'VE NEVER HEARD THIS SOUND.
I CAN'T FIND MY FACE...
I'M NOT HERE.
I'VE GONE SOMEWHERE ELSE.

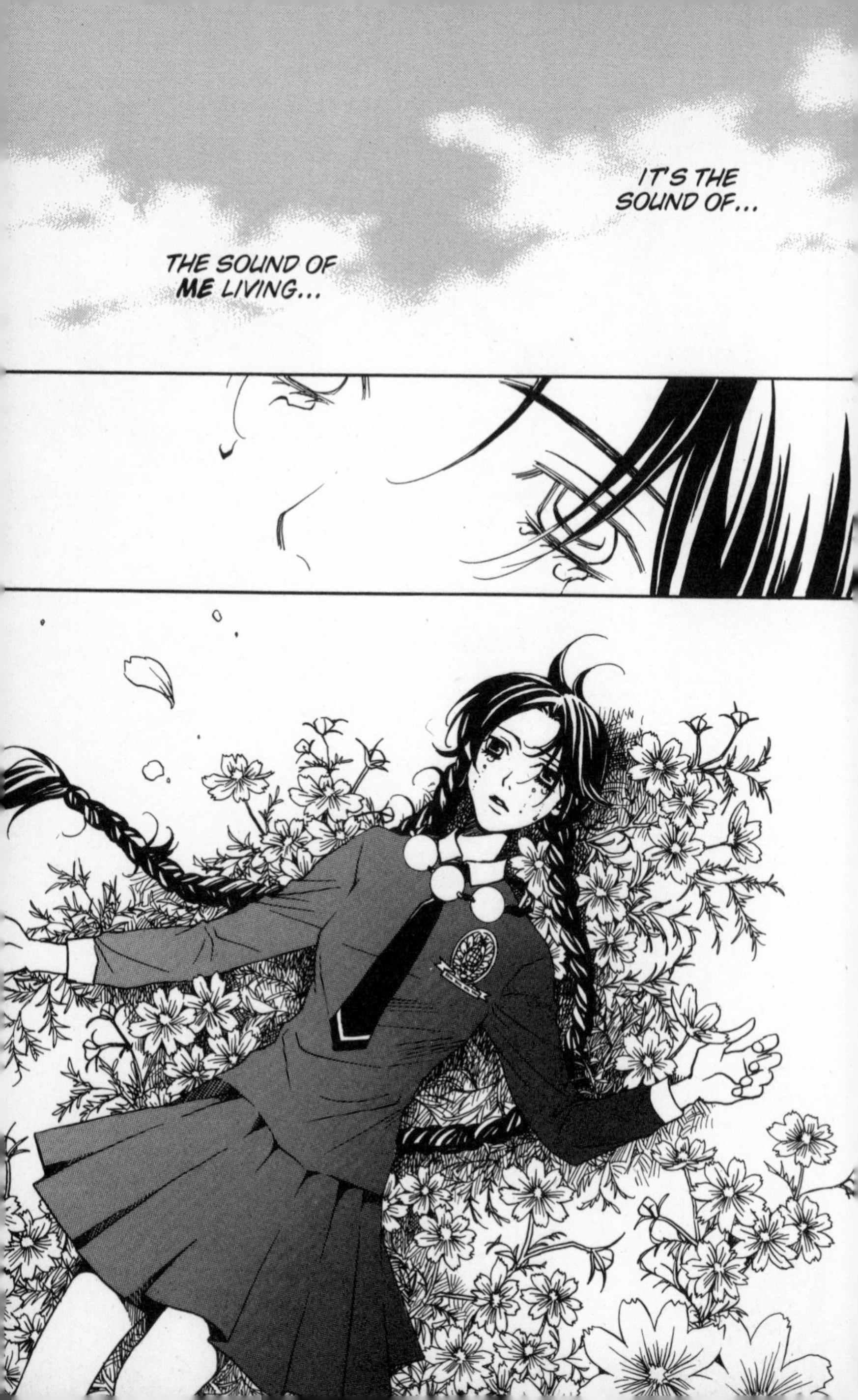
IT'S THE SOUND OF...
THE SOUND OF ME LIVING...

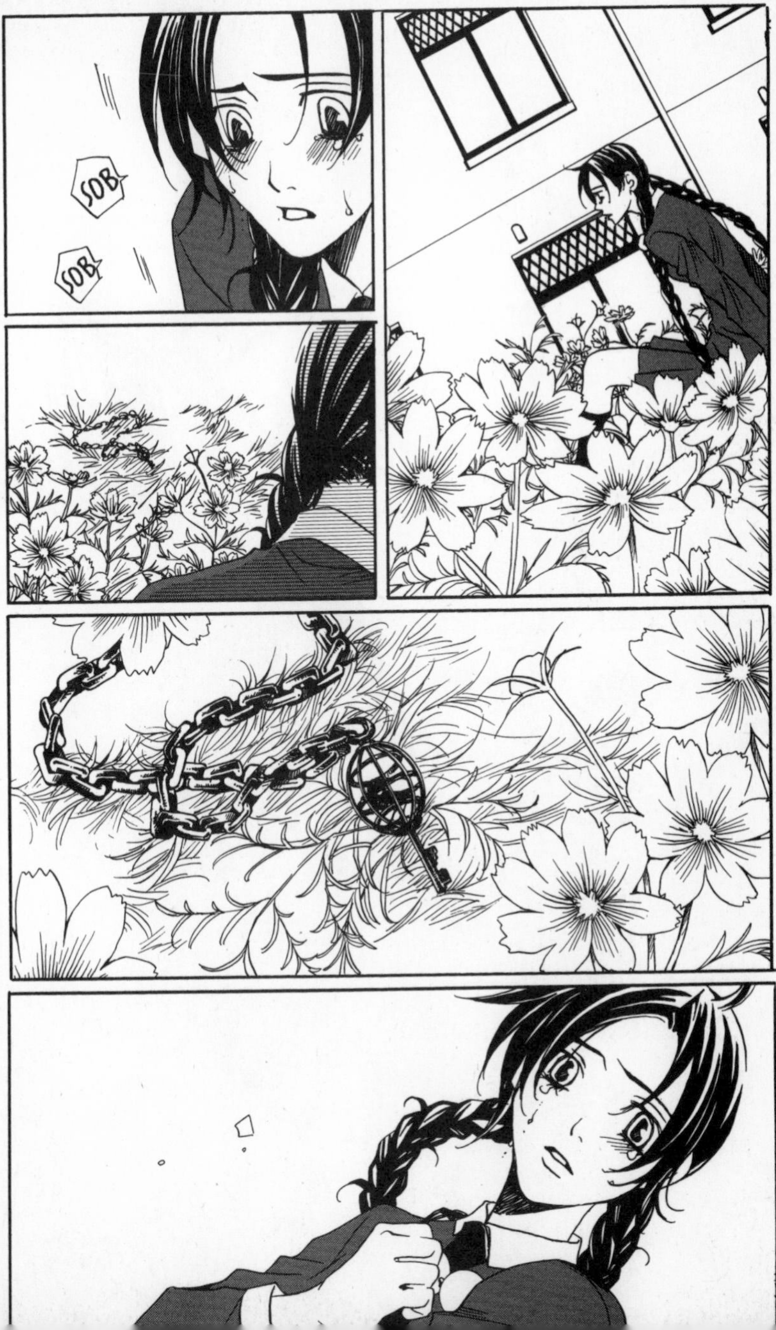
SOB
SOB

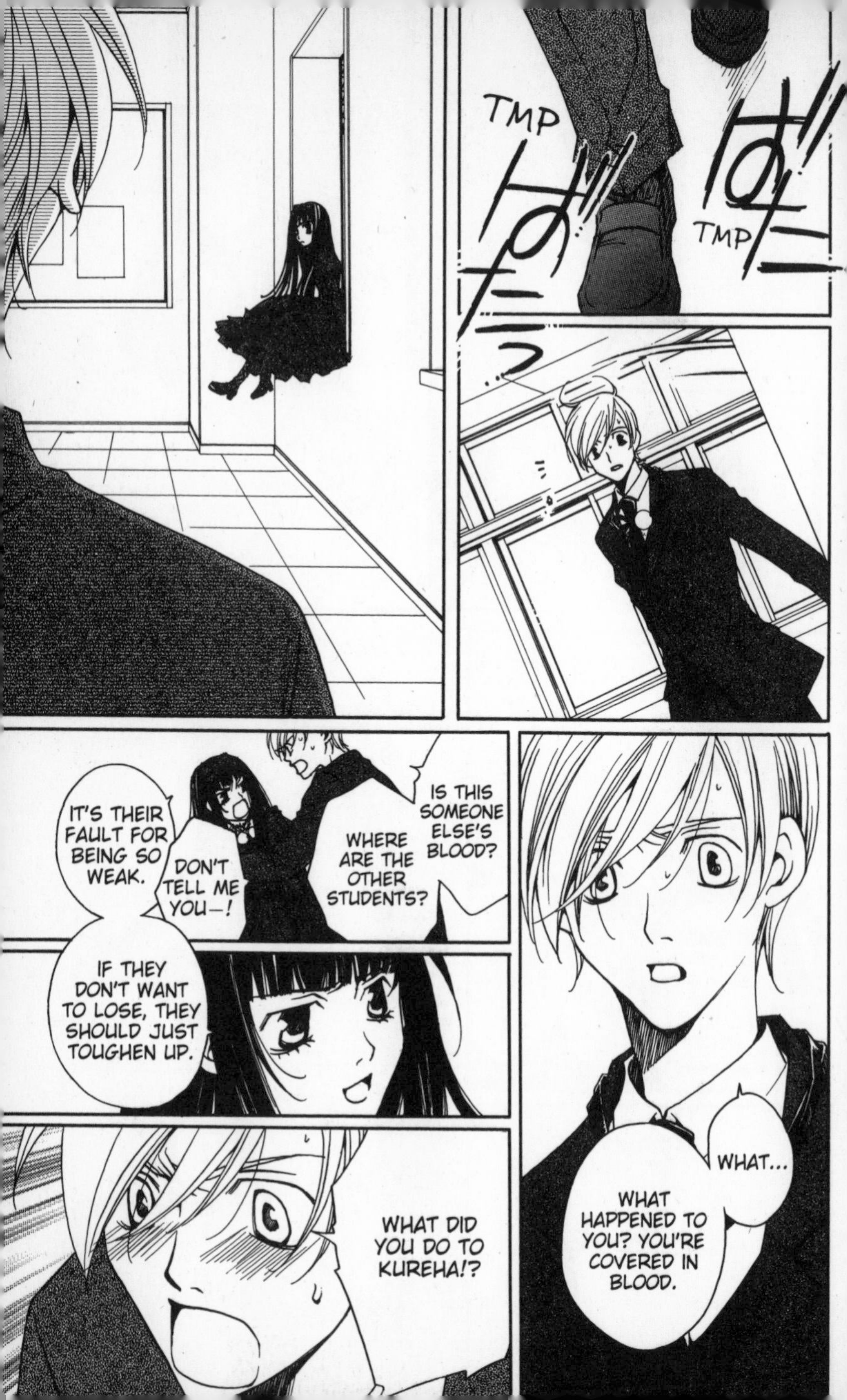
TMP
TMP
WHAT...
WHAT HAPPENED TO YOU? YOU'RE COVERED IN BLOOD.
IS THIS SOMEONE ELSE'S BLOOD?
WHERE ARE THE OTHER STUDENTS?
DON'T TELL ME YOU—!
IT'S THEIR FAULT FOR BEING SO WEAK.
IF THEY DON'T WANT TO LOSE, THEY SHOULD JUST TOUGHEN UP.
WHAT DID YOU DO TO KUREHA!?

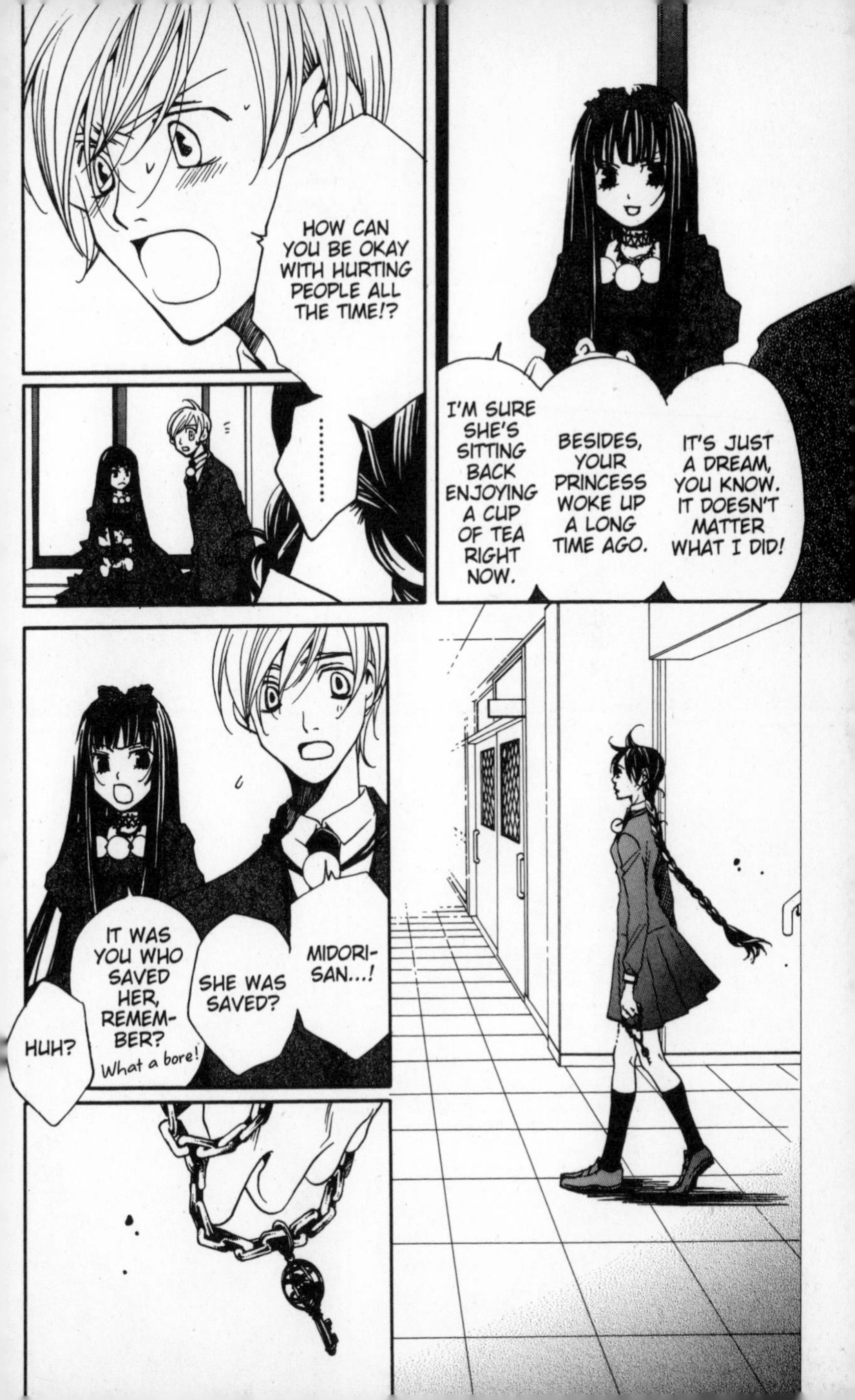
IT'S JUST A DREAM, YOU KNOW. IT DOESN'T MATTER WHAT I DID!
BESIDES, YOUR PRINCESS WOKE UP A LONG TIME AGO.
I'M SURE SHE'S SITTING BACK ENJOYING A CUP OF TEA RIGHT NOW.
HOW CAN YOU BE OKAY WITH HURTING PEOPLE ALL THE TIME!?
......
MIDORI-SAN...!
SHE WAS SAVED?
IT WAS YOU WHO SAVED HER, REMEMBER?
What a bore!
HUH?

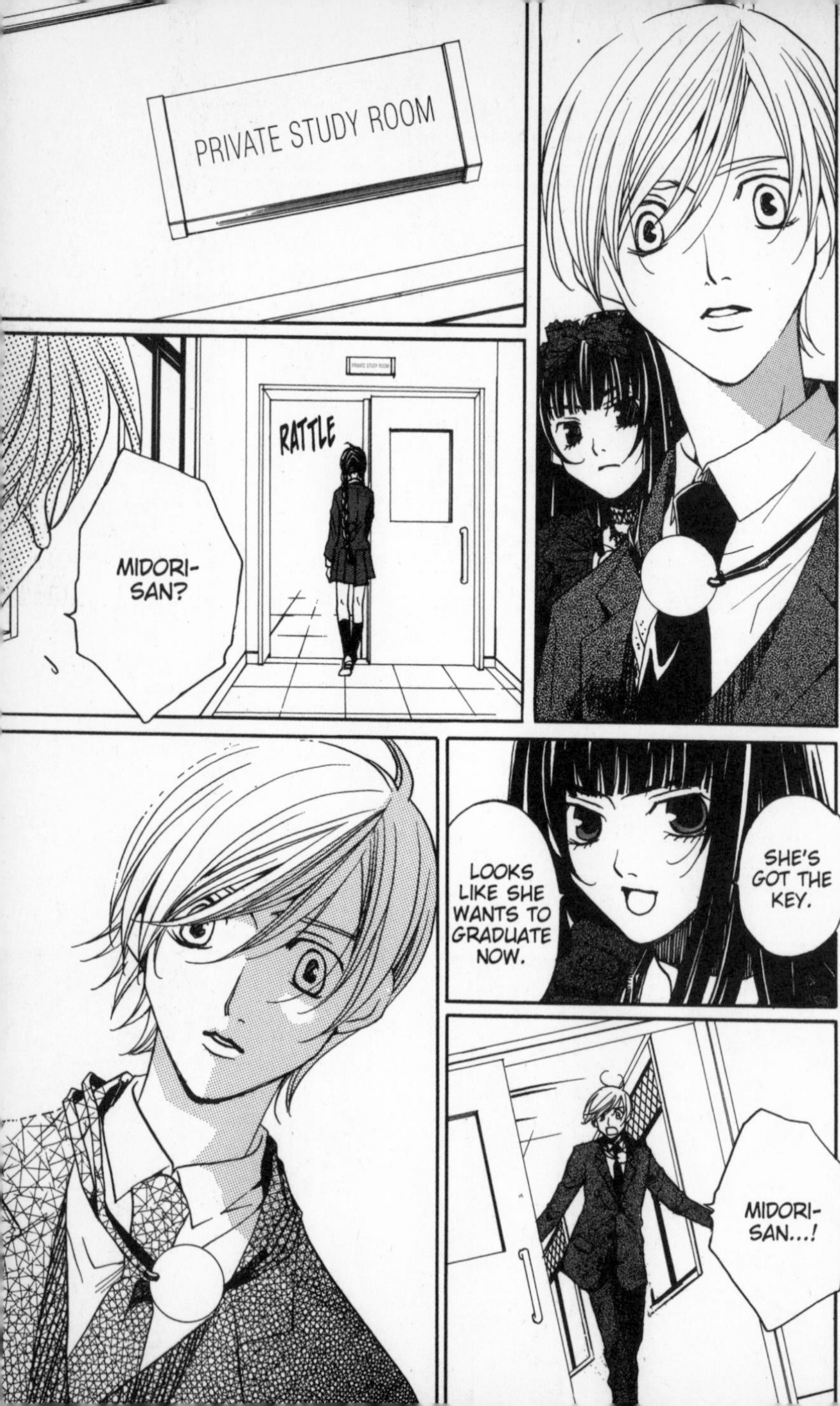
PRIVATE STUDY ROOM
RATTLE
MIDORI-SAN?
SHE'S GOT THE KEY.
LOOKS LIKE SHE WANTS TO GRADUATE NOW.
MIDORI-SAN...!

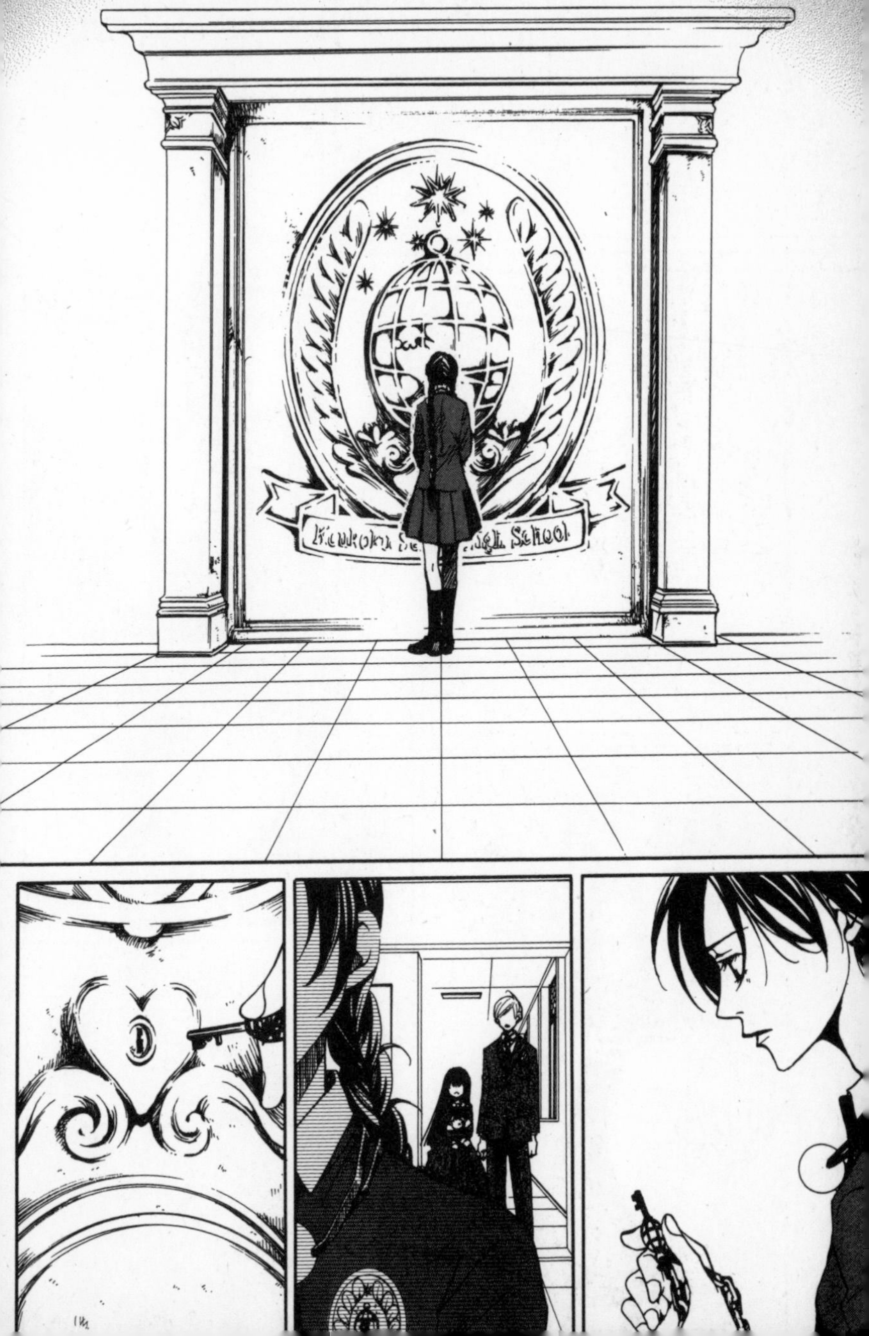
School

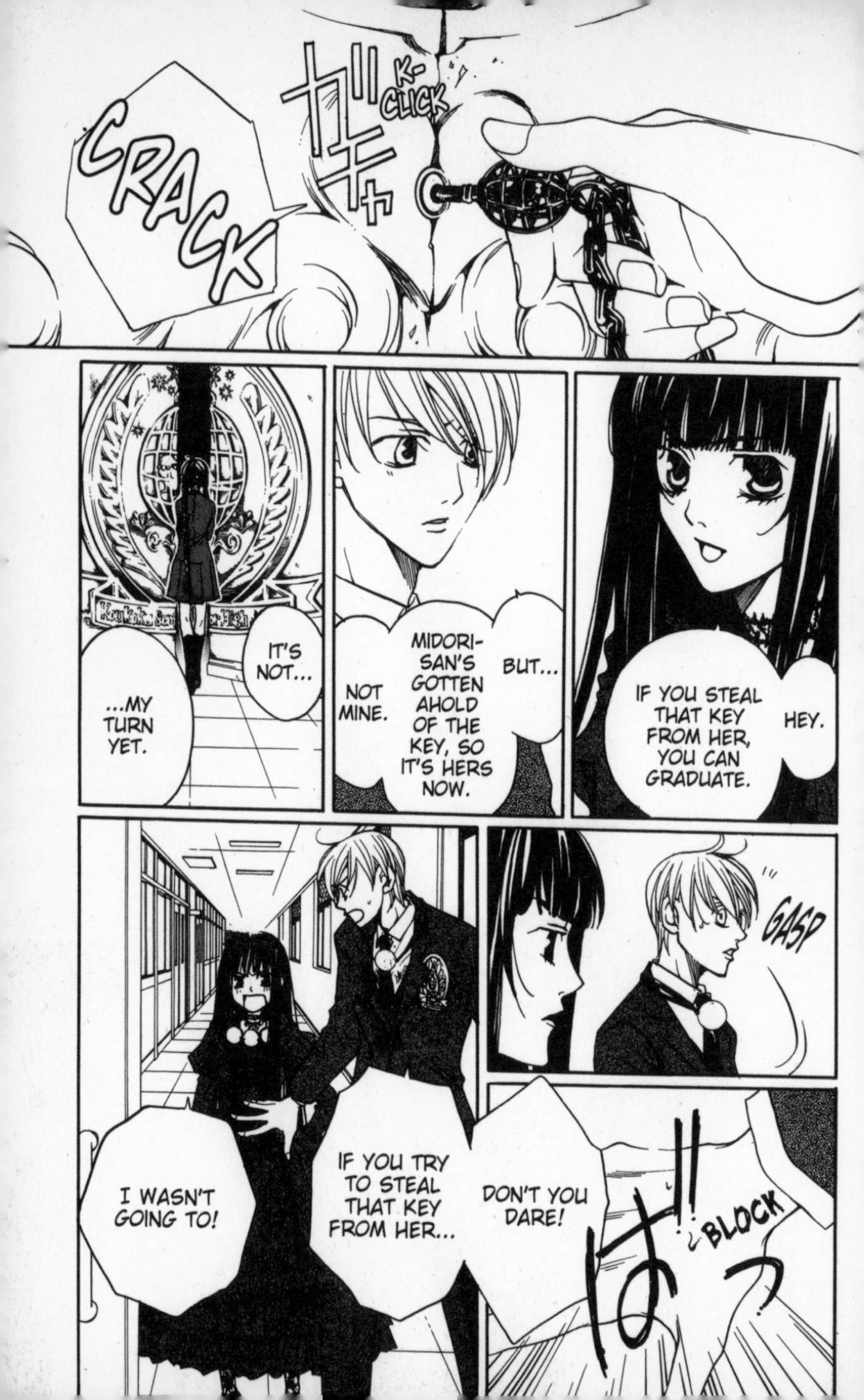
K-CLICK
CRACK
HEY.
IF YOU STEAL THAT KEY FROM HER, YOU CAN GRADUATE.
BUT...
MIDORI-SAN'S GOTTEN AHOLD OF THE KEY, SO IT'S HERS NOW.
NOT MINE.
IT'S NOT...
...MY TURN YET.
GASP
BLOCK
DON'T YOU DARE!
IF YOU TRY TO STEAL THAT KEY FROM HER...
I WASN'T GOING TO!

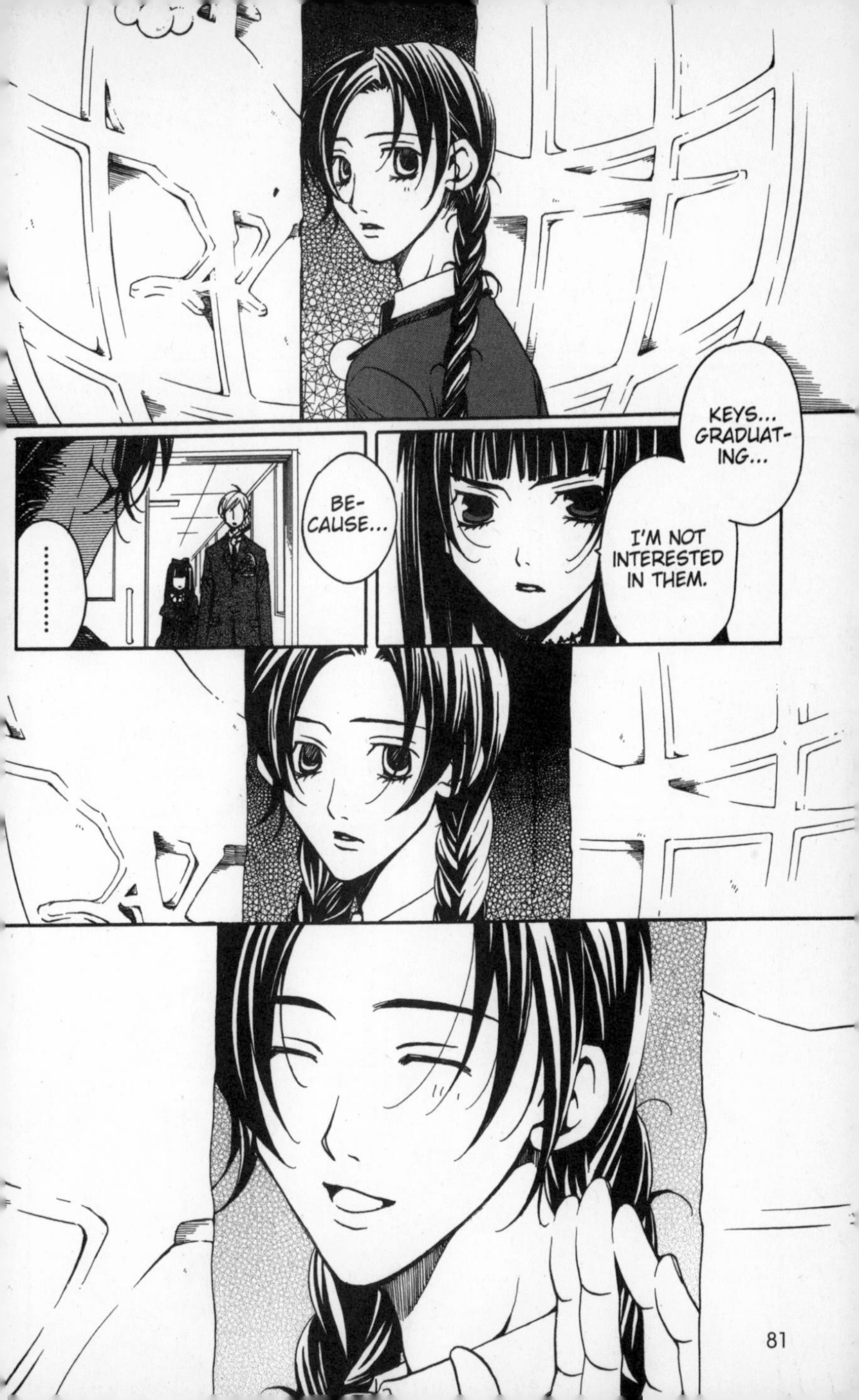
KEYS... GRADUAT-ING...
I'M NOT INTERESTED IN THEM.
BE-CAUSE...
......

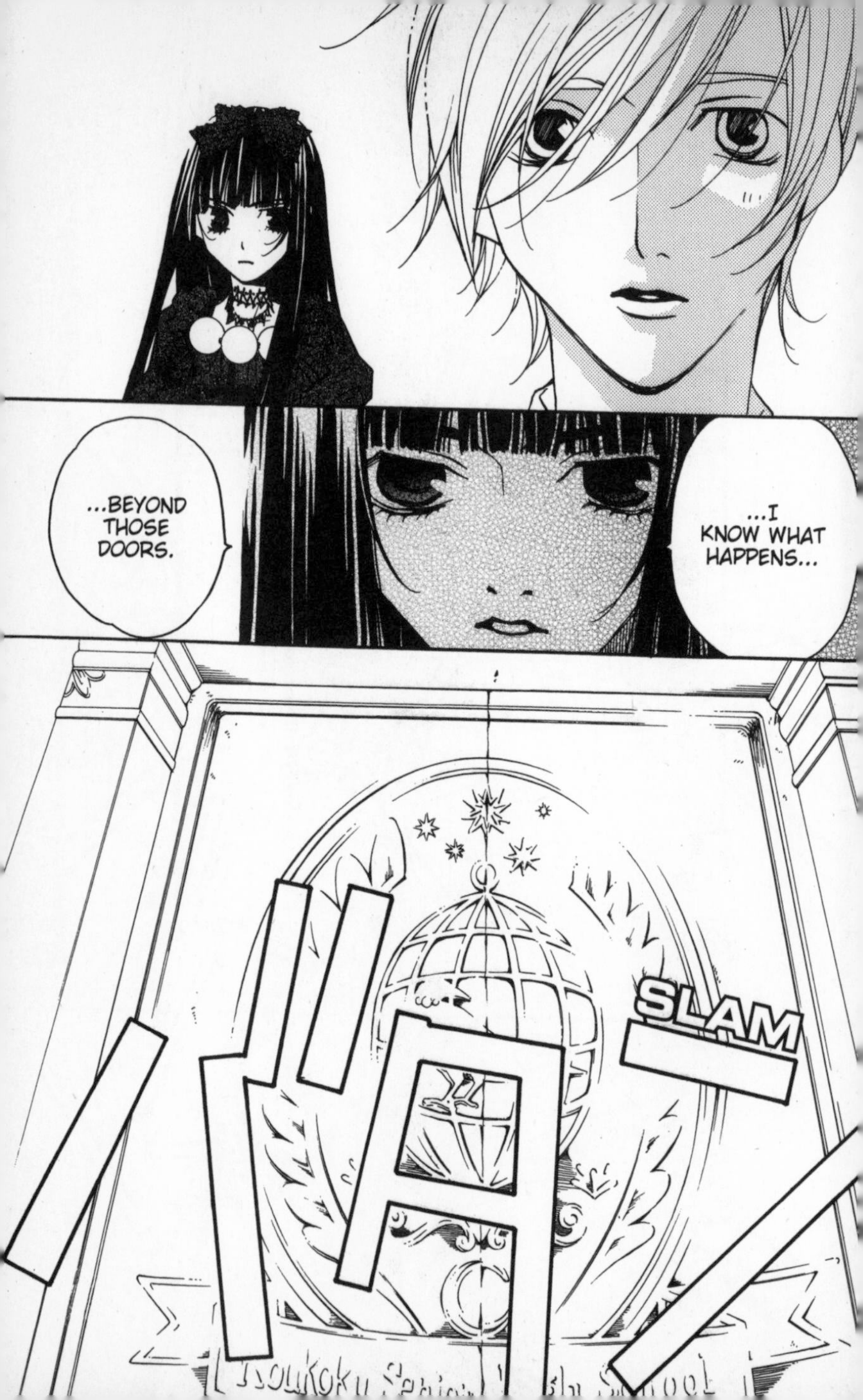
...I KNOW WHAT HAPPENS...
...BEYOND THOSE DOORS.
SLAM

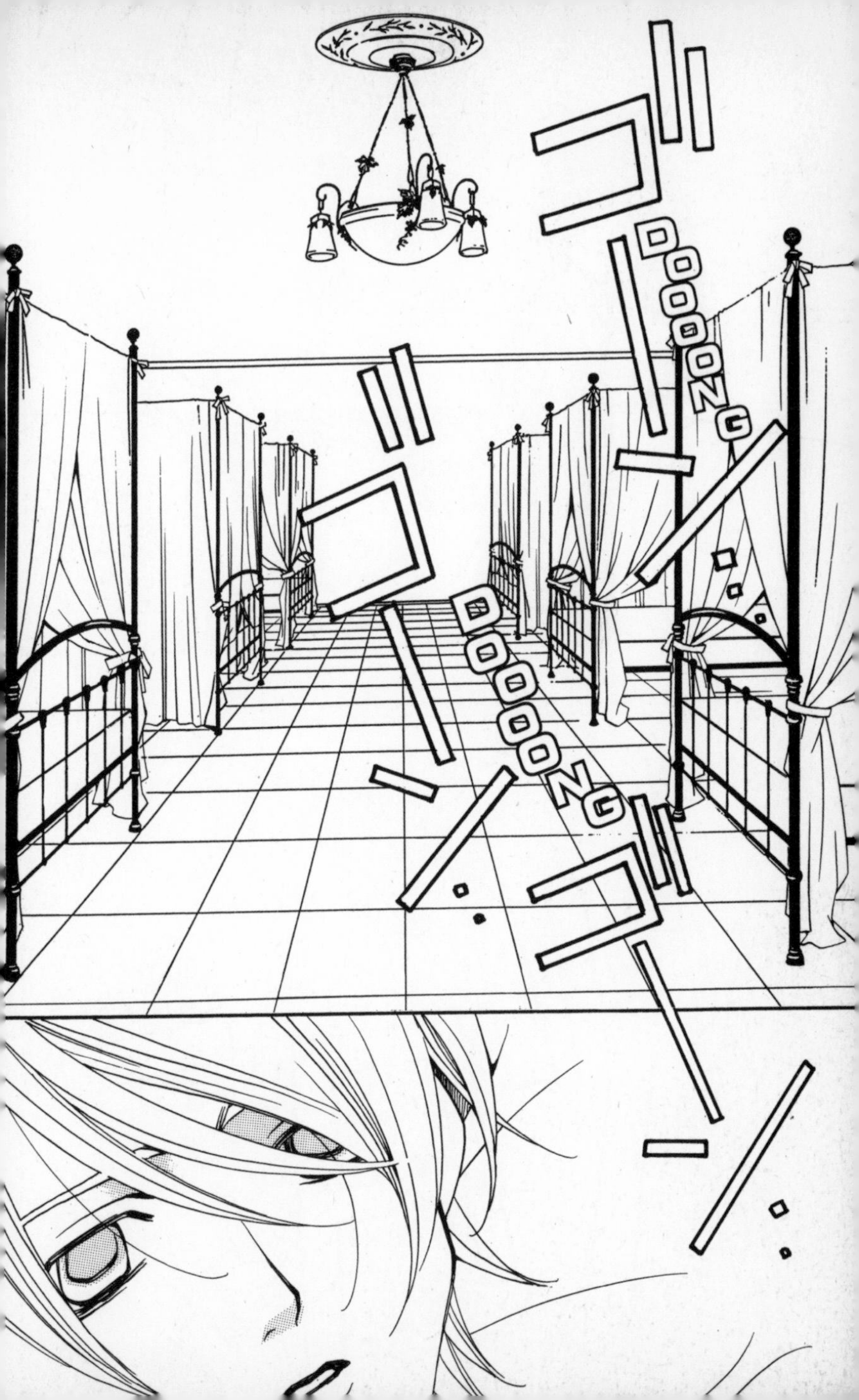
DOOOONG
DOOOOONG

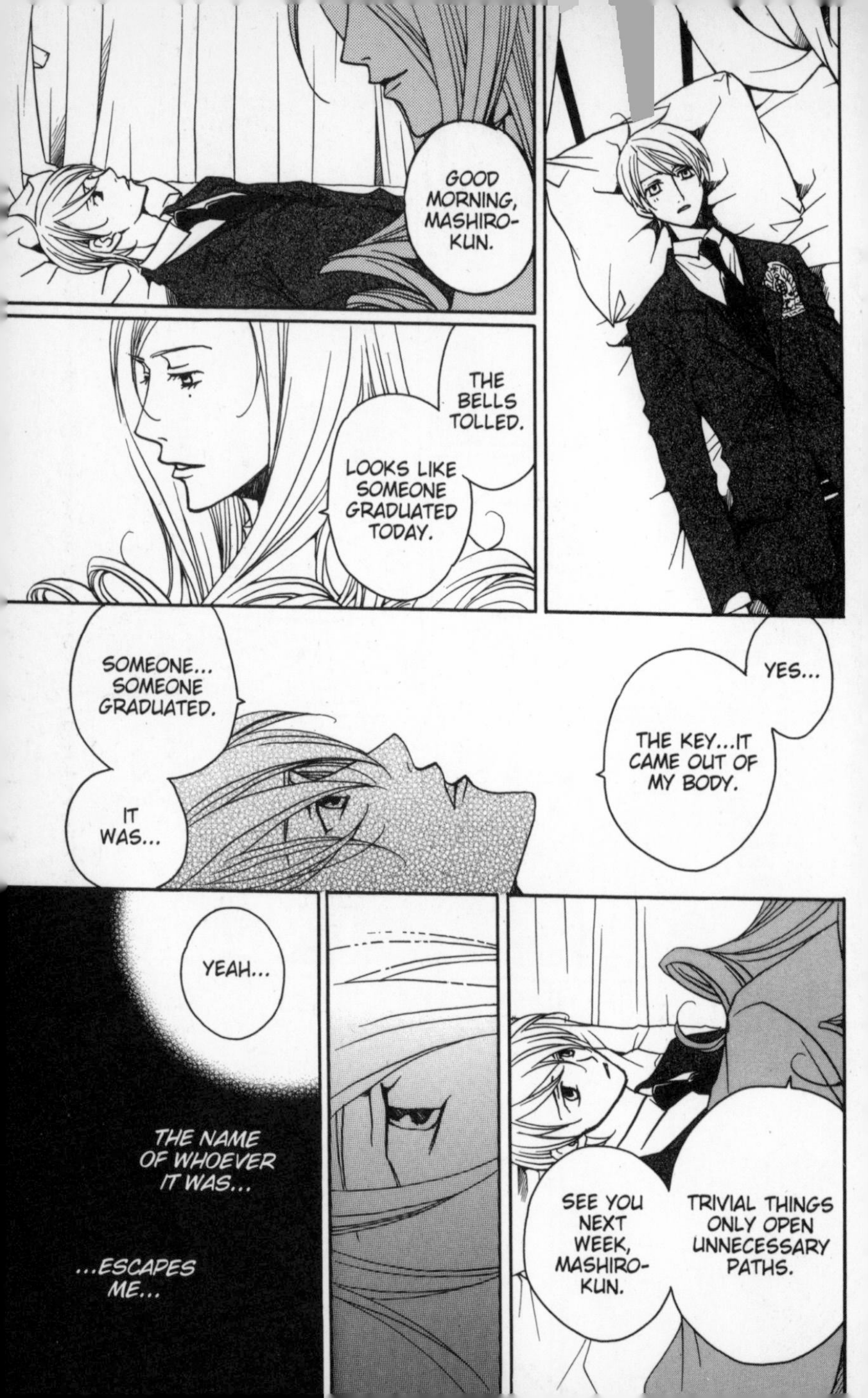
GOOD MORNING, MASHIRO-KUN.
THE BELLS TOLLED.
LOOKS LIKE SOMEONE GRADUATED TODAY.
YES...
THE KEY...IT CAME OUT OF MY BODY.
SOMEONE... SOMEONE GRADUATED.
IT WAS...
TRIVIAL THINGS ONLY OPEN UNNECESSARY PATHS.
SEE YOU NEXT WEEK, MASHIRO-KUN.
YEAH...
THE NAME OF WHOEVER IT WAS...
...ESCAPES ME...

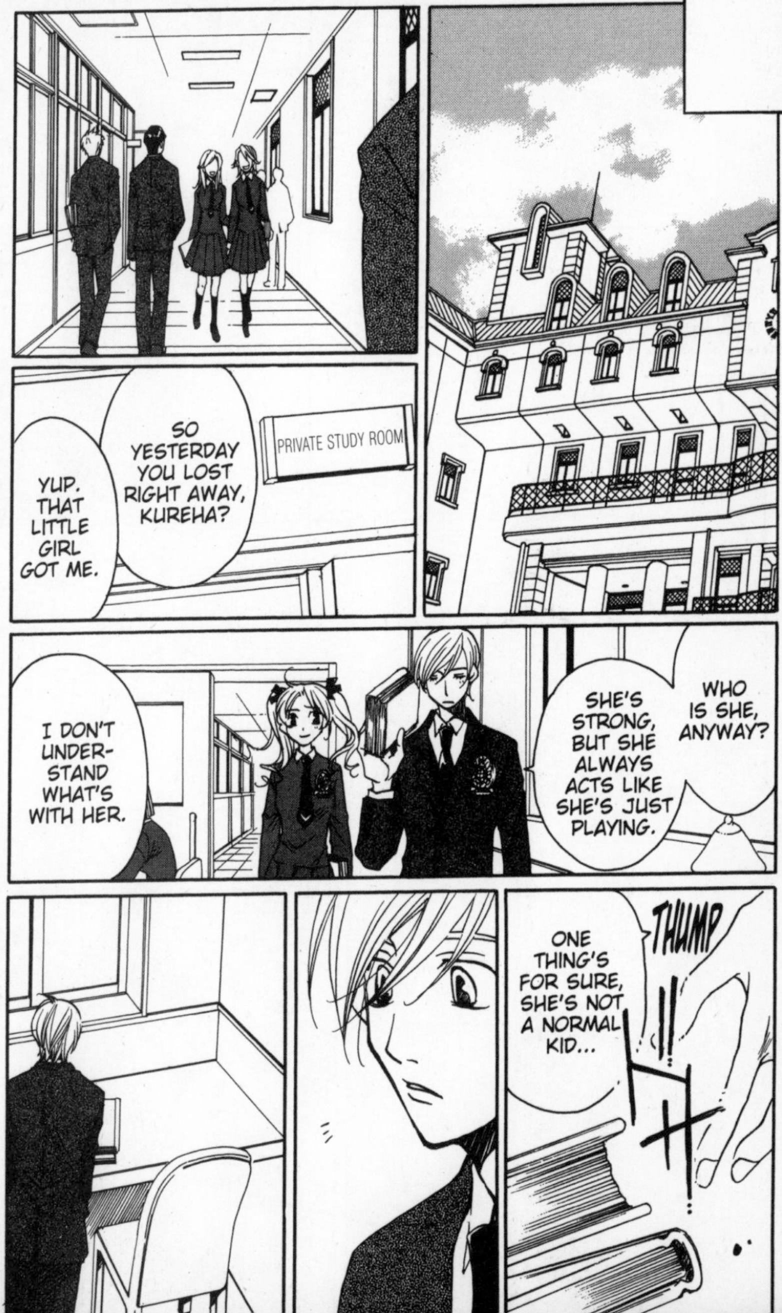
PRIVATE STUDY ROOM
SO YESTERDAY YOU LOST RIGHT AWAY, KUREHA?
YUP. THAT LITTLE GIRL GOT ME.
WHO IS SHE, ANYWAY?
SHE'S STRONG, BUT SHE ALWAYS ACTS LIKE SHE'S JUST PLAYING.
I DON'T UNDER-STAND WHAT'S WITH HER.
THUMP
ONE THING'S FOR SURE, SHE'S NOT A NORMAL KID...

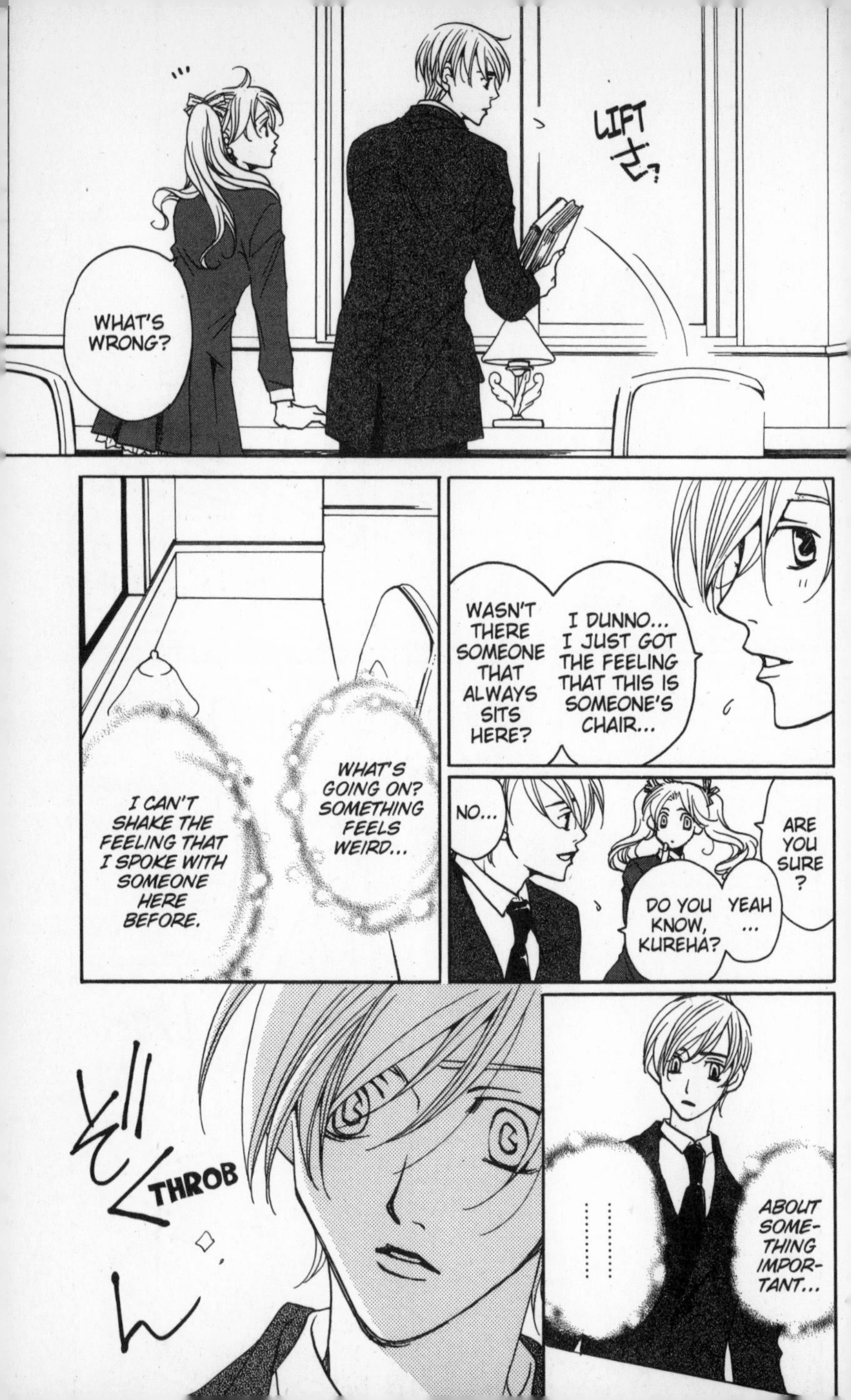
...
LIFT さっ
WHAT'S WRONG?
I DUNNO... I JUST GOT THE FEELING THAT THIS IS SOMEONE'S CHAIR...
WASN'T THERE SOMEONE THAT ALWAYS SITS HERE?
ARE YOU SURE?
YEAH ...
DO YOU KNOW, KUREHA?
NO...
WHAT'S GOING ON? SOMETHING FEELS WEIRD...
I CAN'T SHAKE THE FEELING THAT I SPOKE WITH SOMEONE HERE BEFORE.
......
ABOUT SOME-THING IMPOR-TANT...
どくん
THROB

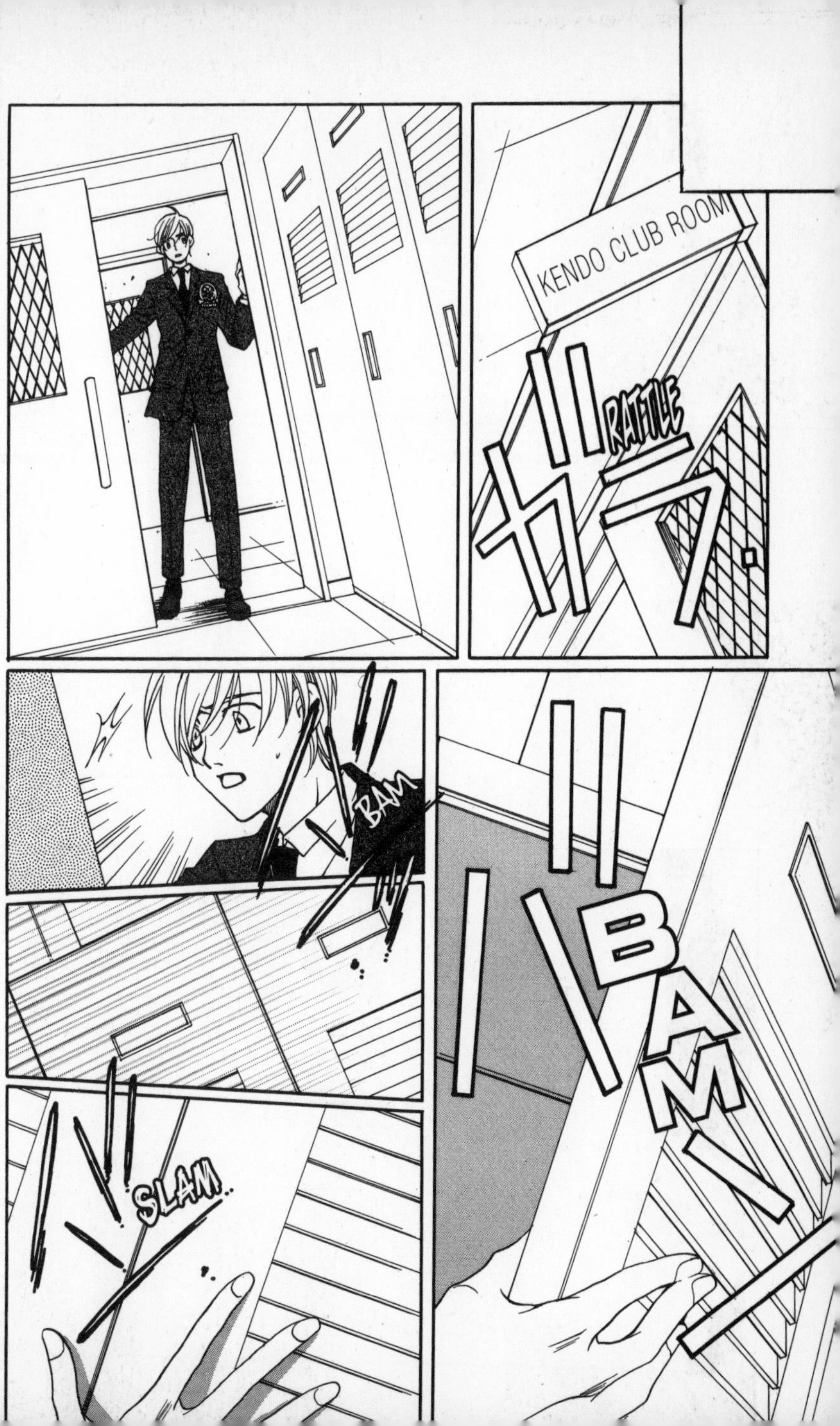
KENDO CLUB ROOM
カラ.
RATTLE
BAM!
BAM
SLAM

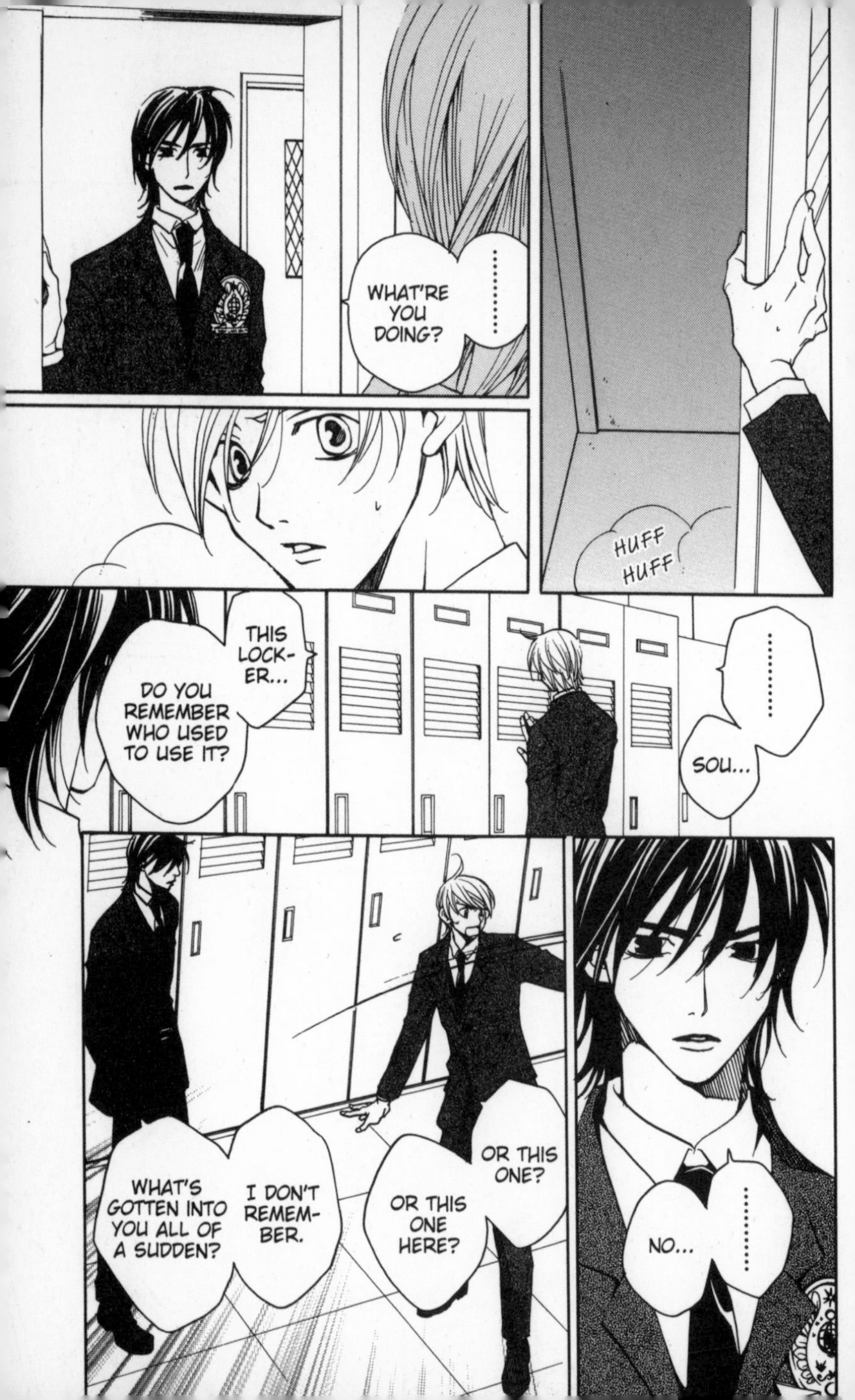
HUFF HUFF
......
WHAT'RE YOU DOING?
......
SOU...
THIS LOCKER...
DO YOU REMEMBER WHO USED TO USE IT?
......
NO...
OR THIS ONE?
OR THIS ONE HERE?
I DON'T REMEMBER.
WHAT'S GOTTEN INTO YOU ALL OF A SUDDEN?

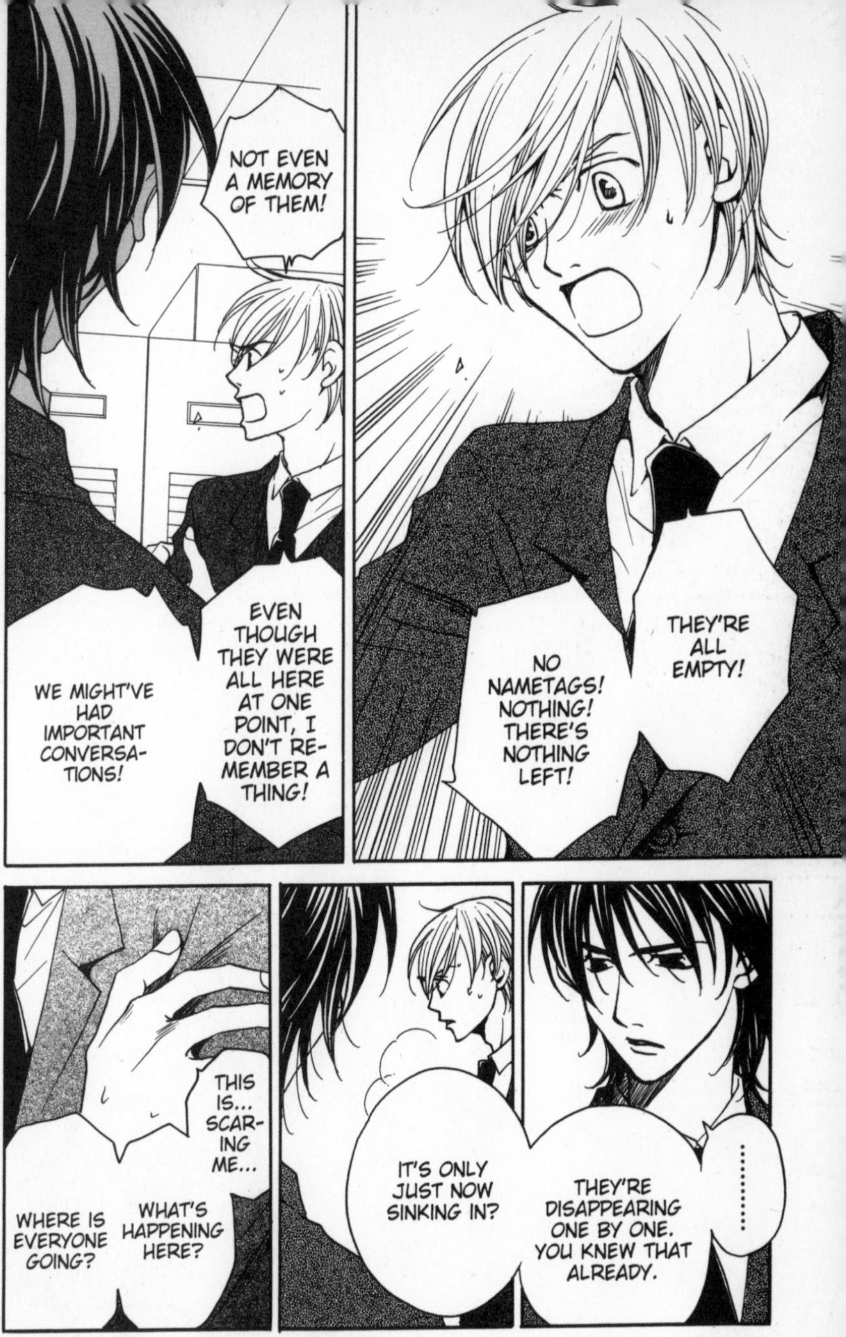
THEY'RE ALL EMPTY!
NO NAMETAGS! NOTHING! THERE'S NOTHING LEFT!
NOT EVEN A MEMORY OF THEM!
EVEN THOUGH THEY WERE ALL HERE AT ONE POINT, I DON'T RE-MEMBER A THING!
WE MIGHT'VE HAD IMPORTANT CONVERSA-TIONS!
......
THEY'RE DISAPPEARING ONE BY ONE. YOU KNEW THAT ALREADY.
IT'S ONLY JUST NOW SINKING IN?
THIS IS... SCAR-ING ME...
WHAT'S HAPPENING HERE?
WHERE IS EVERYONE GOING?

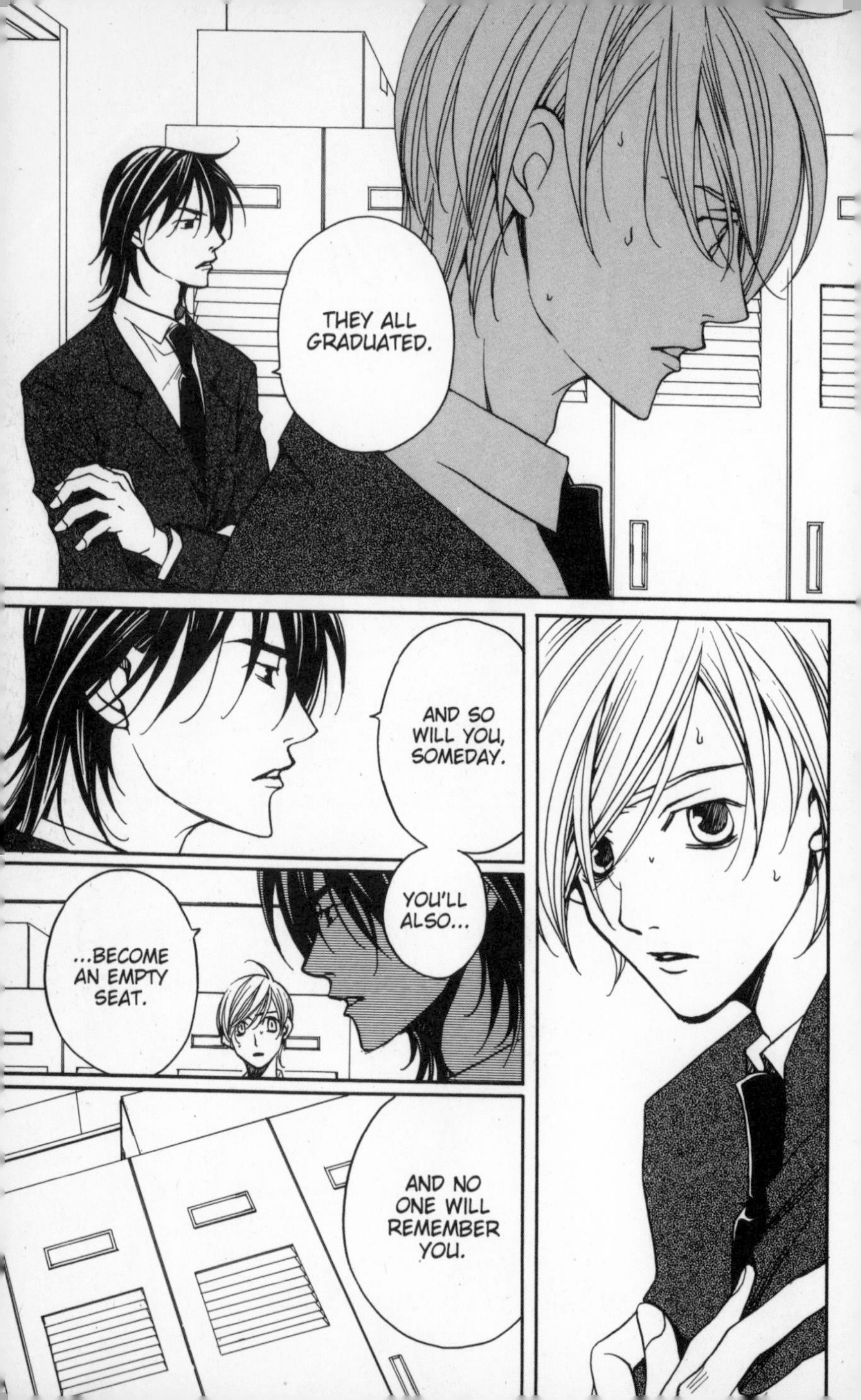
THEY ALL GRADUATED.
AND SO WILL YOU, SOMEDAY.
YOU'LL ALSO...
...BECOME AN EMPTY SEAT.
AND NO ONE WILL REMEMBER YOU.

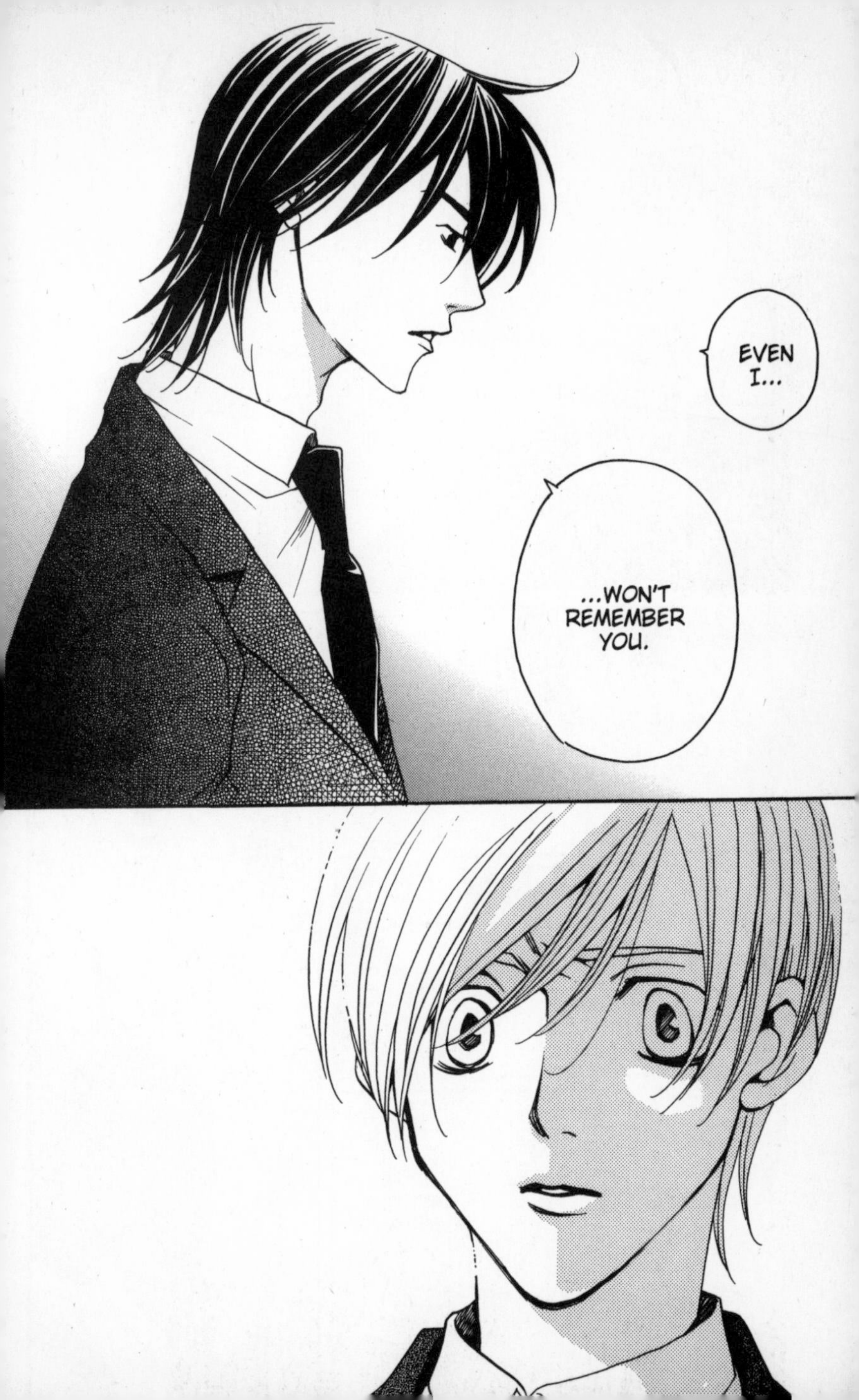
EVEN I...
...WON'T REMEMBER YOU.

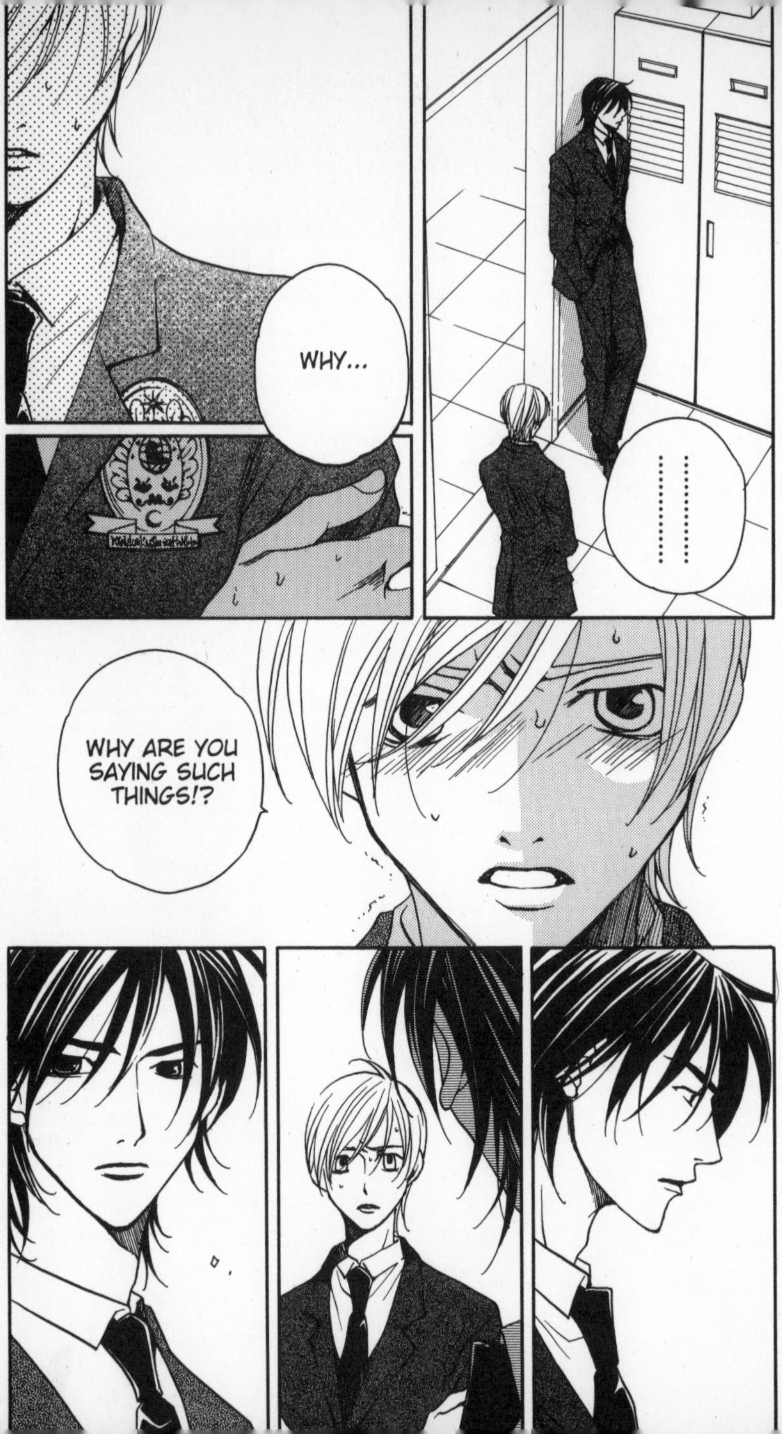
......
WHY...
WHY ARE YOU SAYING SUCH THINGS!?

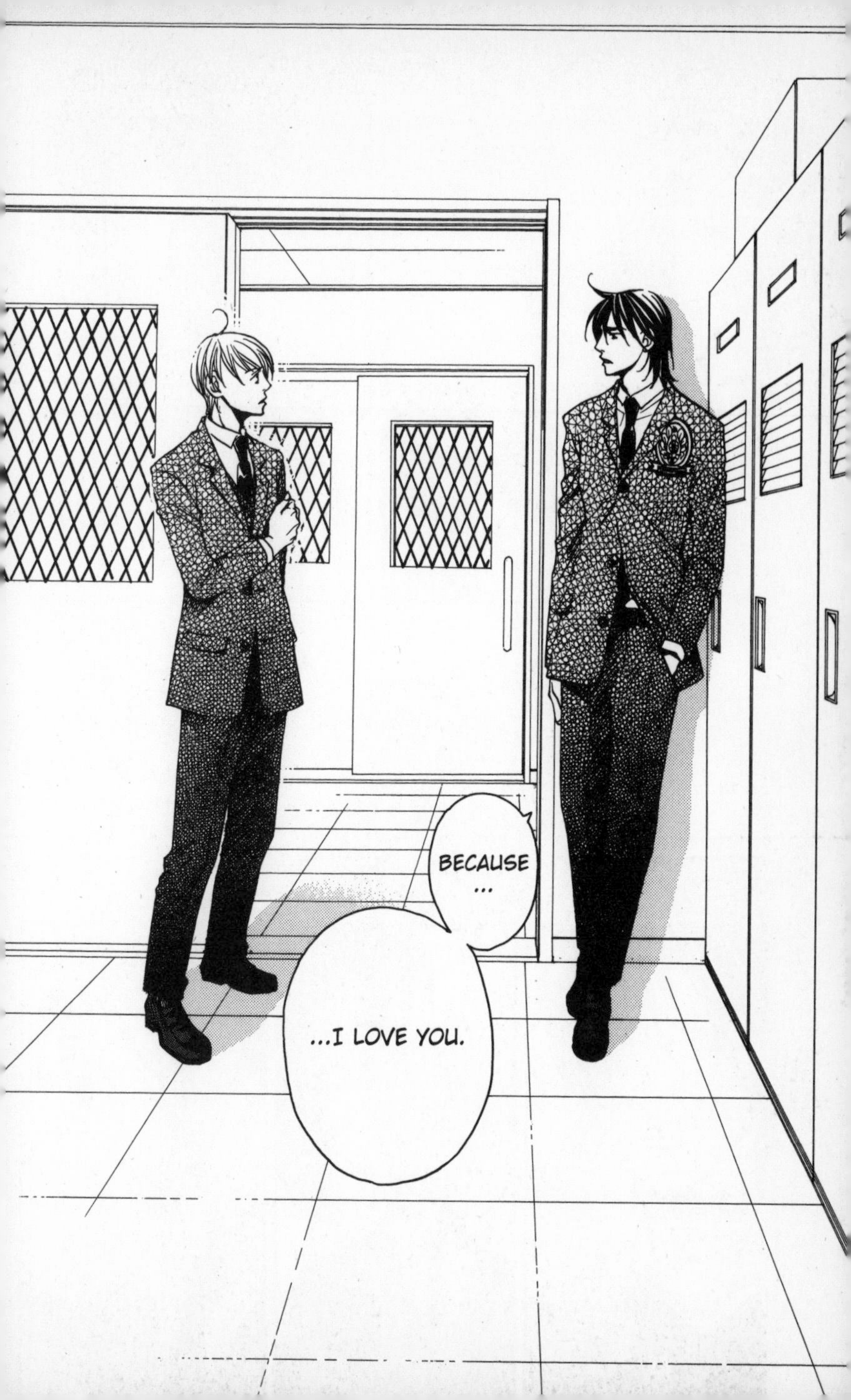
BECAUSE ...
...I LOVE YOU.

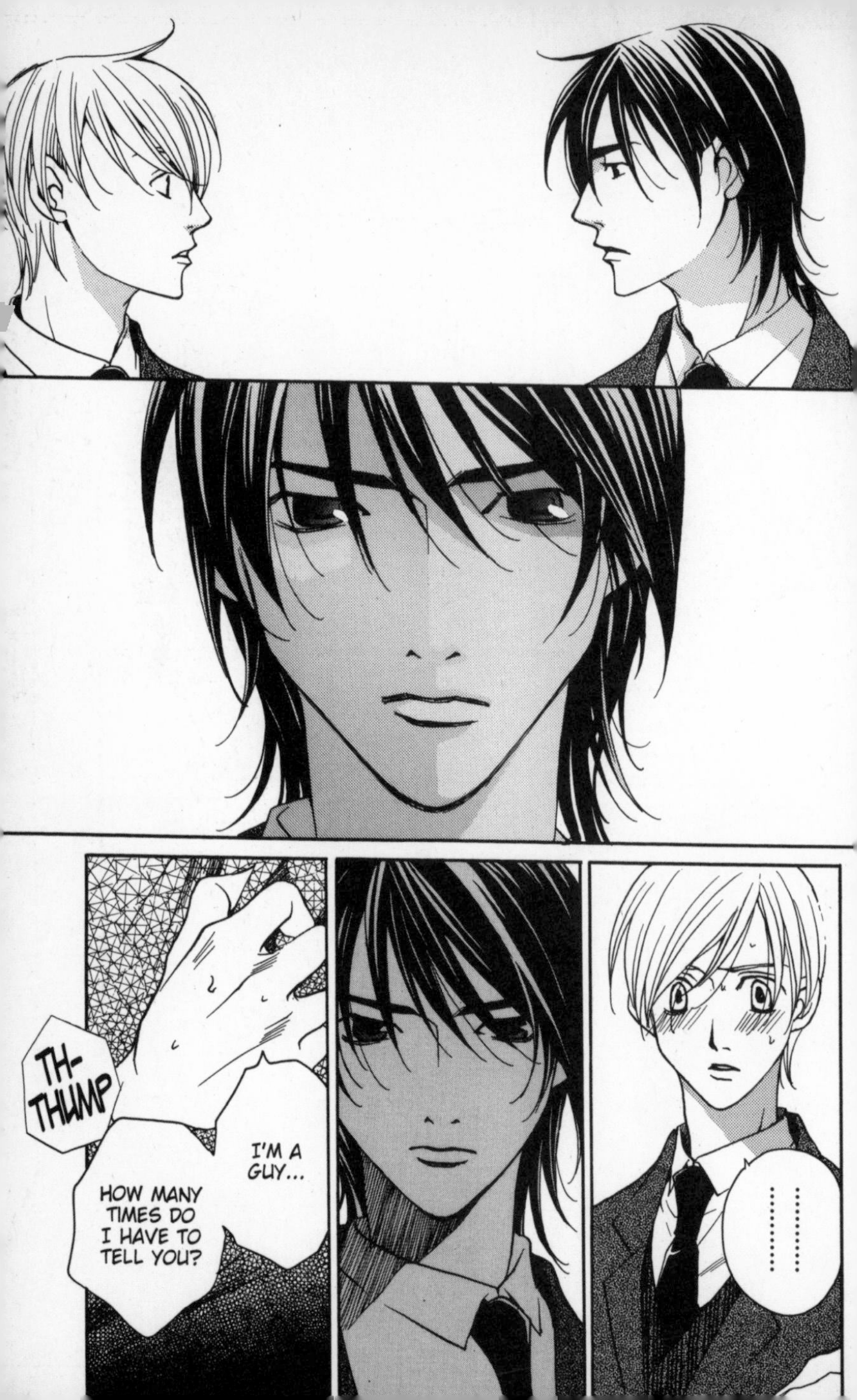
......
TH-THUMP
I'M A GUY...
HOW MANY TIMES DO I HAVE TO TELL YOU?

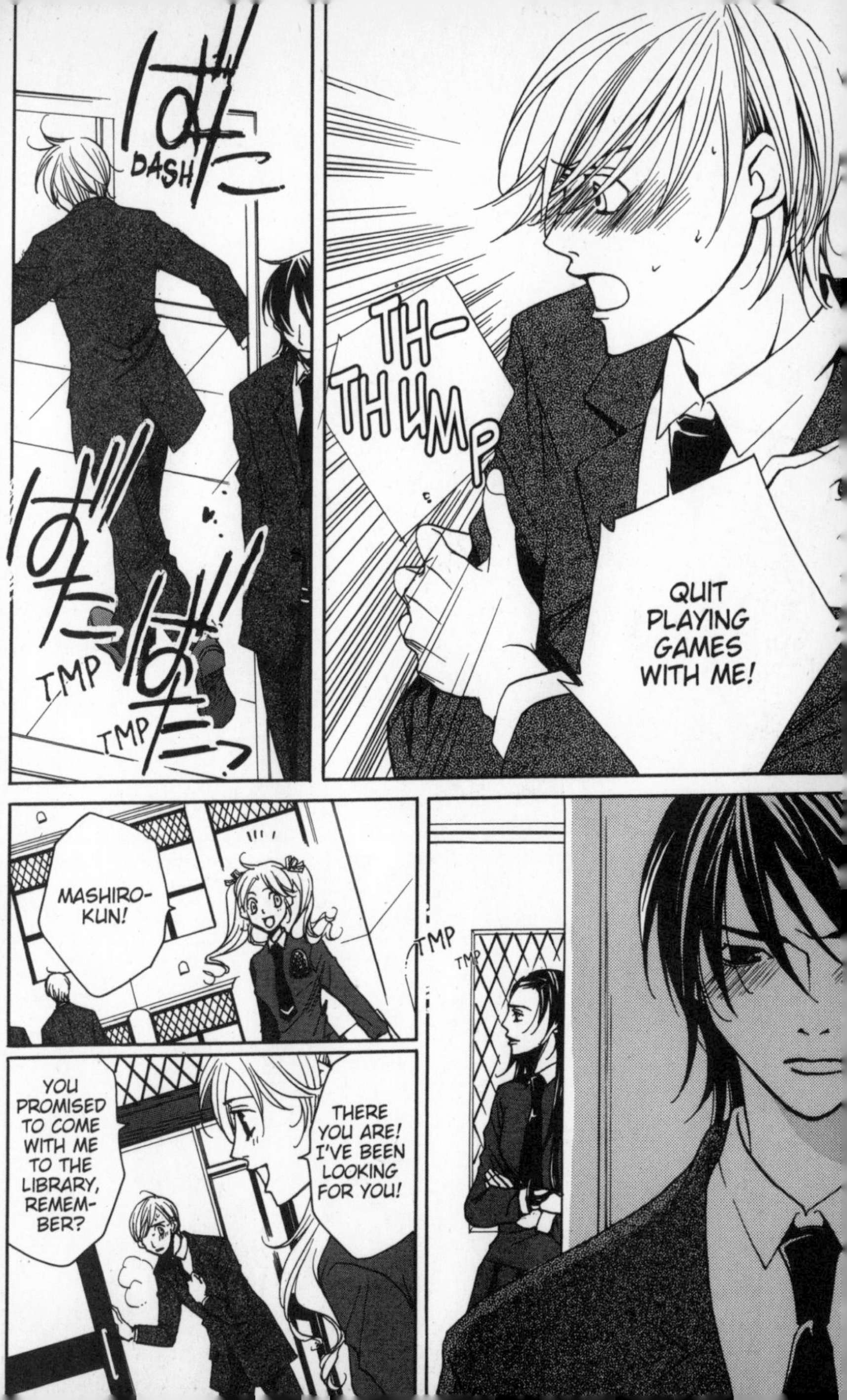
TH-THUMP
QUIT PLAYING GAMES WITH ME!
DASH
TMP
TMP
TMP
TMP
MASHIRO-KUN!
THERE YOU ARE! I'VE BEEN LOOKING FOR YOU!
YOU PROMISED TO COME WITH ME TO THE LIBRARY, REMEMBER?

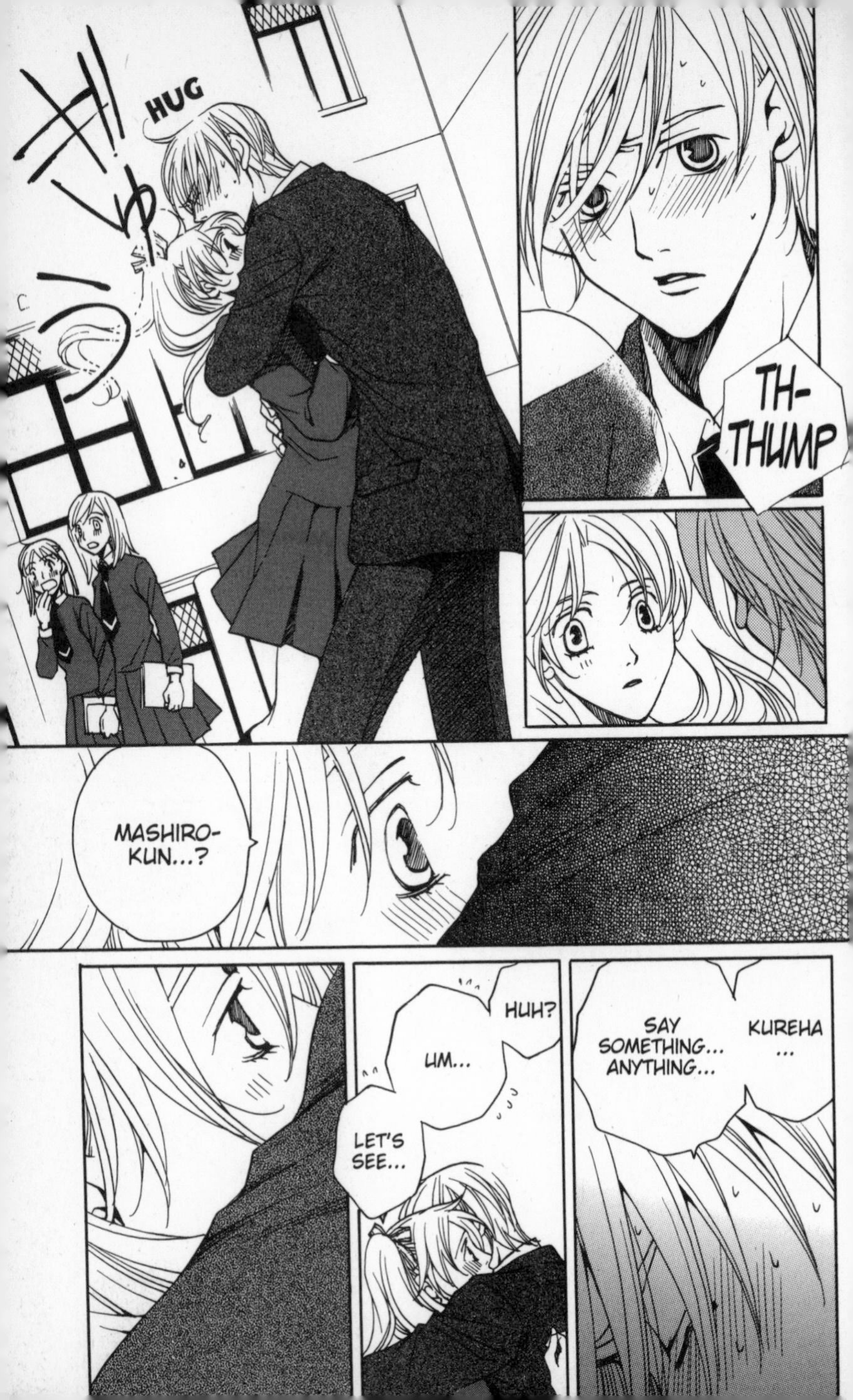
TH-THUMP
HUG
MASHIRO-KUN...?
KUREHA ...
SAY SOMETHING... ANYTHING...
HUH?
UM...
LET'S SEE...

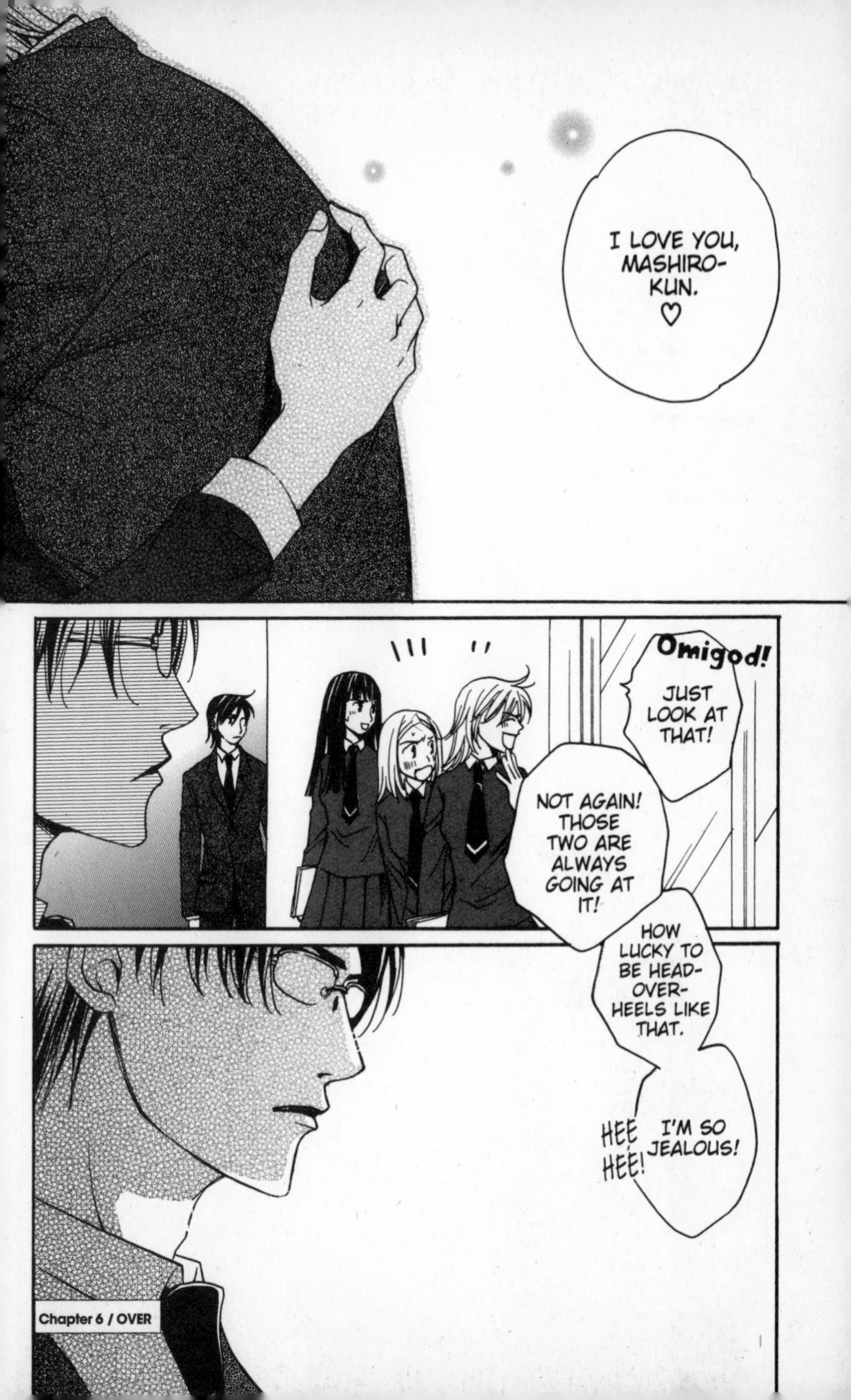
I LOVE YOU, MASHIRO-KUN. ♡
Omigod!
JUST LOOK AT THAT!
NOT AGAIN! THOSE TWO ARE ALWAYS GOING AT IT!
HOW LUCKY TO BE HEAD-OVER-HEELS LIKE THAT.
I'M SO JEALOUS!
HEE HEE!
Chapter 6 / OVER

AFTER SCHOOL NIGHTMARE Chapter 7

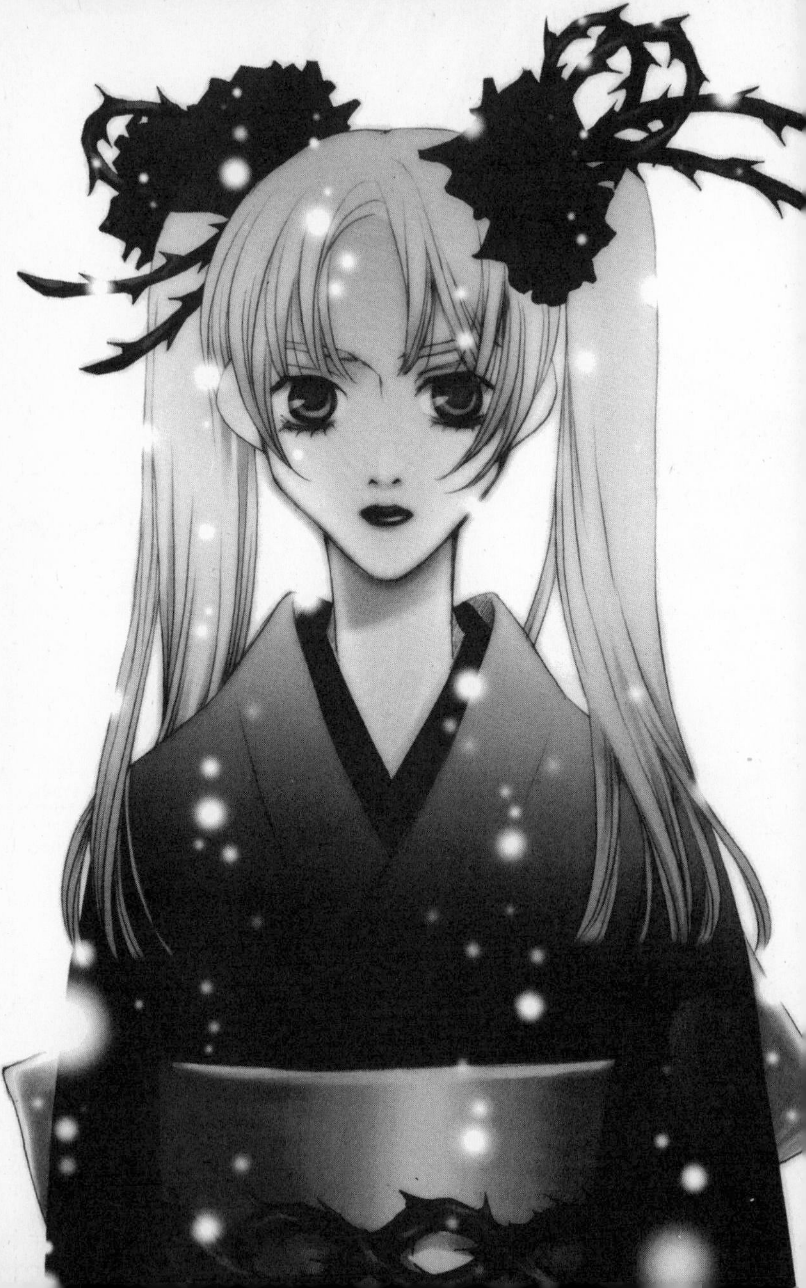

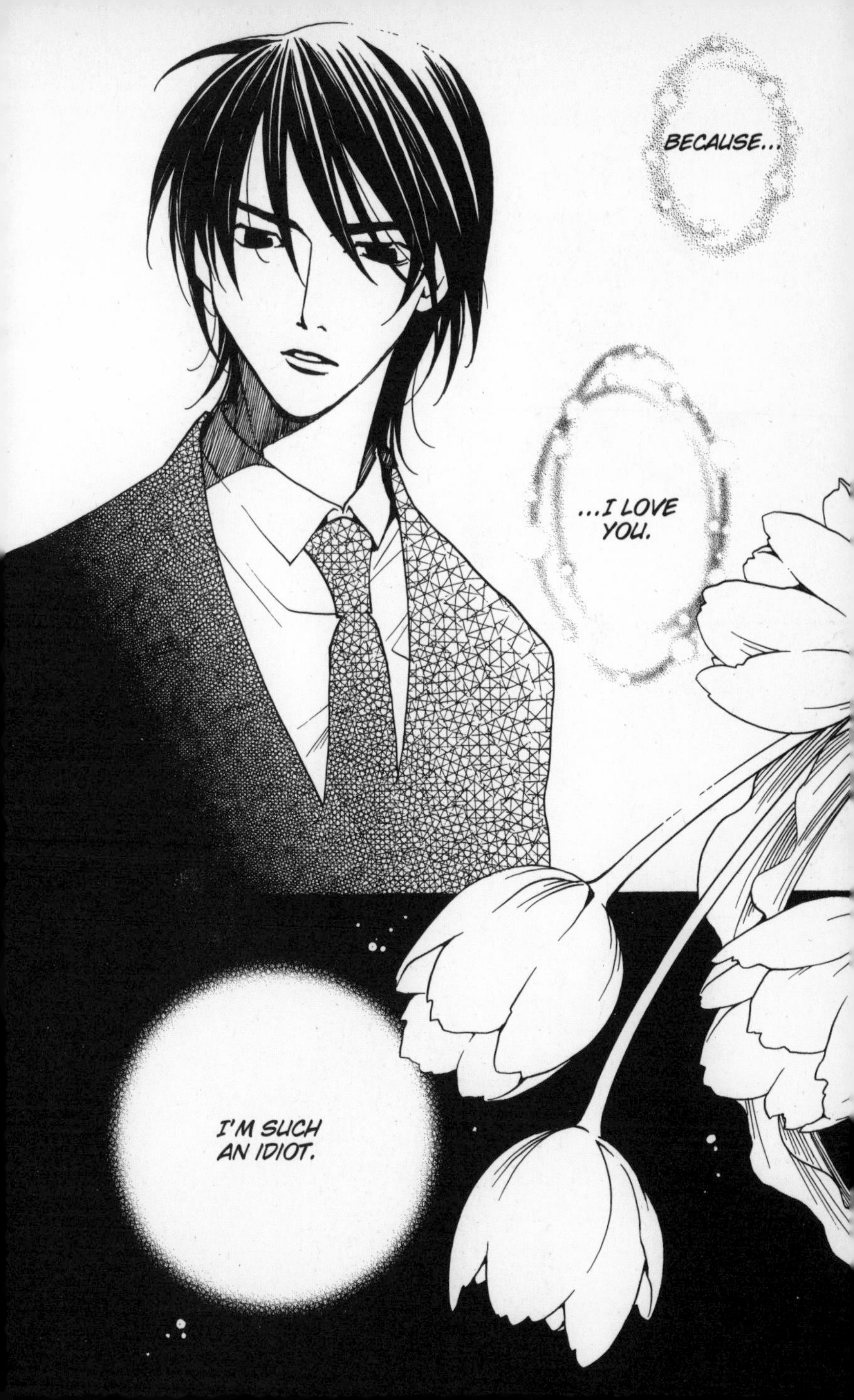
BECAUSE...
...I LOVE YOU.
I'M SUCH AN IDIOT.

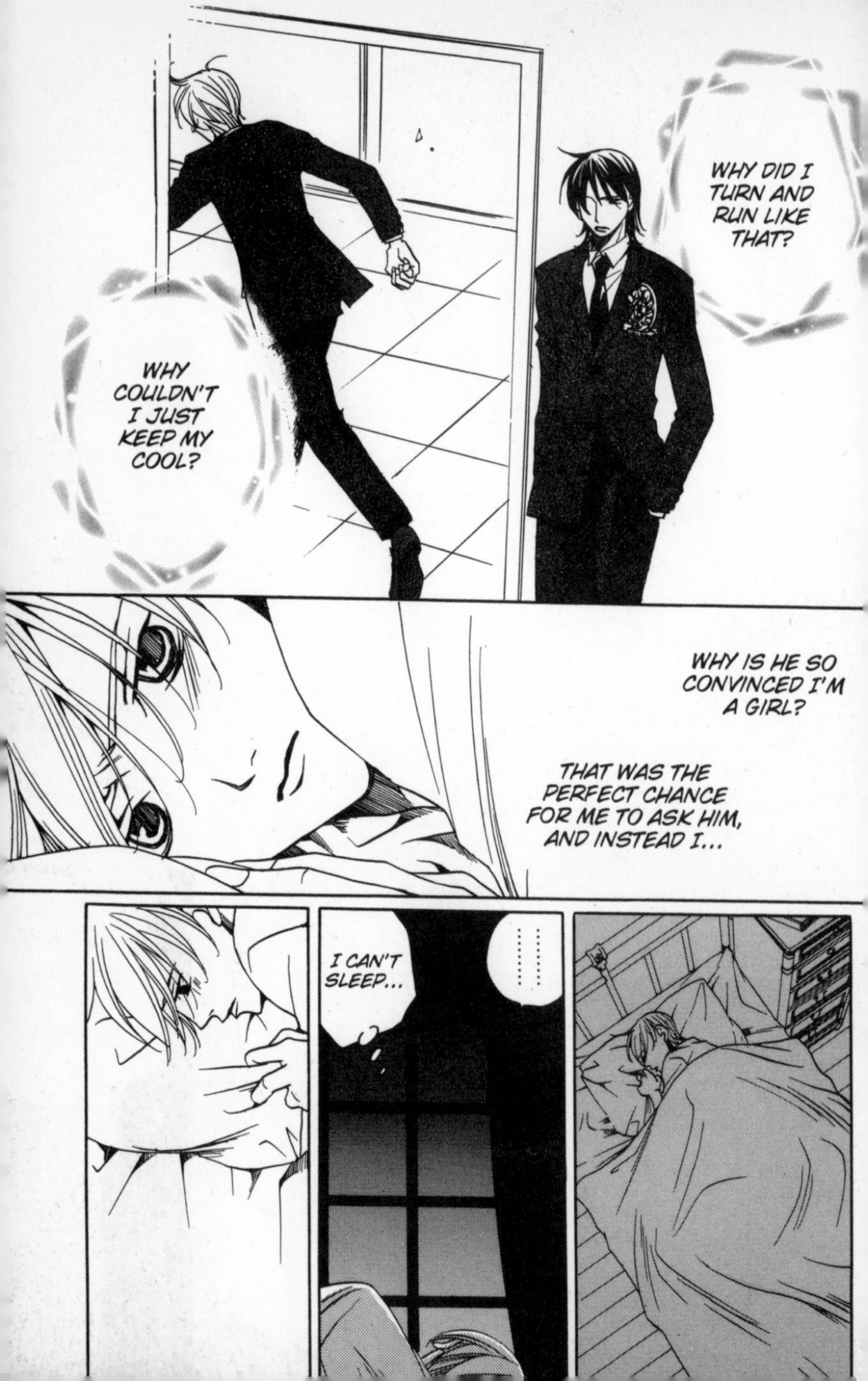
WHY DID I TURN AND RUN LIKE THAT?
WHY COULDN'T I JUST KEEP MY COOL?
WHY IS HE SO CONVINCED I'M A GIRL?
THAT WAS THE PERFECT CHANCE FOR ME TO ASK HIM, AND INSTEAD I...
......
I CAN'T SLEEP...

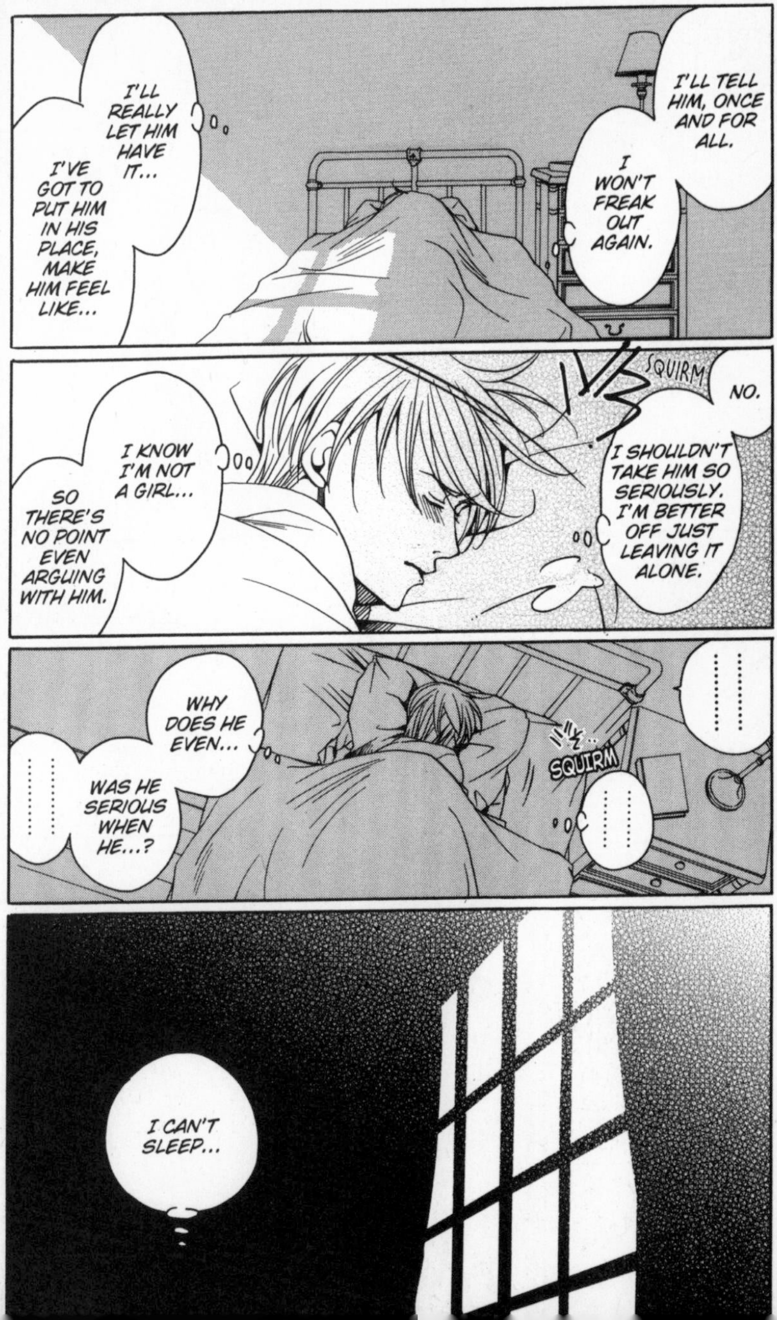
I'LL TELL HIM, ONCE AND FOR ALL.
I WON'T FREAK OUT AGAIN.
I'LL REALLY LET HIM HAVE IT...
I'VE GOT TO PUT HIM IN HIS PLACE, MAKE HIM FEEL LIKE...
SQUIRM
NO.
I SHOULDN'T TAKE HIM SO SERIOUSLY. I'M BETTER OFF JUST LEAVING IT ALONE.
I KNOW I'M NOT A GIRL...
SO THERE'S NO POINT EVEN ARGUING WITH HIM.
......
SQUIRM
......
WHY DOES HE EVEN...
WAS HE SERIOUS WHEN HE...?
......
I CAN'T SLEEP...

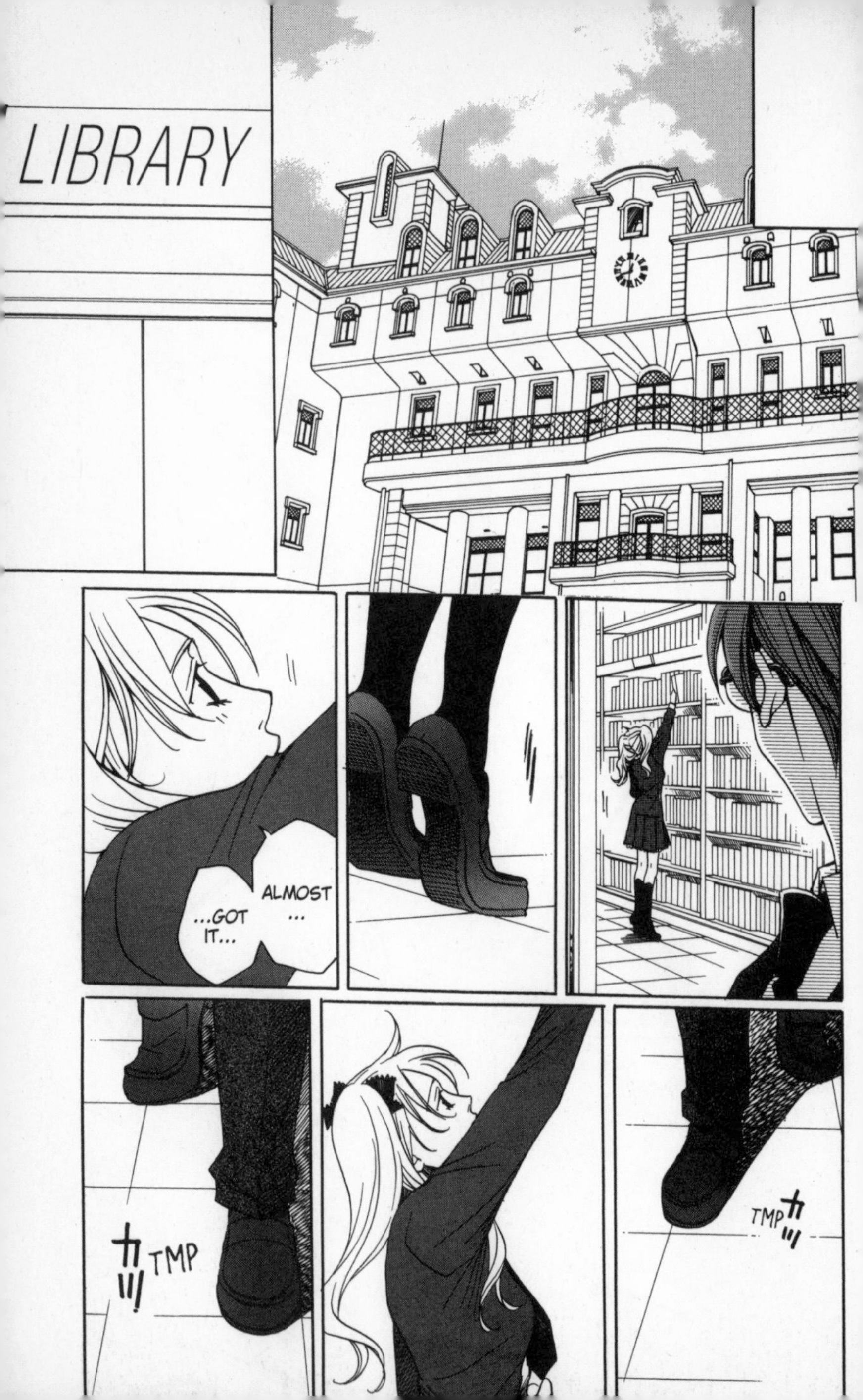
LIBRARY
ALMOST...
...GOT IT...
TMP
TMP

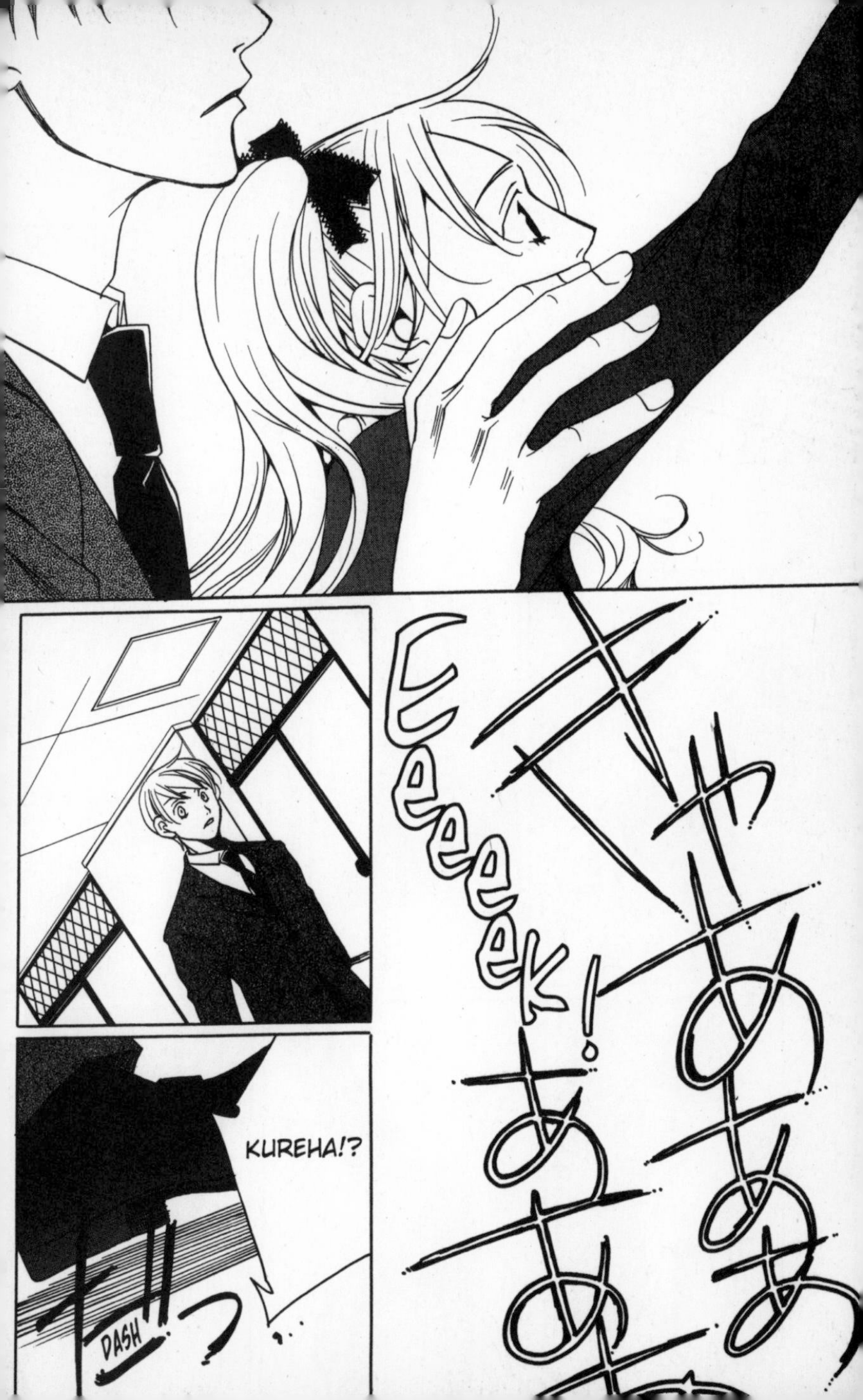

Eeeeek!
KUREHA!?
DASH

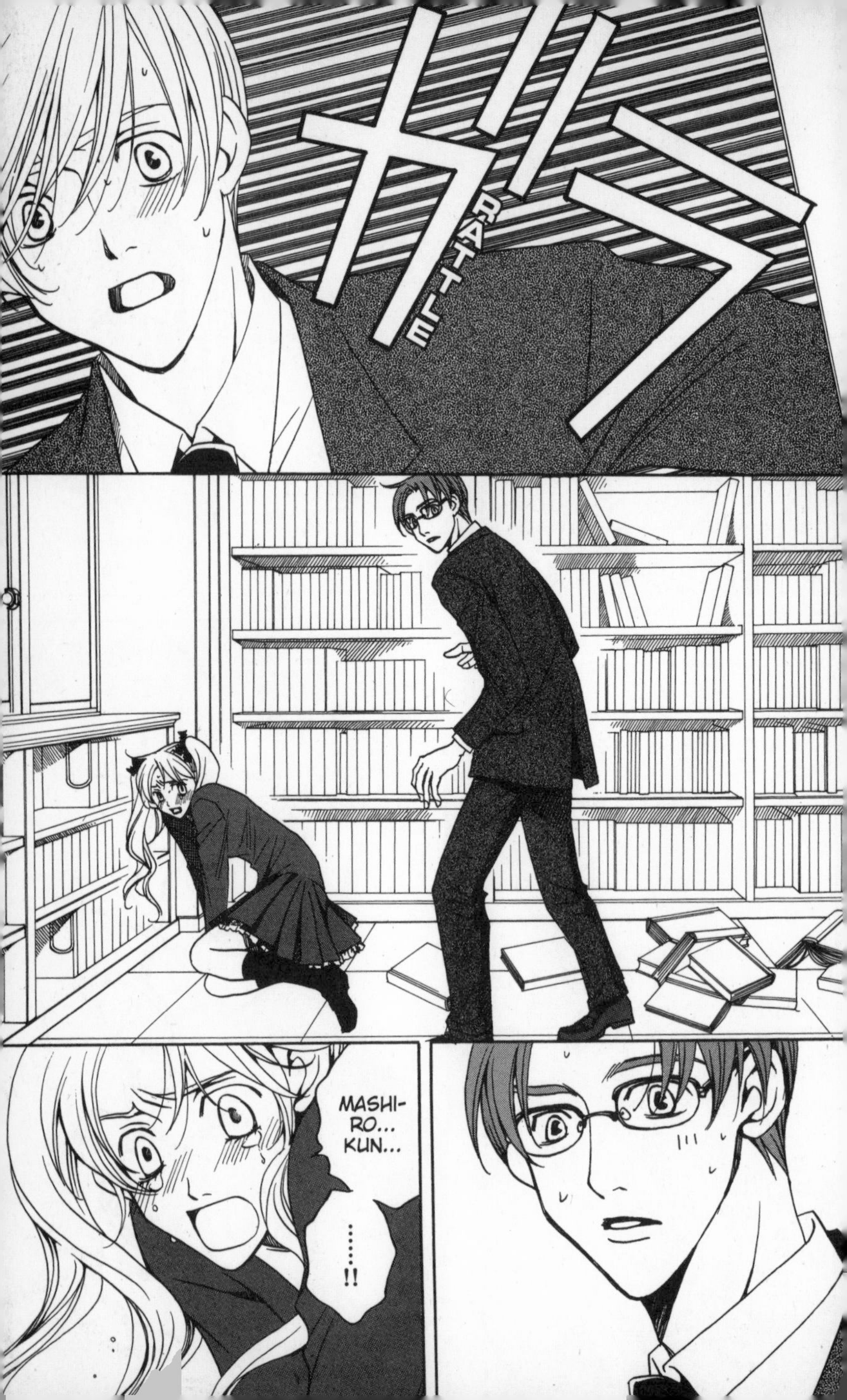
RATTLE
MASHIRO... KUN...
......!!

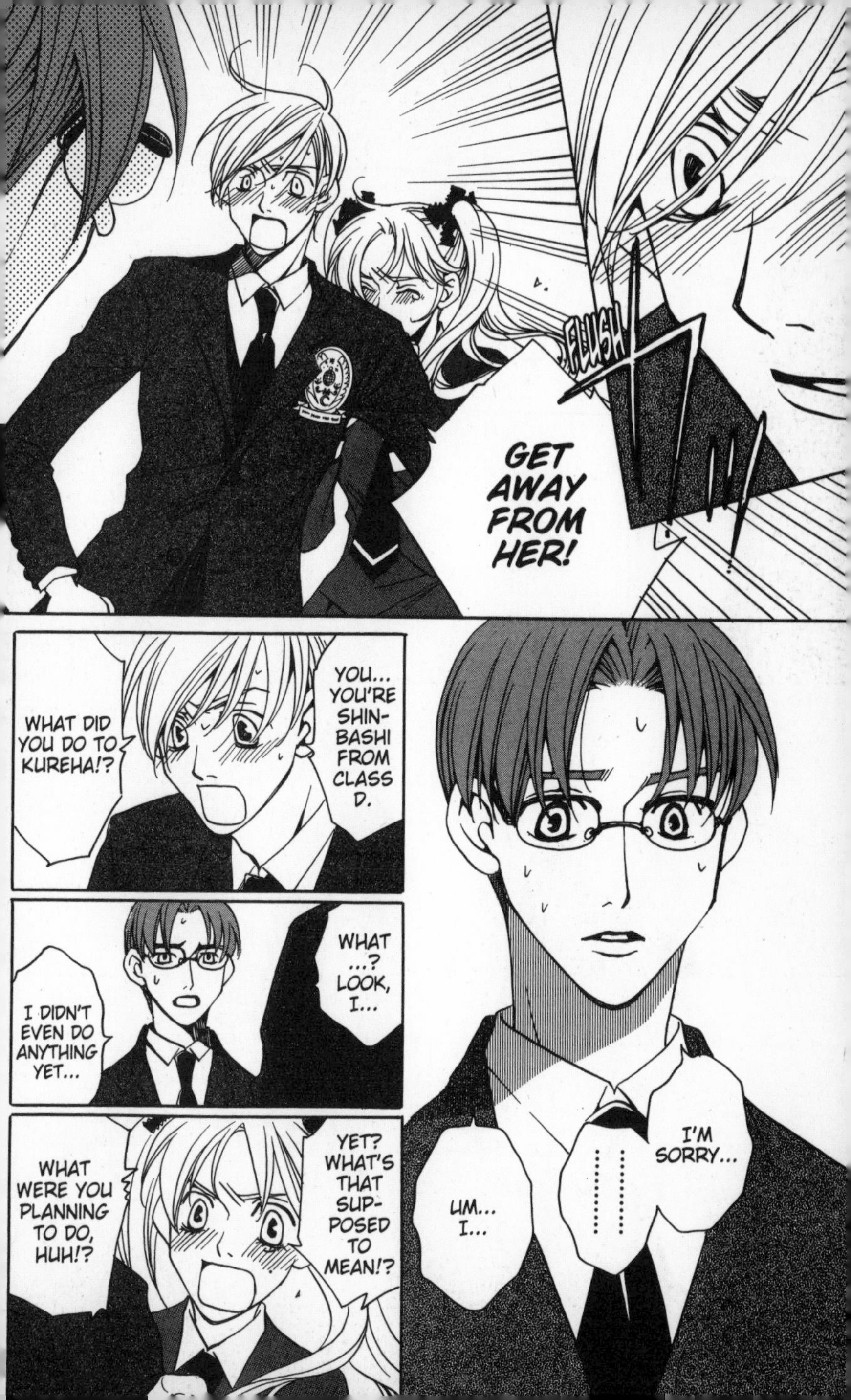
FLUSH
GET AWAY FROM HER!
I'M SORRY...
......
UM... I...
YOU... YOU'RE SHIN-BASHI FROM CLASS D.
WHAT DID YOU DO TO KUREHA!?
WHAT ...? LOOK, I...
I DIDN'T EVEN DO ANYTHING YET...
YET? WHAT'S THAT SUP-POSED TO MEAN!?
WHAT WERE YOU PLANNING TO DO, HUH!?

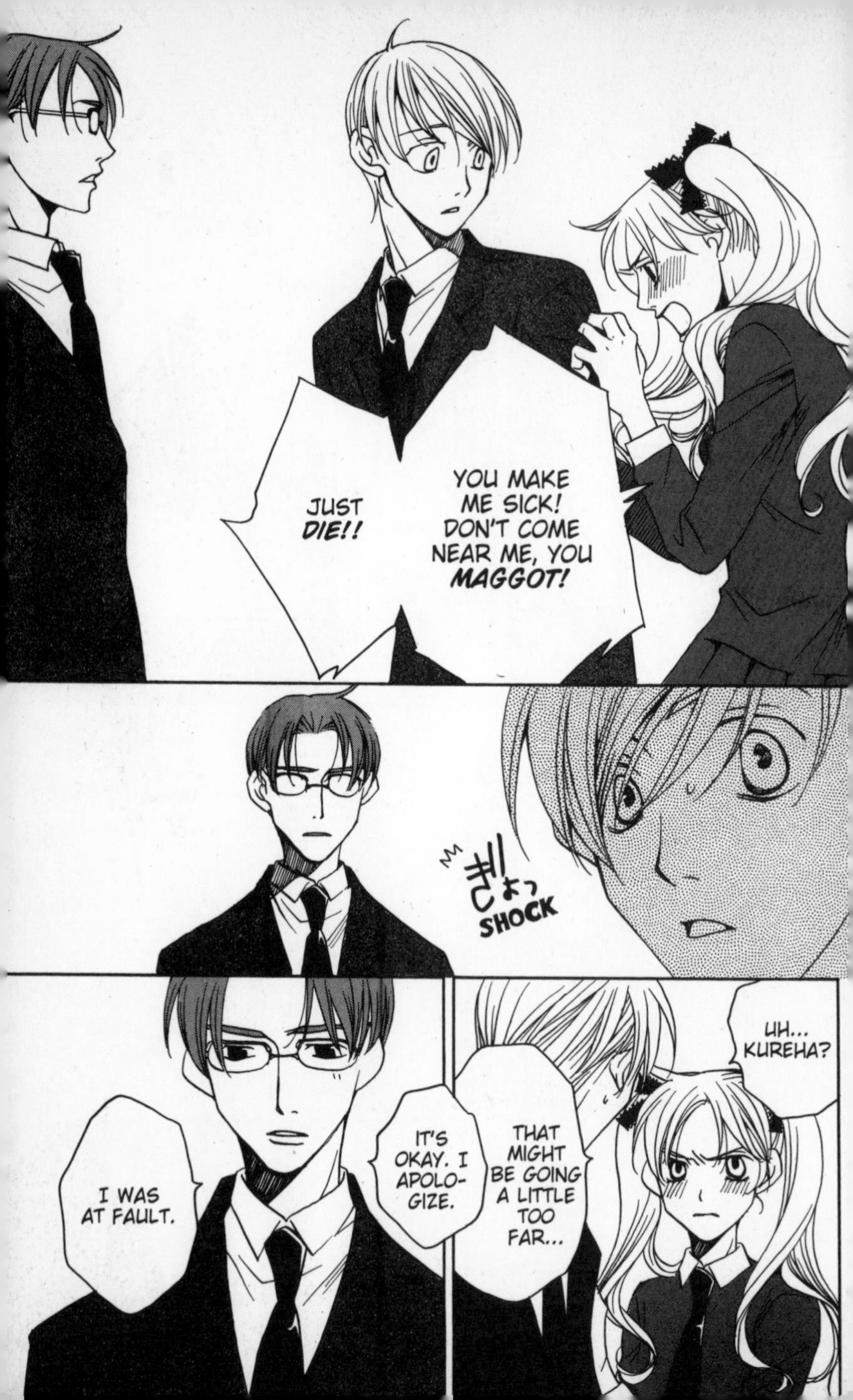
YOU MAKE ME SICK! DON'T COME NEAR ME, YOU MAGGOT!
JUST DIE!!
ぎょっ
SHOCK
UH... KUREHA?
THAT MIGHT BE GOING A LITTLE TOO FAR...
IT'S OKAY. I APOLOGIZE.
I WAS AT FAULT.

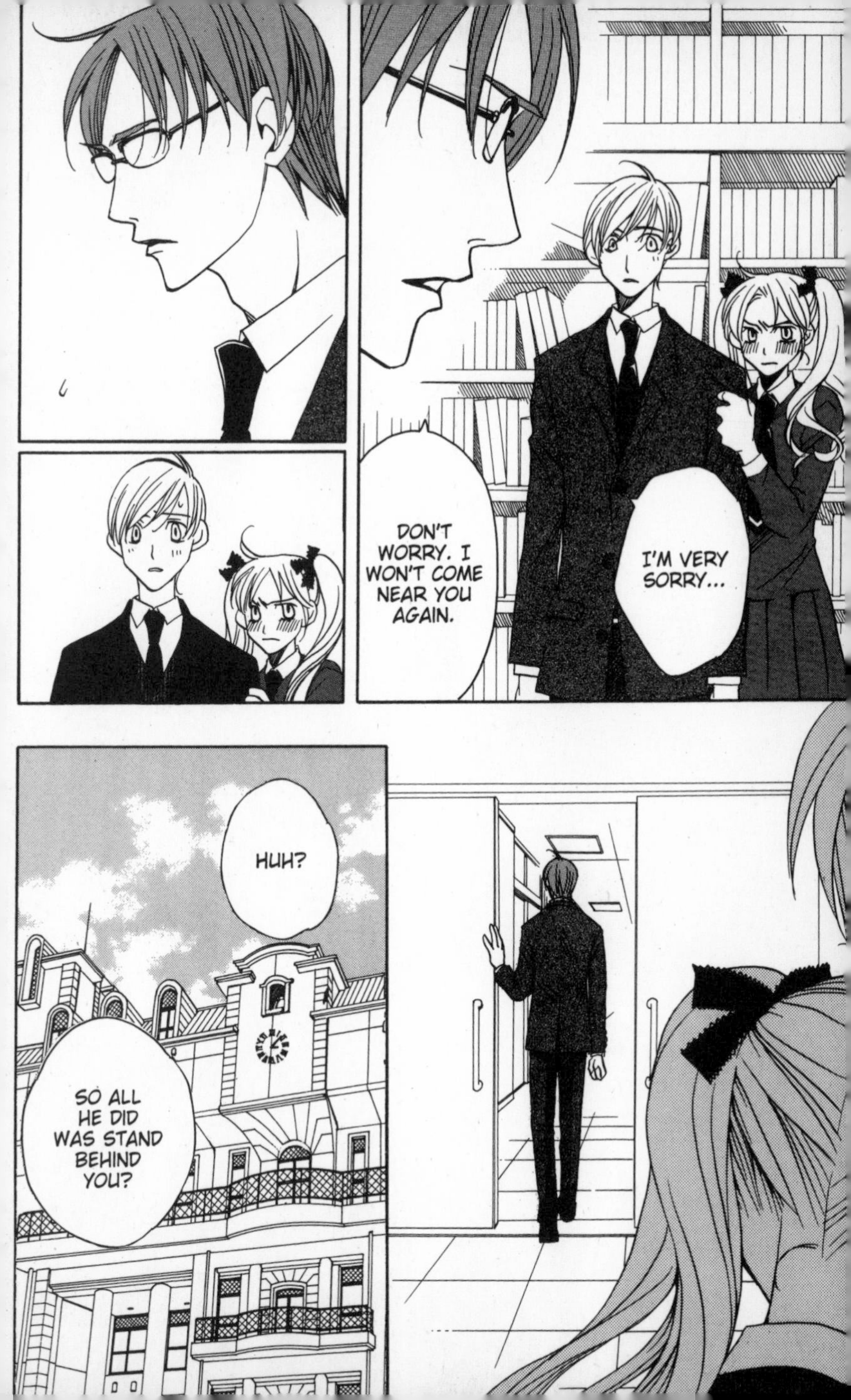
I'M VERY SORRY...
DON'T WORRY. I WON'T COME NEAR YOU AGAIN.
HUH?
SO ALL HE DID WAS STAND BEHIND YOU?

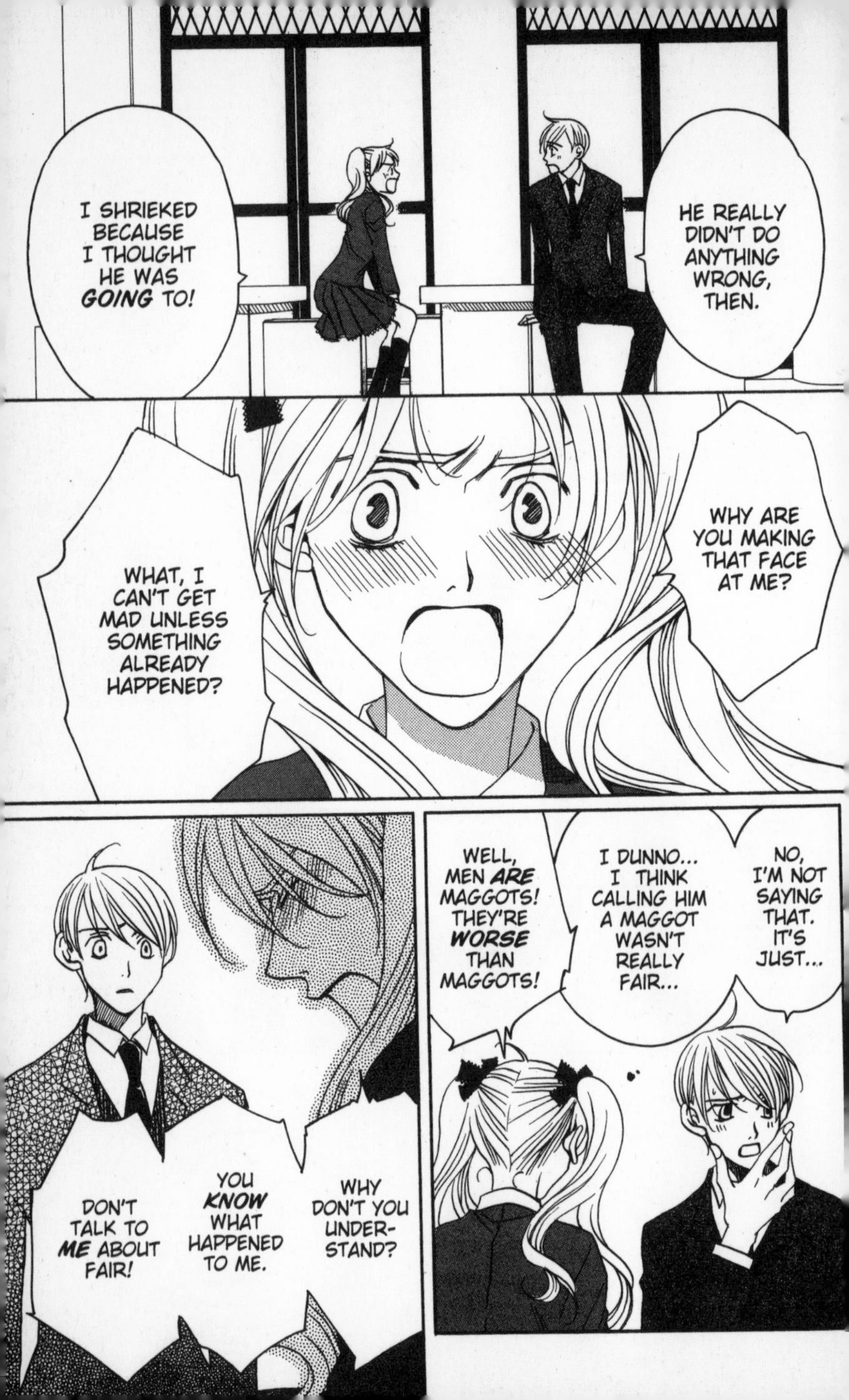
HE REALLY DIDN'T DO ANYTHING WRONG, THEN.
I SHRIEKED BECAUSE I THOUGHT HE WAS *GOING* TO!
WHY ARE YOU MAKING THAT FACE AT ME?
WHAT, I CAN'T GET MAD UNLESS SOMETHING ALREADY HAPPENED?
NO, I'M NOT SAYING THAT. IT'S JUST...
I DUNNO... I THINK CALLING HIM A MAGGOT WASN'T REALLY FAIR...
WELL, MEN *ARE* MAGGOTS! THEY'RE *WORSE* THAN MAGGOTS!
WHY DON'T YOU UNDERSTAND?
YOU *KNOW* WHAT HAPPENED TO ME.
DON'T TALK TO *ME* ABOUT FAIR!

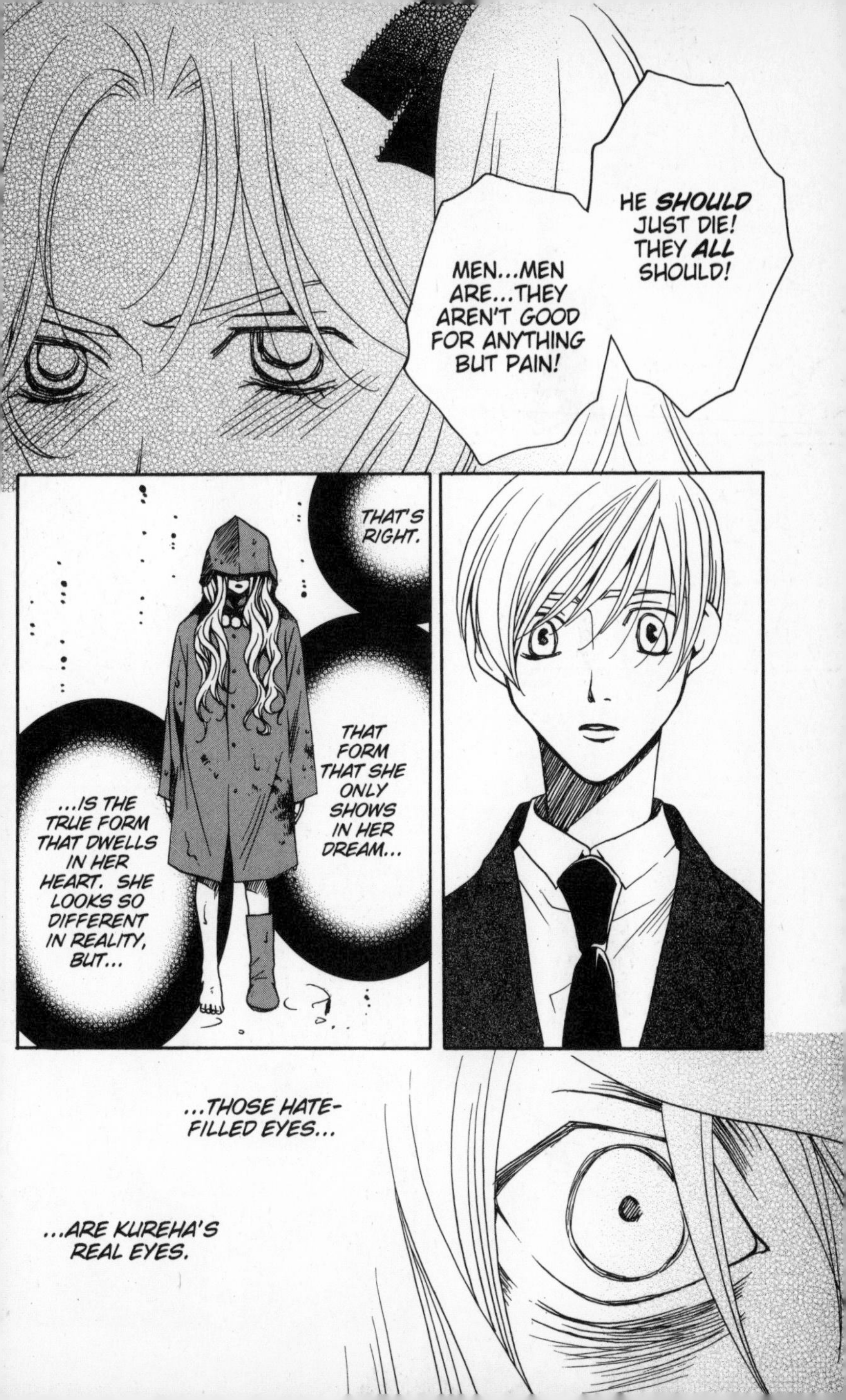
HE SHOULD JUST DIE! THEY ALL SHOULD!
MEN...MEN ARE...THEY AREN'T GOOD FOR ANYTHING BUT PAIN!
THAT'S RIGHT.
THAT FORM THAT SHE ONLY SHOWS IN HER DREAM...
...IS THE TRUE FORM THAT DWELLS IN HER HEART. SHE LOOKS SO DIFFERENT IN REALITY, BUT...
...THOSE HATE-FILLED EYES...
...ARE KUREHA'S REAL EYES.

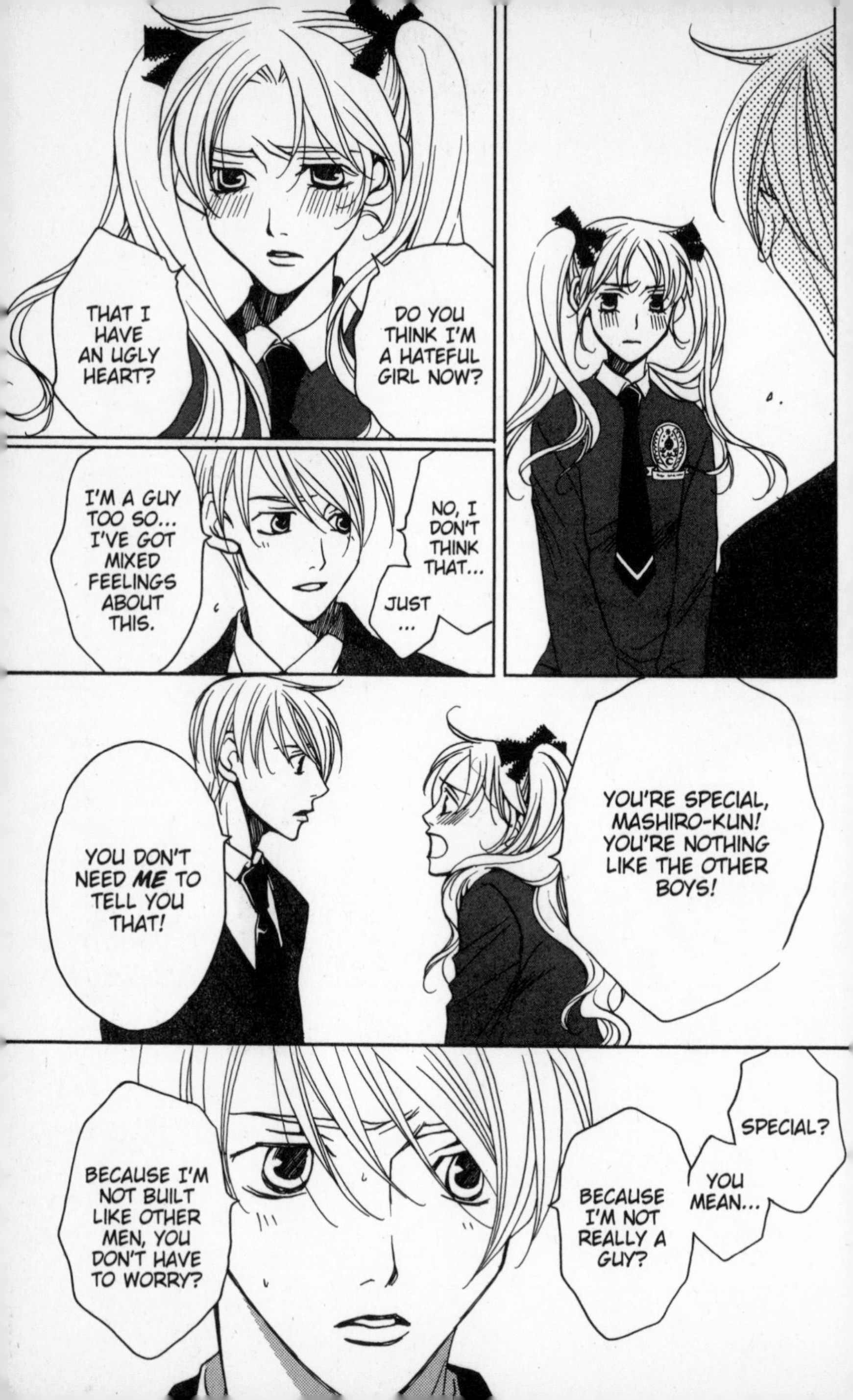
DO YOU THINK I'M A HATEFUL GIRL NOW?
THAT I HAVE AN UGLY HEART?
NO, I DON'T THINK THAT...
JUST ...
I'M A GUY TOO SO... I'VE GOT MIXED FEELINGS ABOUT THIS.
YOU'RE SPECIAL, MASHIRO-KUN! YOU'RE NOTHING LIKE THE OTHER BOYS!
YOU DON'T NEED *ME* TO TELL YOU THAT!
SPECIAL?
YOU MEAN...
BECAUSE I'M NOT REALLY A GUY?
BECAUSE I'M NOT BUILT LIKE OTHER MEN, YOU DON'T HAVE TO WORRY?

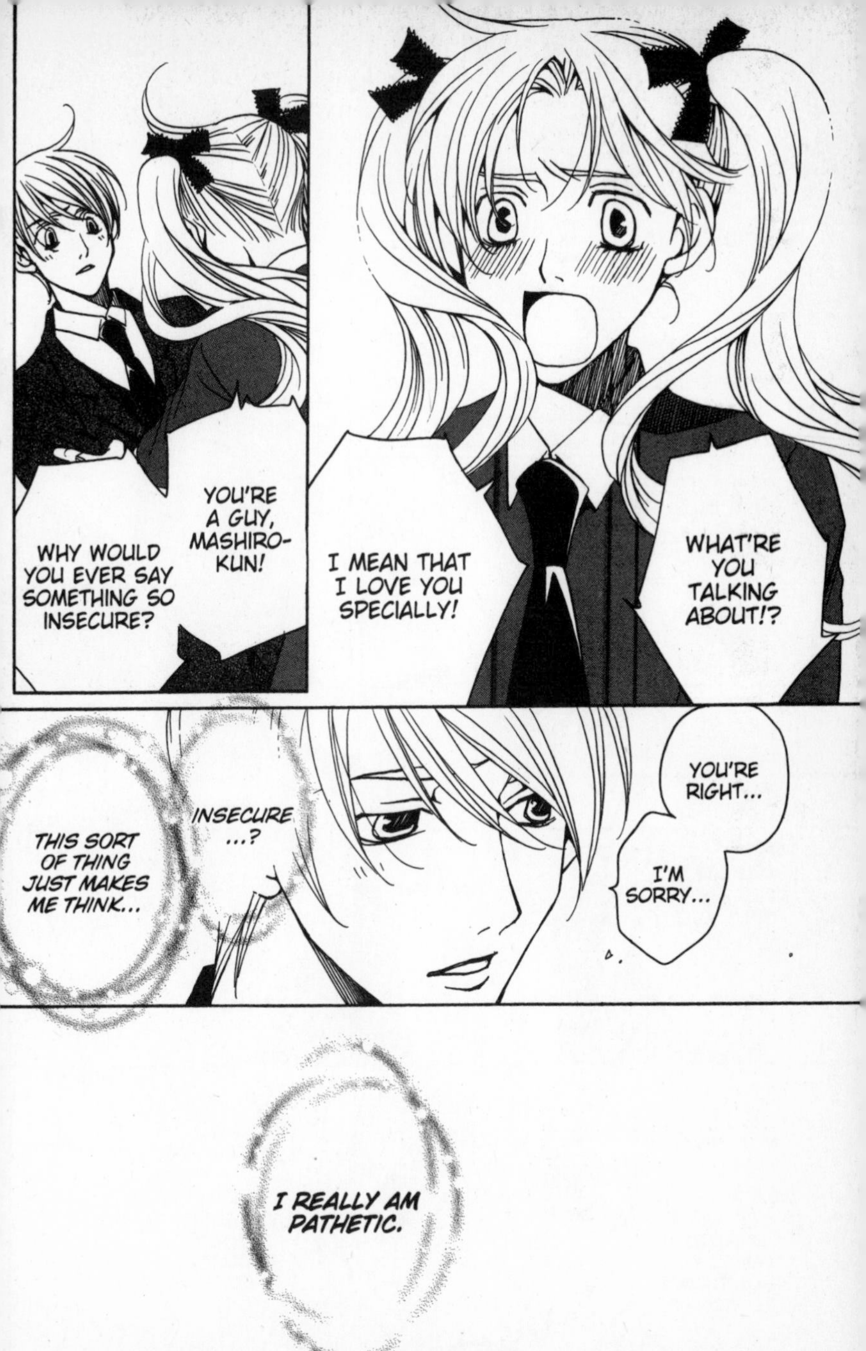
WHAT'RE YOU TALKING ABOUT!?
I MEAN THAT I LOVE YOU SPECIALLY!
YOU'RE A GUY, MASHIRO-KUN!
WHY WOULD YOU EVER SAY SOMETHING SO INSECURE?
YOU'RE RIGHT...
I'M SORRY...
INSECURE ...?
THIS SORT OF THING JUST MAKES ME THINK...
I REALLY AM PATHETIC.

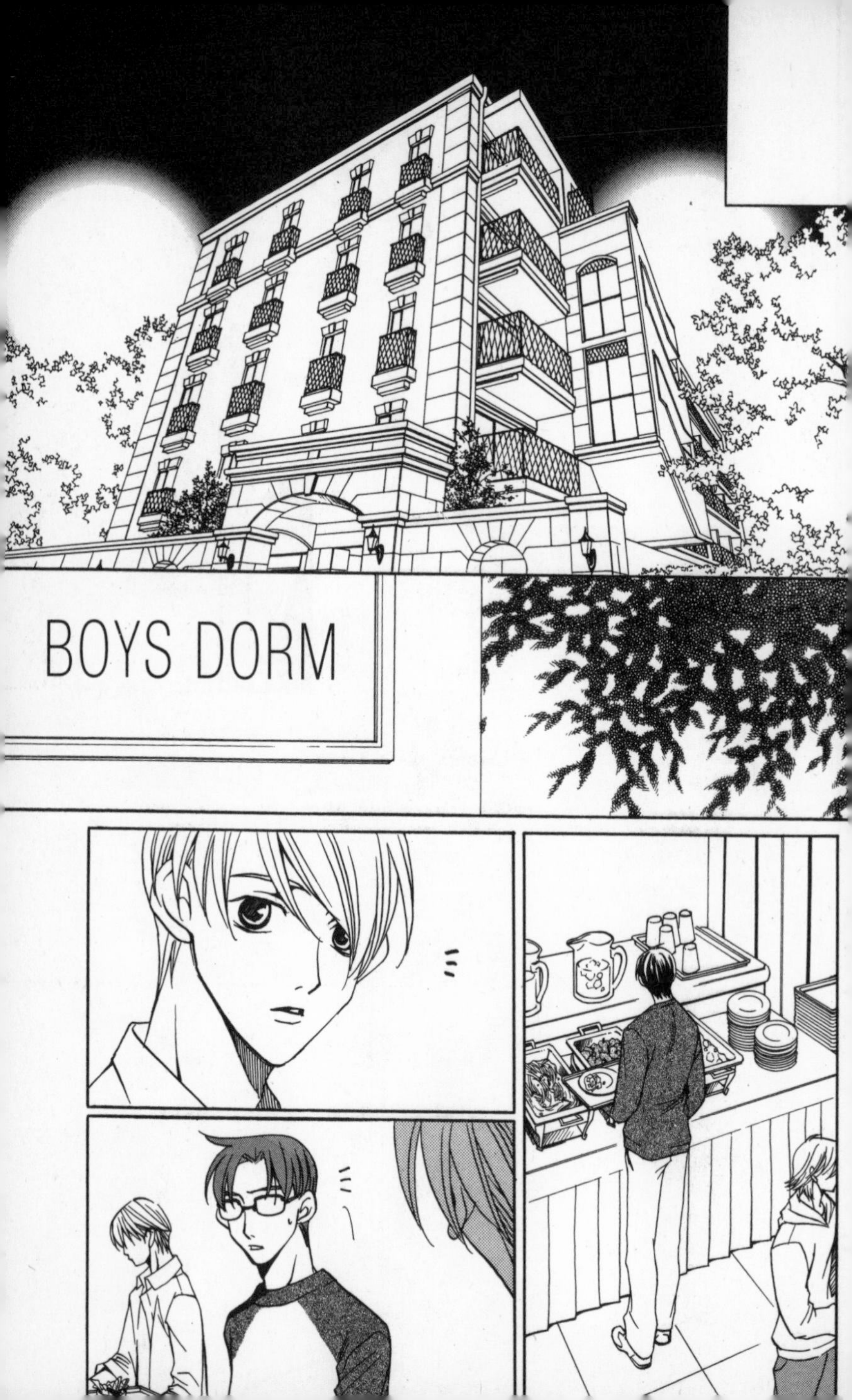
BOYS DORM

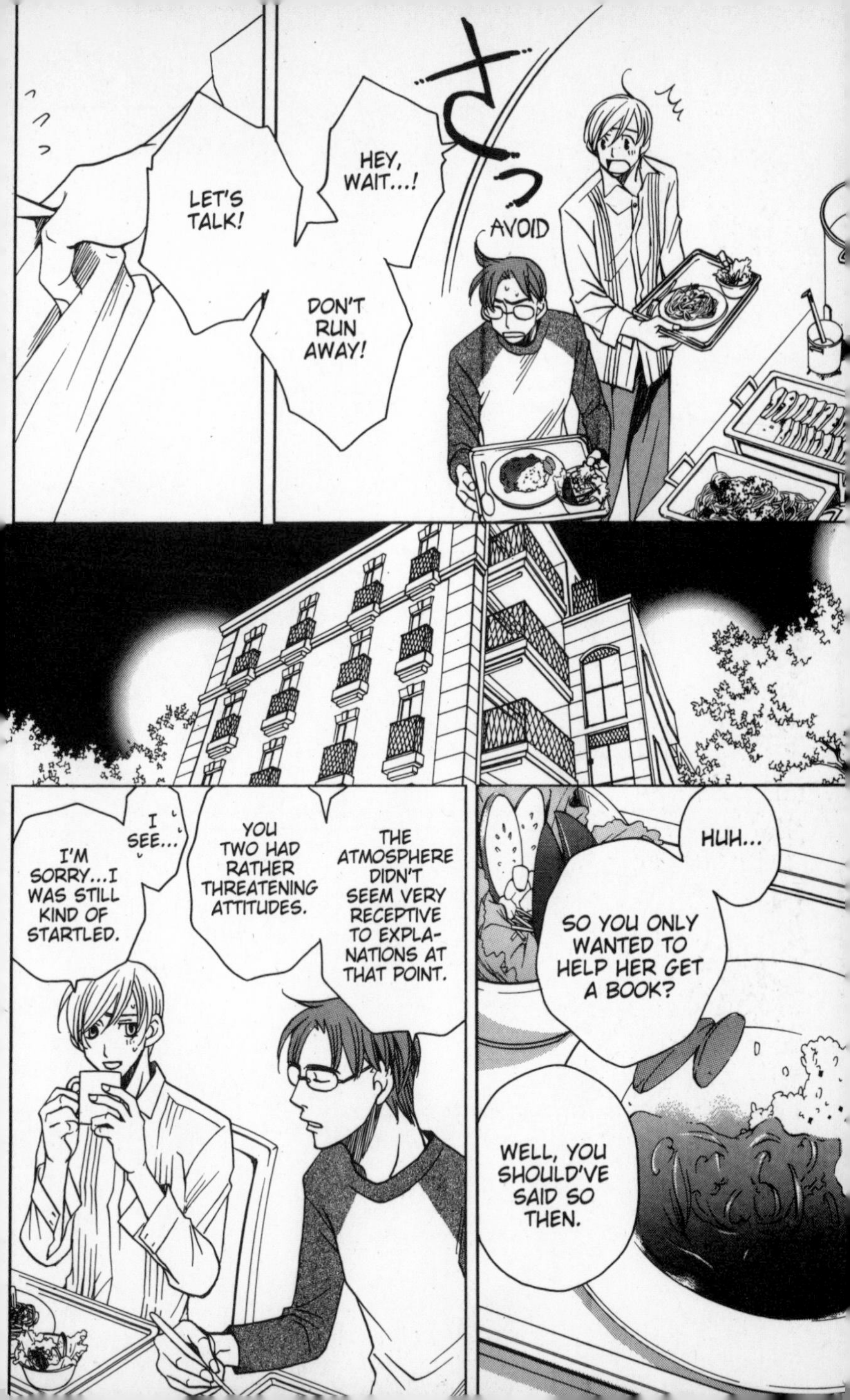

さっ
AVOID
HEY, WAIT...!
DON'T RUN AWAY!
LET'S TALK!
HUH...
SO YOU ONLY WANTED TO HELP HER GET A BOOK?
WELL, YOU SHOULD'VE SAID SO THEN.
THE ATMOSPHERE DIDN'T SEEM VERY RECEPTIVE TO EXPLA-NATIONS AT THAT POINT.
YOU TWO HAD RATHER THREATENING ATTITUDES.
I SEE...
I'M SORRY...I WAS STILL KIND OF STARTLED.

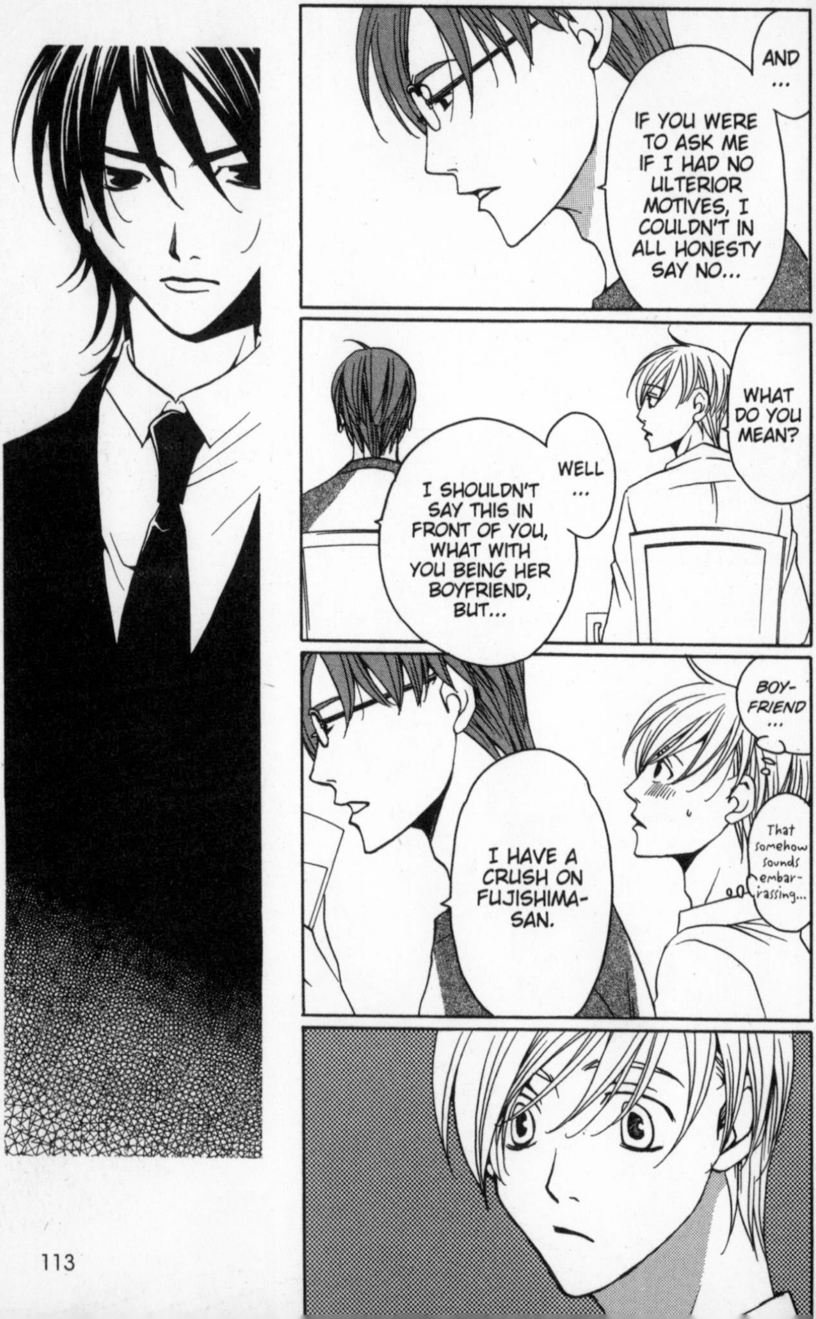
AND...
IF YOU WERE TO ASK ME IF I HAD NO ULTERIOR MOTIVES, I COULDN'T IN ALL HONESTY SAY NO...
WHAT DO YOU MEAN?
WELL...
I SHOULDN'T SAY THIS IN FRONT OF YOU, WHAT WITH YOU BEING HER BOYFRIEND, BUT...
BOY-FRIEND...
That somehow sounds embar-rassing...
I HAVE A CRUSH ON FUJISHIMA-SAN.

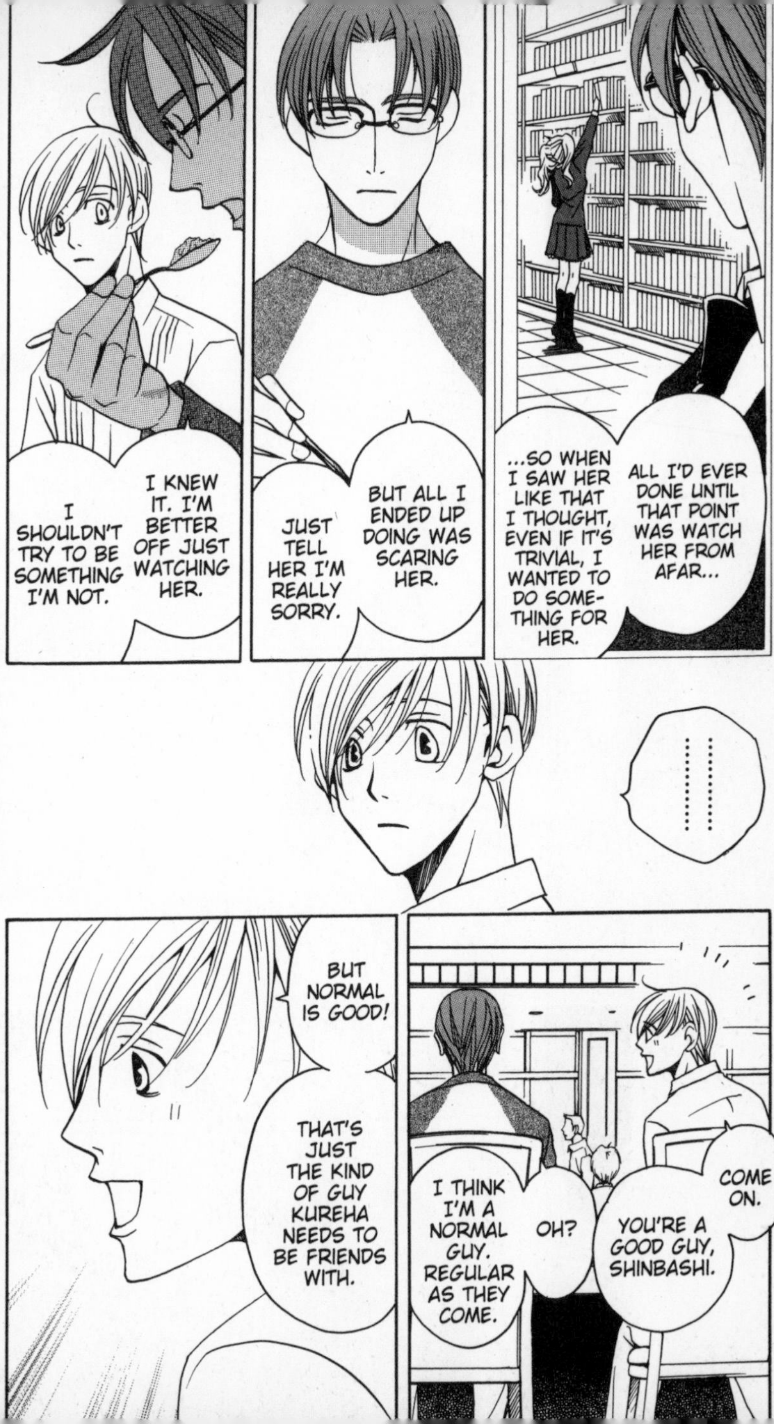
ALL I'D EVER DONE UNTIL THAT POINT WAS WATCH HER FROM AFAR...
...SO WHEN I SAW HER LIKE THAT I THOUGHT, EVEN IF IT'S TRIVIAL, I WANTED TO DO SOME-THING FOR HER.
BUT ALL I ENDED UP DOING WAS SCARING HER.
JUST TELL HER I'M REALLY SORRY.
I KNEW IT. I'M BETTER OFF JUST WATCHING HER.
I SHOULDN'T TRY TO BE SOMETHING I'M NOT.
......
COME ON.
YOU'RE A GOOD GUY, SHINBASHI.
OH?
I THINK I'M A NORMAL GUY. REGULAR AS THEY COME.
BUT NORMAL IS GOOD!
THAT'S JUST THE KIND OF GUY KUREHA NEEDS TO BE FRIENDS WITH.

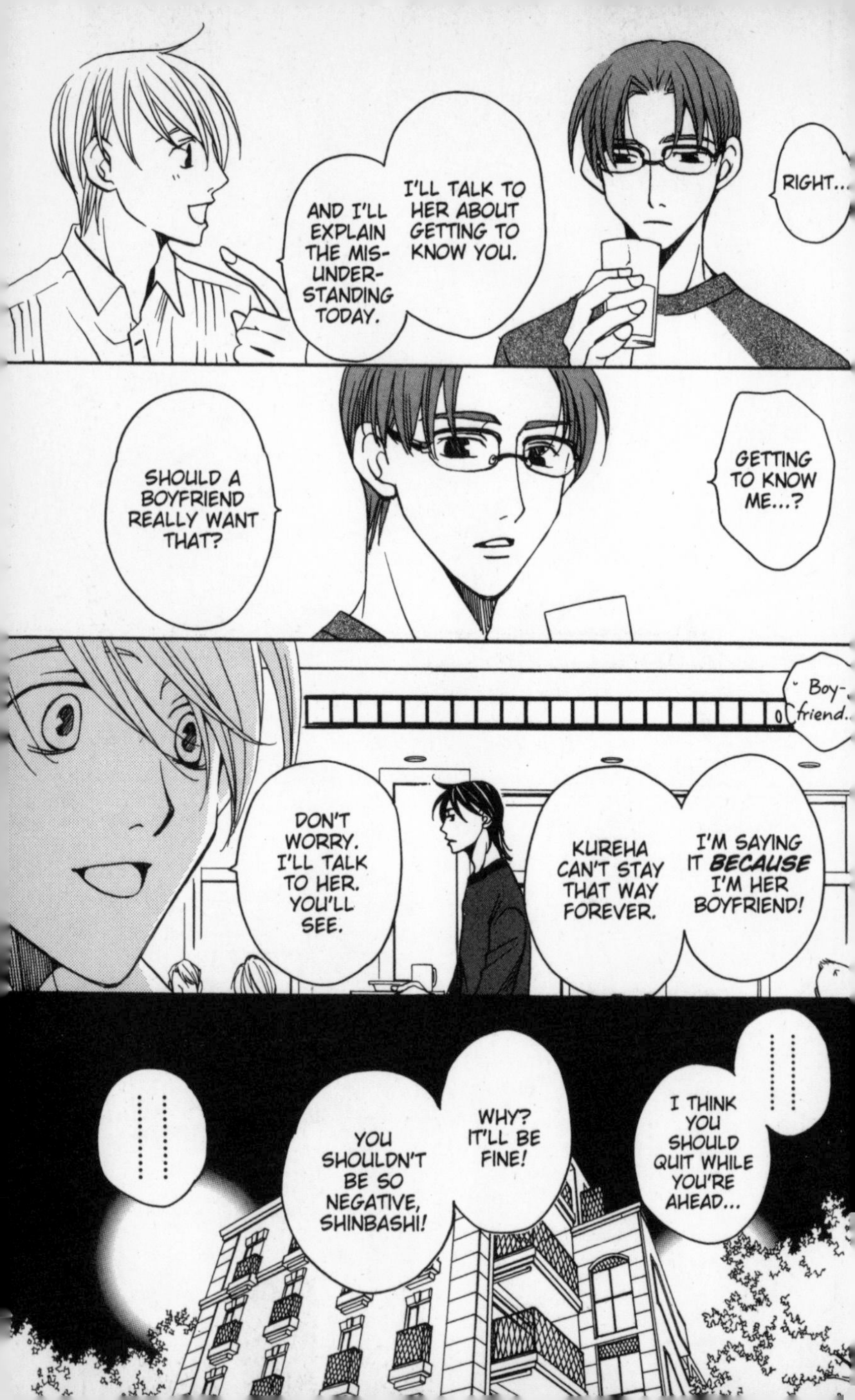
RIGHT...
I'LL TALK TO HER ABOUT GETTING TO KNOW YOU.
AND I'LL EXPLAIN THE MIS-UNDER-STANDING TODAY.
GETTING TO KNOW ME...?
SHOULD A BOYFRIEND REALLY WANT THAT?
Boy-friend..
I'M SAYING IT *BECAUSE* I'M HER BOYFRIEND!
KUREHA CAN'T STAY THAT WAY FOREVER.
DON'T WORRY. I'LL TALK TO HER. YOU'LL SEE.
......
I THINK YOU SHOULD QUIT WHILE YOU'RE AHEAD...
WHY? IT'LL BE FINE!
YOU SHOULDN'T BE SO NEGATIVE, SHINBASHI!
......

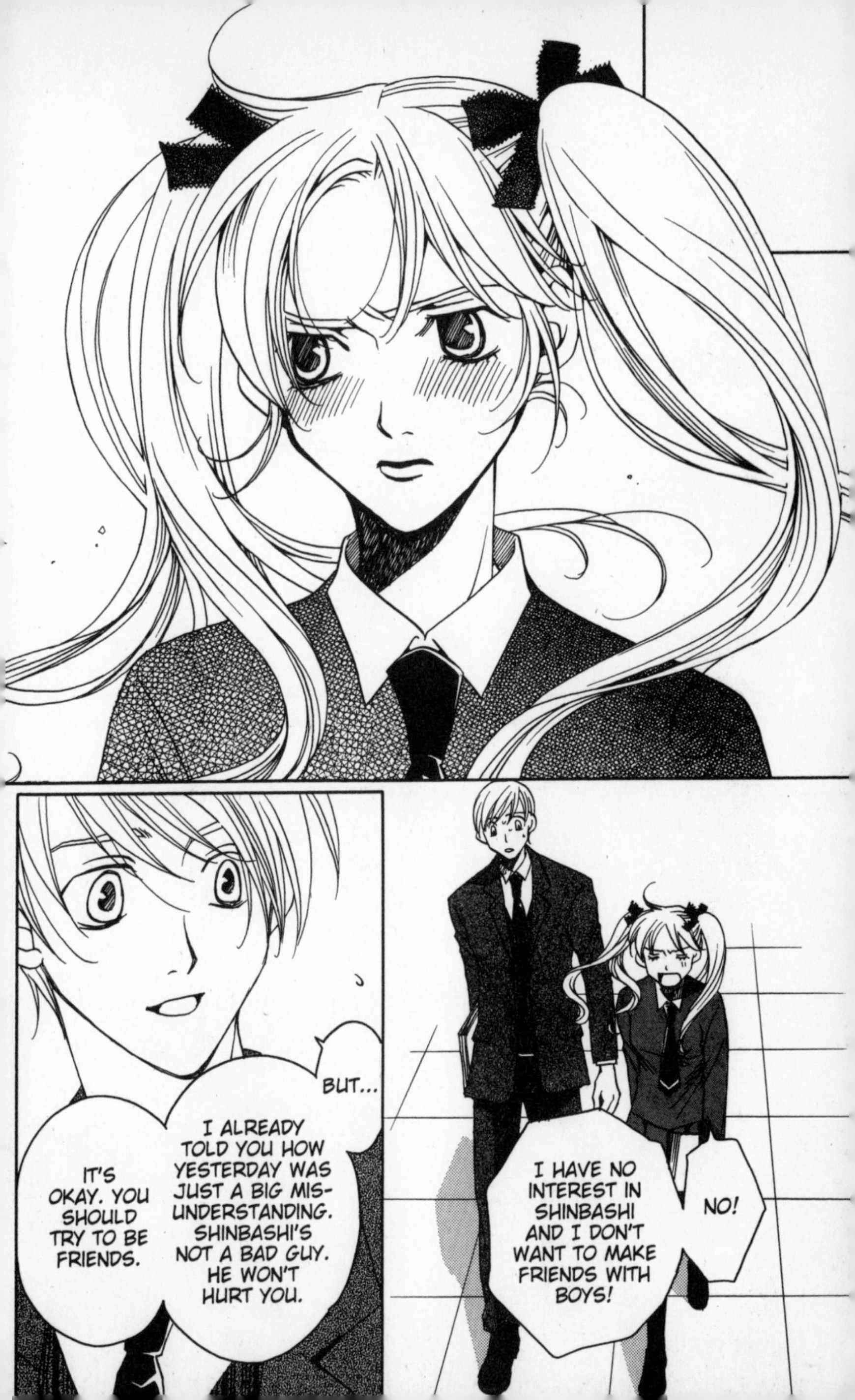
NO!
I HAVE NO INTEREST IN SHINBASHI AND I DON'T WANT TO MAKE FRIENDS WITH BOYS!
BUT...
I ALREADY TOLD YOU HOW YESTERDAY WAS JUST A BIG MIS-UNDERSTANDING. SHINBASHI'S NOT A BAD GUY. HE WON'T HURT YOU.
IT'S OKAY. YOU SHOULD TRY TO BE FRIENDS.

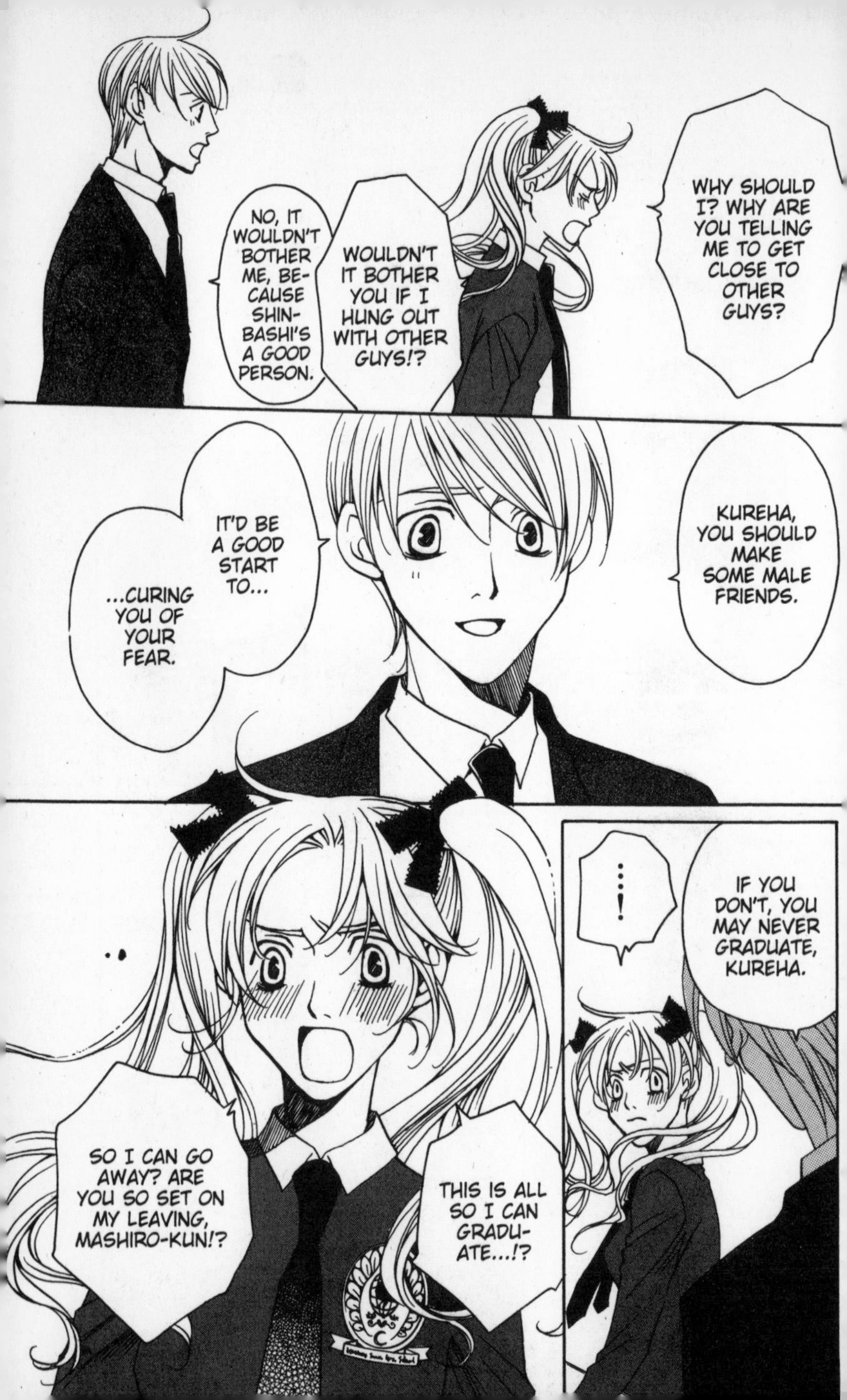
WHY SHOULD I? WHY ARE YOU TELLING ME TO GET CLOSE TO OTHER GUYS?
WOULDN'T IT BOTHER YOU IF I HUNG OUT WITH OTHER GUYS!?
NO, IT WOULDN'T BOTHER ME, BECAUSE SHINBASHI'S A GOOD PERSON.
KUREHA, YOU SHOULD MAKE SOME MALE FRIENDS.
IT'D BE A GOOD START TO...
...CURING YOU OF YOUR FEAR.
IF YOU DON'T, YOU MAY NEVER GRADUATE, KUREHA.
...!
THIS IS ALL SO I CAN GRADUATE...!?
SO I CAN GO AWAY? ARE YOU SO SET ON MY LEAVING, MASHIRO-KUN!?

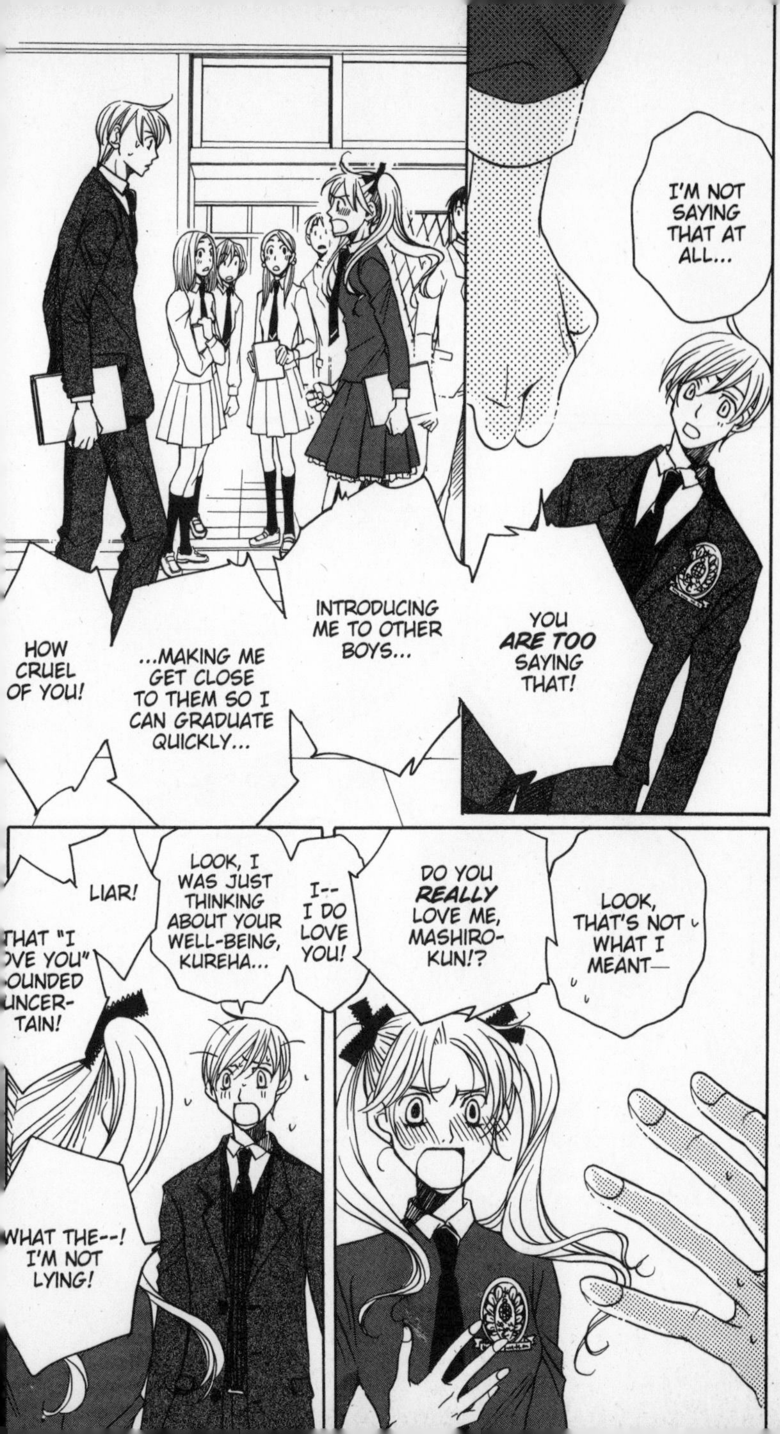
I'M NOT SAYING THAT AT ALL...
YOU ARE TOO SAYING THAT!
INTRODUCING ME TO OTHER BOYS...
...MAKING ME GET CLOSE TO THEM SO I CAN GRADUATE QUICKLY...
HOW CRUEL OF YOU!
LOOK, THAT'S NOT WHAT I MEANT—
DO YOU REALLY LOVE ME, MASHIRO-KUN!?
I-- I DO LOVE YOU!
LOOK, I WAS JUST THINKING ABOUT YOUR WELL-BEING, KUREHA...
LIAR!
THAT "I OVE YOU" OUNDED NCER-TAIN!
WHAT THE--! I'M NOT LYING!

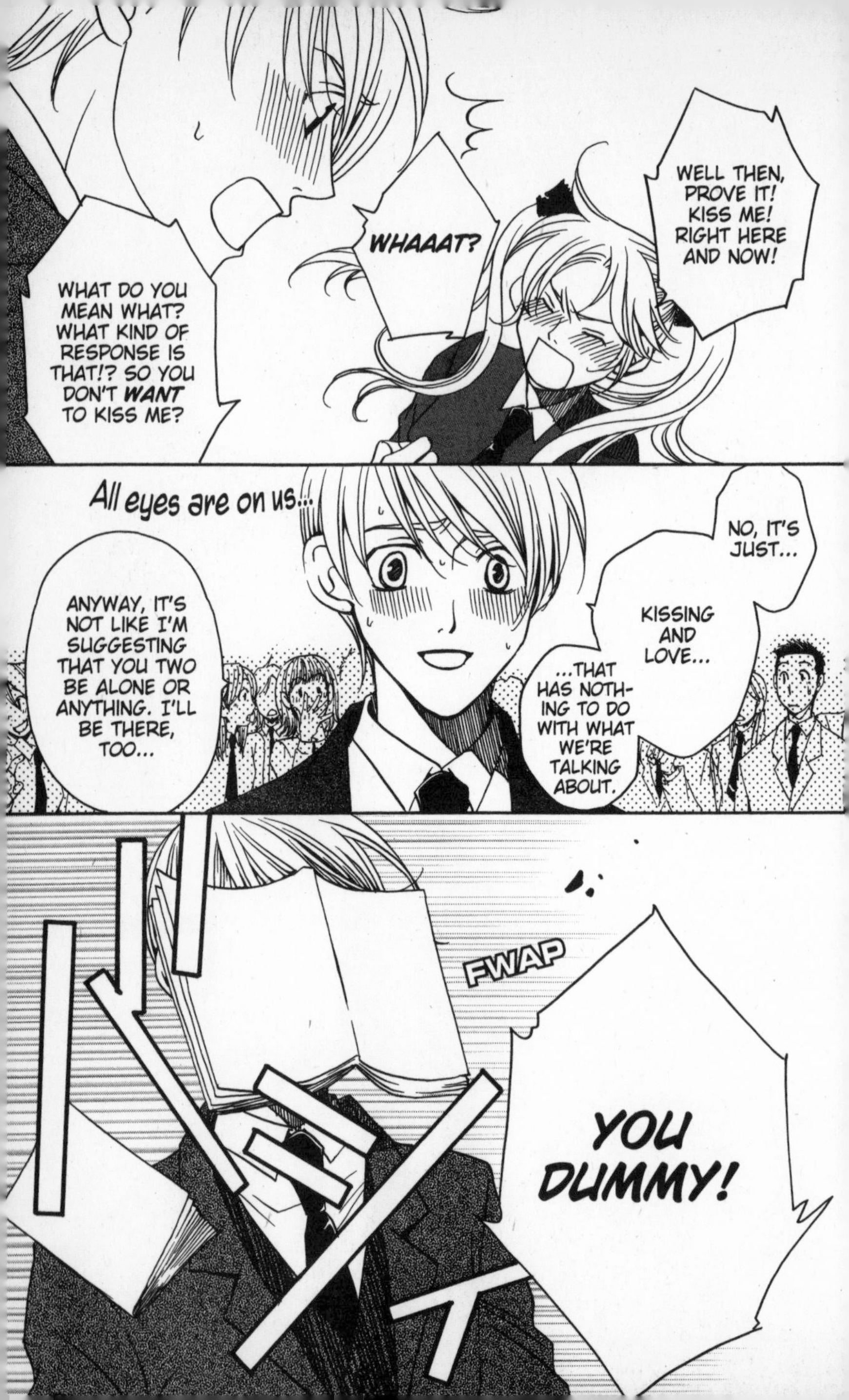
WELL THEN, PROVE IT! KISS ME! RIGHT HERE AND NOW!
WHAAAT?
WHAT DO YOU MEAN WHAT? WHAT KIND OF RESPONSE IS THAT!? SO YOU DON'T ***WANT*** TO KISS ME?
NO, IT'S JUST...
KISSING AND LOVE...
...THAT HAS NOTH-ING TO DO WITH WHAT WE'RE TALKING ABOUT.
All eyes are on us...
ANYWAY, IT'S NOT LIKE I'M SUGGESTING THAT YOU TWO BE ALONE OR ANYTHING. I'LL BE THERE, TOO...
FWAP
YOU DUMMY!

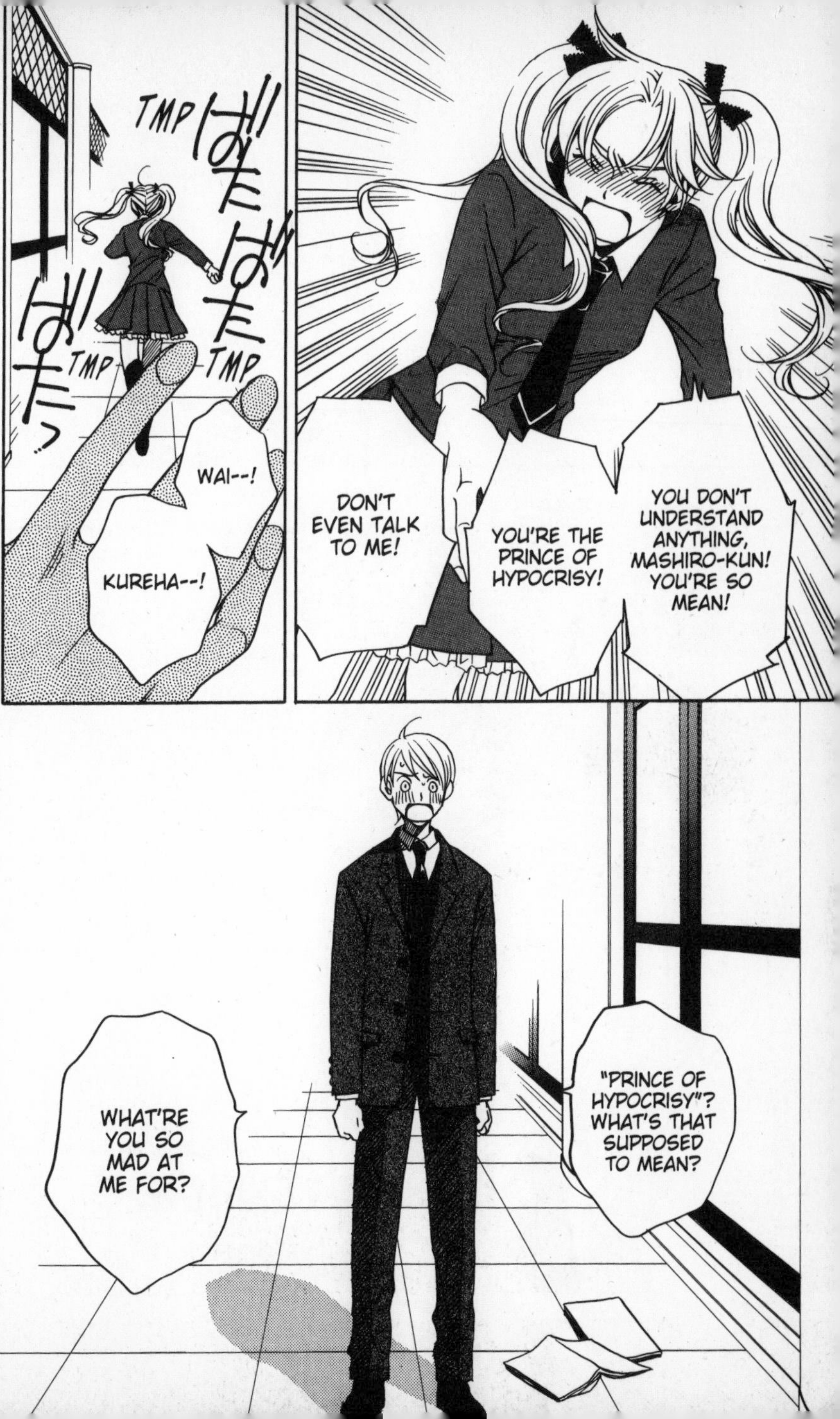
YOU DON'T UNDERSTAND ANYTHING, MASHIRO-KUN! YOU'RE SO MEAN!
YOU'RE THE PRINCE OF HYPOCRISY!
DON'T EVEN TALK TO ME!
TMP
TMP
TMP
WAI--!
KUREHA--!
"PRINCE OF HYPOCRISY"? WHAT'S THAT SUPPOSED TO MEAN?
WHAT'RE YOU SO MAD AT ME FOR?

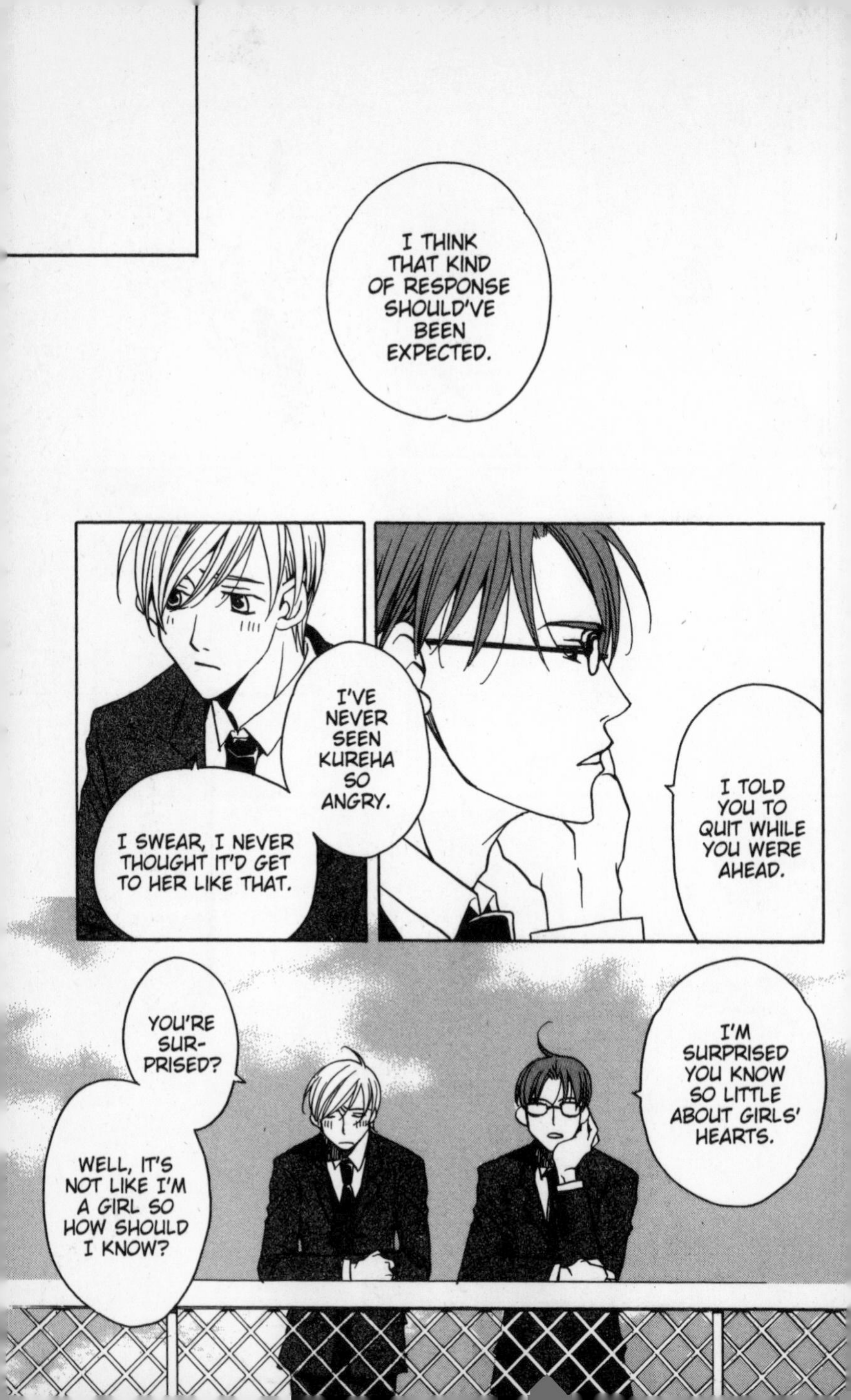
I THINK THAT KIND OF RESPONSE SHOULD'VE BEEN EXPECTED.
I TOLD YOU TO QUIT WHILE YOU WERE AHEAD.
I'VE NEVER SEEN KUREHA SO ANGRY.
I SWEAR, I NEVER THOUGHT IT'D GET TO HER LIKE THAT.
I'M SURPRISED YOU KNOW SO LITTLE ABOUT GIRLS' HEARTS.
YOU'RE SURPRISED?
WELL, IT'S NOT LIKE I'M A GIRL SO HOW SHOULD I KNOW?

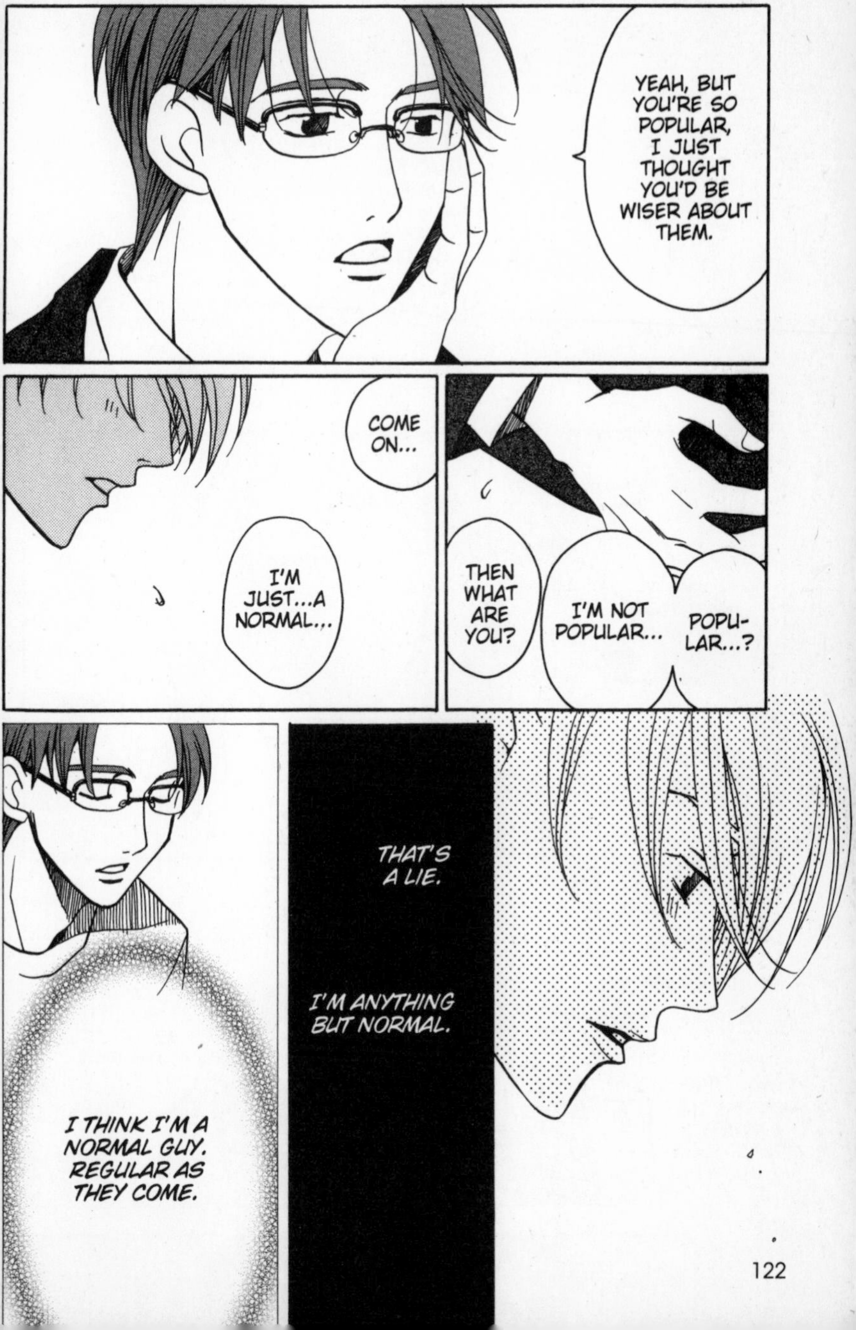
YEAH, BUT YOU'RE SO POPULAR, I JUST THOUGHT YOU'D BE WISER ABOUT THEM.
POPU-LAR...?
I'M NOT POPULAR...
THEN WHAT ARE YOU?
COME ON...
I'M JUST...A NORMAL...
THAT'S A LIE.
I'M ANYTHING BUT NORMAL.
I THINK I'M A NORMAL GUY. REGULAR AS THEY COME.

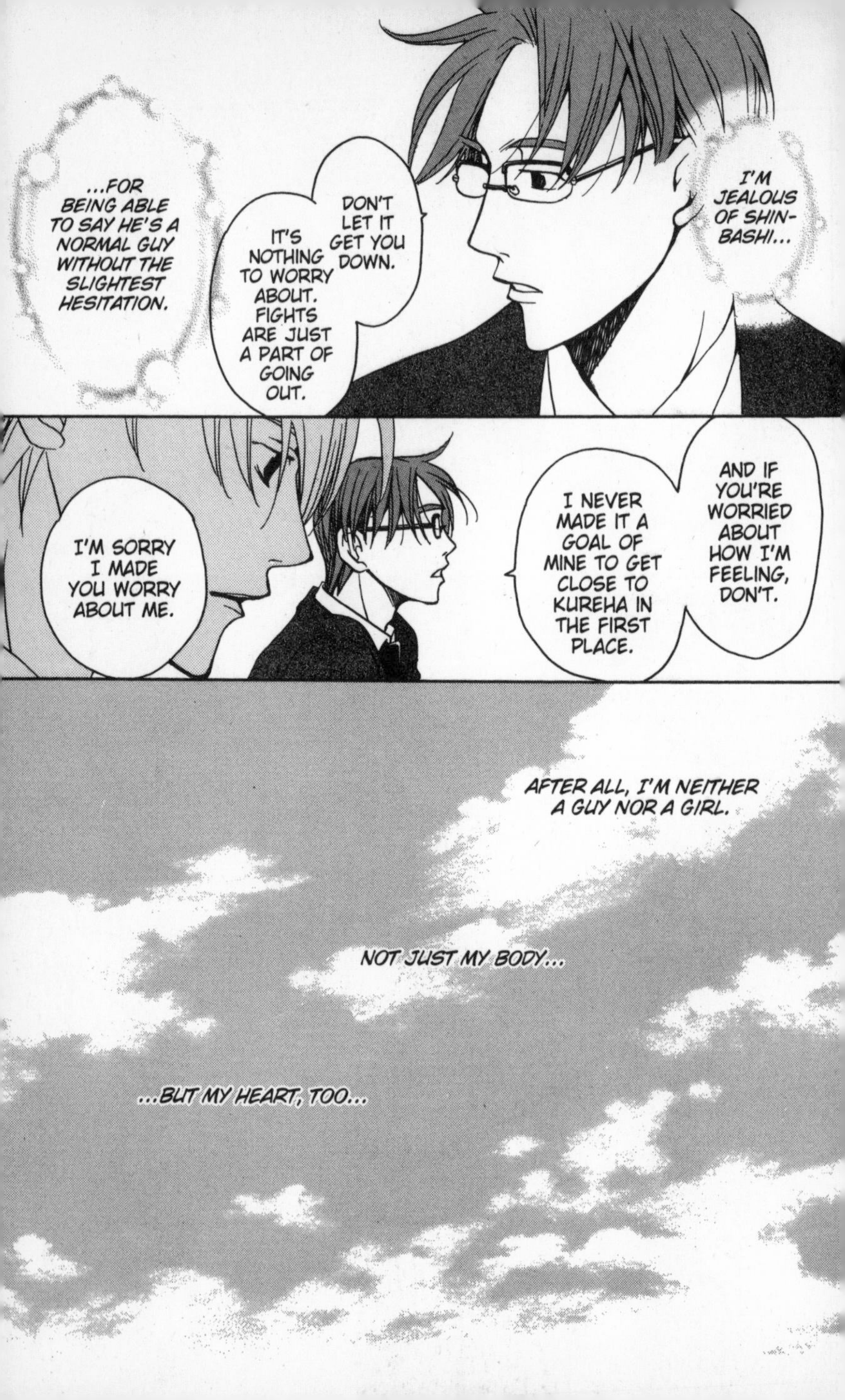
I'M JEALOUS OF SHIN-BASHI...
DON'T LET IT GET YOU DOWN. IT'S NOTHING TO WORRY ABOUT. FIGHTS ARE JUST A PART OF GOING OUT.
...FOR BEING ABLE TO SAY HE'S A NORMAL GUY WITHOUT THE SLIGHTEST HESITATION.
AND IF YOU'RE WORRIED ABOUT HOW I'M FEELING, DON'T.
I NEVER MADE IT A GOAL OF MINE TO GET CLOSE TO KUREHA IN THE FIRST PLACE.
I'M SORRY I MADE YOU WORRY ABOUT ME.
AFTER ALL, I'M NEITHER A GUY NOR A GIRL.
NOT JUST MY BODY...
...BUT MY HEART, TOO...

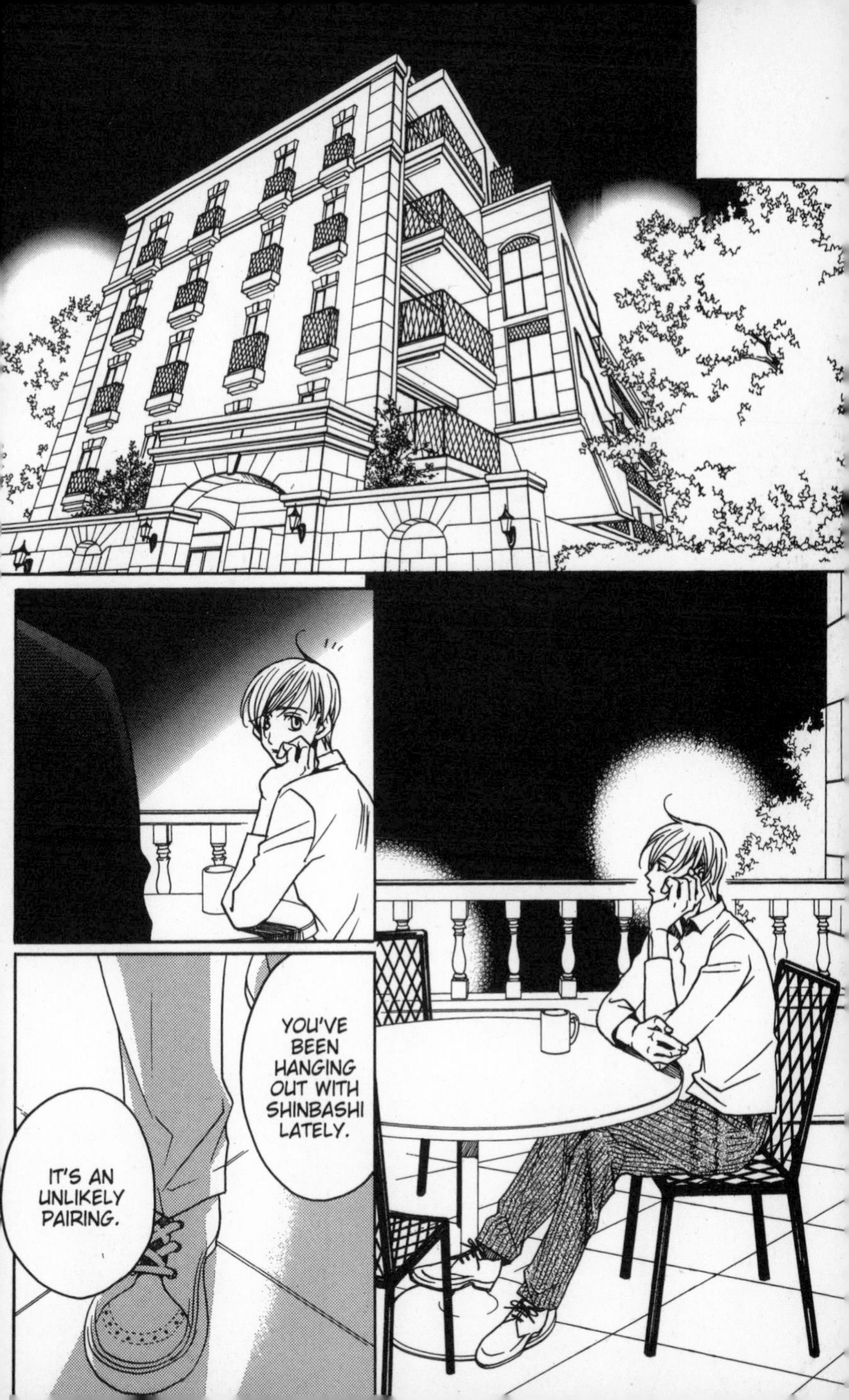
YOU'VE BEEN HANGING OUT WITH SHINBASHI LATELY.
IT'S AN UNLIKELY PAIRING.

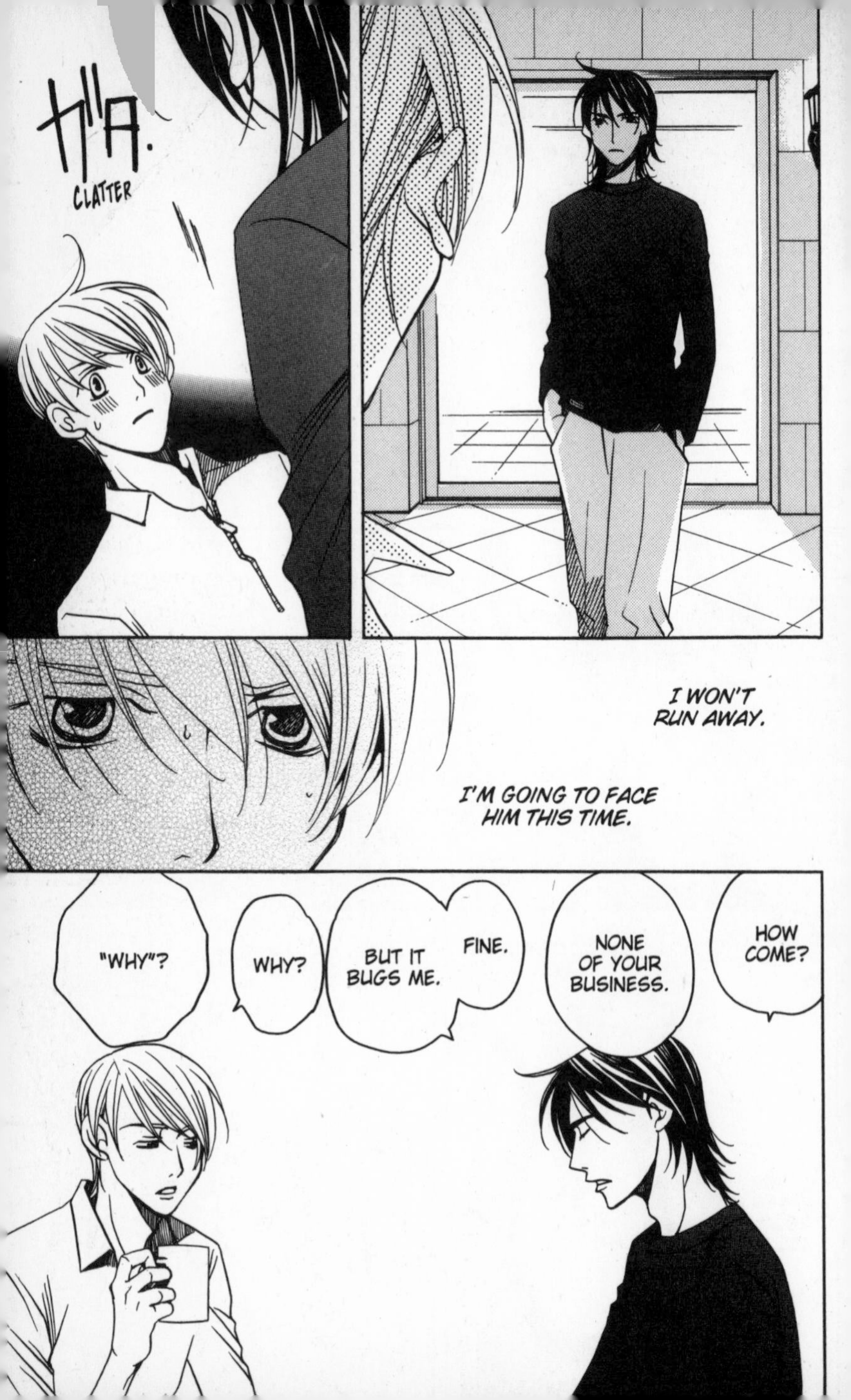
ガタ
CLATTER
I WON'T RUN AWAY.
I'M GOING TO FACE HIM THIS TIME.
HOW COME?
NONE OF YOUR BUSINESS.
FINE.
BUT IT BUGS ME.
WHY?
"WHY"?

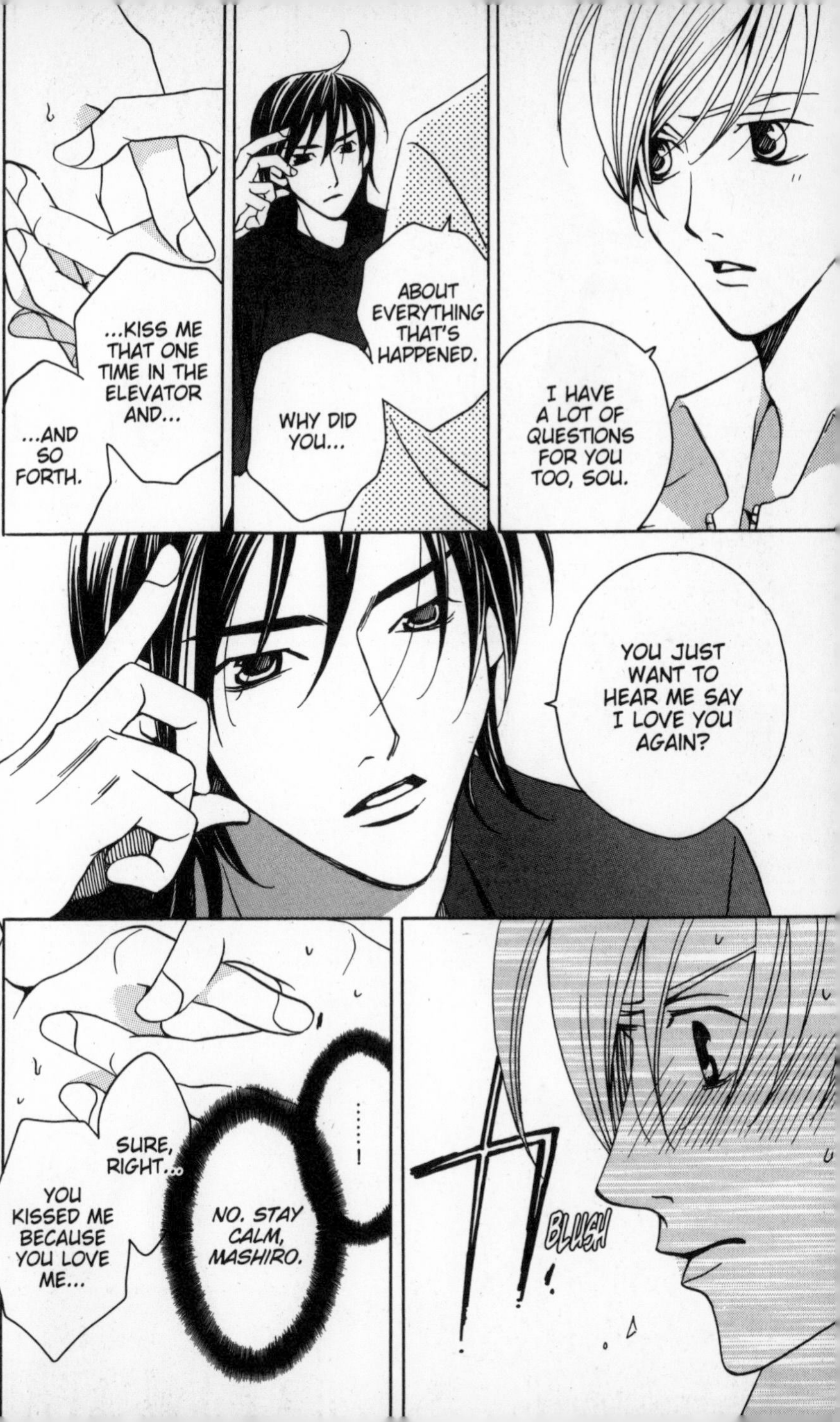
I HAVE A LOT OF QUESTIONS FOR YOU TOO, SOU.
ABOUT EVERYTHING THAT'S HAPPENED.
WHY DID YOU...
...KISS ME THAT ONE TIME IN THE ELEVATOR AND...
...AND SO FORTH.
YOU JUST WANT TO HEAR ME SAY I LOVE YOU AGAIN?
BLUSH
......!
NO. STAY CALM, MASHIRO.
SURE, RIGHT...
YOU KISSED ME BECAUSE YOU LOVE ME...

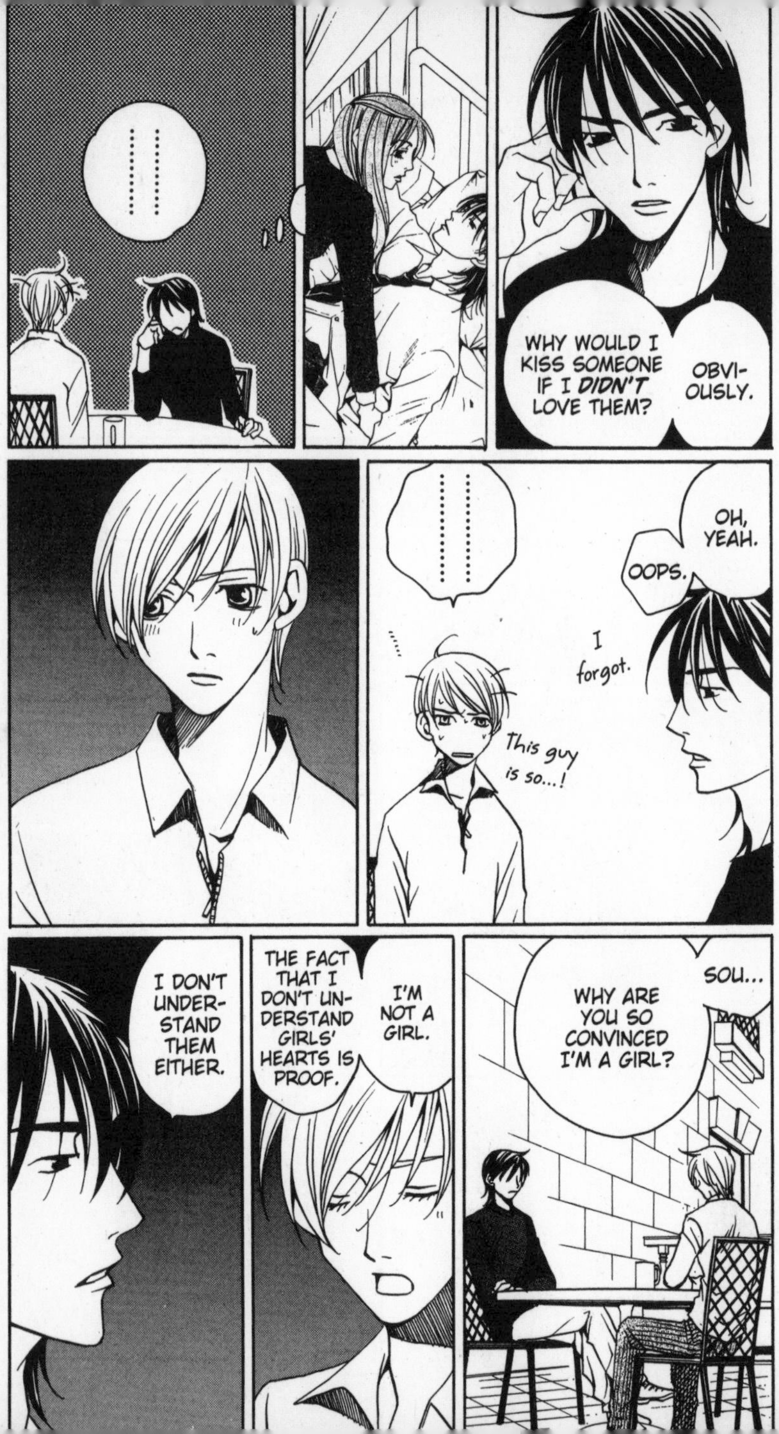
OBVI-OUSLY.
WHY WOULD I KISS SOMEONE IF I *DIDN'T* LOVE THEM?
......
OH, YEAH.
OOPS.
I forgot.
......
This guy is so...!
SOU...
WHY ARE YOU SO CONVINCED I'M A GIRL?
I'M NOT A GIRL.
THE FACT THAT I DON'T UNDERSTAND GIRLS' HEARTS IS PROOF.
I DON'T UNDERSTAND THEM EITHER.

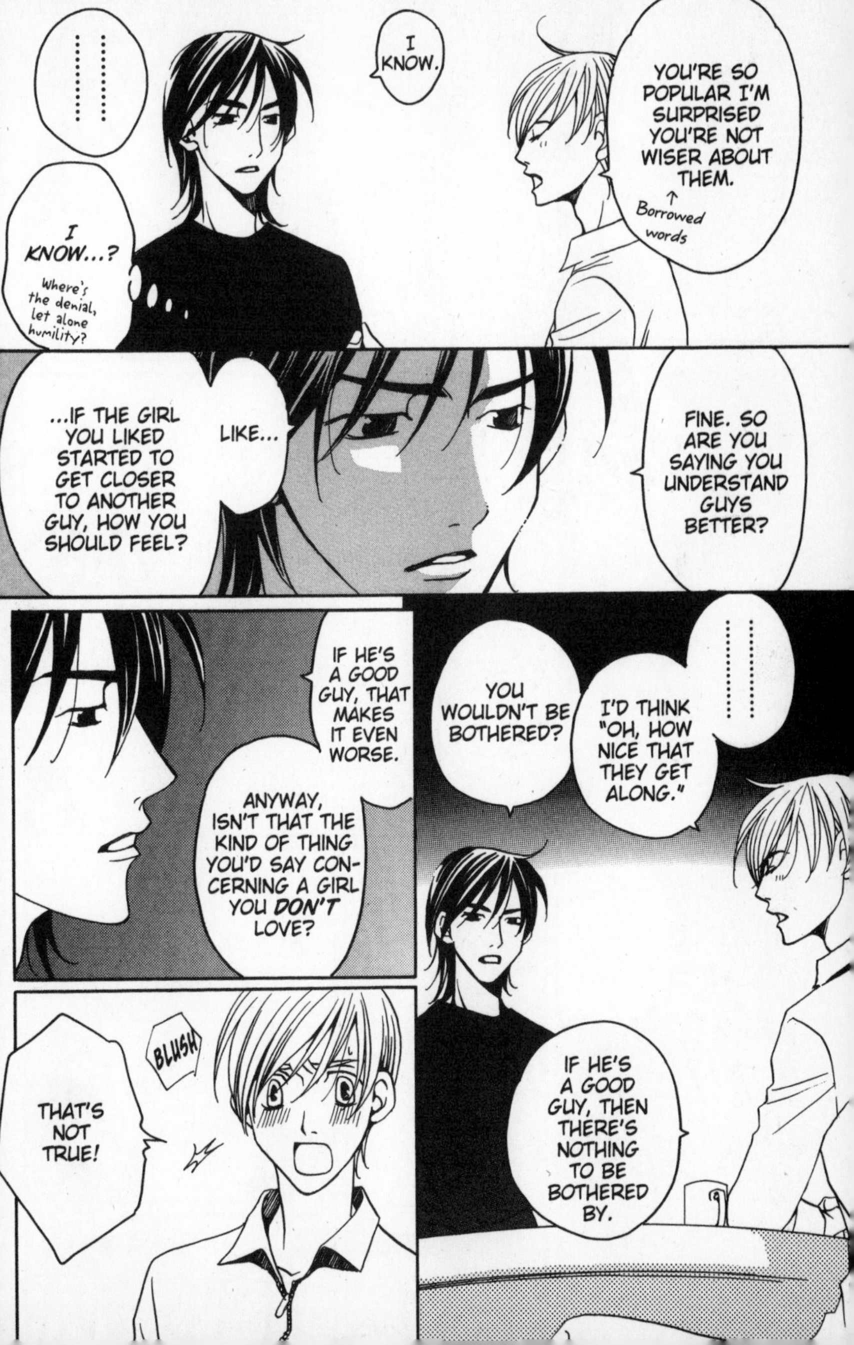
YOU'RE SO POPULAR I'M SURPRISED YOU'RE NOT WISER ABOUT THEM.
↑ Borrowed words
I KNOW.
......
I KNOW...?
Where's the denial, let alone humility?
FINE. SO ARE YOU SAYING YOU UNDERSTAND GUYS BETTER?
LIKE...
...IF THE GIRL YOU LIKED STARTED TO GET CLOSER TO ANOTHER GUY, HOW YOU SHOULD FEEL?
......
I'D THINK "OH, HOW NICE THAT THEY GET ALONG."
YOU WOULDN'T BE BOTHERED?
IF HE'S A GOOD GUY, THEN THERE'S NOTHING TO BE BOTHERED BY.
IF HE'S A GOOD GUY, THAT MAKES IT EVEN WORSE.
ANYWAY, ISN'T THAT THE KIND OF THING YOU'D SAY CONCERNING A GIRL YOU DON'T LOVE?
BLUSH
THAT'S NOT TRUE!

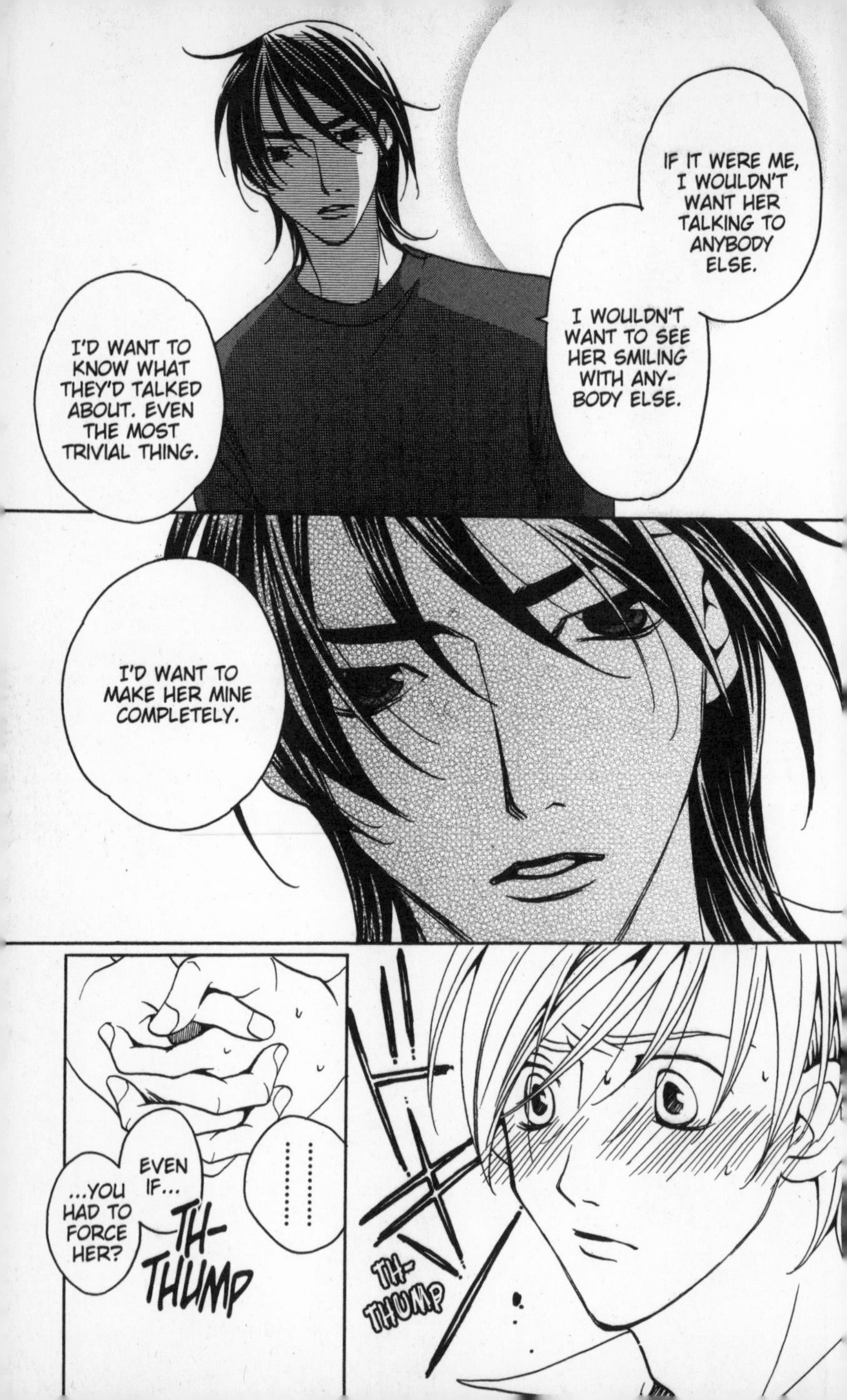
IF IT WERE ME, I WOULDN'T WANT HER TALKING TO ANYBODY ELSE.
I WOULDN'T WANT TO SEE HER SMILING WITH ANY-BODY ELSE.
I'D WANT TO KNOW WHAT THEY'D TALKED ABOUT. EVEN THE MOST TRIVIAL THING.
I'D WANT TO MAKE HER MINE COMPLETELY.
!!
TH-THUMP
......
EVEN IF...
...YOU HAD TO FORCE HER?
TH-THUMP

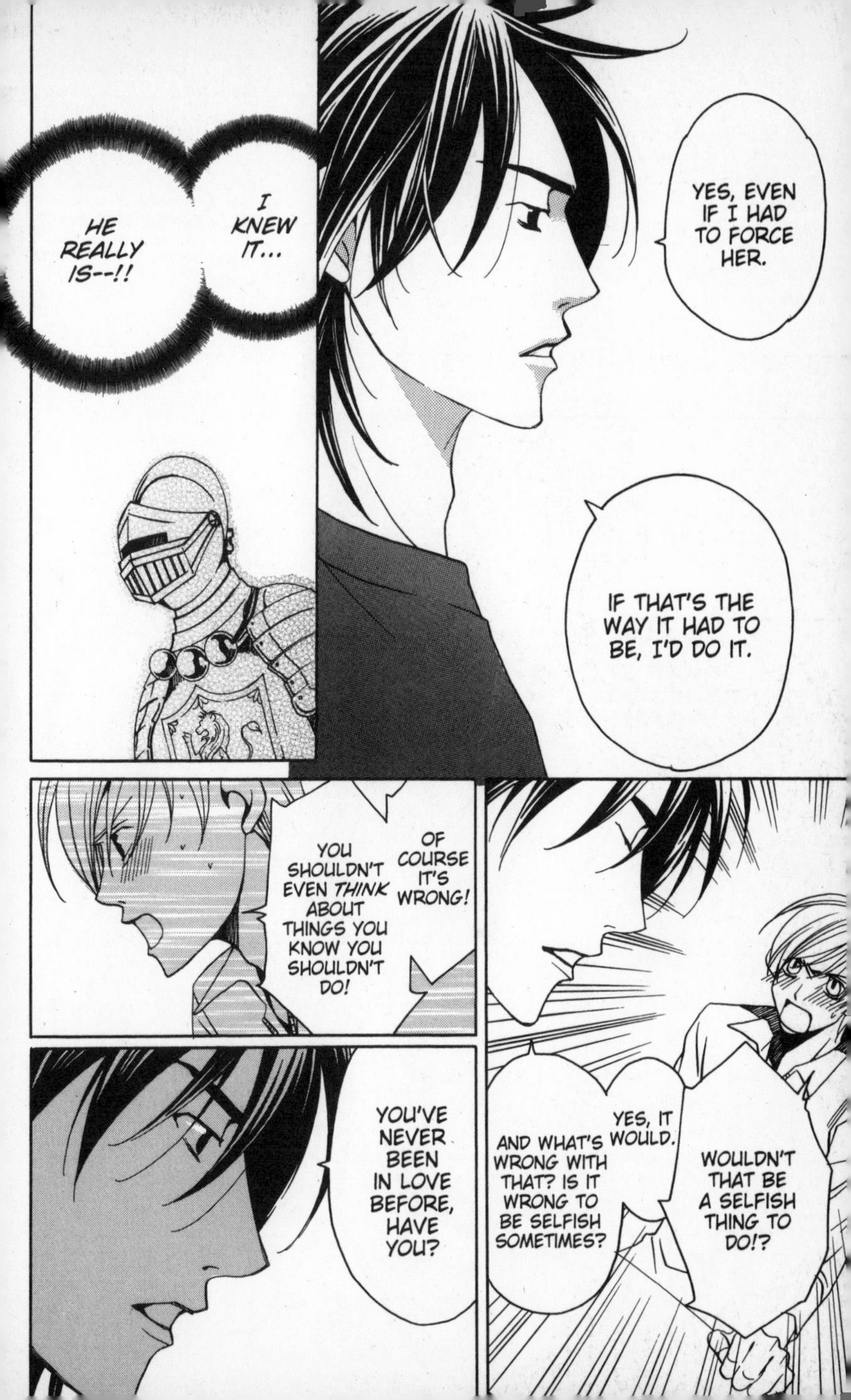
YES, EVEN IF I HAD TO FORCE HER.
IF THAT'S THE WAY IT HAD TO BE, I'D DO IT.
I KNEW IT...
HE REALLY IS--!!
WOULDN'T THAT BE A SELFISH THING TO DO!?
YES, IT WOULD.
AND WHAT'S WRONG WITH THAT? IS IT WRONG TO BE SELFISH SOMETIMES?
OF COURSE IT'S WRONG!
YOU SHOULDN'T EVEN *THINK* ABOUT THINGS YOU KNOW YOU SHOULDN'T DO!
YOU'VE NEVER BEEN IN LOVE BEFORE, HAVE YOU?

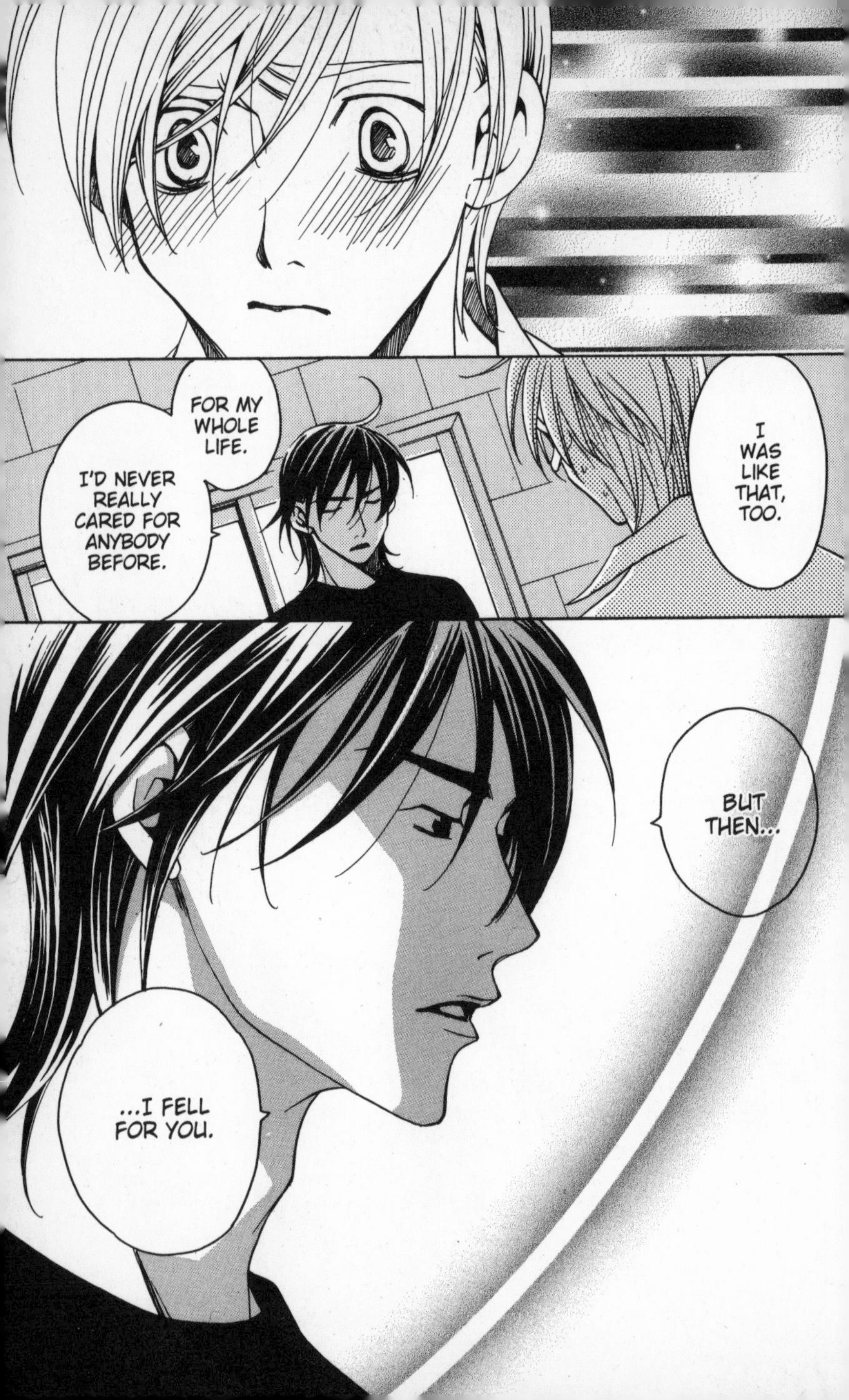
I WAS LIKE THAT, TOO.
FOR MY WHOLE LIFE.
I'D NEVER REALLY CARED FOR ANYBODY BEFORE.
BUT THEN...
...I FELL FOR YOU.

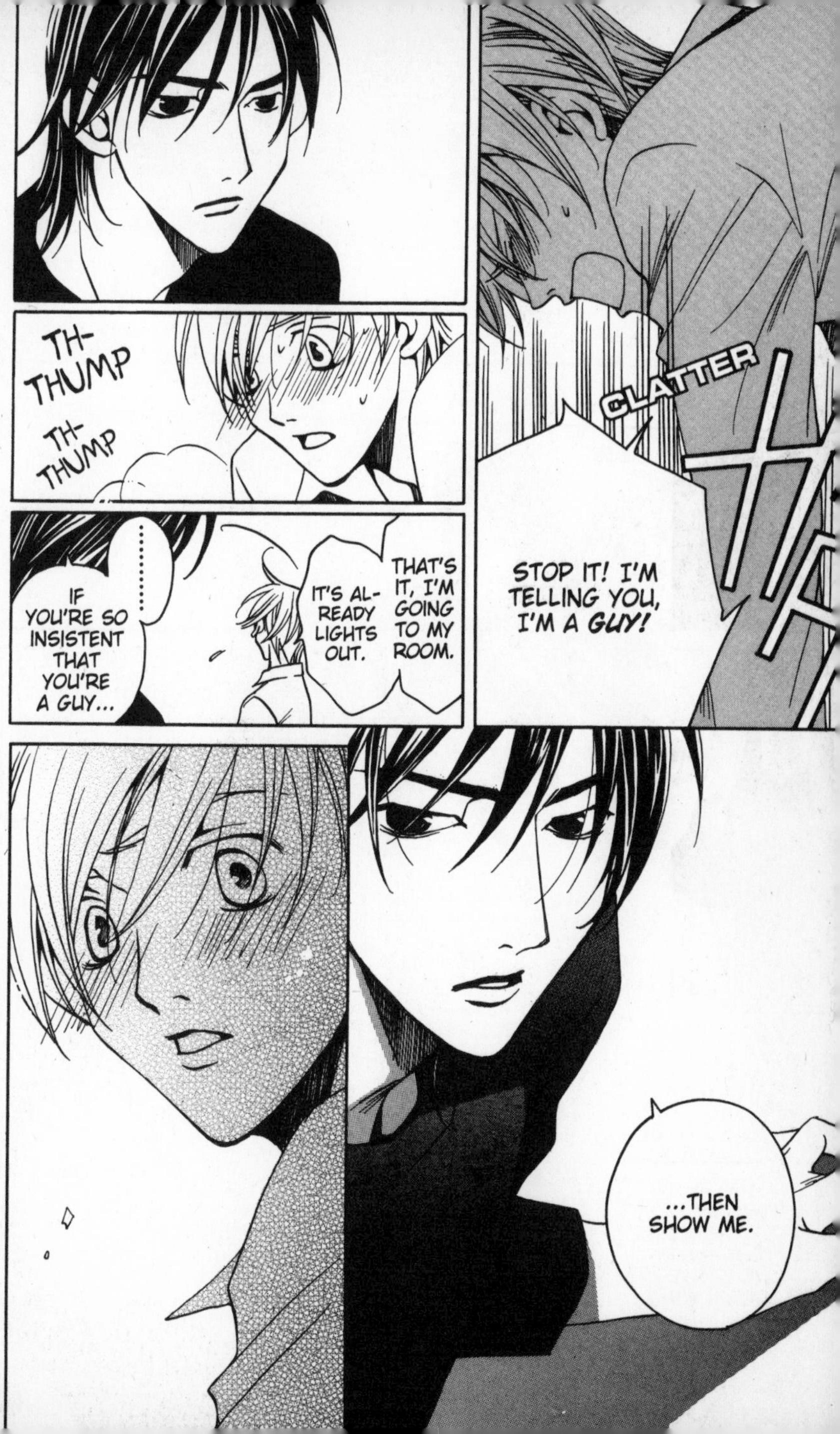
CLATTER
STOP IT! I'M TELLING YOU, I'M A GUY!
TH-THUMP
TH-THUMP
THAT'S IT, I'M GOING TO MY ROOM.
IT'S AL-READY LIGHTS OUT.
......
IF YOU'RE SO INSISTENT THAT YOU'RE A GUY...
...THEN SHOW ME.

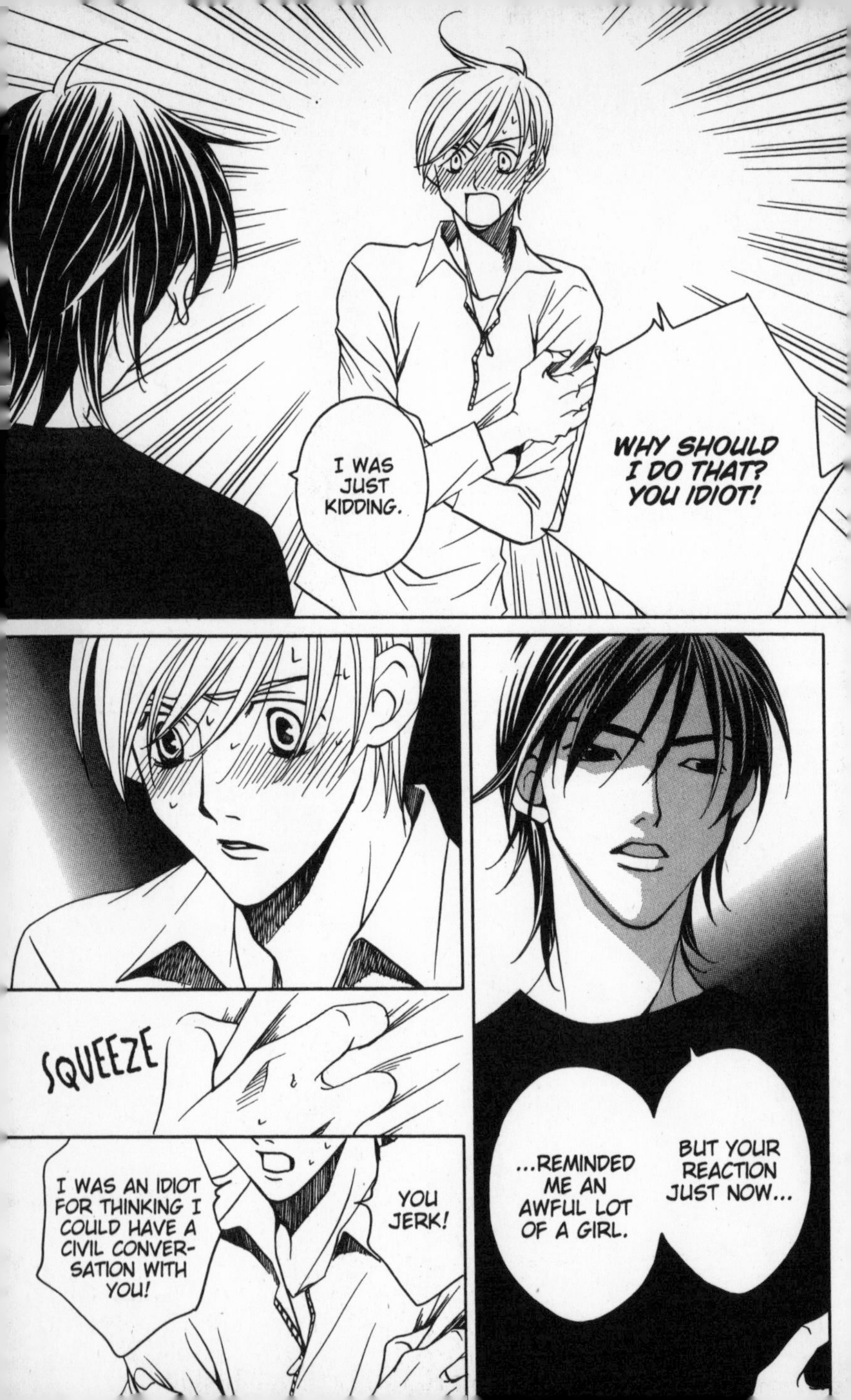
WHY SHOULD I DO THAT? YOU IDIOT!
I WAS JUST KIDDING.
BUT YOUR REACTION JUST NOW...
...REMINDED ME AN AWFUL LOT OF A GIRL.
SQUEEZE
YOU JERK!
I WAS AN IDIOT FOR THINKING I COULD HAVE A CIVIL CONVERSATION WITH YOU!

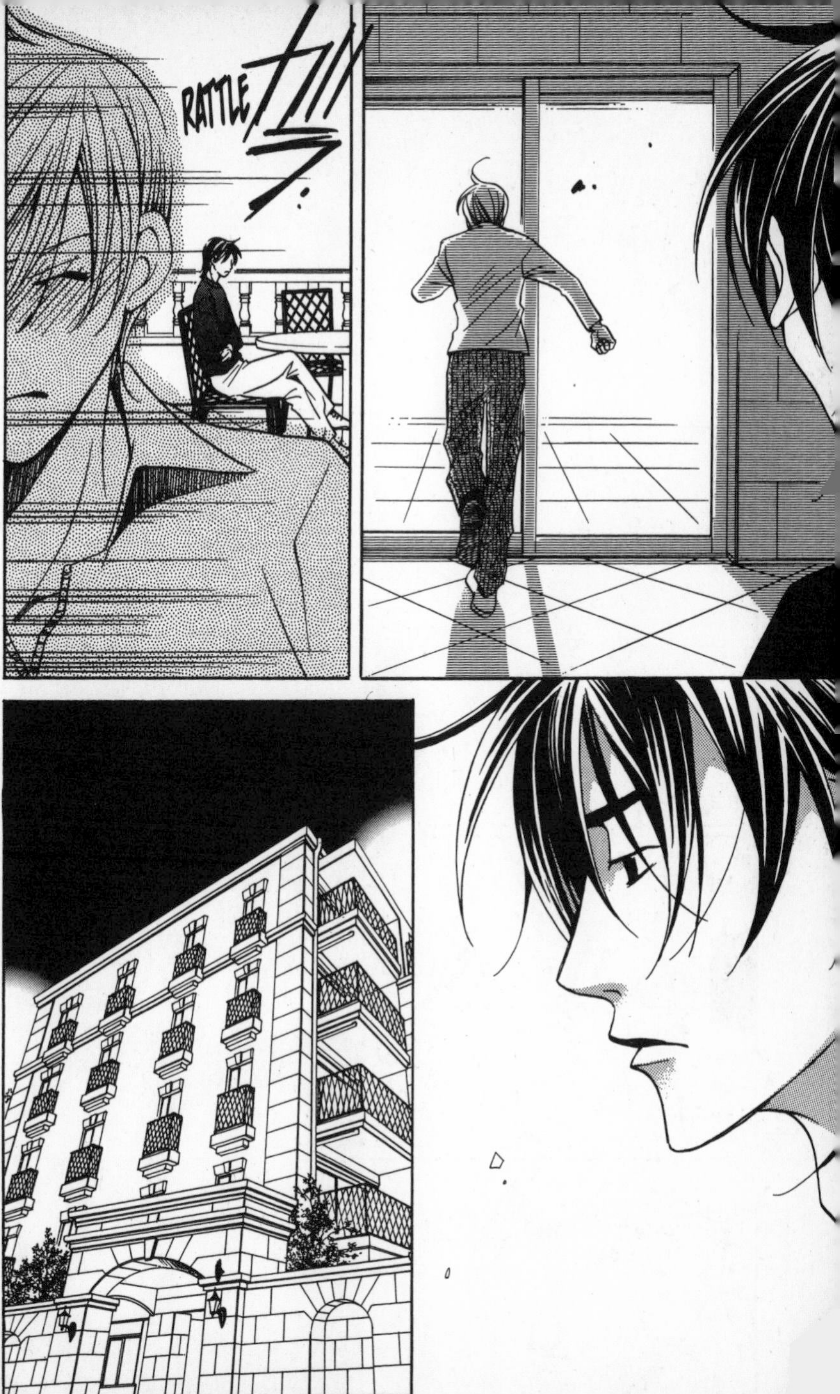
RATTLE

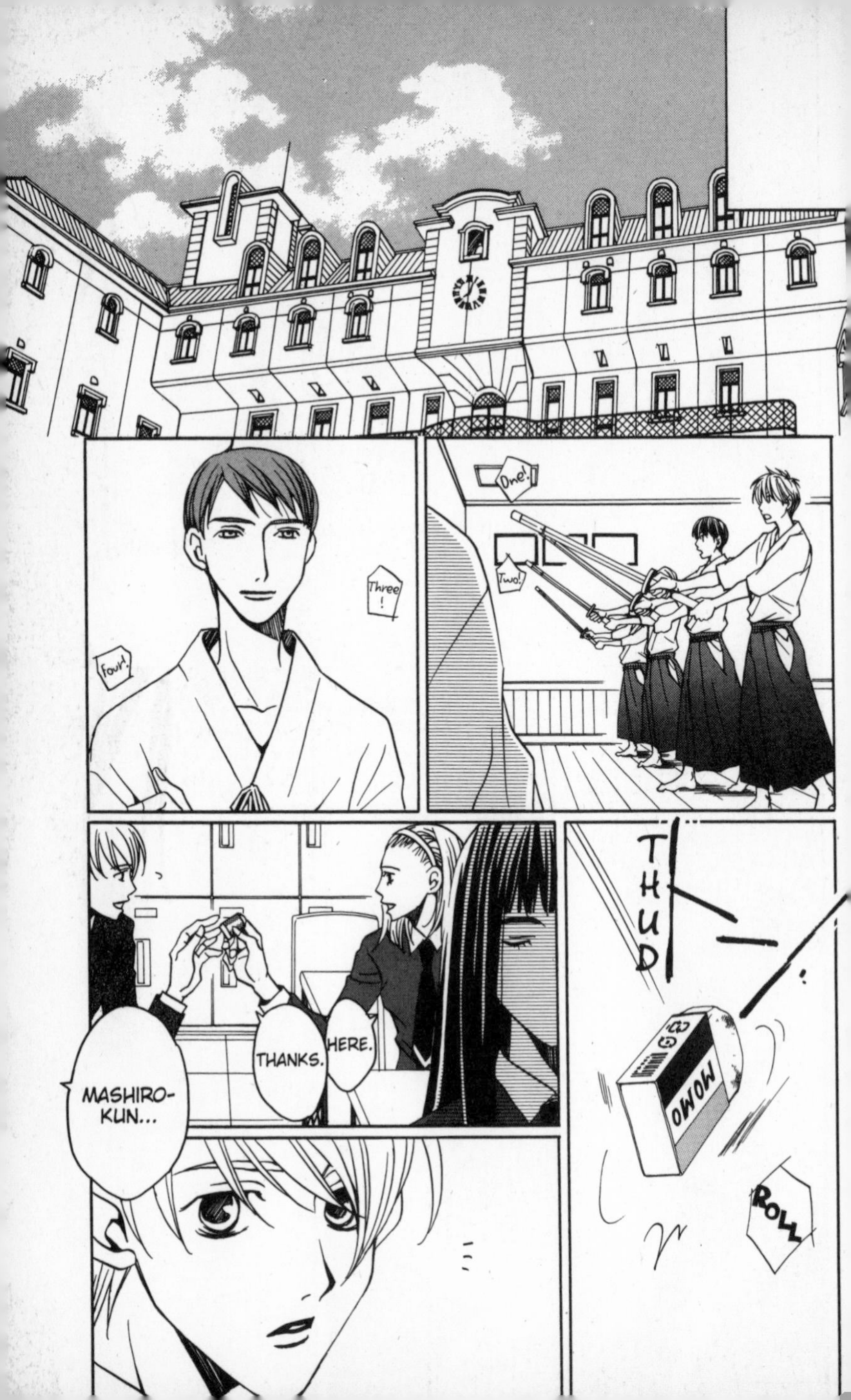
One!
Two!
Three!
Four!
THUD
ROLL
MOMO
HERE.
THANKS.
MASHIRO-KUN...

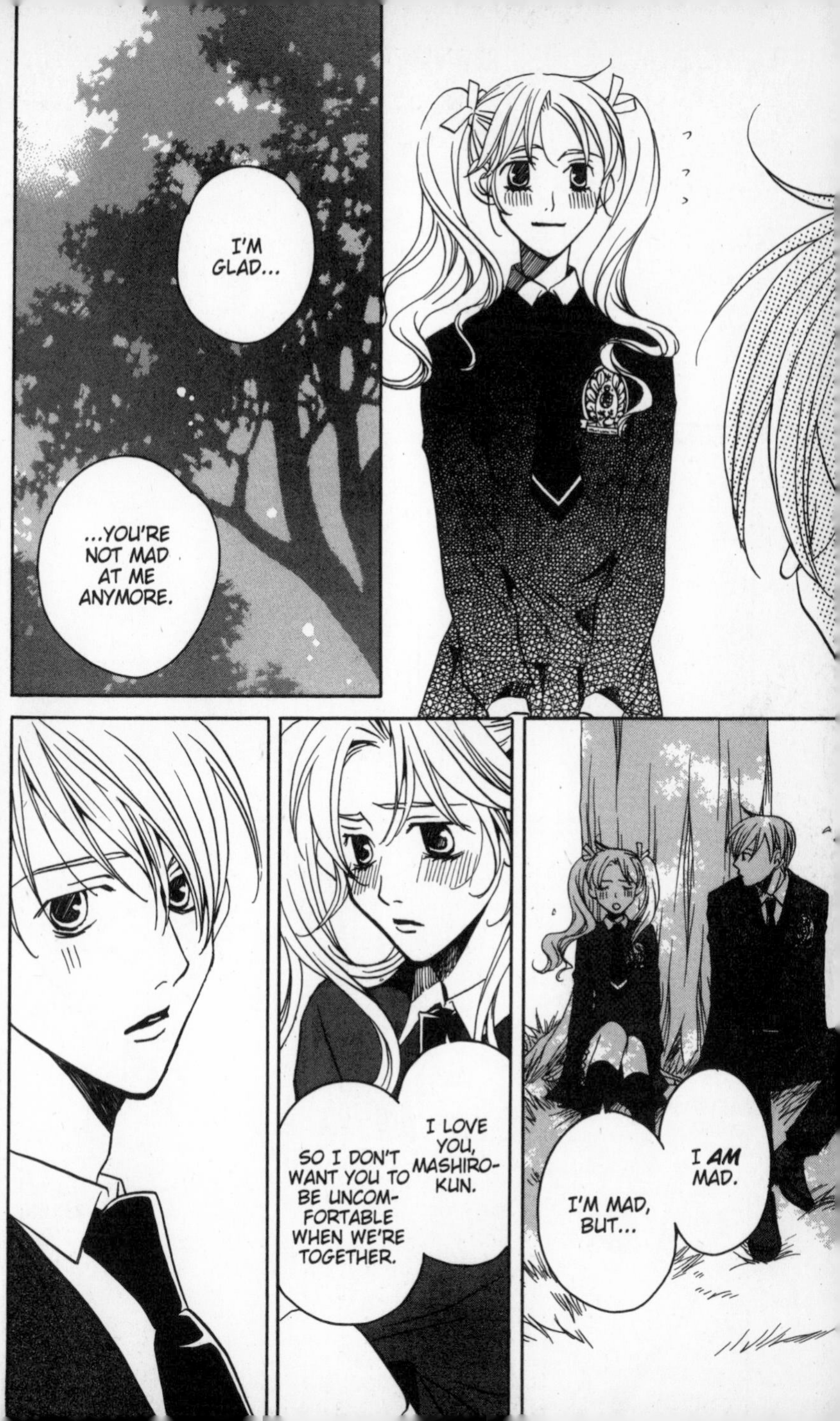
I'M GLAD...
...YOU'RE NOT MAD AT ME ANYMORE.
I *AM* MAD.
I'M MAD, BUT...
I LOVE YOU, MASHIRO-KUN.
SO I DON'T WANT YOU TO BE UNCOMFORTABLE WHEN WE'RE TOGETHER.

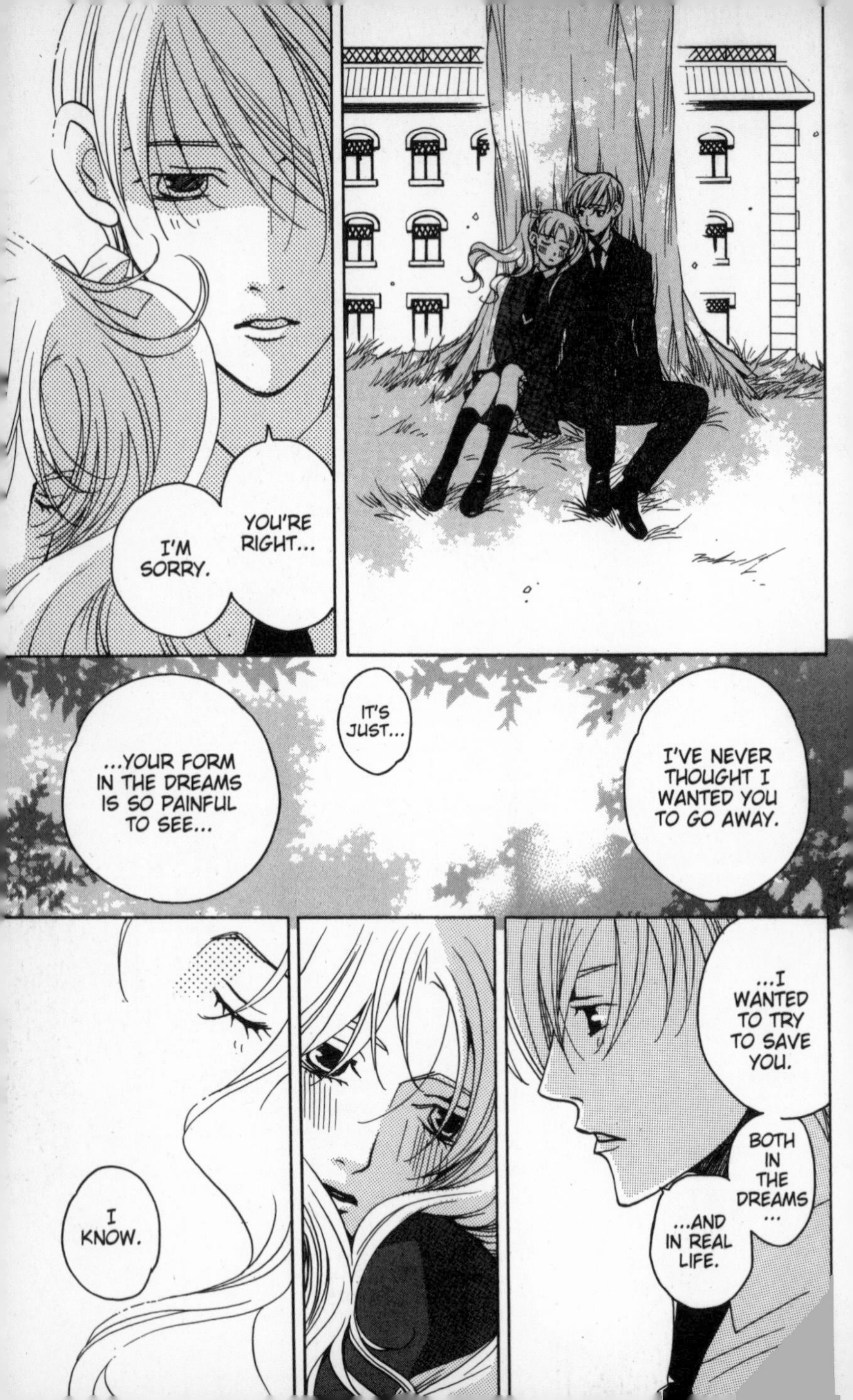
YOU'RE RIGHT...
I'M SORRY.
I'VE NEVER THOUGHT I WANTED YOU TO GO AWAY.
IT'S JUST...
...YOUR FORM IN THE DREAMS IS SO PAINFUL TO SEE...
...I WANTED TO TRY TO SAVE YOU.
BOTH IN THE DREAMS...
...AND IN REAL LIFE.
I KNOW.

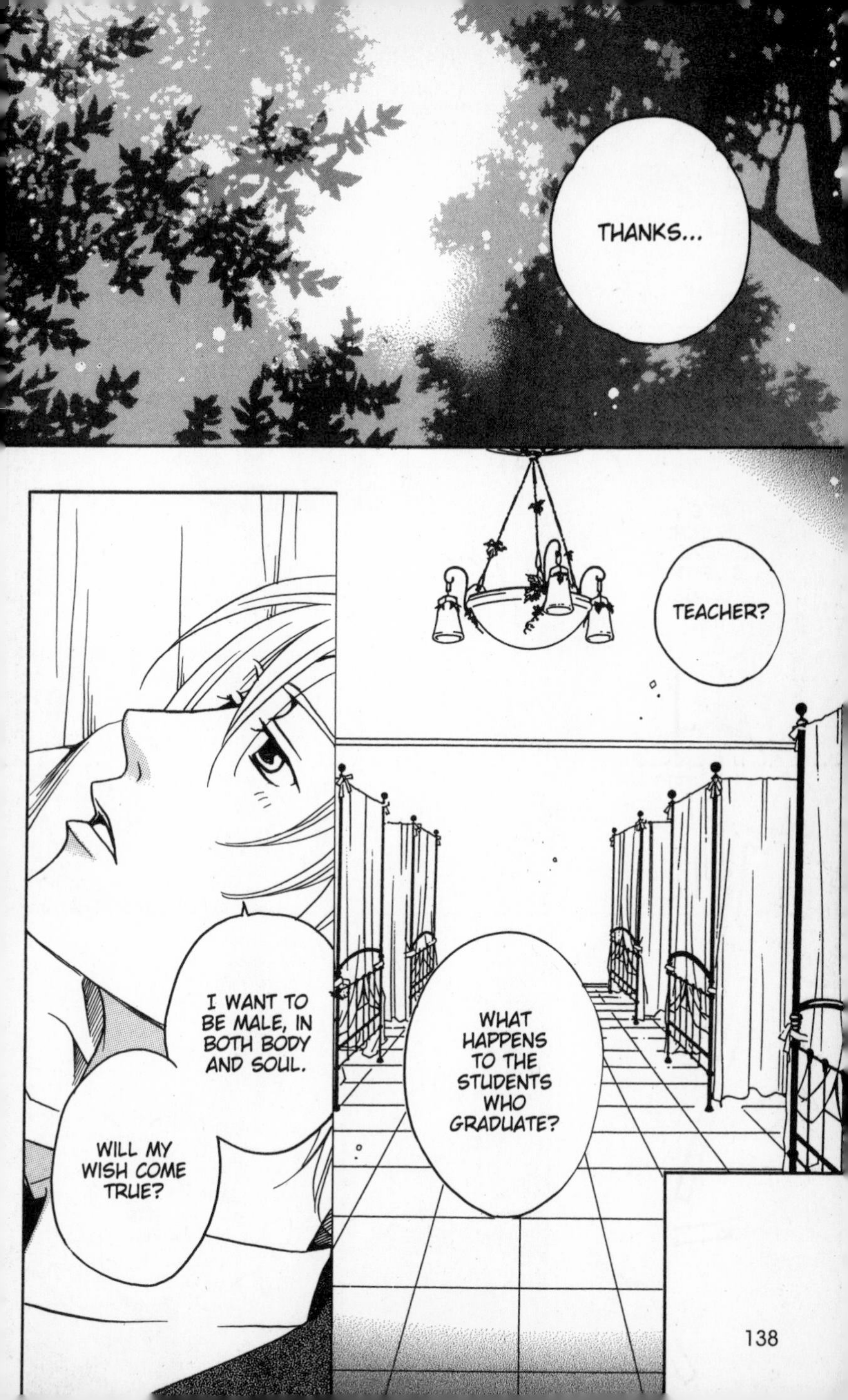
THANKS...
TEACHER?
WHAT HAPPENS TO THE STUDENTS WHO GRADUATE?
I WANT TO BE MALE, IN BOTH BODY AND SOUL.
WILL MY WISH COME TRUE?

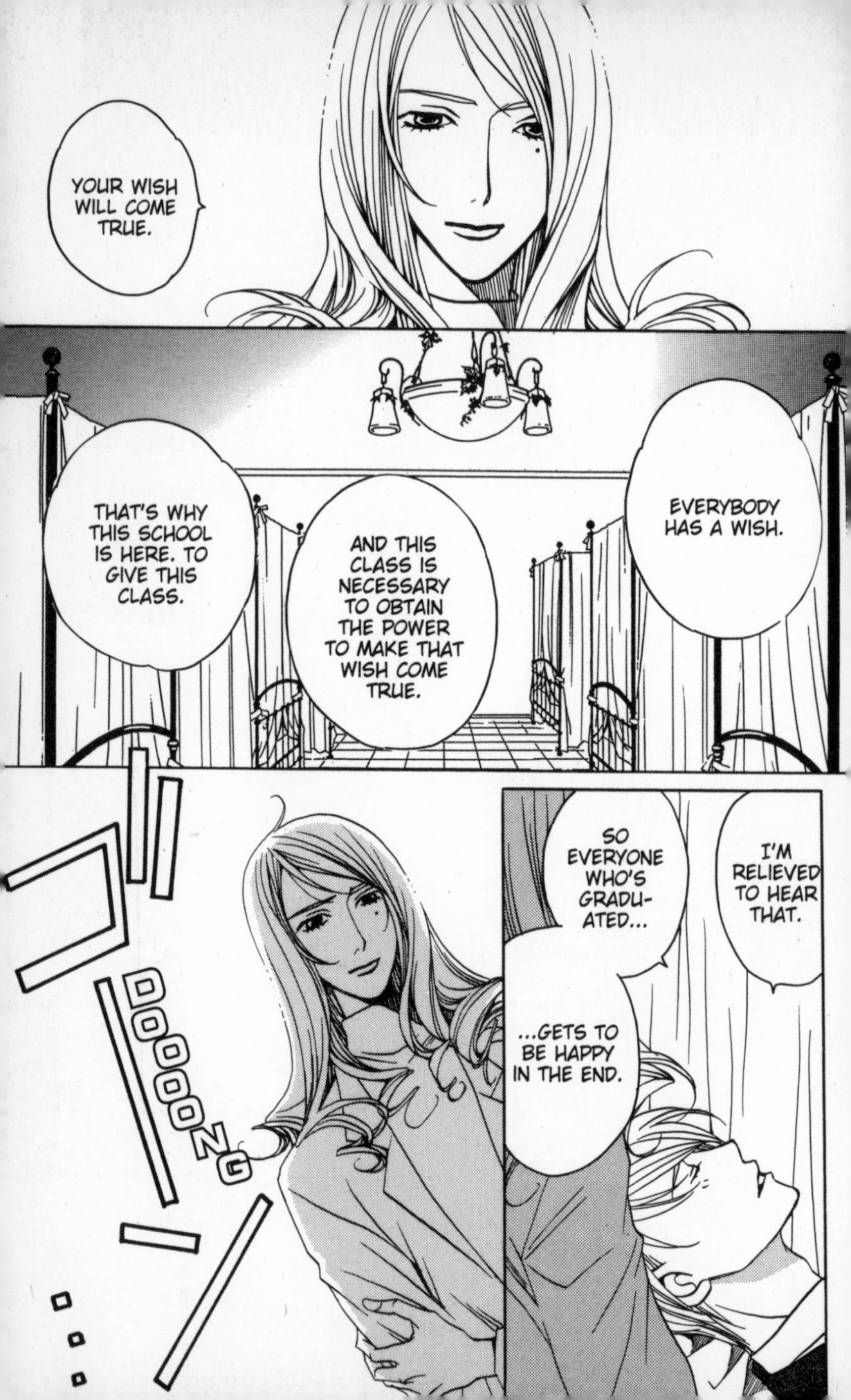
YOUR WISH WILL COME TRUE.
EVERYBODY HAS A WISH.
AND THIS CLASS IS NECESSARY TO OBTAIN THE POWER TO MAKE THAT WISH COME TRUE.
THAT'S WHY THIS SCHOOL IS HERE. TO GIVE THIS CLASS.
I'M RELIEVED TO HEAR THAT.
SO EVERYONE WHO'S GRADU-ATED...
...GETS TO BE HAPPY IN THE END.
DOOOONG
...

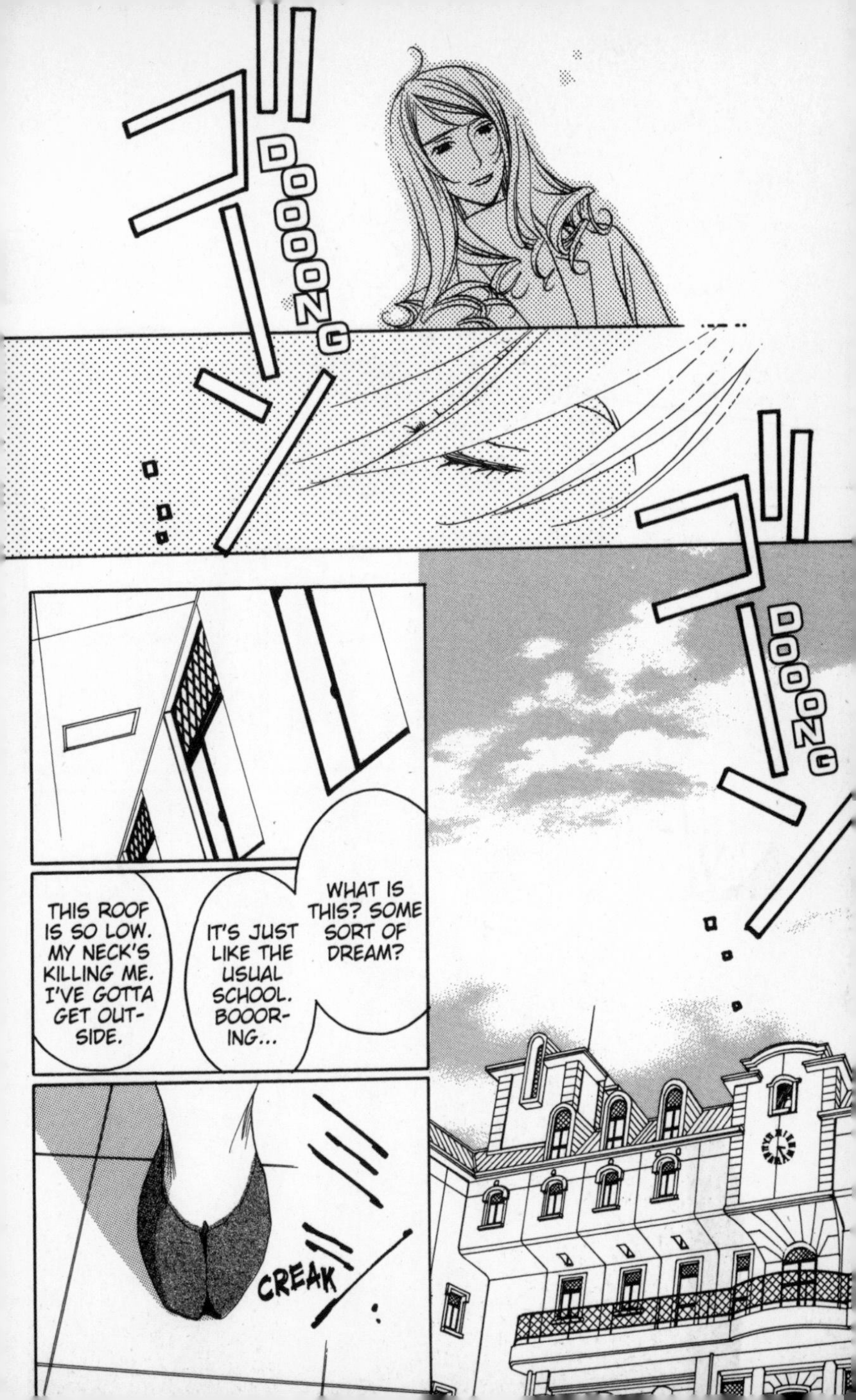
DOOONG
DOOONG
WHAT IS THIS? SOME SORT OF DREAM?
IT'S JUST LIKE THE USUAL SCHOOL. BOOOR-ING...
THIS ROOF IS SO LOW. MY NECK'S KILLING ME. I'VE GOTTA GET OUT-SIDE.
CREAK

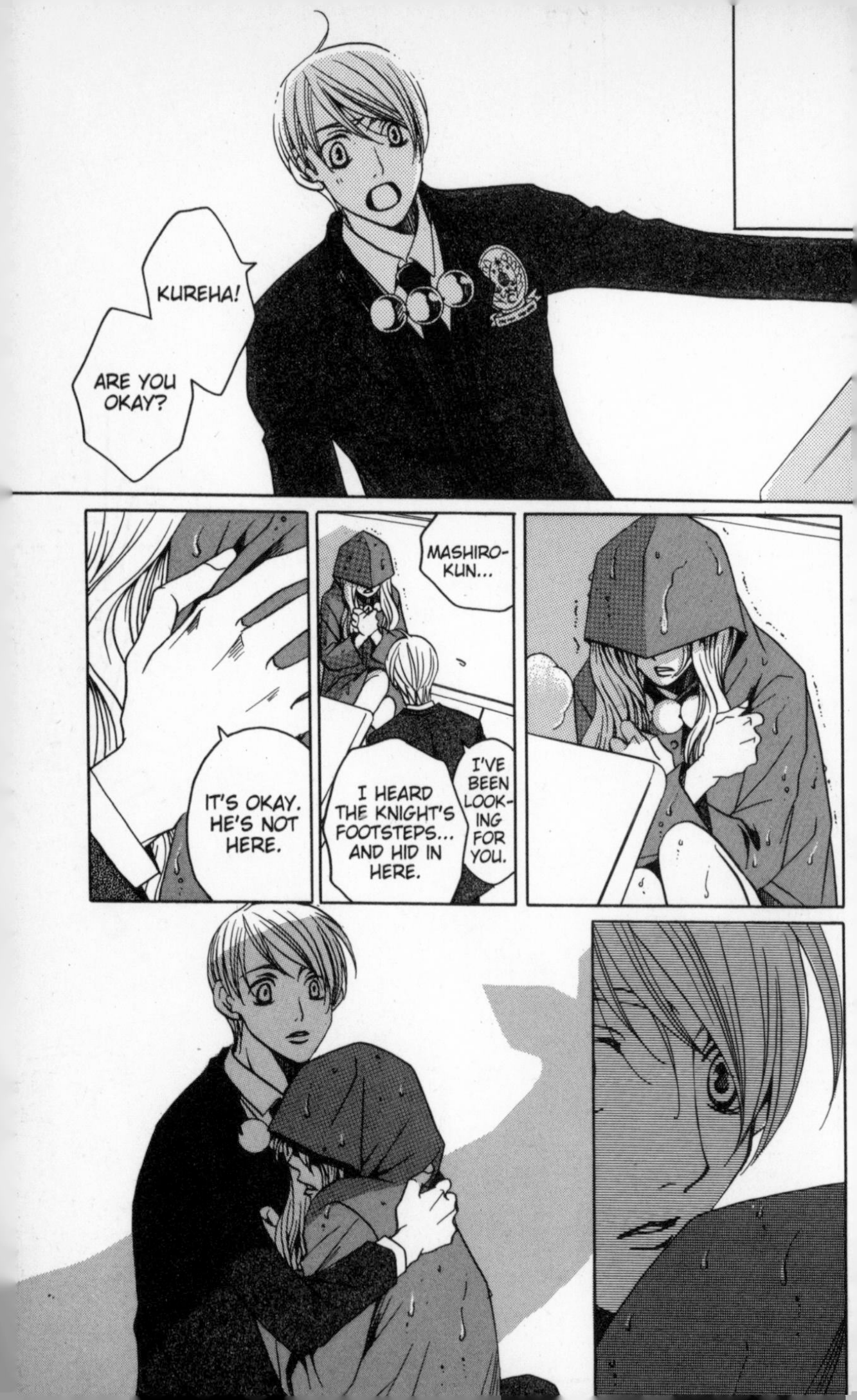
KUREHA!
ARE YOU OKAY?
MASHIRO-KUN...
I'VE BEEN LOOKING FOR YOU.
I HEARD THE KNIGHT'S FOOTSTEPS... AND HID IN HERE.
IT'S OKAY. HE'S NOT HERE.

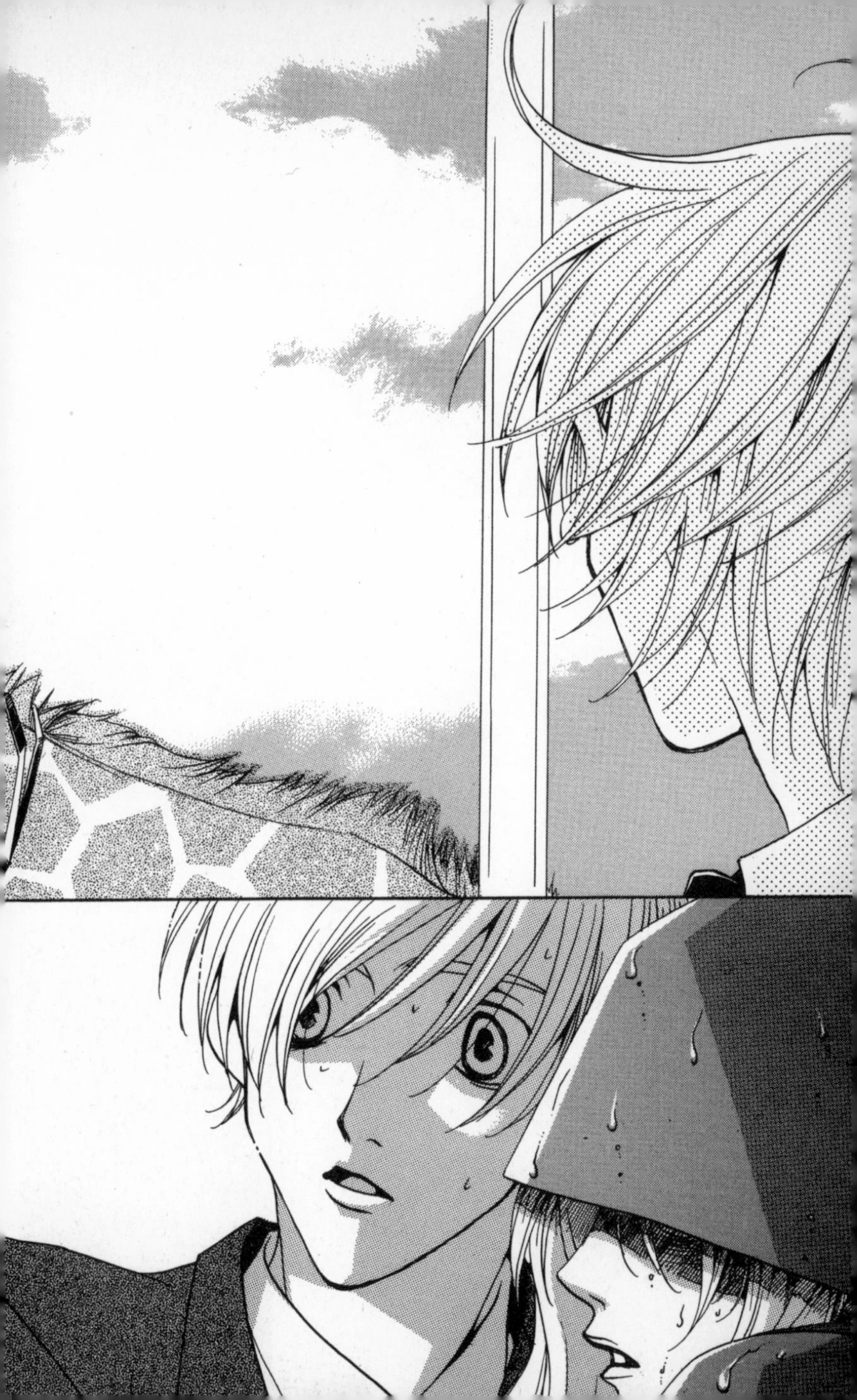

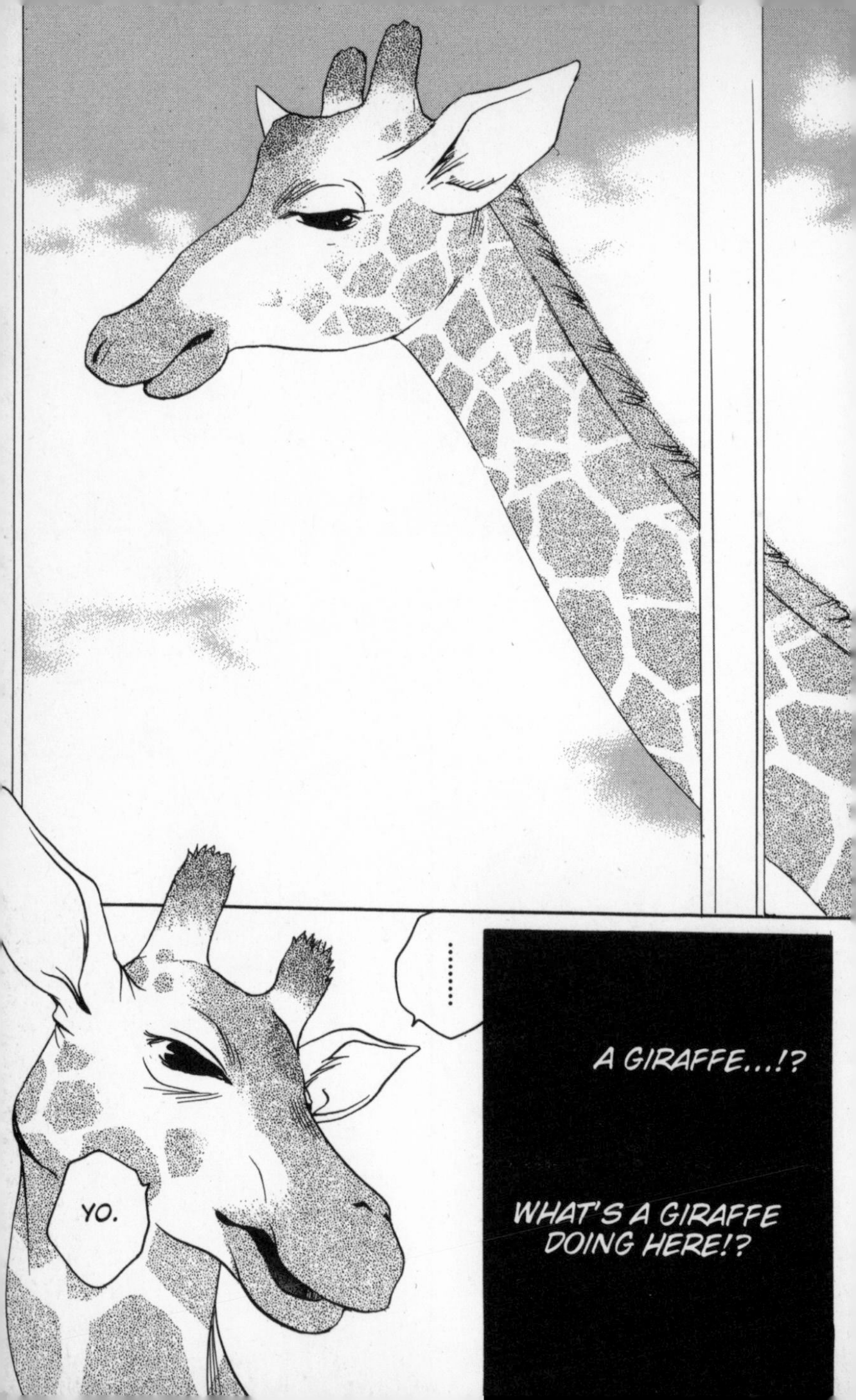
A GIRAFFE...!?
WHAT'S A GIRAFFE DOING HERE!?
....
YO.

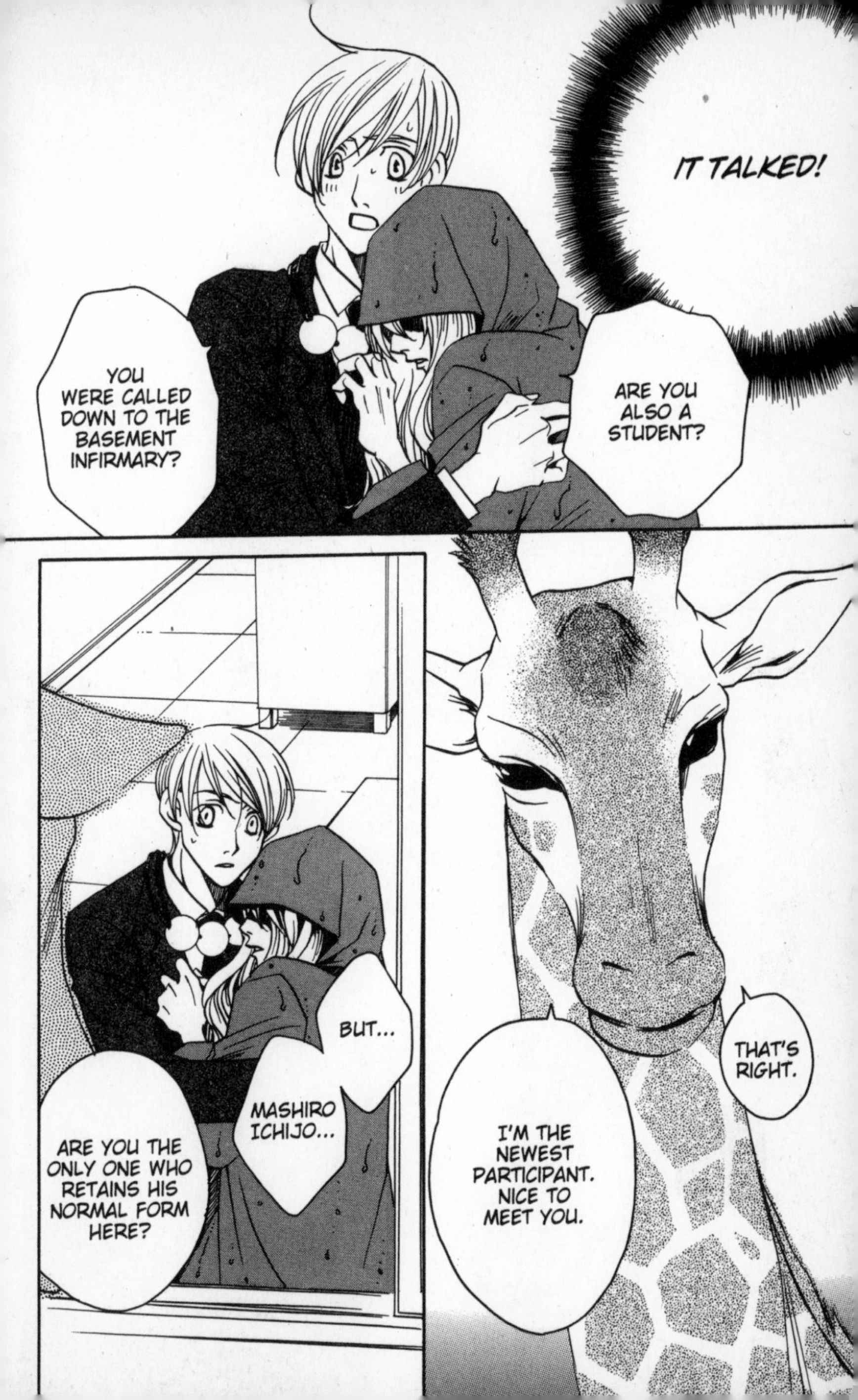
IT TALKED!
ARE YOU ALSO A STUDENT?
YOU WERE CALLED DOWN TO THE BASEMENT INFIRMARY?
THAT'S RIGHT.
I'M THE NEWEST PARTICIPANT. NICE TO MEET YOU.
BUT...
MASHIRO ICHIJO...
ARE YOU THE ONLY ONE WHO RETAINS HIS NORMAL FORM HERE?

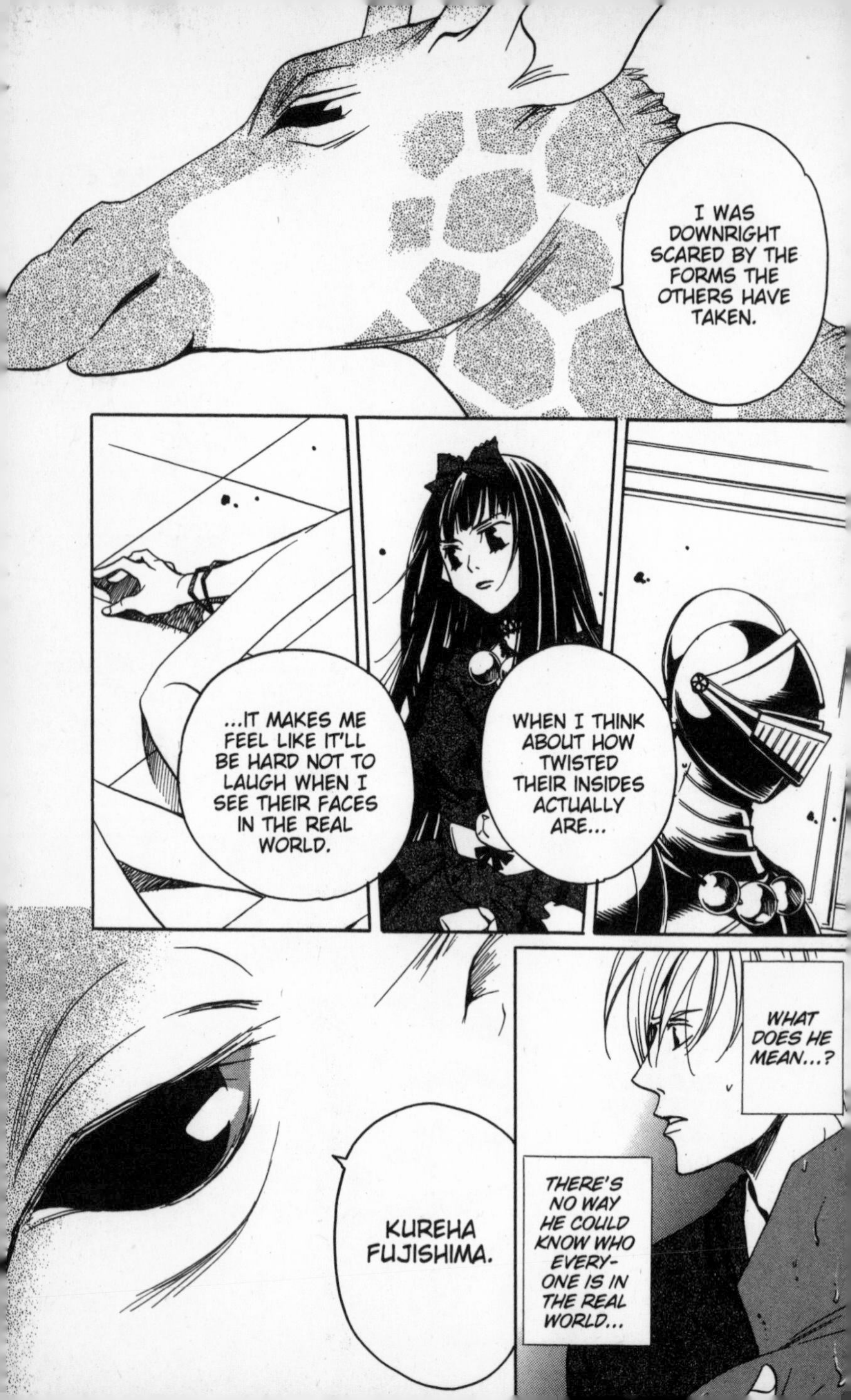
I WAS DOWNRIGHT SCARED BY THE FORMS THE OTHERS HAVE TAKEN.
WHEN I THINK ABOUT HOW TWISTED THEIR INSIDES ACTUALLY ARE...
...IT MAKES ME FEEL LIKE IT'LL BE HARD NOT TO LAUGH WHEN I SEE THEIR FACES IN THE REAL WORLD.
WHAT DOES HE MEAN...?
THERE'S NO WAY HE COULD KNOW WHO EVERY-ONE IS IN THE REAL WORLD...
KUREHA FUJISHIMA.

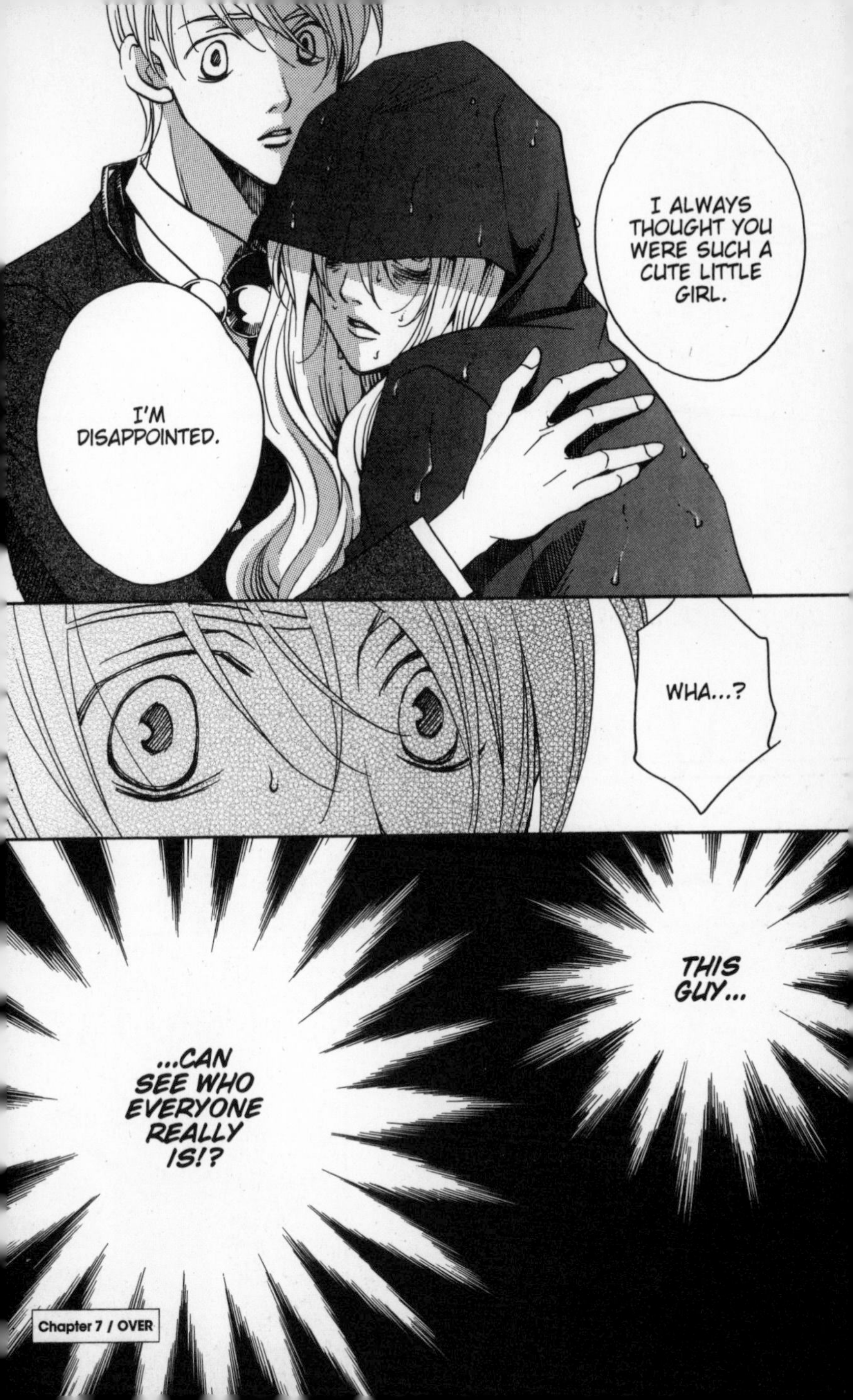
I ALWAYS THOUGHT YOU WERE SUCH A CUTE LITTLE GIRL.
I'M DISAPPOINTED.
WHA...?
THIS GUY...
...CAN SEE WHO EVERYONE REALLY IS!?
Chapter 7 / OVER

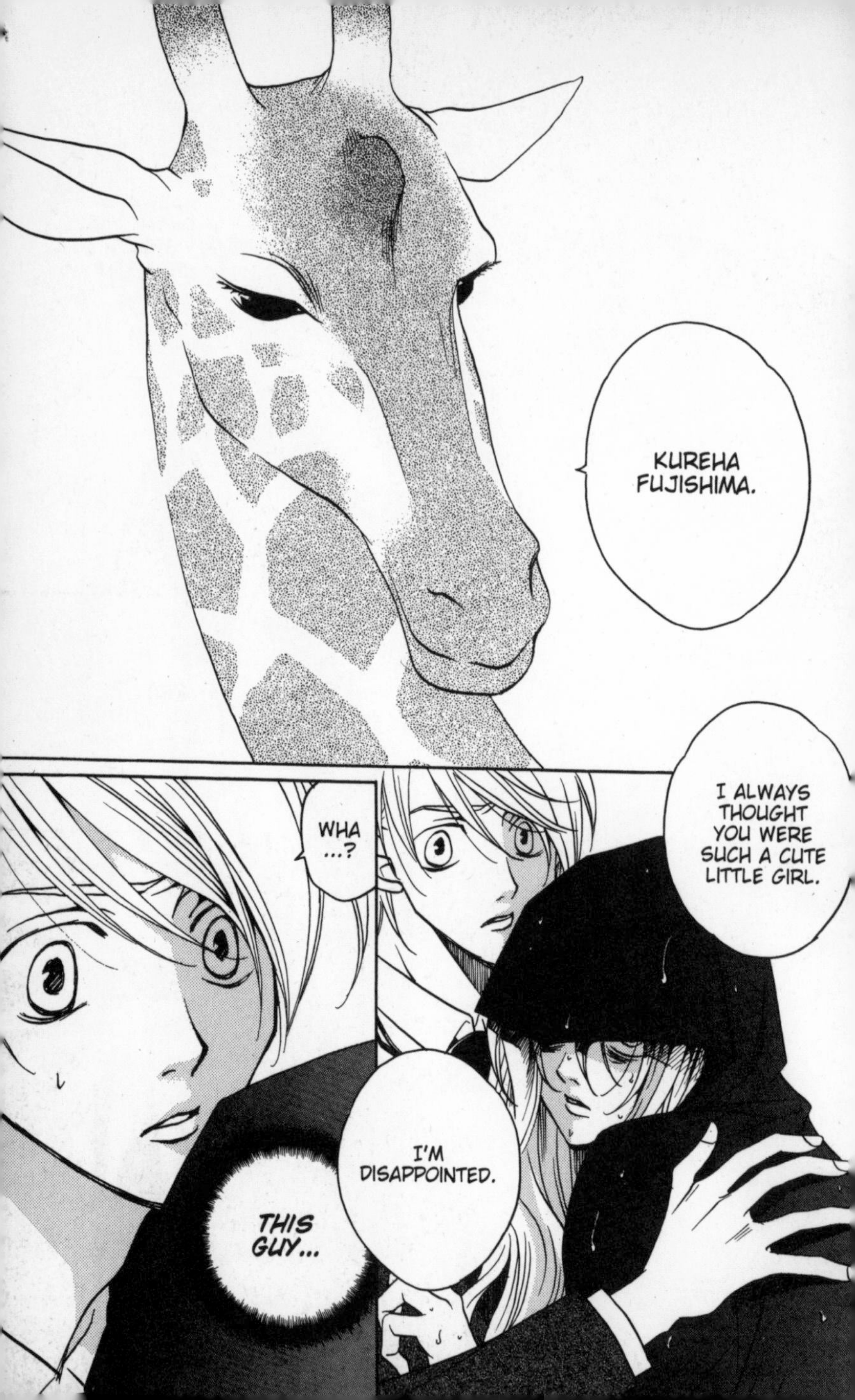
KUREHA FUJISHIMA.
I ALWAYS THOUGHT YOU WERE SUCH A CUTE LITTLE GIRL.
I'M DISAPPOINTED.
WHA ...?
THIS GUY...

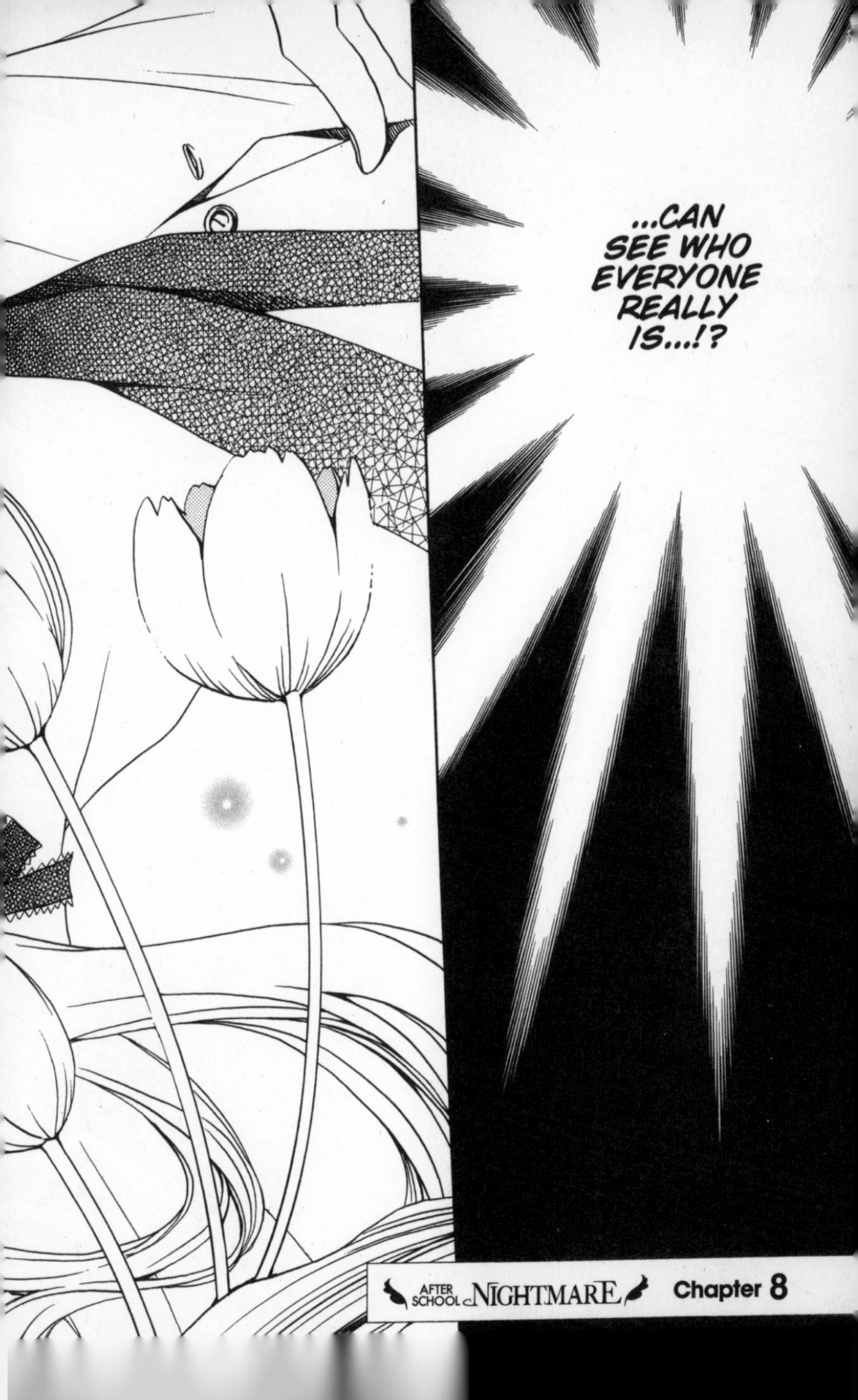
...CAN SEE WHO EVERYONE REALLY IS...!?
AFTER SCHOOL NIGHTMARE Chapter 8

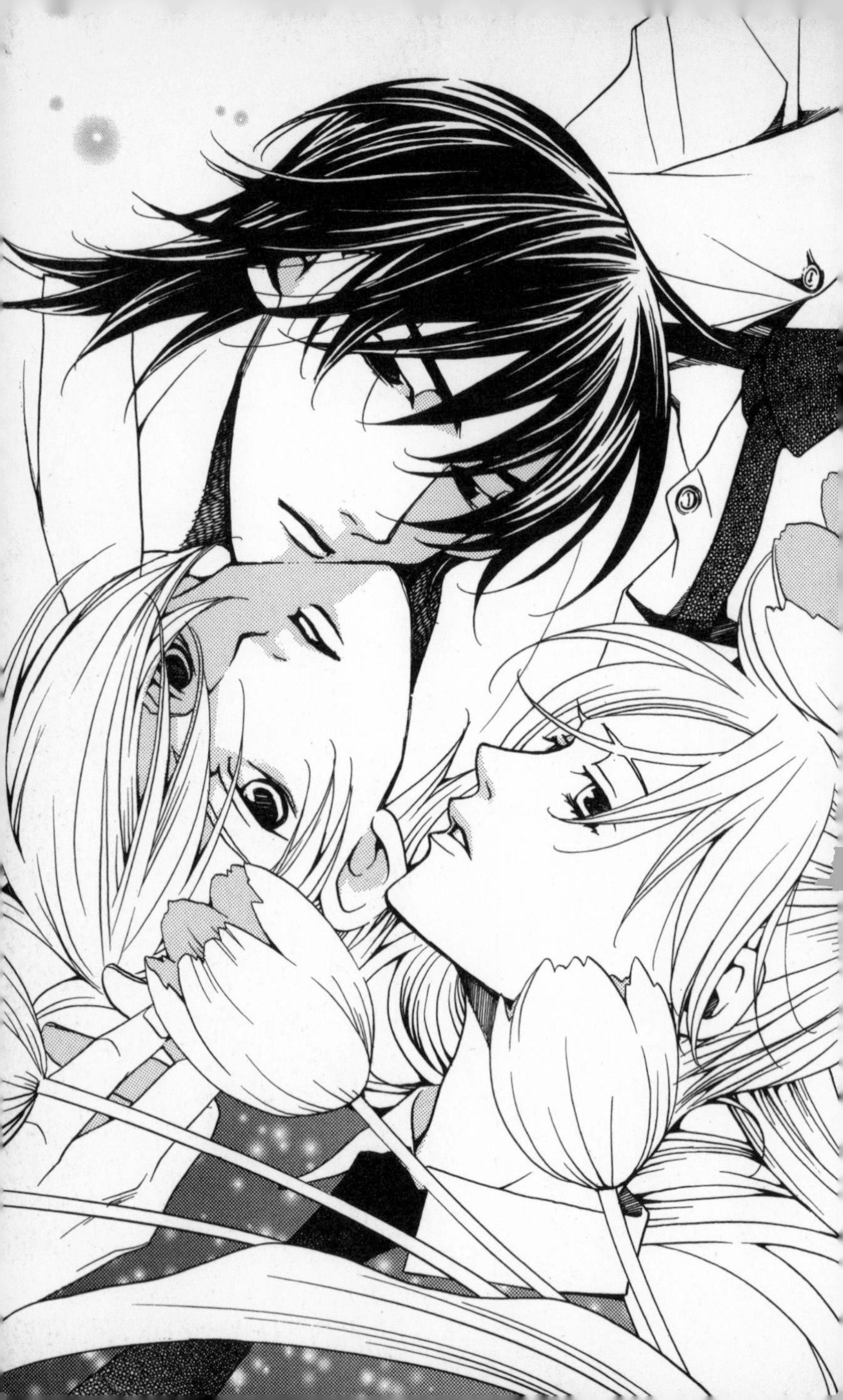

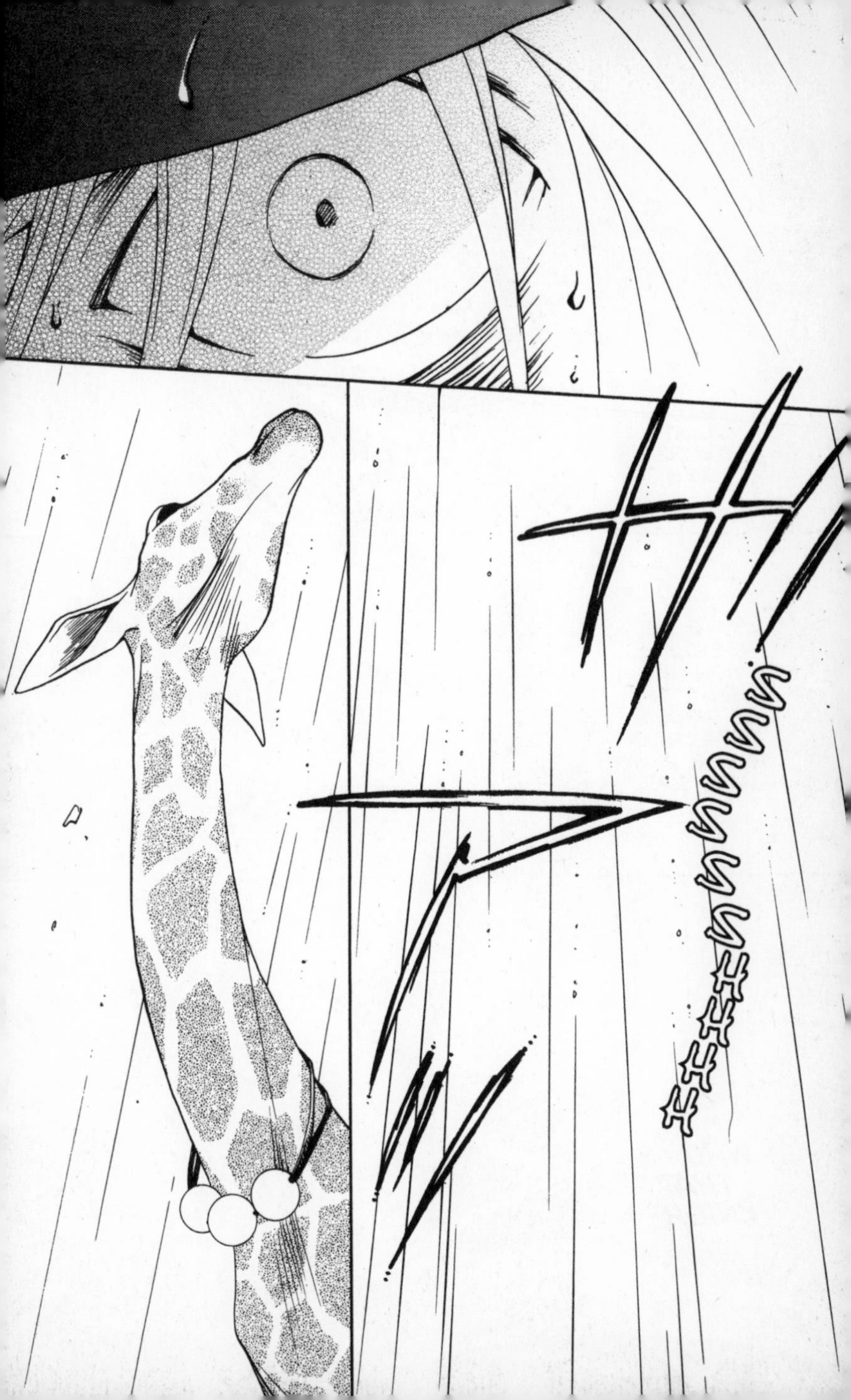
SSSSSSHHHH

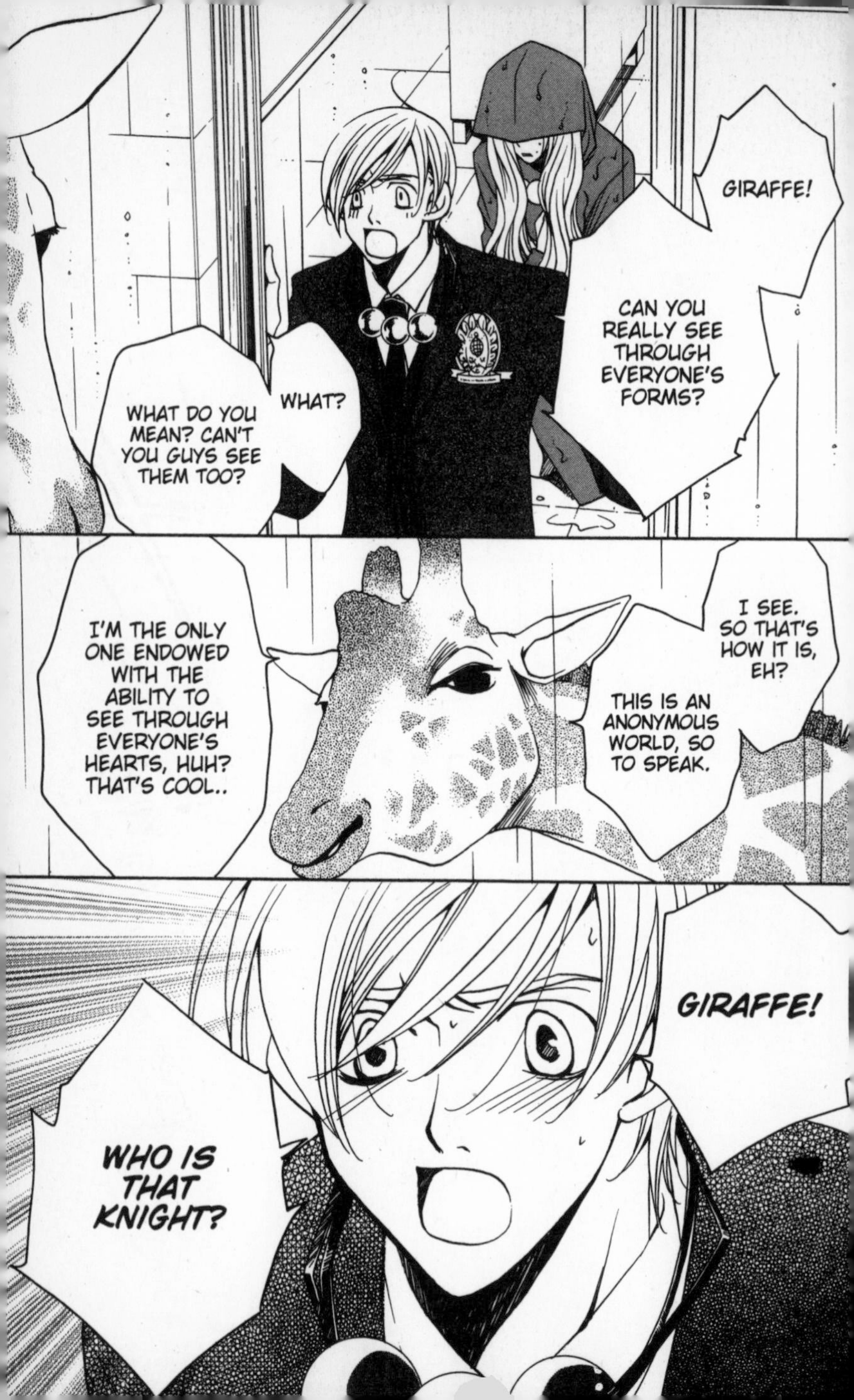
GIRAFFE!
CAN YOU REALLY SEE THROUGH EVERYONE'S FORMS?
WHAT?
WHAT DO YOU MEAN? CAN'T YOU GUYS SEE THEM TOO?
I SEE. SO THAT'S HOW IT IS, EH?
THIS IS AN ANONYMOUS WORLD, SO TO SPEAK.
I'M THE ONLY ONE ENDOWED WITH THE ABILITY TO SEE THROUGH EVERYONE'S HEARTS, HUH? THAT'S COOL..
GIRAFFE!
WHO IS THAT KNIGHT?

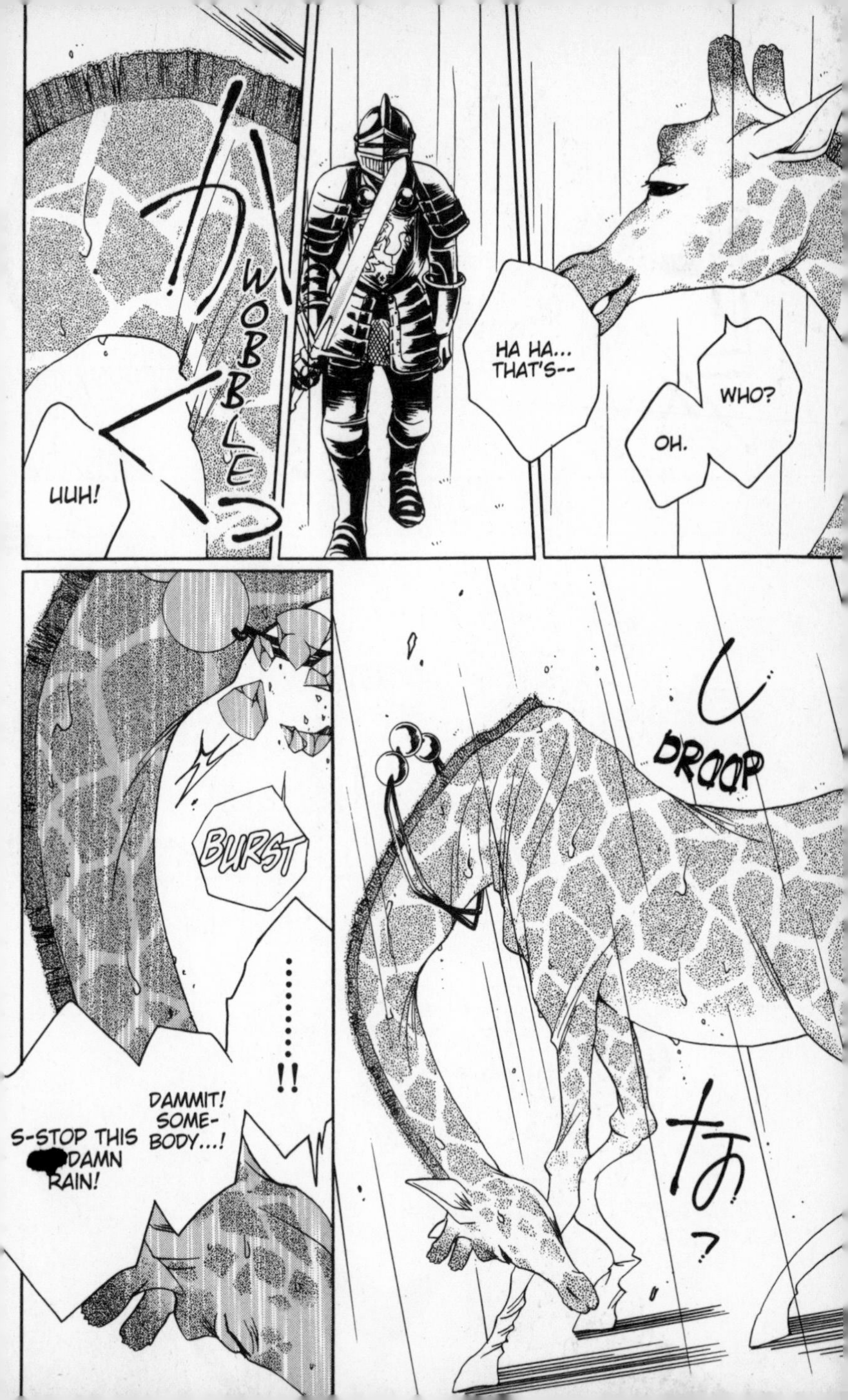
WHO?
OH.
HA HA... THAT'S--
UUH!
WOBBLE
DROOP
BURST
......!!
DAMMIT! SOME-BODY...!
S-STOP THIS [redacted] DAMN RAIN!

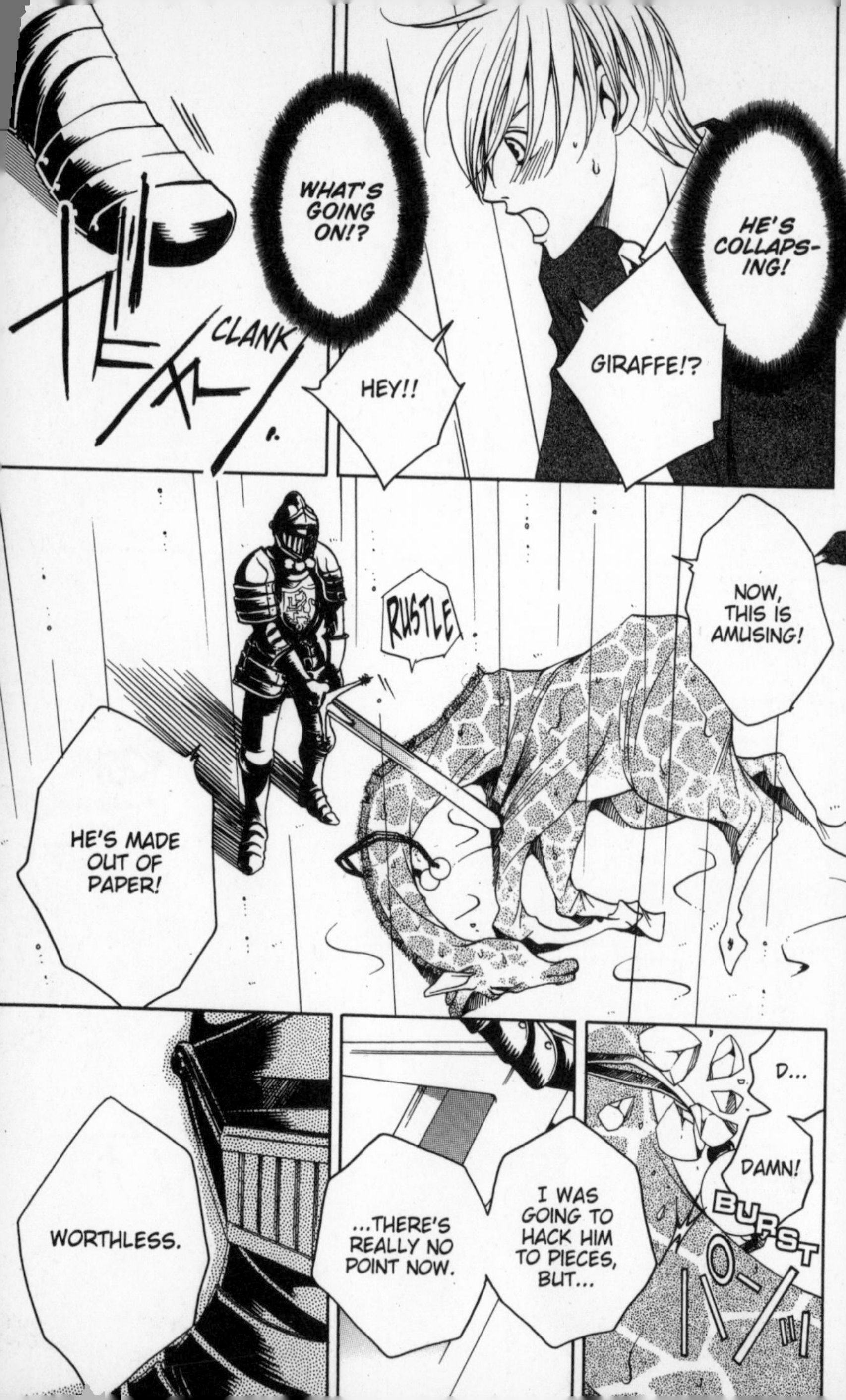
HE'S COLLAPS-ING!
GIRAFFE!?
WHAT'S GOING ON!?
HEY!!
CLANK
NOW, THIS IS AMUSING!
RUSTLE
HE'S MADE OUT OF PAPER!
D...
DAMN!
BURST
I WAS GOING TO HACK HIM TO PIECES, BUT...
...THERE'S REALLY NO POINT NOW.
WORTHLESS.

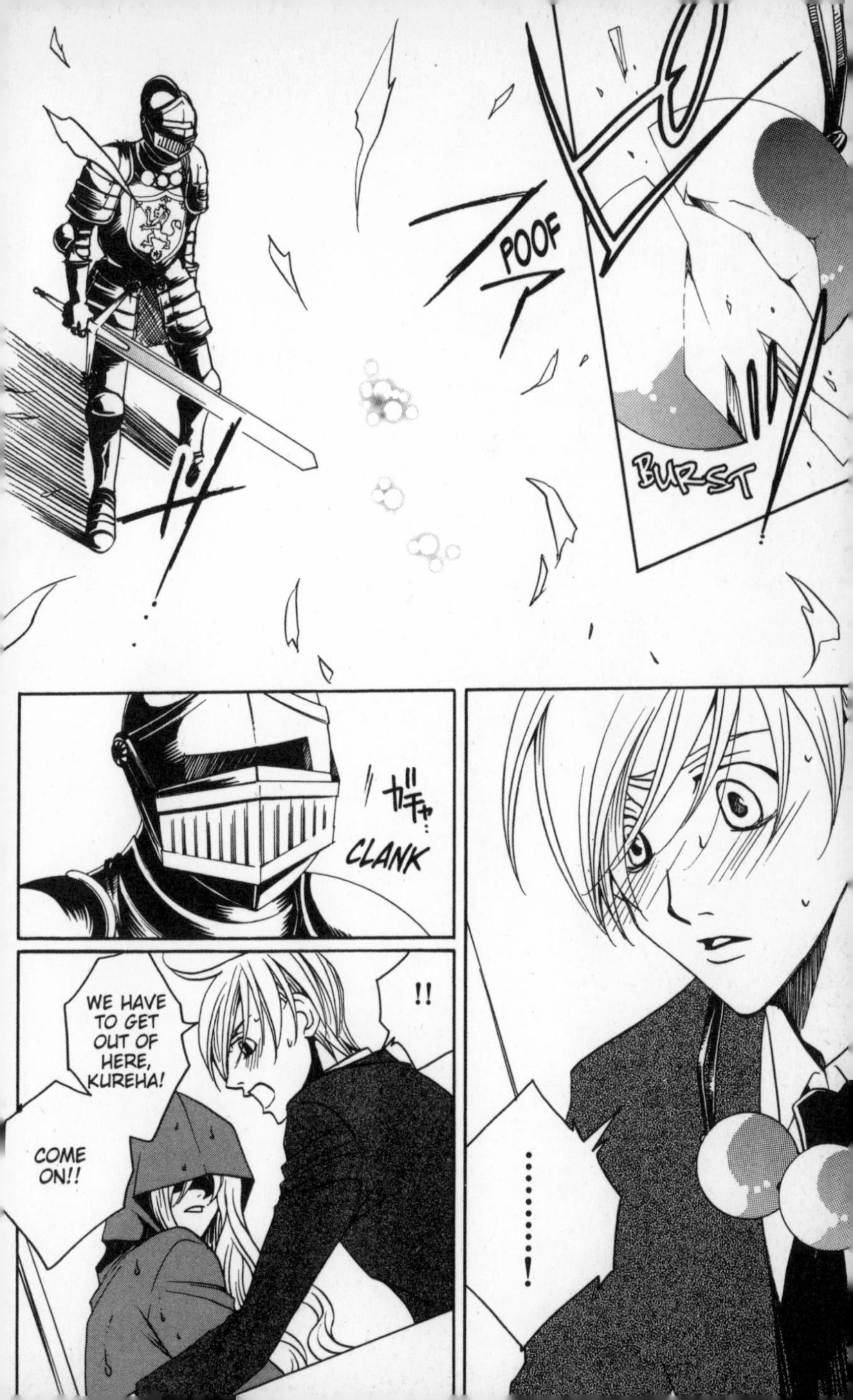
POOF
BURST
......!
ガチャ
CLANK
!!
WE HAVE TO GET OUT OF HERE, KUREHA!
COME ON!!

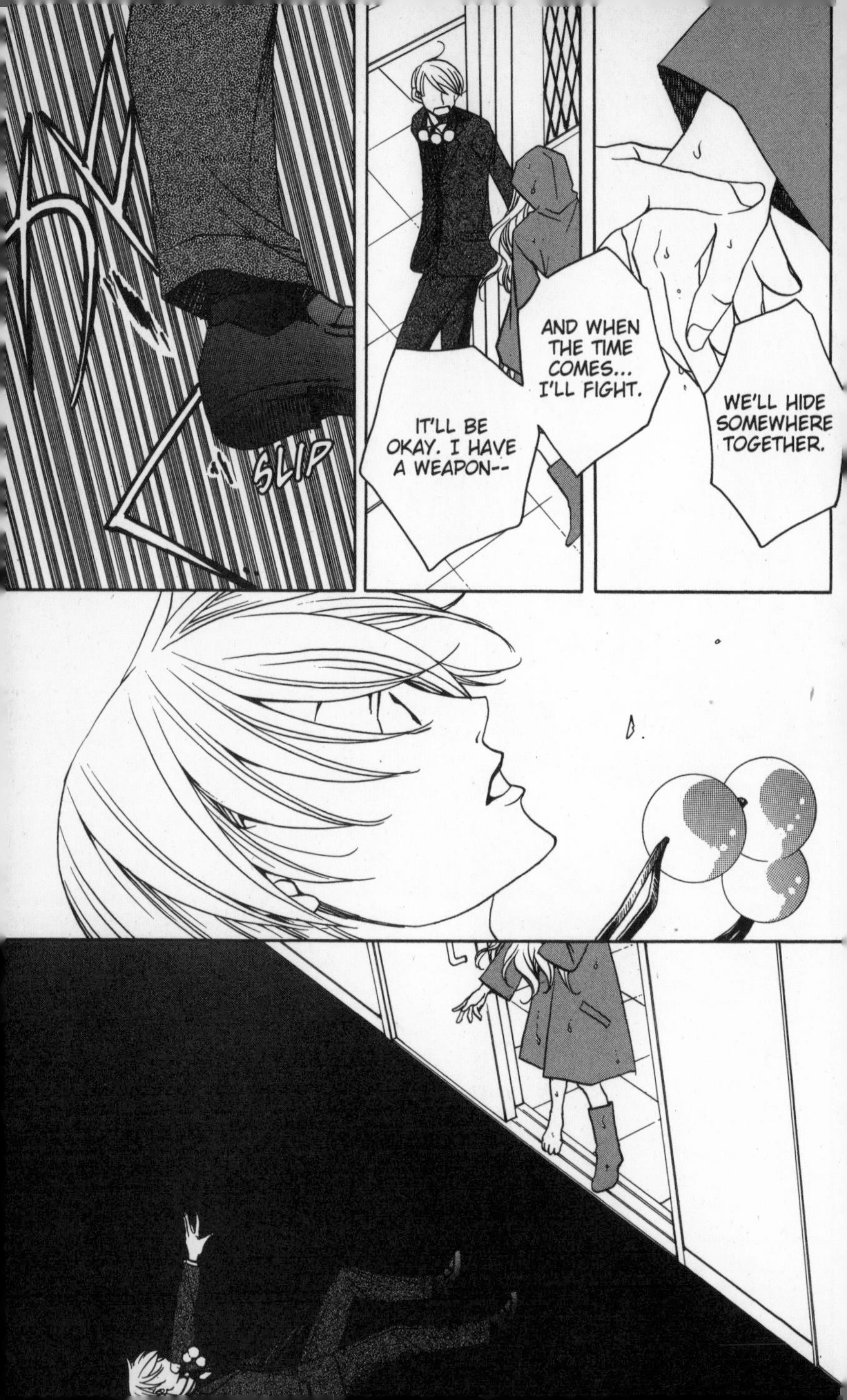
WE'LL HIDE SOMEWHERE TOGETHER.
AND WHEN THE TIME COMES... I'LL FIGHT.
IT'LL BE OKAY. I HAVE A WEAPON--
SLIP

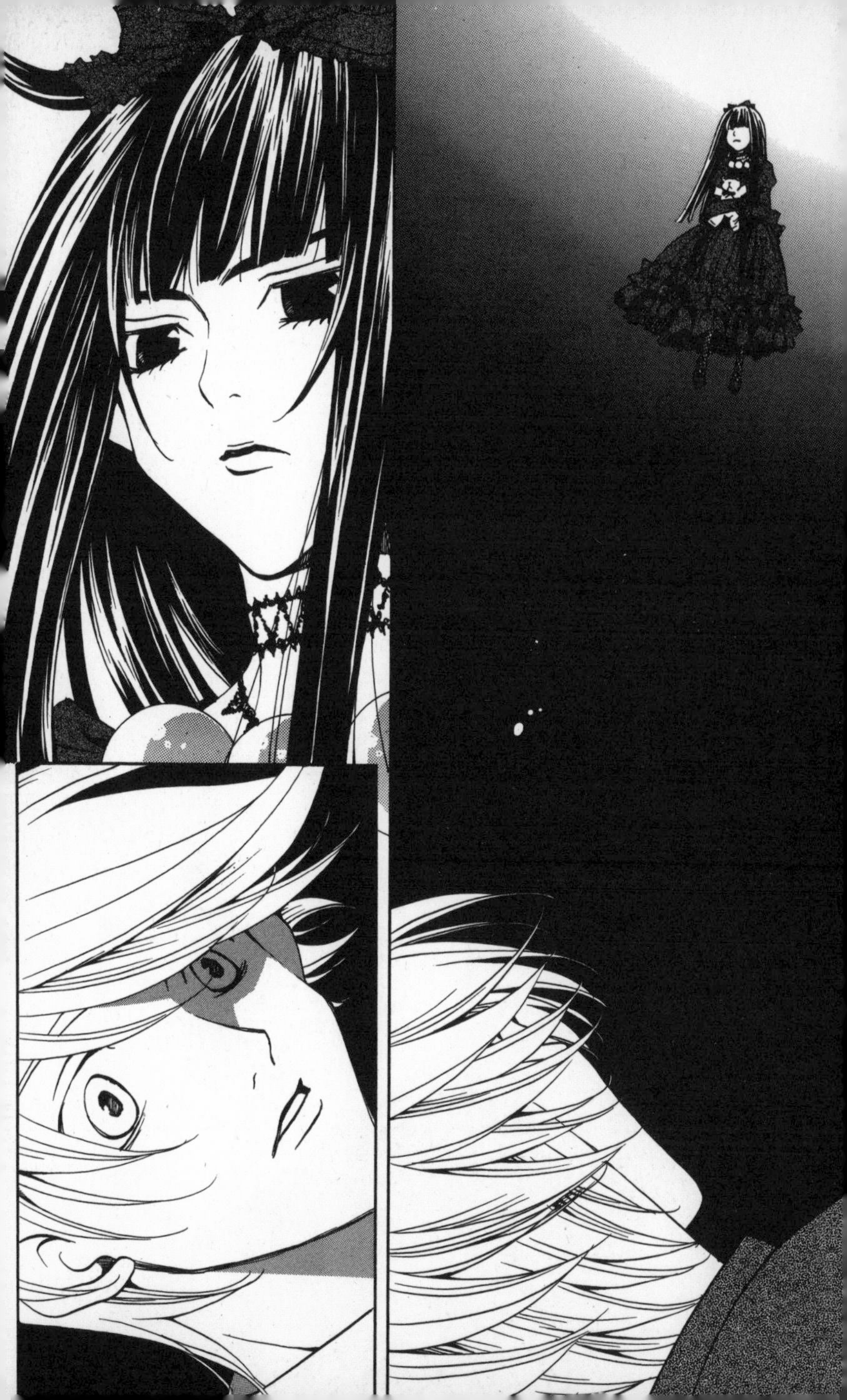

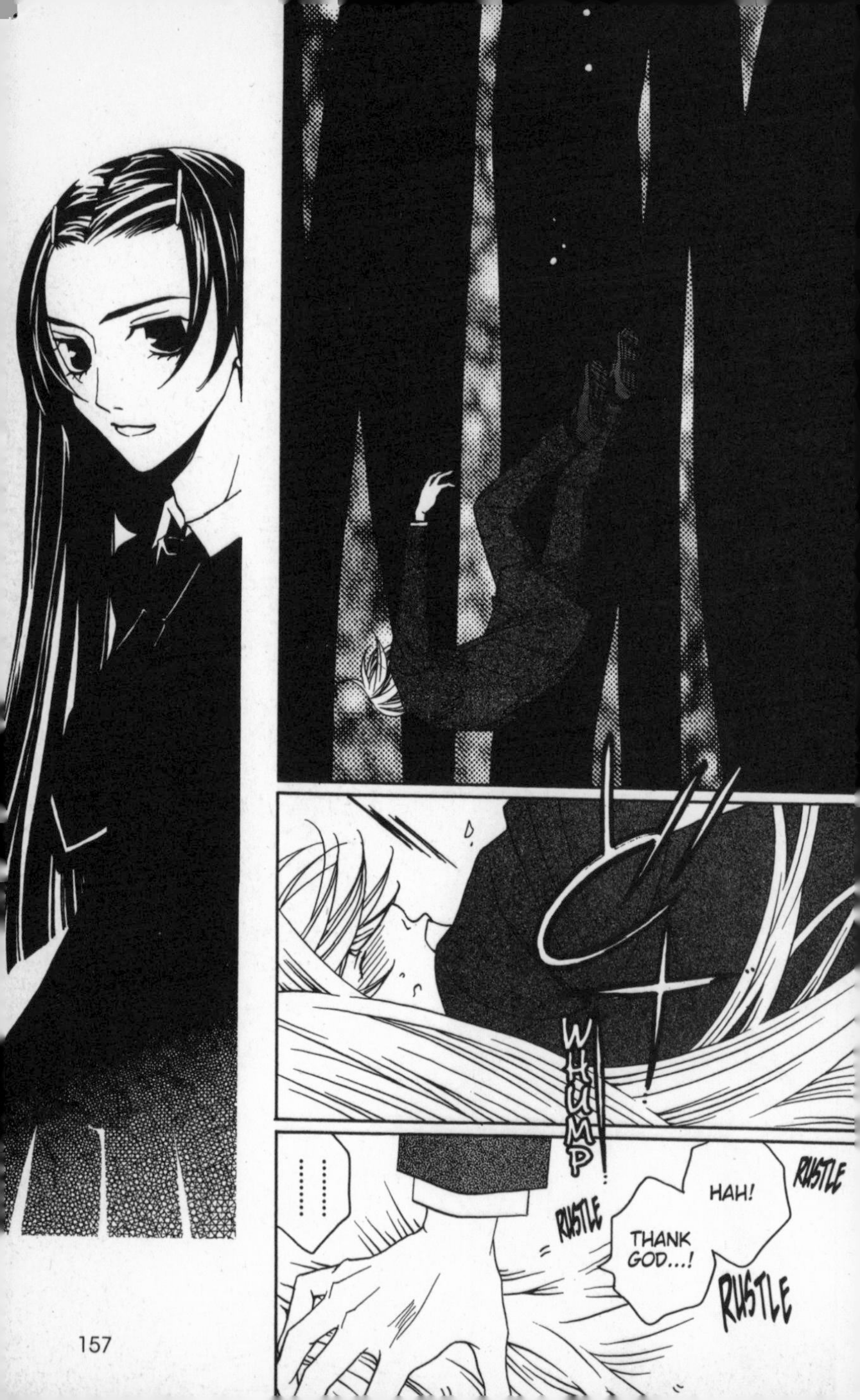

WHUMP
RUSTLE
HAH!
THANK GOD...!
RUSTLE
......
RUSTLE

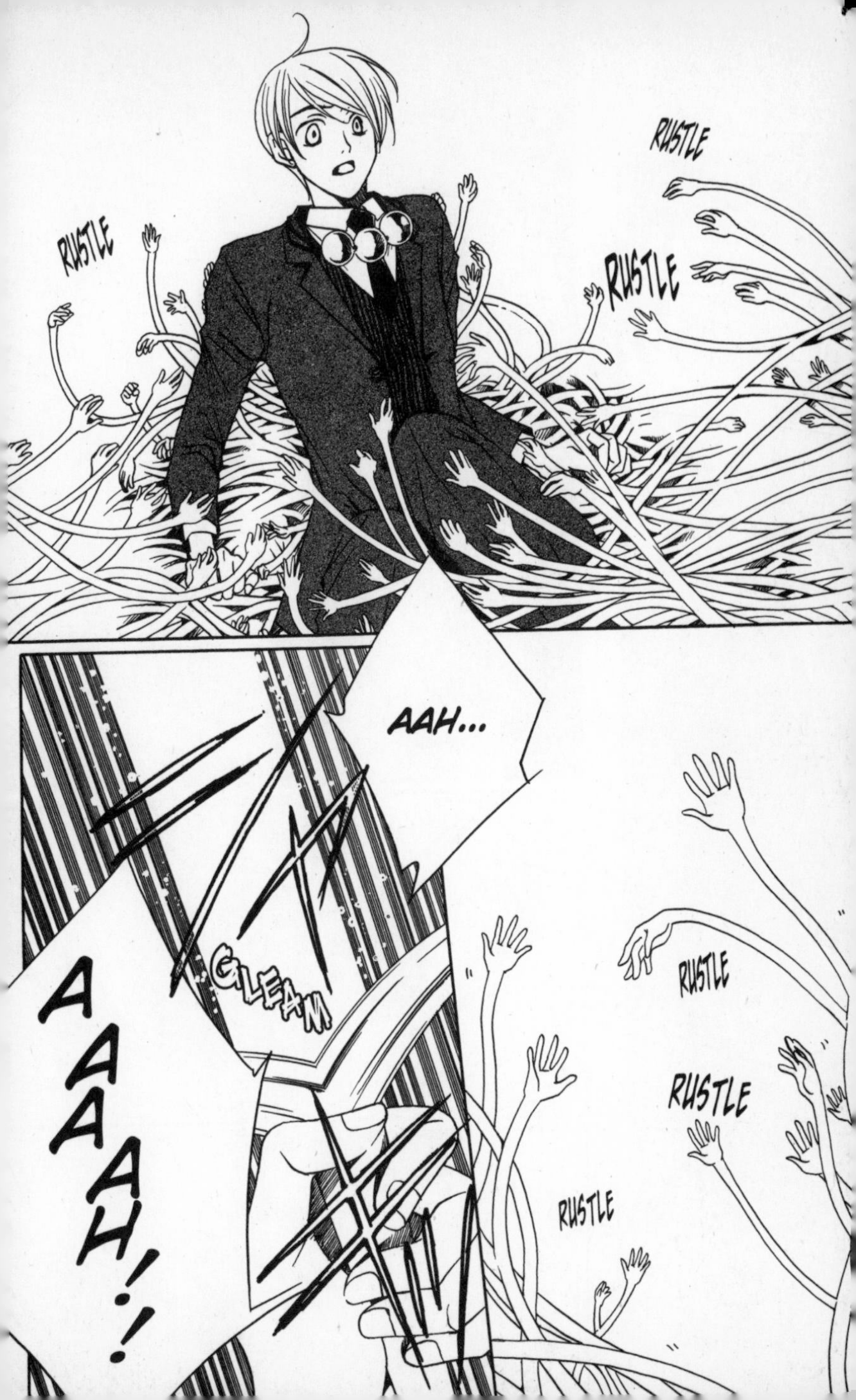
RUSTLE
RUSTLE
RUSTLE
AAH...
RUSTLE
RUSTLE
GLEAM
RUSTLE
AAAAH!!

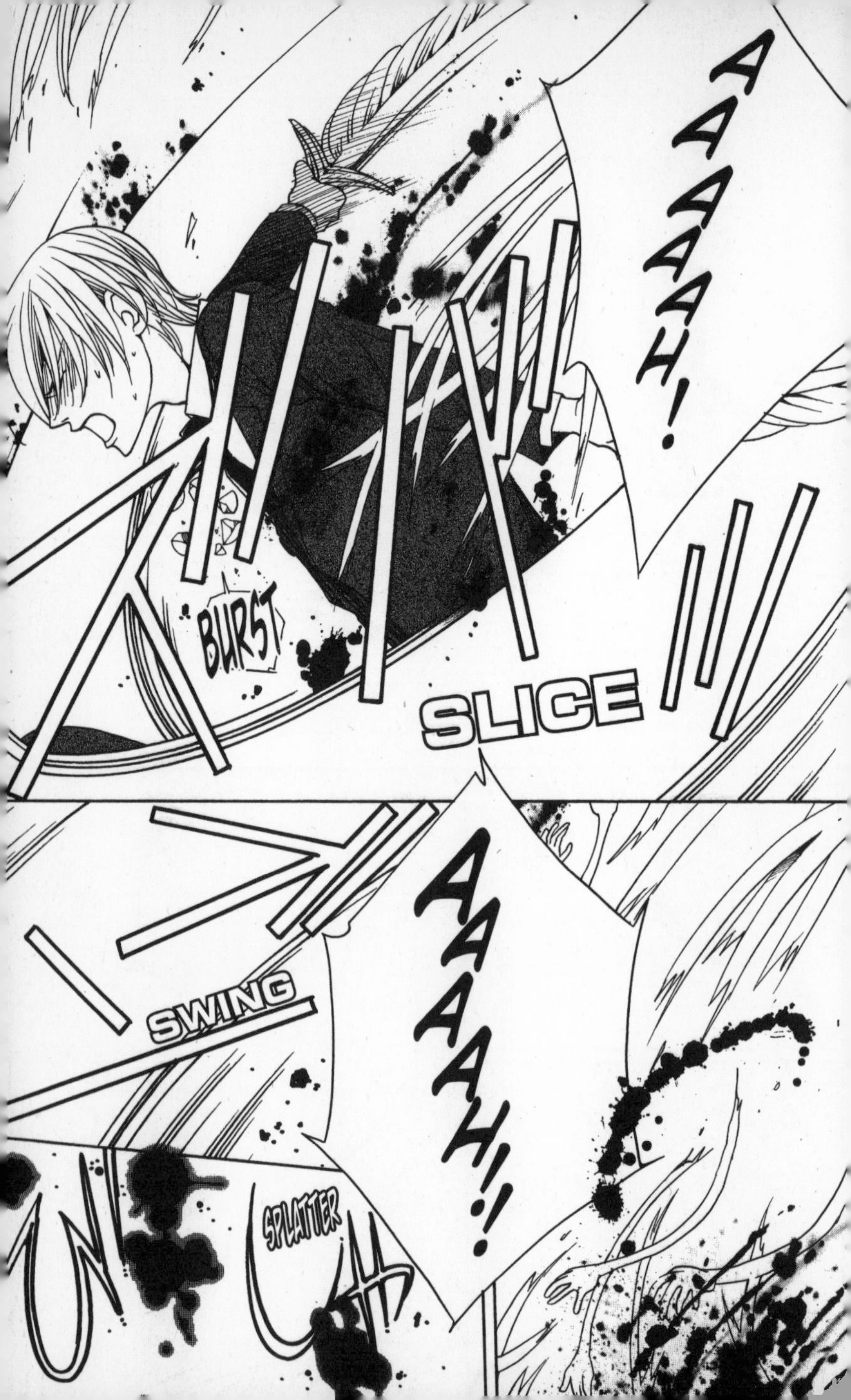
AAAAAAH!
SLICE
BURST
AAAAAH!!!
SWING
SPLATTER

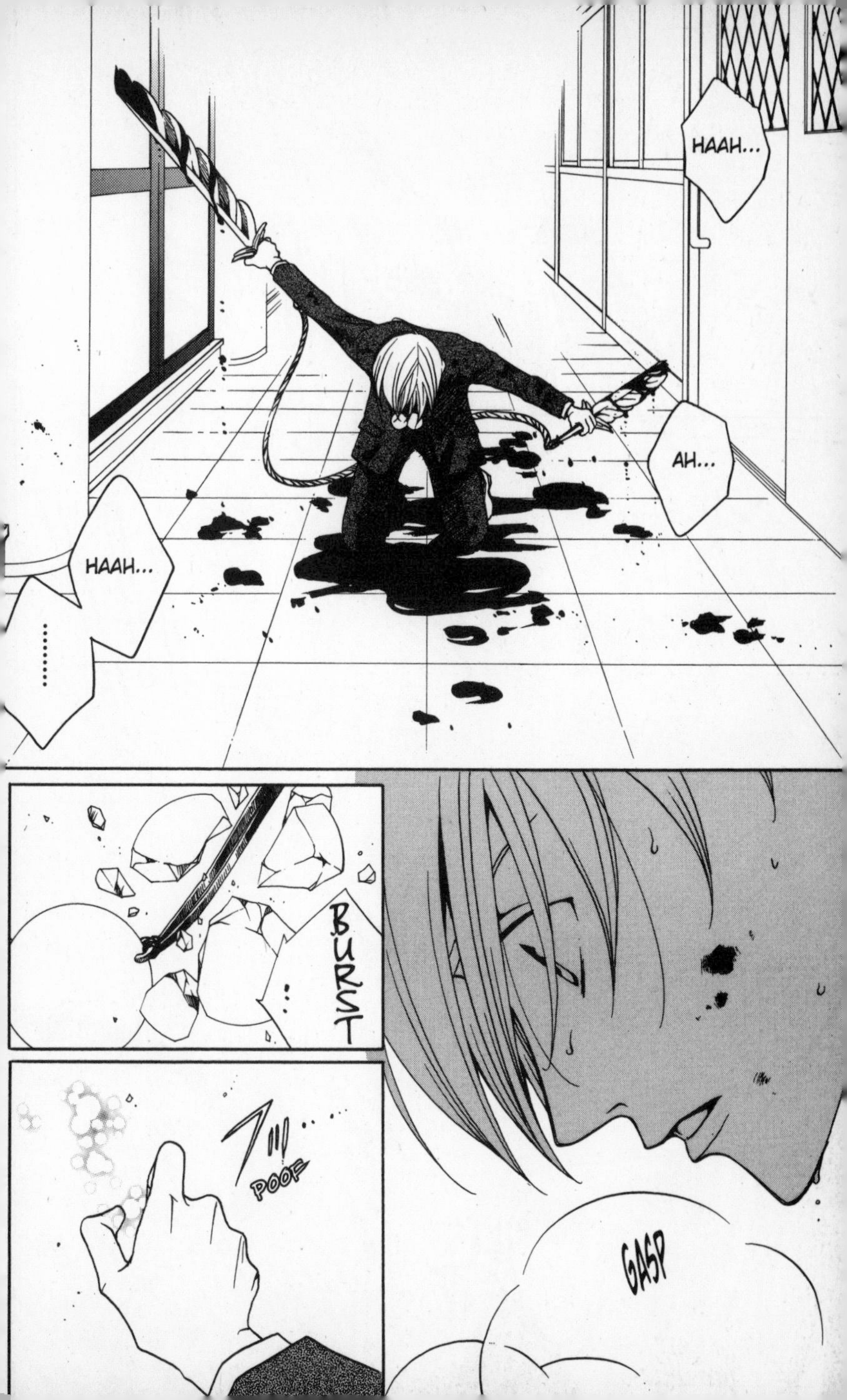
HAAH...
AH...
HAAH...
......
GASP
BURST
POOF

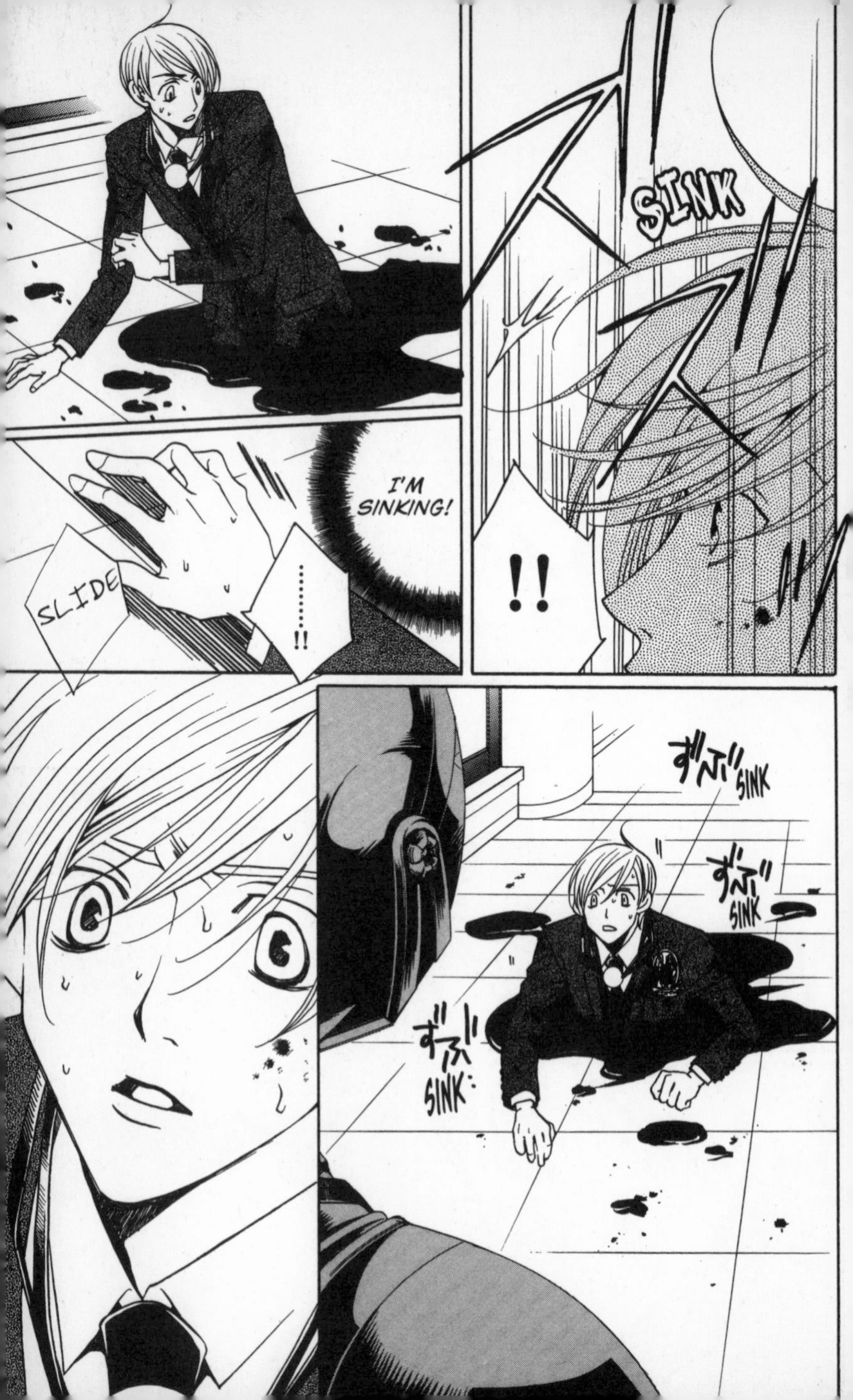

SINK
!!
I'M SINKING!
......!!
SLIDE
ずぶ SINK
ずぶ SINK
ずぶ SINK

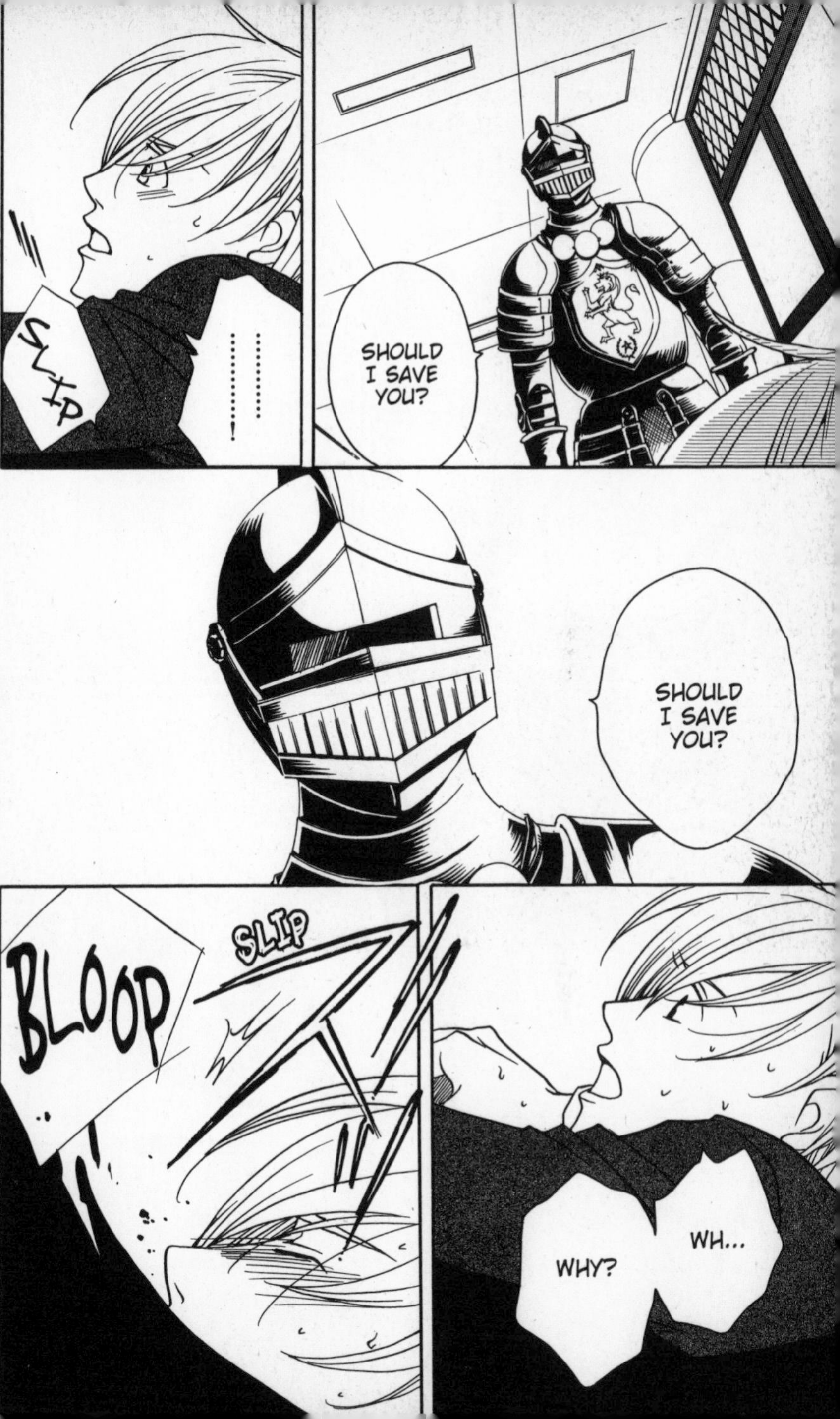
SHOULD I SAVE YOU?
......!
SLIP
SHOULD I SAVE YOU?
WH...
WHY?
SLIP
BLOOP

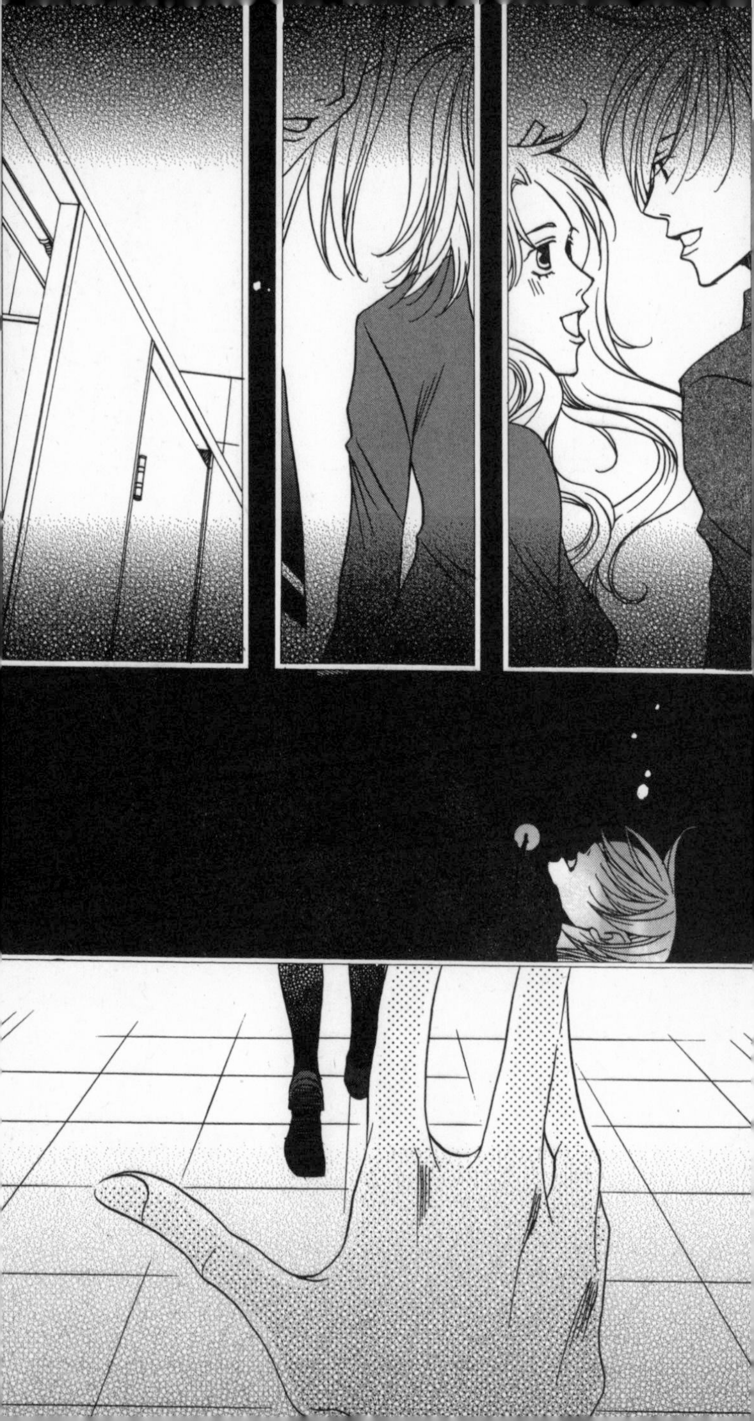

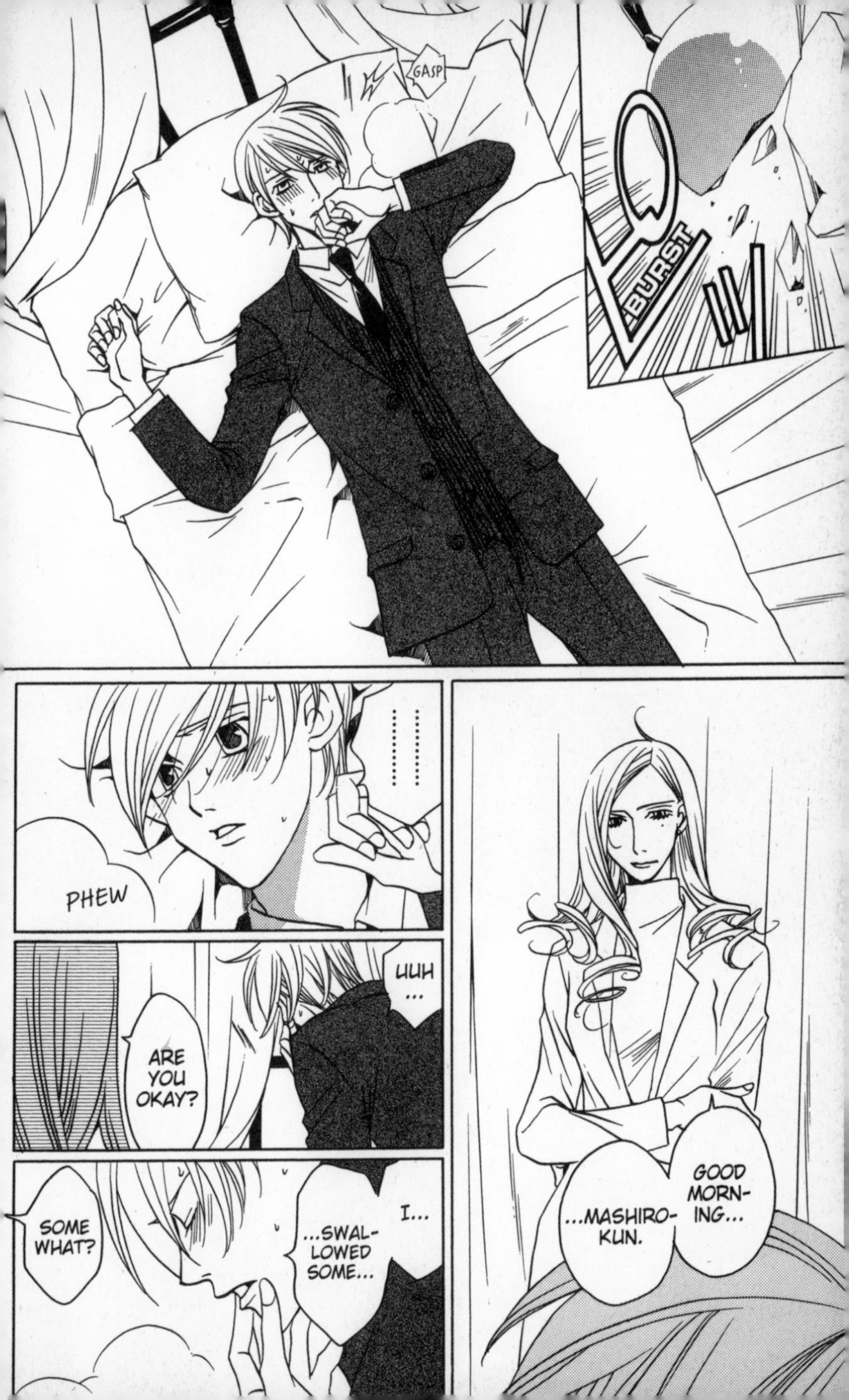
BURST
GASP
GOOD MORN-ING...
...MASHIRO-KUN.
......
PHEW
UUH...
ARE YOU OKAY?
I...
...SWAL-LOWED SOME...
SOME WHAT?

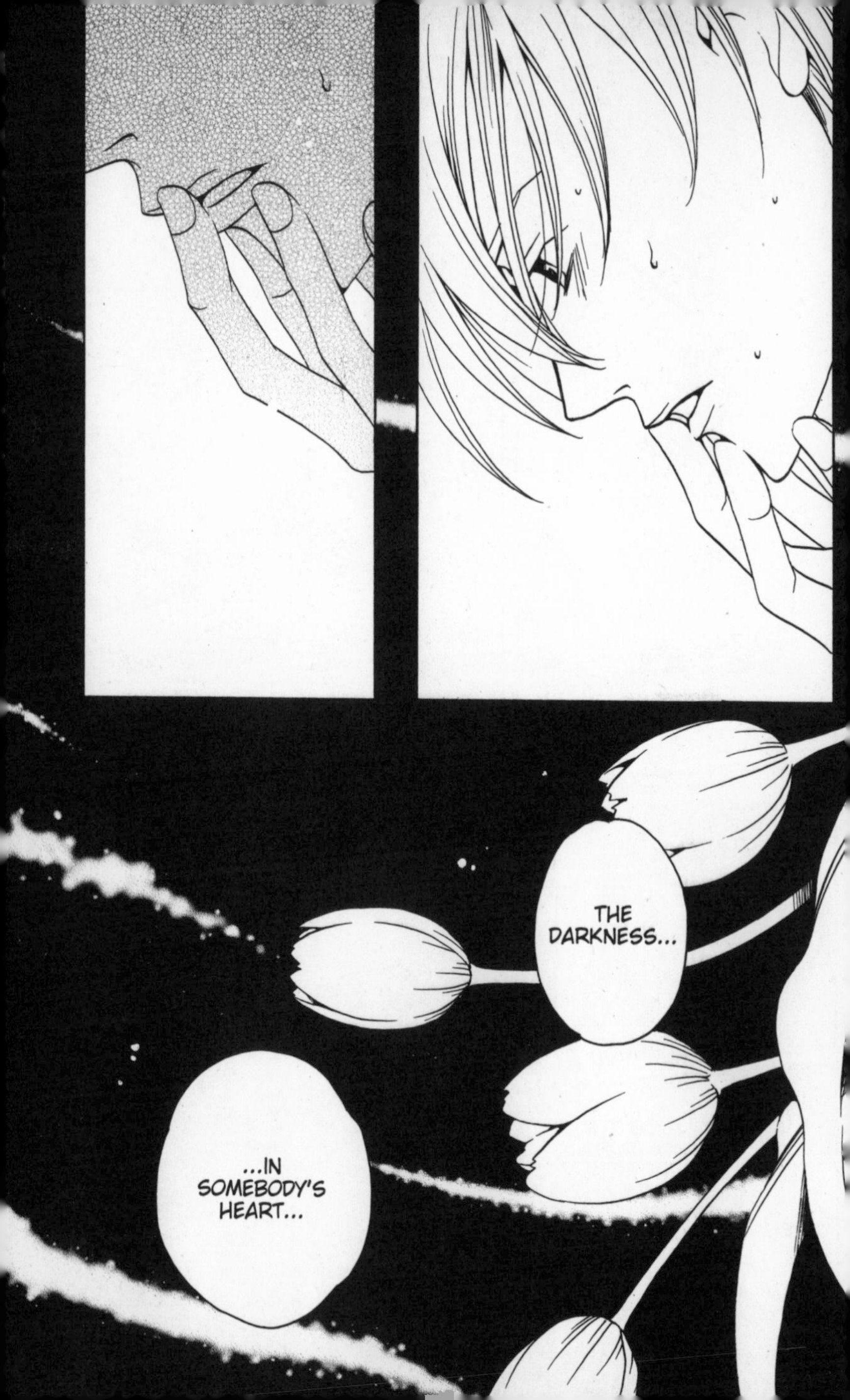
THE DARKNESS...
...IN SOMEBODY'S HEART...

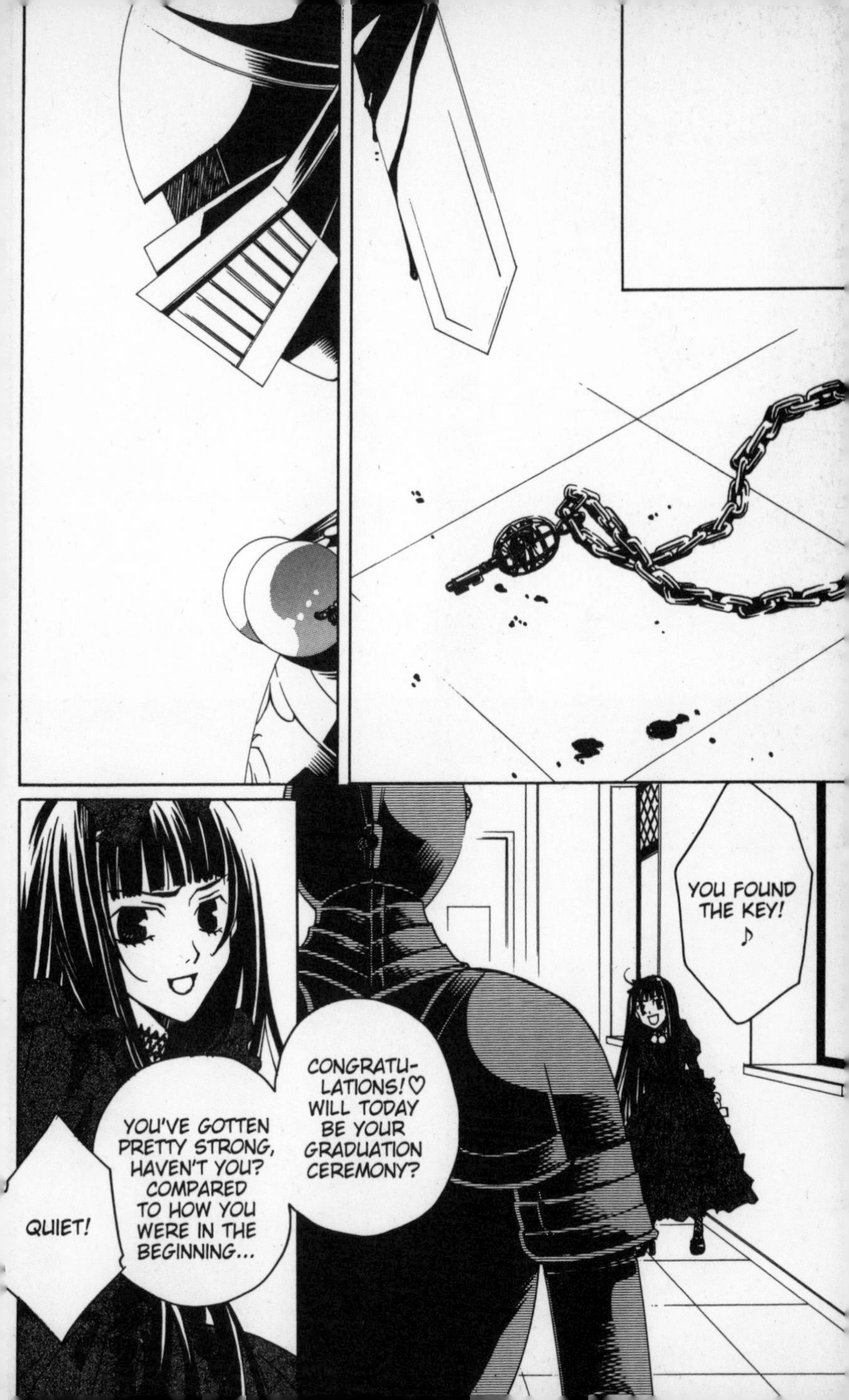
YOU FOUND THE KEY! ♪
CONGRATULATIONS!♡ WILL TODAY BE YOUR GRADUATION CEREMONY?
YOU'VE GOTTEN PRETTY STRONG, HAVEN'T YOU? COMPARED TO HOW YOU WERE IN THE BEGINNING...
QUIET!

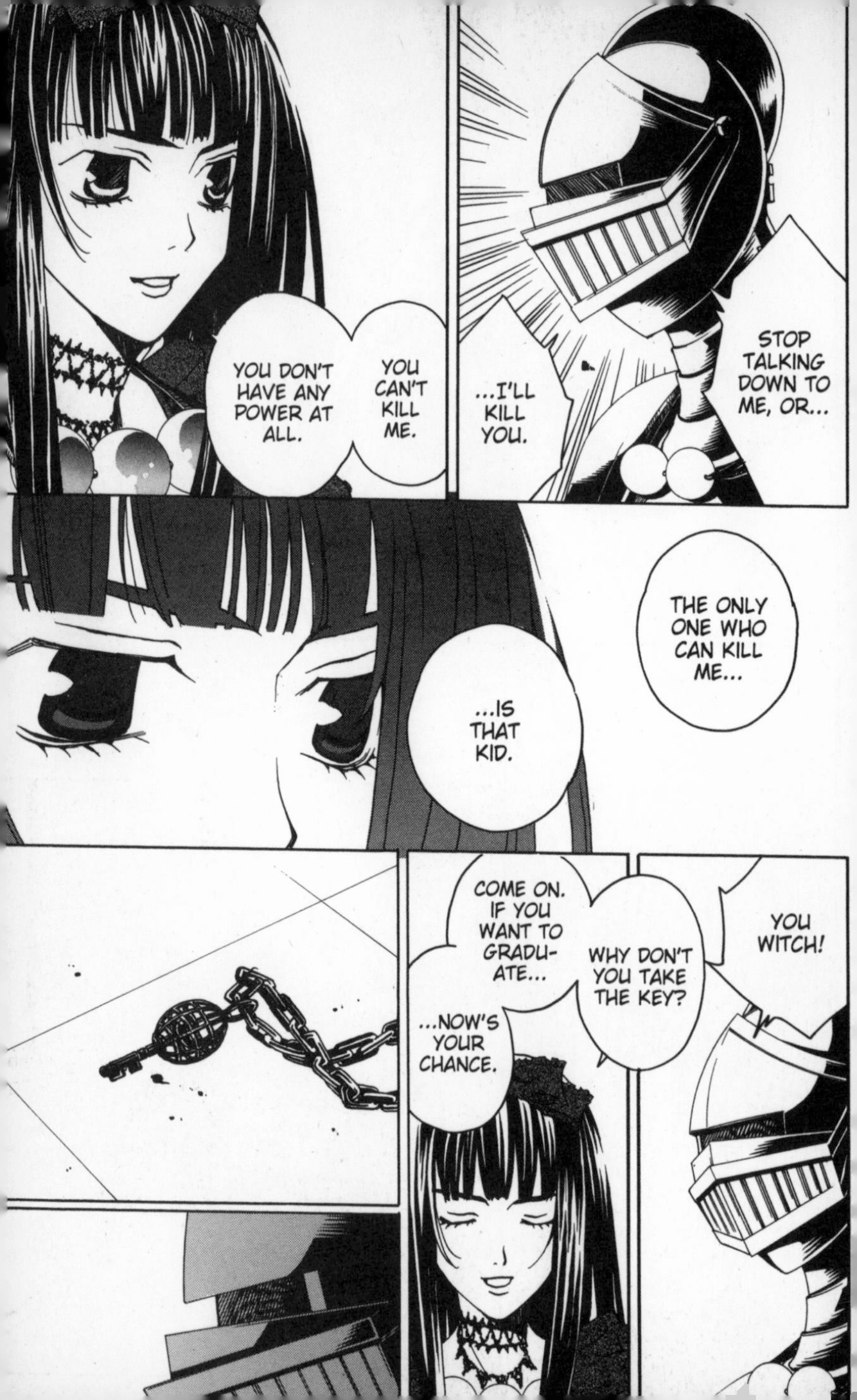
STOP TALKING DOWN TO ME, OR...
...I'LL KILL YOU.
YOU CAN'T KILL ME.
YOU DON'T HAVE ANY POWER AT ALL.
THE ONLY ONE WHO CAN KILL ME...
...IS THAT KID.
YOU WITCH!
COME ON. IF YOU WANT TO GRADU-ATE...
WHY DON'T YOU TAKE THE KEY?
...NOW'S YOUR CHANCE.

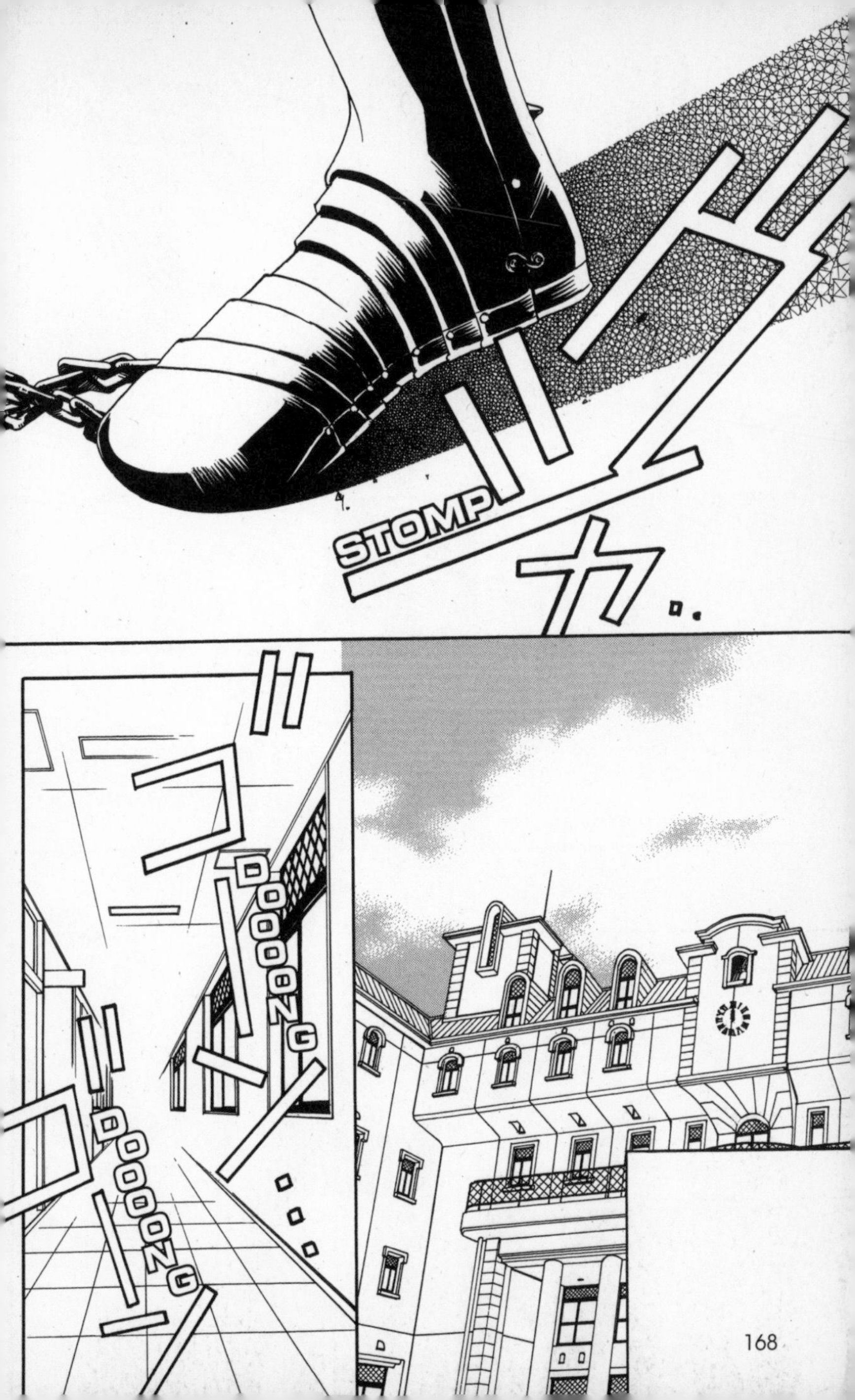
STOMP
DOOOONG
DOOOONG

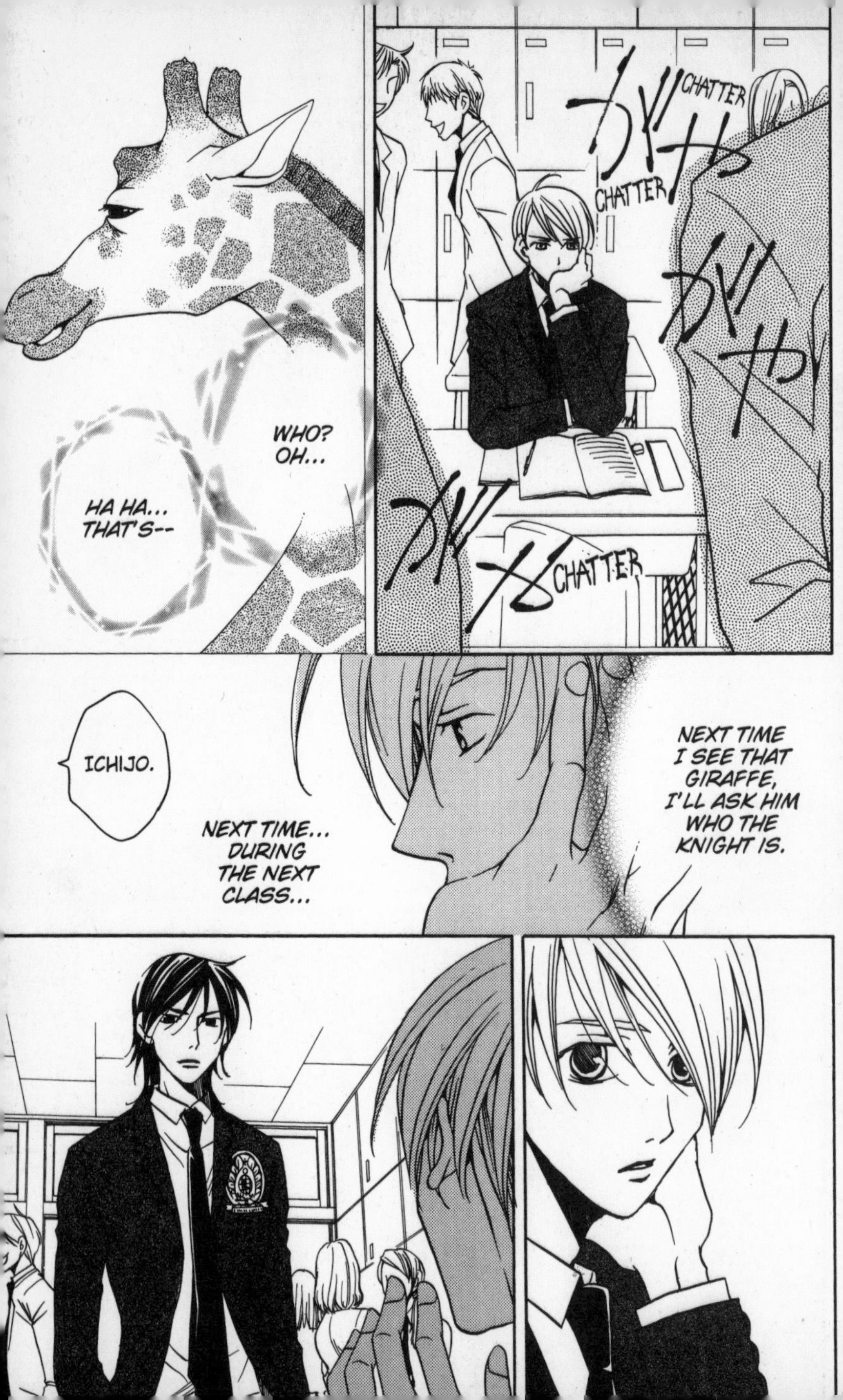
CHATTER
CHATTER
CHATTER
WHO? OH...
HA HA... THAT'S--
NEXT TIME I SEE THAT GIRAFFE, I'LL ASK HIM WHO THE KNIGHT IS.
NEXT TIME... DURING THE NEXT CLASS...
ICHIJO.

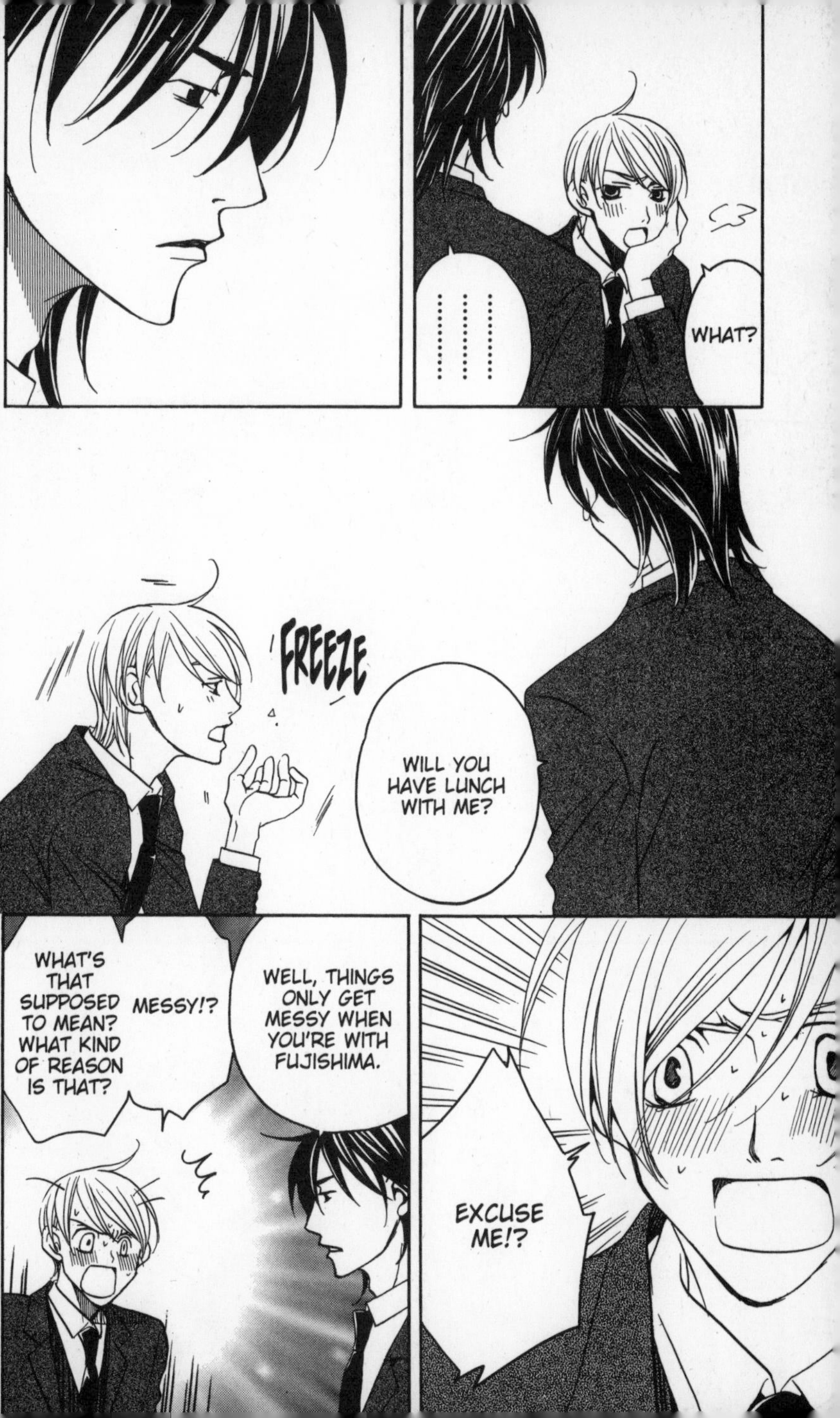
WHAT?
......
WILL YOU HAVE LUNCH WITH ME?
FREEZE
EXCUSE ME!?
WELL, THINGS ONLY GET MESSY WHEN YOU'RE WITH FUJISHIMA.
MESSY!?
WHAT'S THAT SUPPOSED TO MEAN? WHAT KIND OF REASON IS THAT?

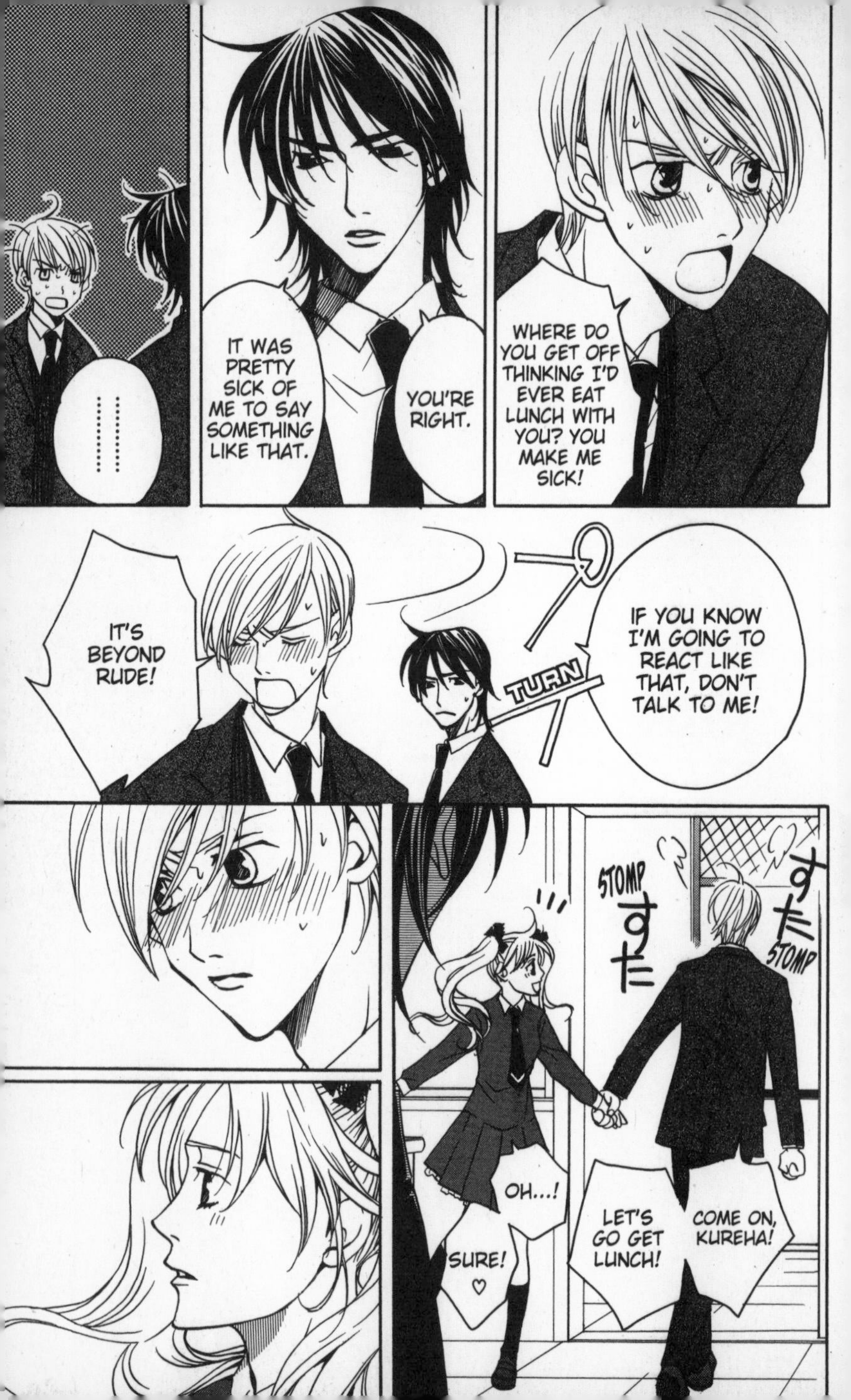
WHERE DO YOU GET OFF THINKING I'D EVER EAT LUNCH WITH YOU? YOU MAKE ME SICK!
YOU'RE RIGHT.
IT WAS PRETTY SICK OF ME TO SAY SOMETHING LIKE THAT.
......
IF YOU KNOW I'M GOING TO REACT LIKE THAT, DON'T TALK TO ME!
TURN
IT'S BEYOND RUDE!
すた
STOMP
STOMP
すた
COME ON, KUREHA!
LET'S GO GET LUNCH!
OH...!
SURE! ♥

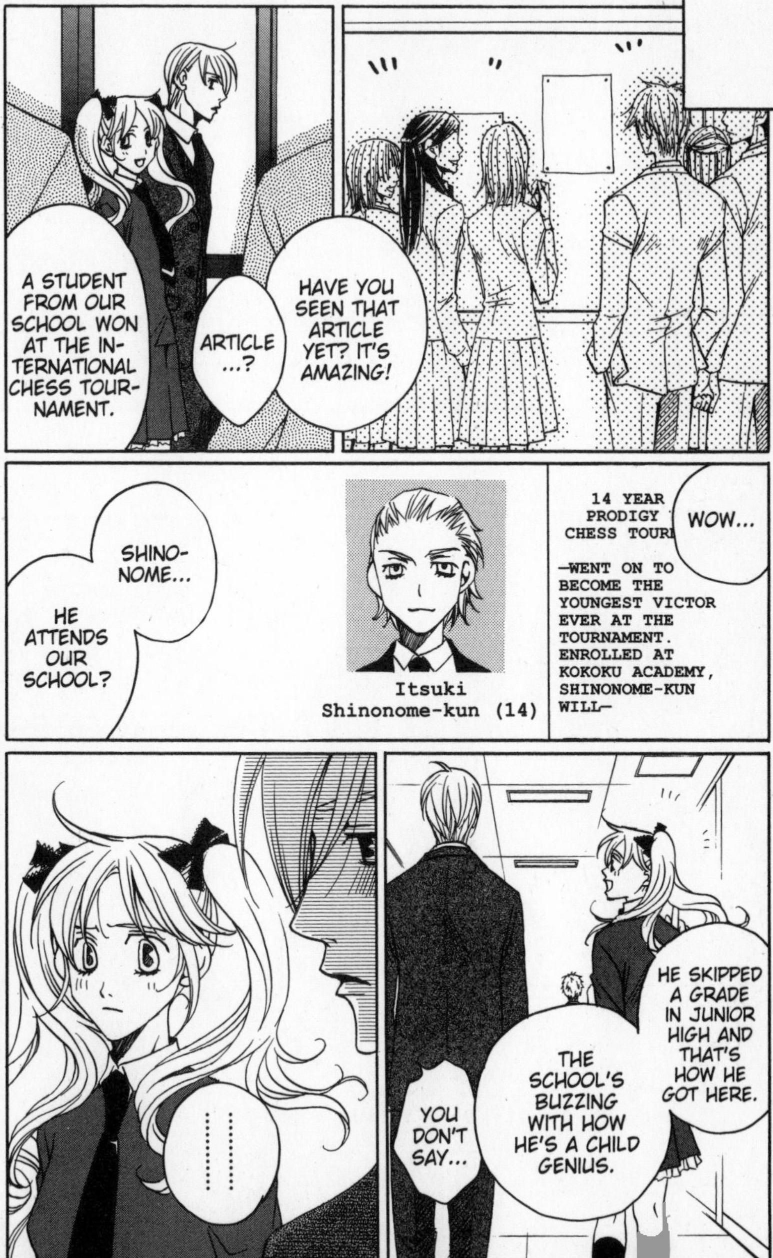
HAVE YOU SEEN THAT ARTICLE YET? IT'S AMAZING!
ARTICLE...?
A STUDENT FROM OUR SCHOOL WON AT THE INTERNATIONAL CHESS TOURNAMENT.
14 YEAR PRODIGY
CHESS TOUR
—WENT ON TO BECOME THE YOUNGEST VICTOR EVER AT THE TOURNAMENT. ENROLLED AT KOKOKU ACADEMY, SHINONOME-KUN WILL—
WOW...
Itsuki Shinonome-kun (14)
SHINONOME...
HE ATTENDS OUR SCHOOL?
HE SKIPPED A GRADE IN JUNIOR HIGH AND THAT'S HOW HE GOT HERE.
THE SCHOOL'S BUZZING WITH HOW HE'S A CHILD GENIUS.
YOU DON'T SAY...
......

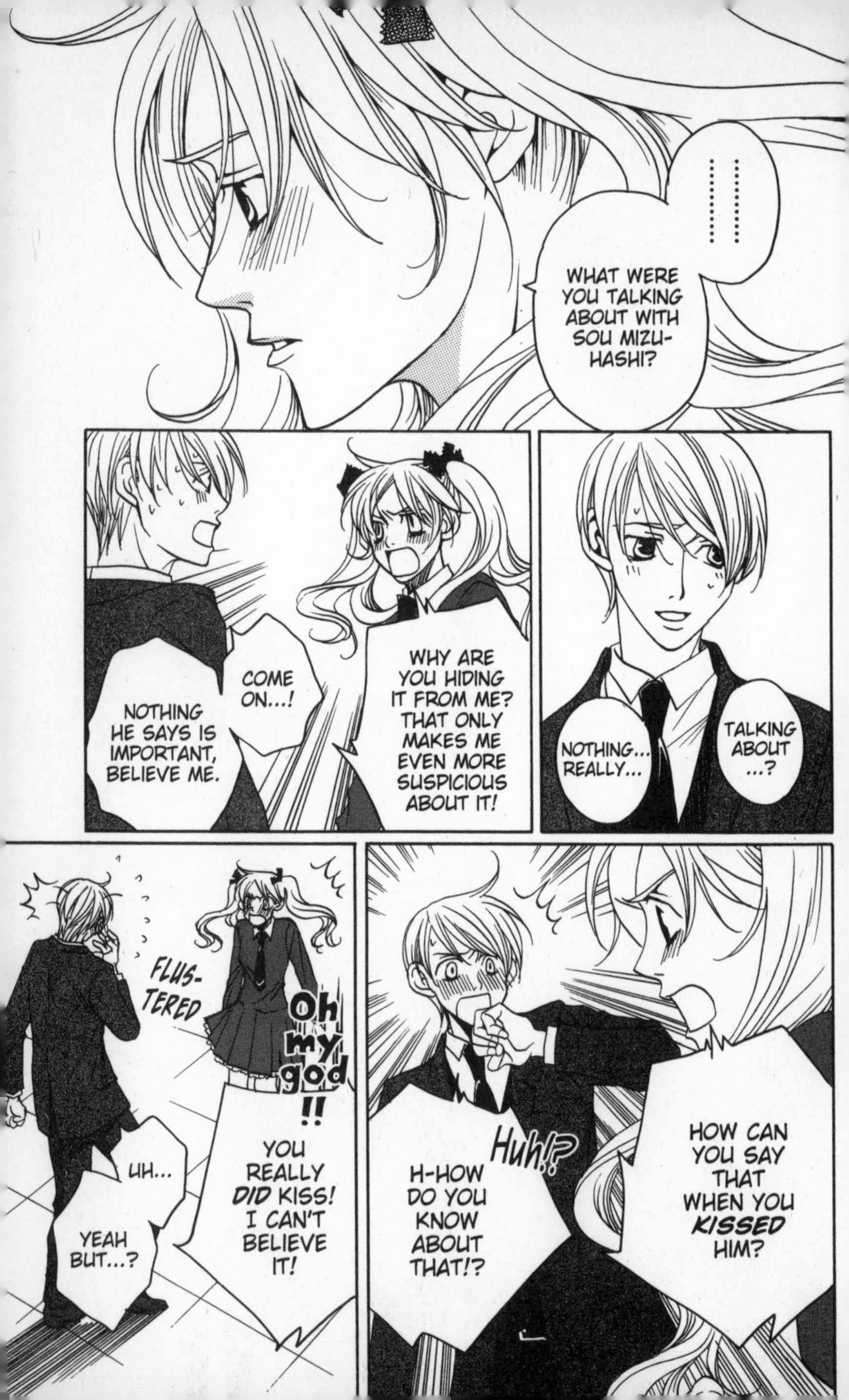
……
WHAT WERE YOU TALKING ABOUT WITH SOU MIZUHASHI?
TALKING ABOUT ...?
NOTHING... REALLY...
WHY ARE YOU HIDING IT FROM ME? THAT ONLY MAKES ME EVEN MORE SUSPICIOUS ABOUT IT!
COME ON...!
NOTHING HE SAYS IS IMPORTANT, BELIEVE ME.
HOW CAN YOU SAY THAT WHEN YOU KISSED HIM?
Huh!?
H-HOW DO YOU KNOW ABOUT THAT!?
Oh my god!!
YOU REALLY DID KISS! I CAN'T BELIEVE IT!
FLUSTERED
UH...
YEAH BUT...?

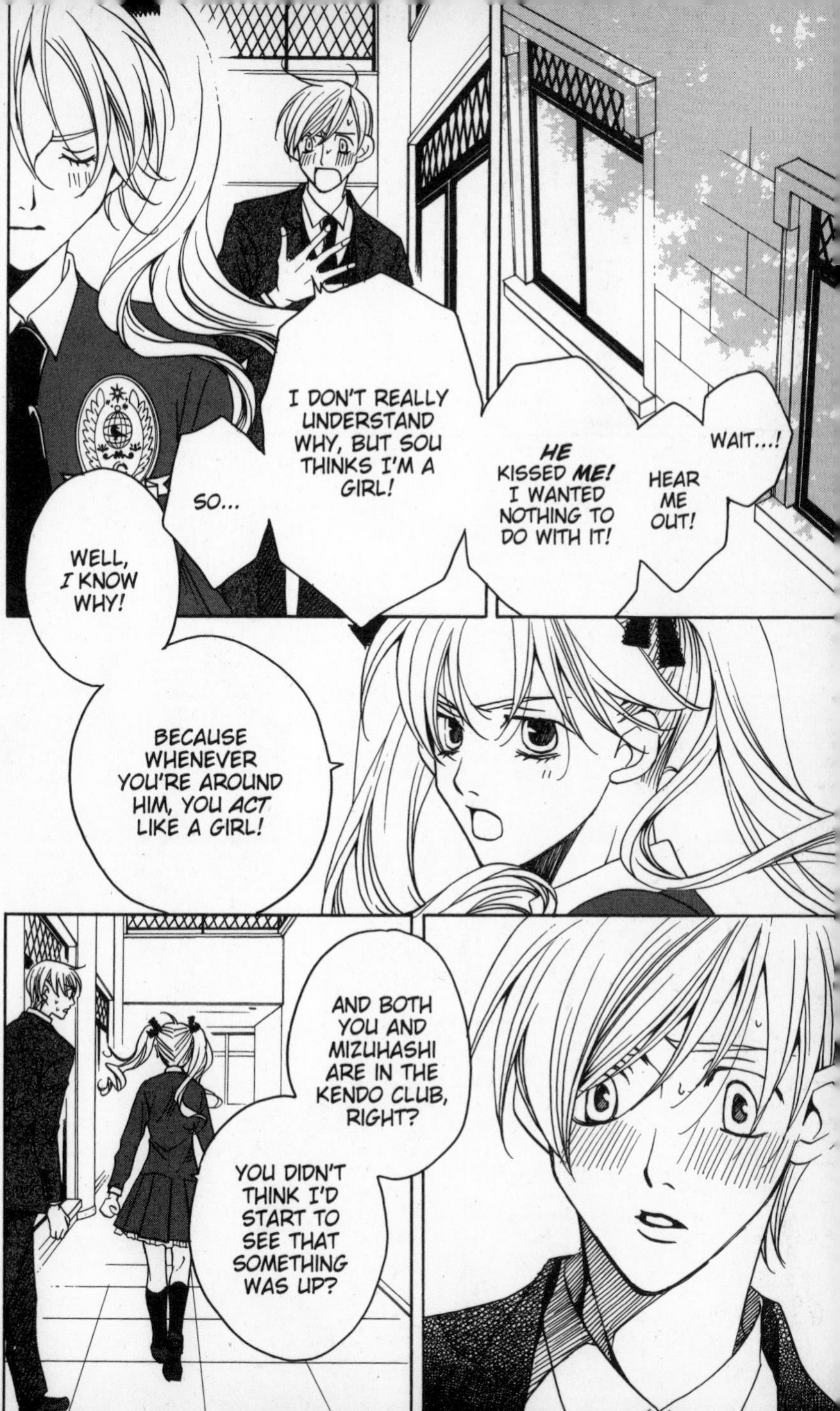
WAIT...!
HEAR ME OUT!
HE KISSED ME! I WANTED NOTHING TO DO WITH IT!
I DON'T REALLY UNDERSTAND WHY, BUT SOU THINKS I'M A GIRL!
SO...
WELL, I KNOW WHY!
BECAUSE WHENEVER YOU'RE AROUND HIM, YOU ACT LIKE A GIRL!
AND BOTH YOU AND MIZUHASHI ARE IN THE KENDO CLUB, RIGHT?
YOU DIDN'T THINK I'D START TO SEE THAT SOMETHING WAS UP?

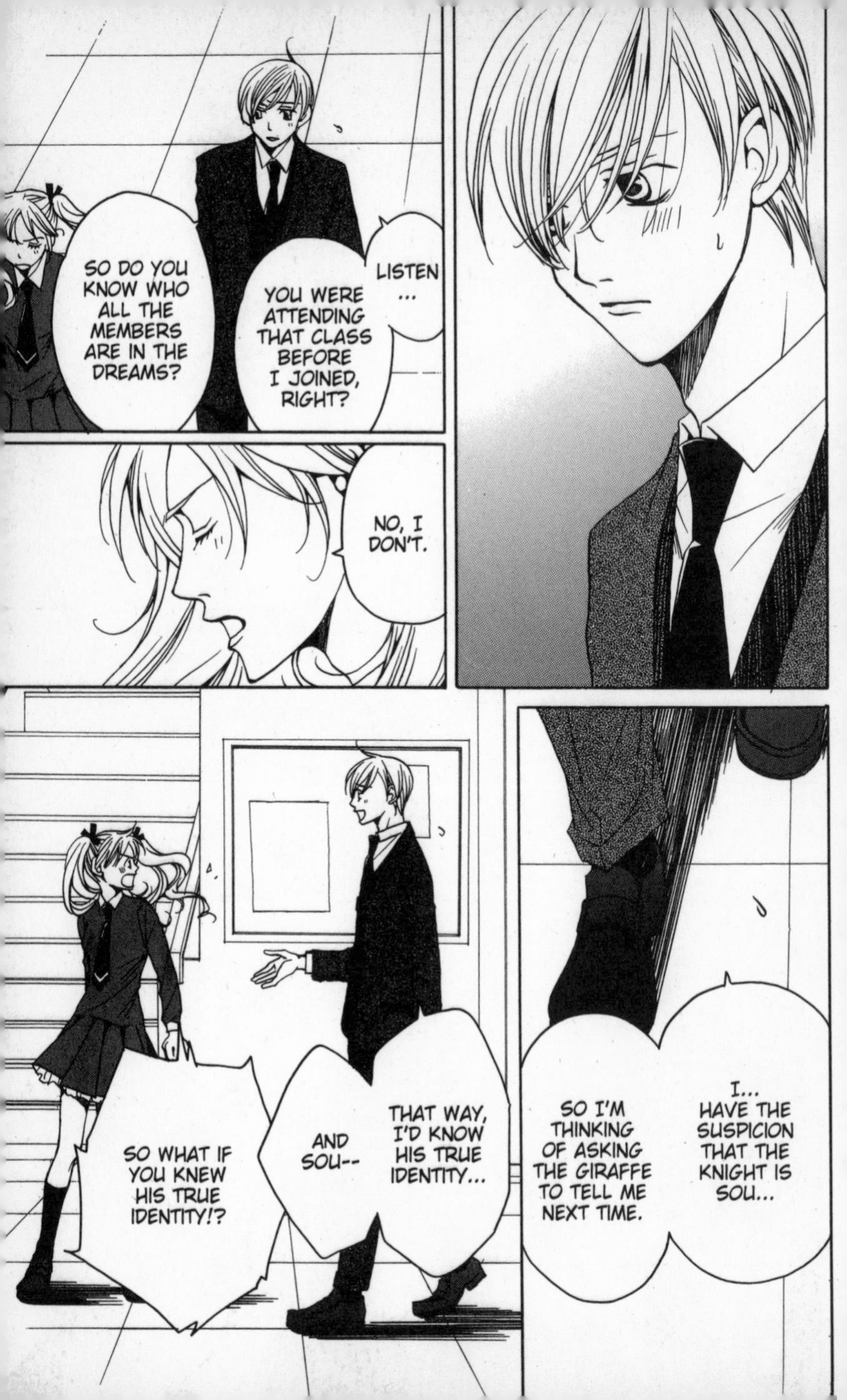
LISTEN...
YOU WERE ATTENDING THAT CLASS BEFORE I JOINED, RIGHT?
SO DO YOU KNOW WHO ALL THE MEMBERS ARE IN THE DREAMS?
NO, I DON'T.
I... HAVE THE SUSPICION THAT THE KNIGHT IS SOU...
SO I'M THINKING OF ASKING THE GIRAFFE TO TELL ME NEXT TIME.
THAT WAY, I'D KNOW HIS TRUE IDENTITY...
AND SOU--
SO WHAT IF YOU KNEW HIS TRUE IDENTITY!?

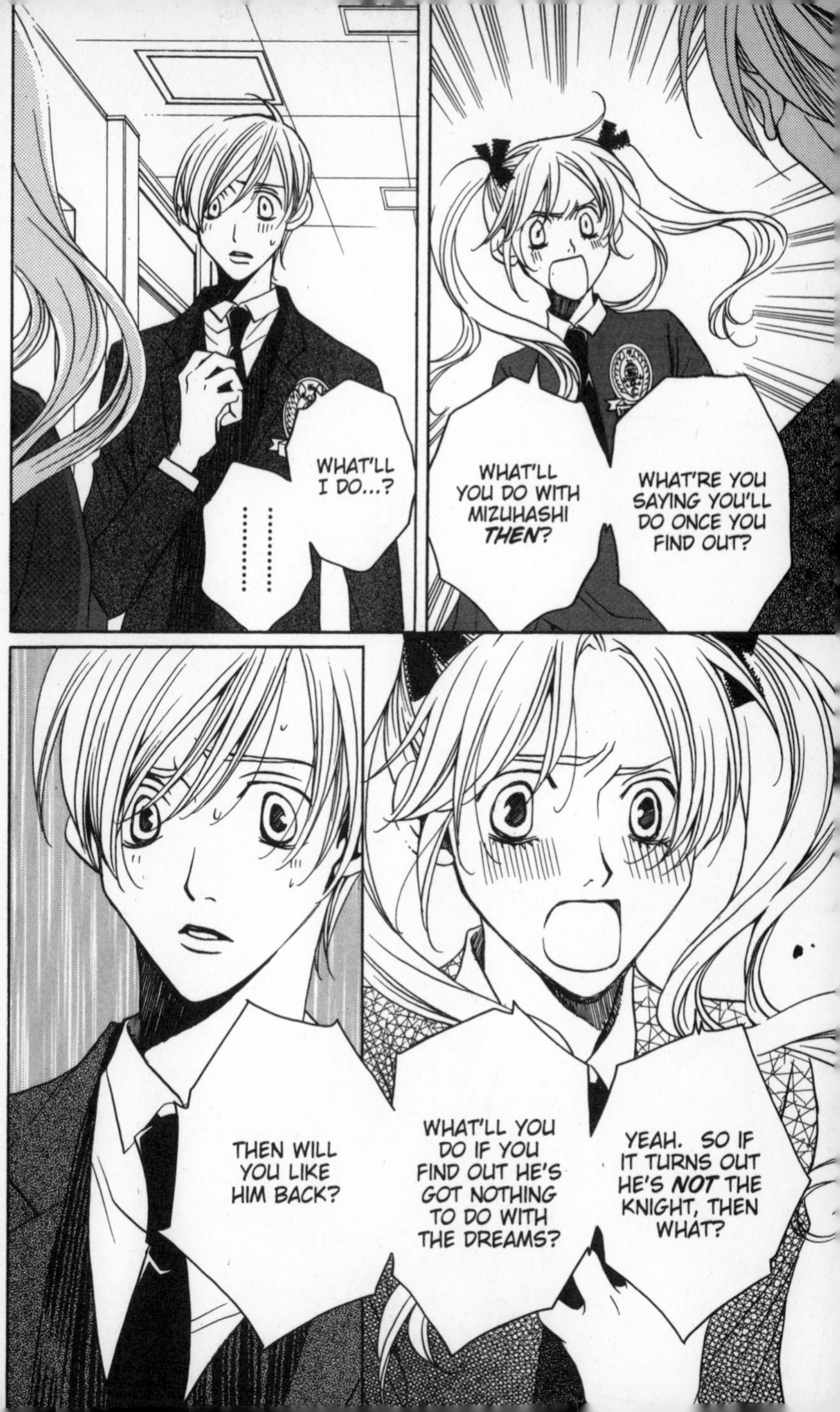
WHAT'RE YOU SAYING YOU'LL DO ONCE YOU FIND OUT?
WHAT'LL YOU DO WITH MIZUHASHI *THEN*?
WHAT'LL I DO...?
......
YEAH. SO IF IT TURNS OUT HE'S *NOT* THE KNIGHT, THEN WHAT?
WHAT'LL YOU DO IF YOU FIND OUT HE'S GOT NOTHING TO DO WITH THE DREAMS?
THEN WILL YOU LIKE HIM BACK?

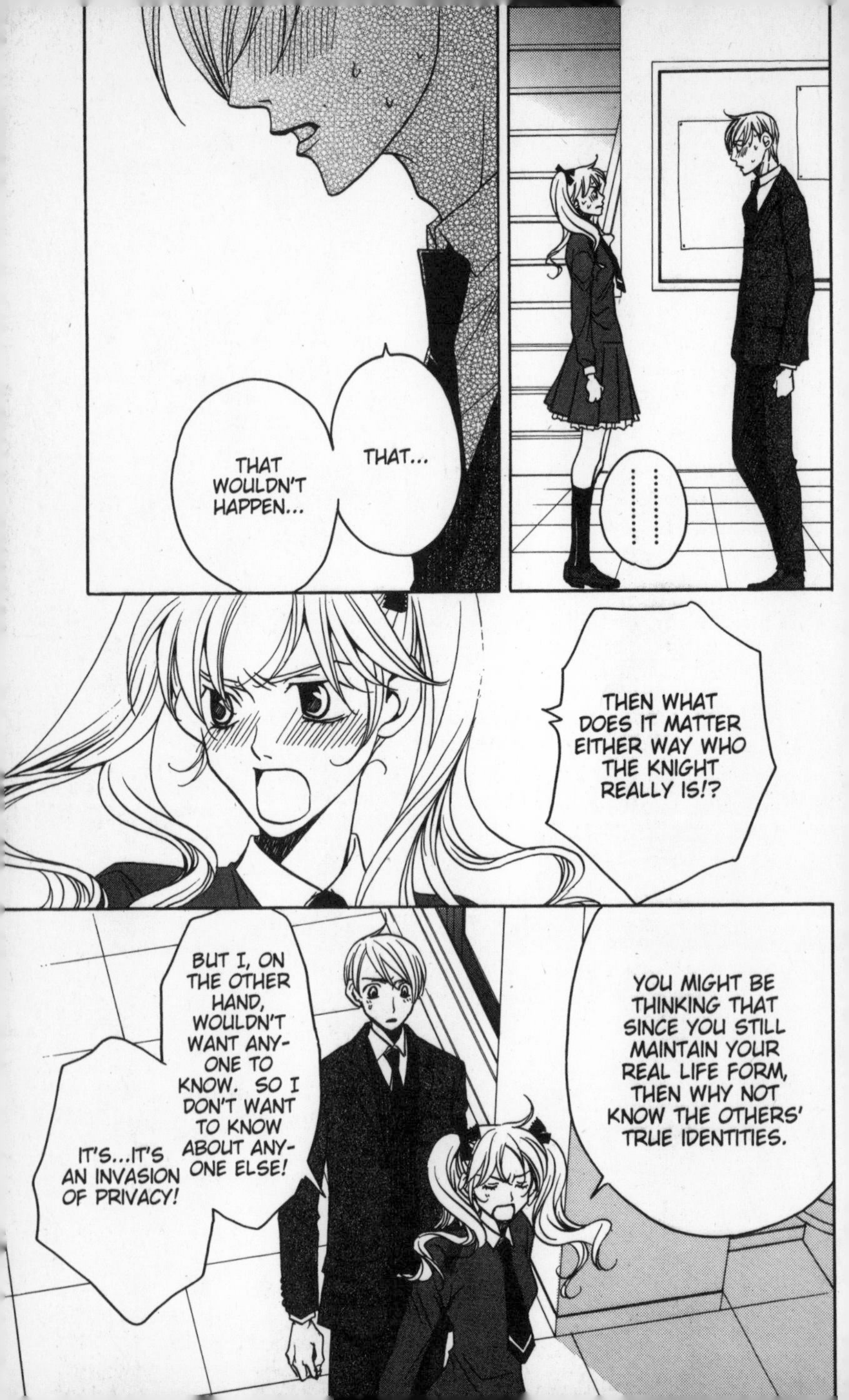
……
THAT...
THAT WOULDN'T HAPPEN...
THEN WHAT DOES IT MATTER EITHER WAY WHO THE KNIGHT REALLY IS!?
YOU MIGHT BE THINKING THAT SINCE YOU STILL MAINTAIN YOUR REAL LIFE FORM, THEN WHY NOT KNOW THE OTHERS' TRUE IDENTITIES.
BUT I, ON THE OTHER HAND, WOULDN'T WANT ANY-ONE TO KNOW. SO I DON'T WANT TO KNOW ABOUT ANY-ONE ELSE!
IT'S...IT'S AN INVASION OF PRIVACY!

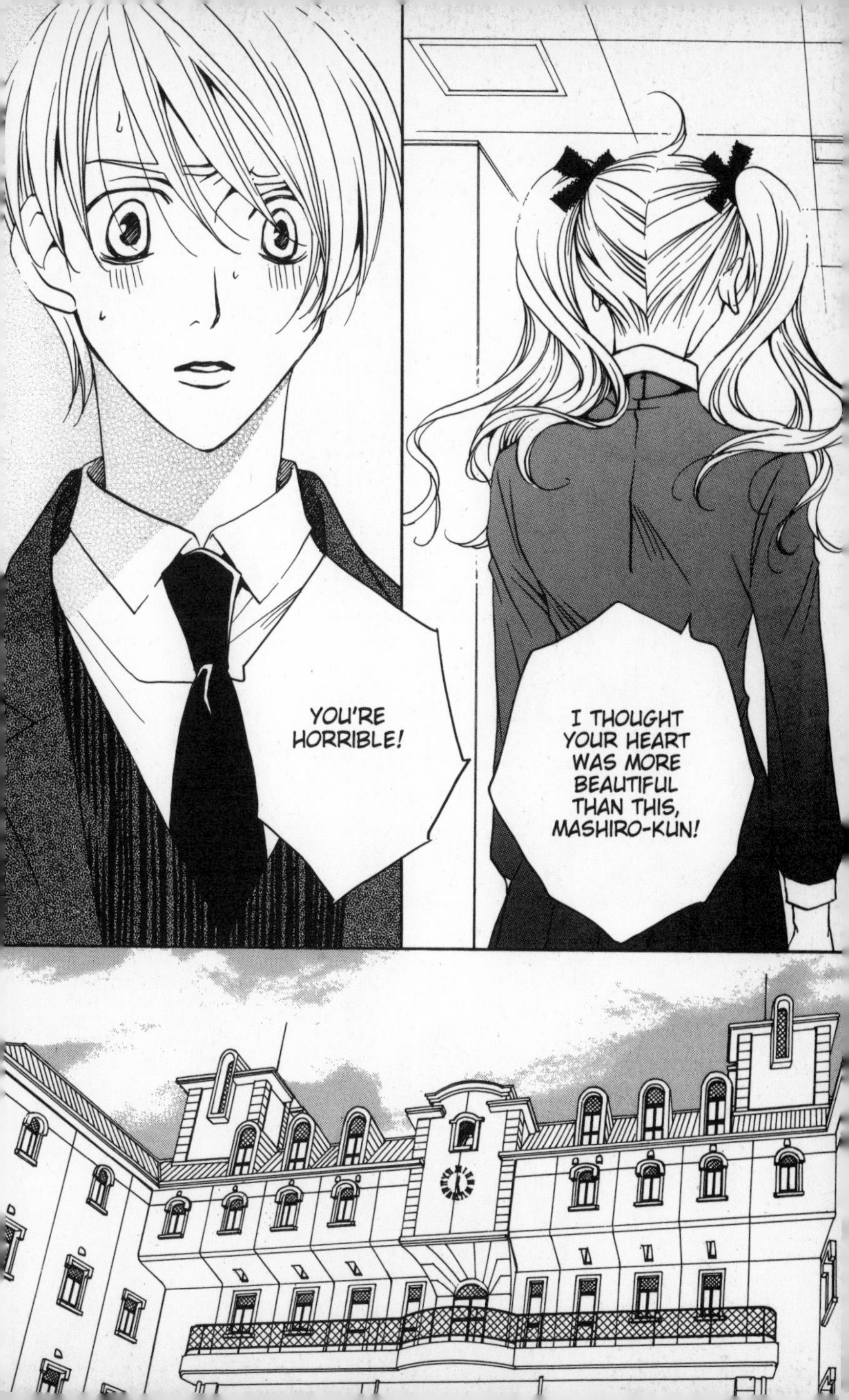
I THOUGHT YOUR HEART WAS MORE BEAUTIFUL THAN THIS, MASHIRO-KUN!
YOU'RE HORRIBLE!

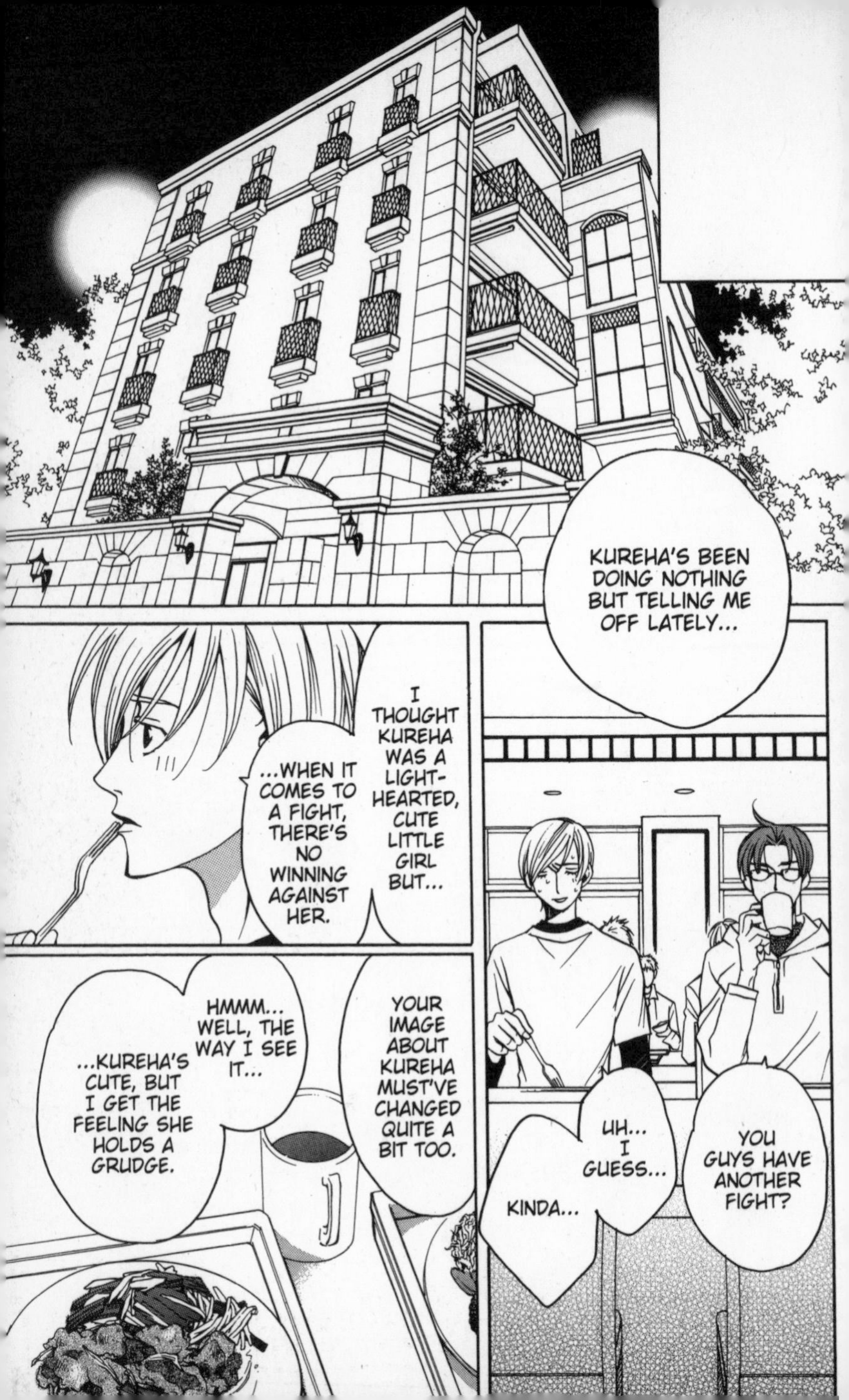
KUREHA'S BEEN DOING NOTHING BUT TELLING ME OFF LATELY...
YOU GUYS HAVE ANOTHER FIGHT?
UH... I GUESS...
KINDA...
I THOUGHT KUREHA WAS A LIGHT-HEARTED, CUTE LITTLE GIRL BUT...
...WHEN IT COMES TO A FIGHT, THERE'S NO WINNING AGAINST HER.
YOUR IMAGE ABOUT KUREHA MUST'VE CHANGED QUITE A BIT TOO.
HMMM... WELL, THE WAY I SEE IT...
...KUREHA'S CUTE, BUT I GET THE FEELING SHE HOLDS A GRUDGE.

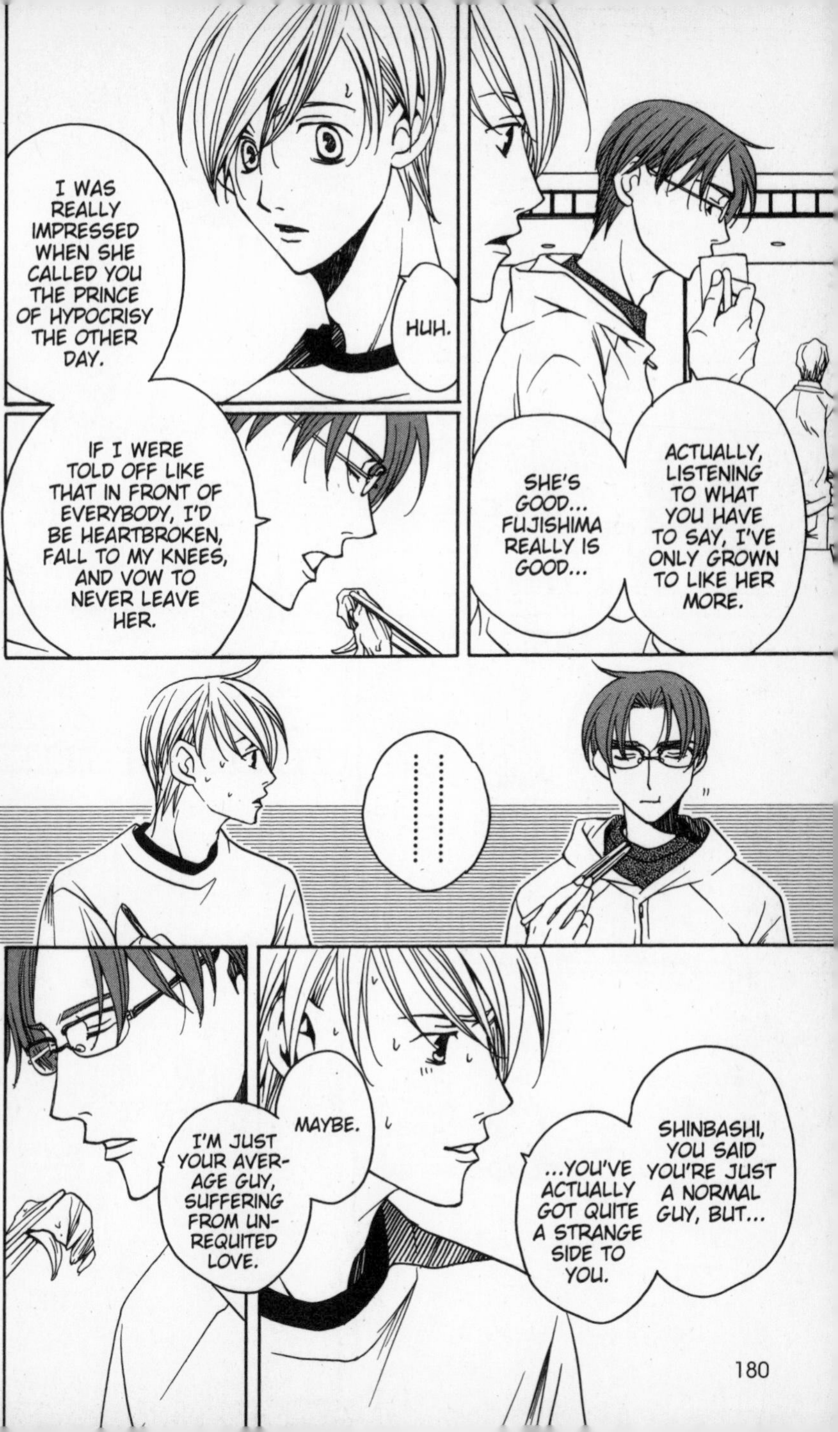
I WAS REALLY IMPRESSED WHEN SHE CALLED YOU THE PRINCE OF HYPOCRISY THE OTHER DAY.
HUH.
IF I WERE TOLD OFF LIKE THAT IN FRONT OF EVERYBODY, I'D BE HEARTBROKEN, FALL TO MY KNEES, AND VOW TO NEVER LEAVE HER.
ACTUALLY, LISTENING TO WHAT YOU HAVE TO SAY, I'VE ONLY GROWN TO LIKE HER MORE.
SHE'S GOOD... FUJISHIMA REALLY IS GOOD...
......
SHINBASHI, YOU SAID YOU'RE JUST A NORMAL GUY, BUT...
...YOU'VE ACTUALLY GOT QUITE A STRANGE SIDE TO YOU.
MAYBE.
I'M JUST YOUR AVER-AGE GUY, SUFFERING FROM UN-REQUITED LOVE.

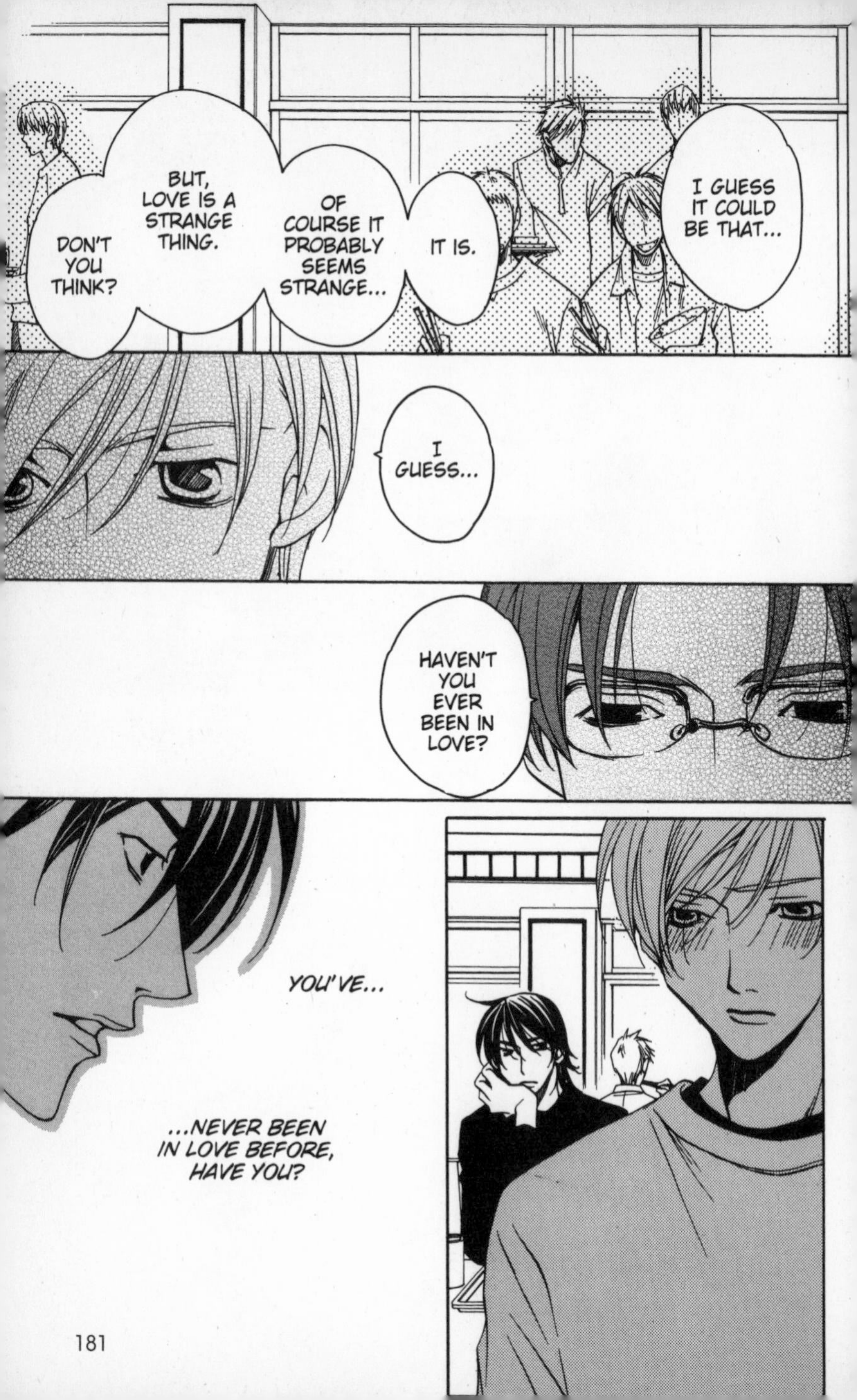
I GUESS IT COULD BE THAT...
IT IS.
OF COURSE IT PROBABLY SEEMS STRANGE...
BUT, LOVE IS A STRANGE THING.
DON'T YOU THINK?
I GUESS...
HAVEN'T YOU EVER BEEN IN LOVE?
YOU'VE...
...NEVER BEEN IN LOVE BEFORE, HAVE YOU?

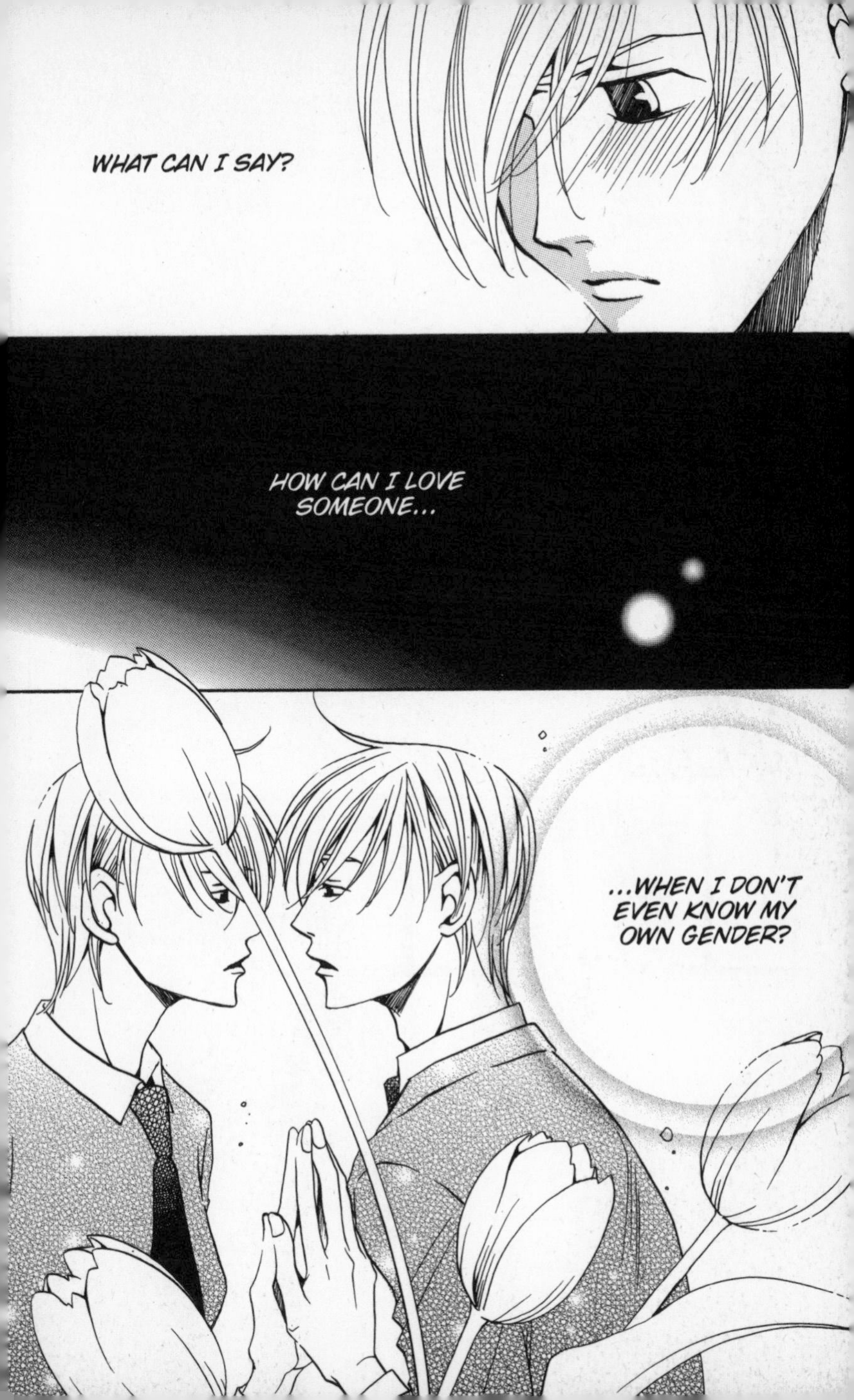
WHAT CAN I SAY?
HOW CAN I LOVE SOMEONE...
...WHEN I DON'T EVEN KNOW MY OWN GENDER?

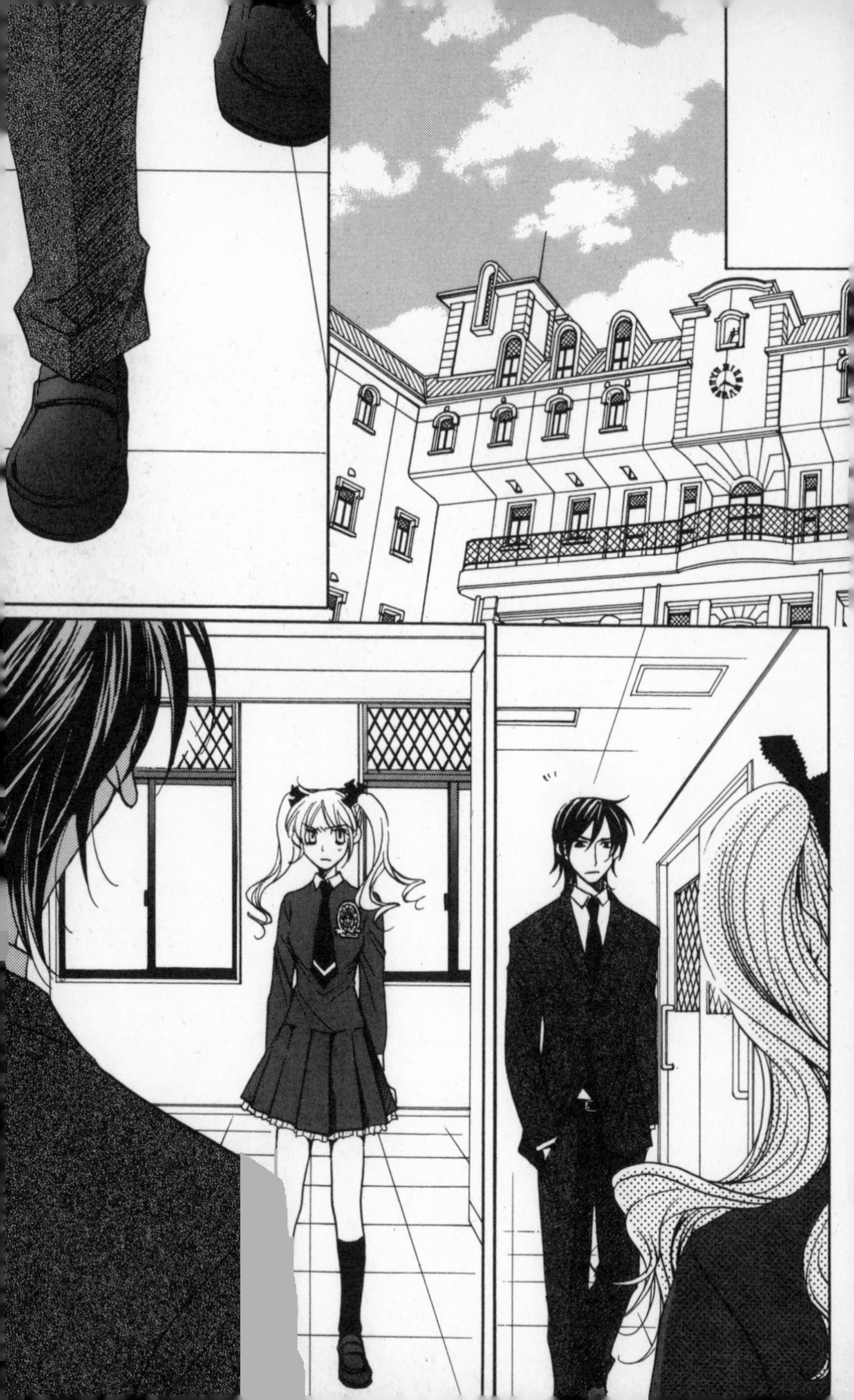

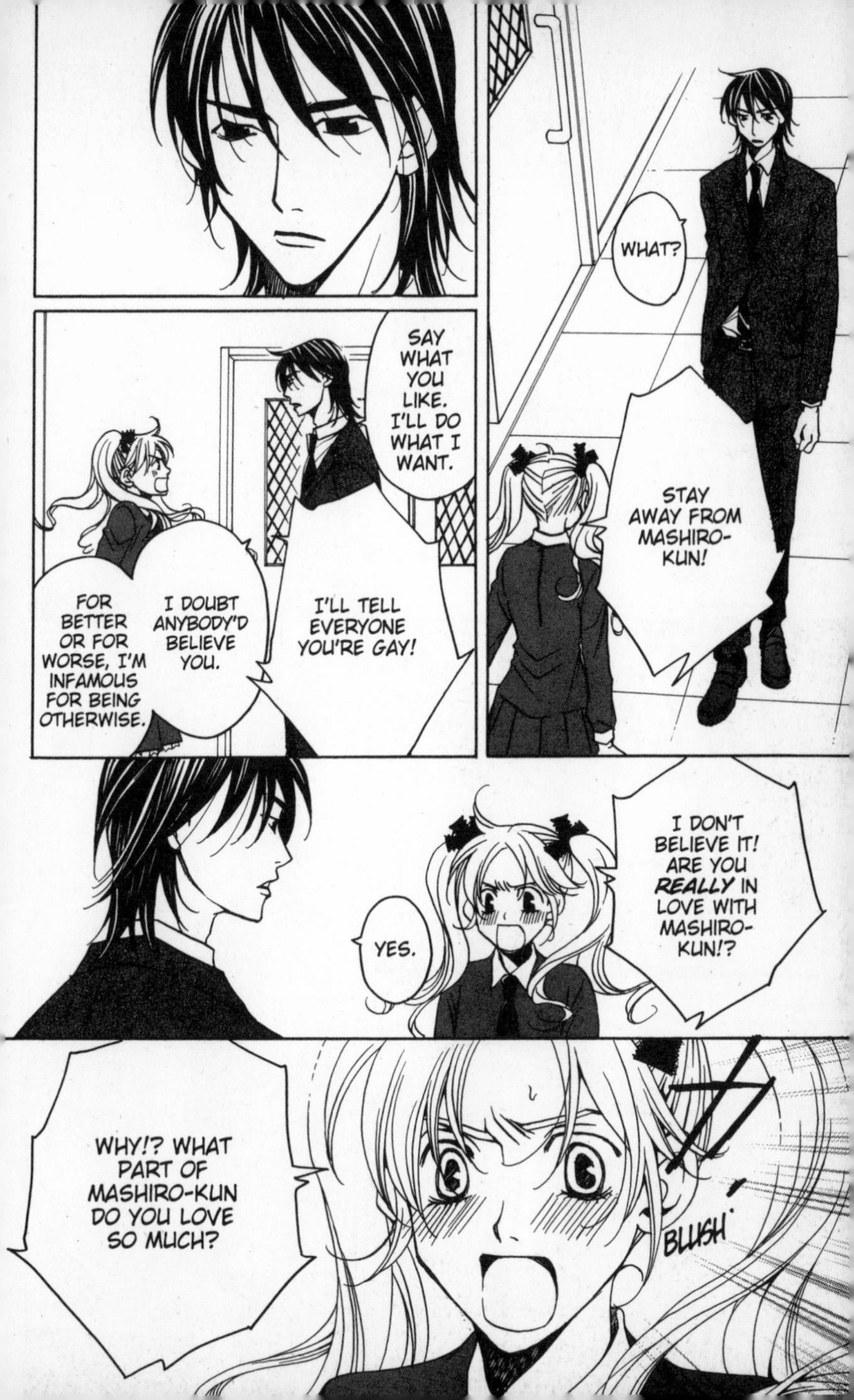
STAY AWAY FROM MASHIRO-KUN!
WHAT?
SAY WHAT YOU LIKE. I'LL DO WHAT I WANT.
I'LL TELL EVERYONE YOU'RE GAY!
I DOUBT ANYBODY'D BELIEVE YOU.
FOR BETTER OR FOR WORSE, I'M INFAMOUS FOR BEING OTHERWISE.
I DON'T BELIEVE IT! ARE YOU *REALLY* IN LOVE WITH MASHIRO-KUN!?
YES.
BLUSH
WHY!? WHAT PART OF MASHIRO-KUN DO YOU LOVE SO MUCH?

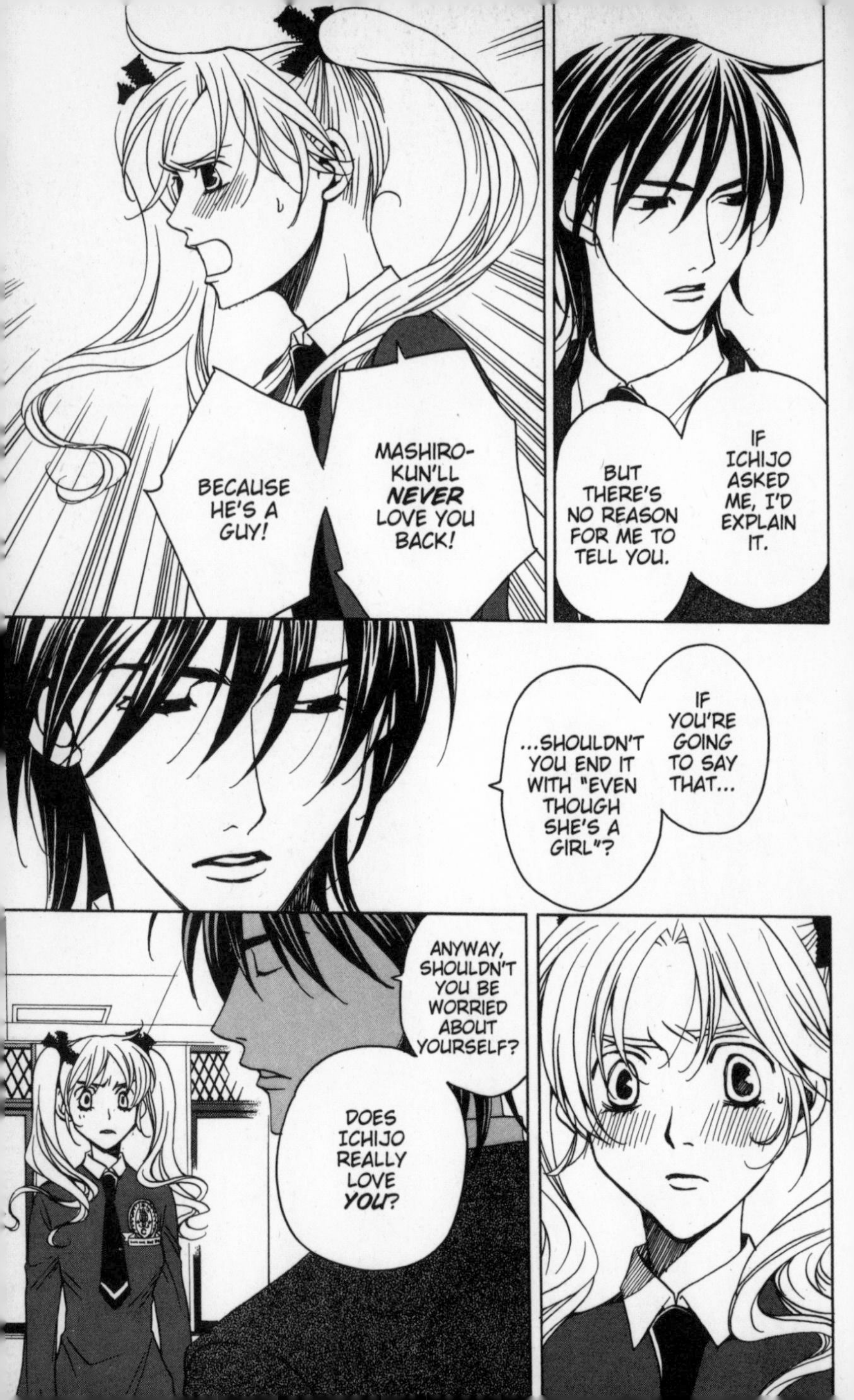
IF ICHIJO ASKED ME, I'D EXPLAIN IT.
BUT THERE'S NO REASON FOR ME TO TELL YOU.
MASHIRO-KUN'LL **NEVER** LOVE YOU BACK!
BECAUSE HE'S A GUY!
IF YOU'RE GOING TO SAY THAT...
...SHOULDN'T YOU END IT WITH "EVEN THOUGH SHE'S A GIRL"?
ANYWAY, SHOULDN'T YOU BE WORRIED ABOUT YOURSELF?
DOES ICHIJO REALLY LOVE **YOU**?

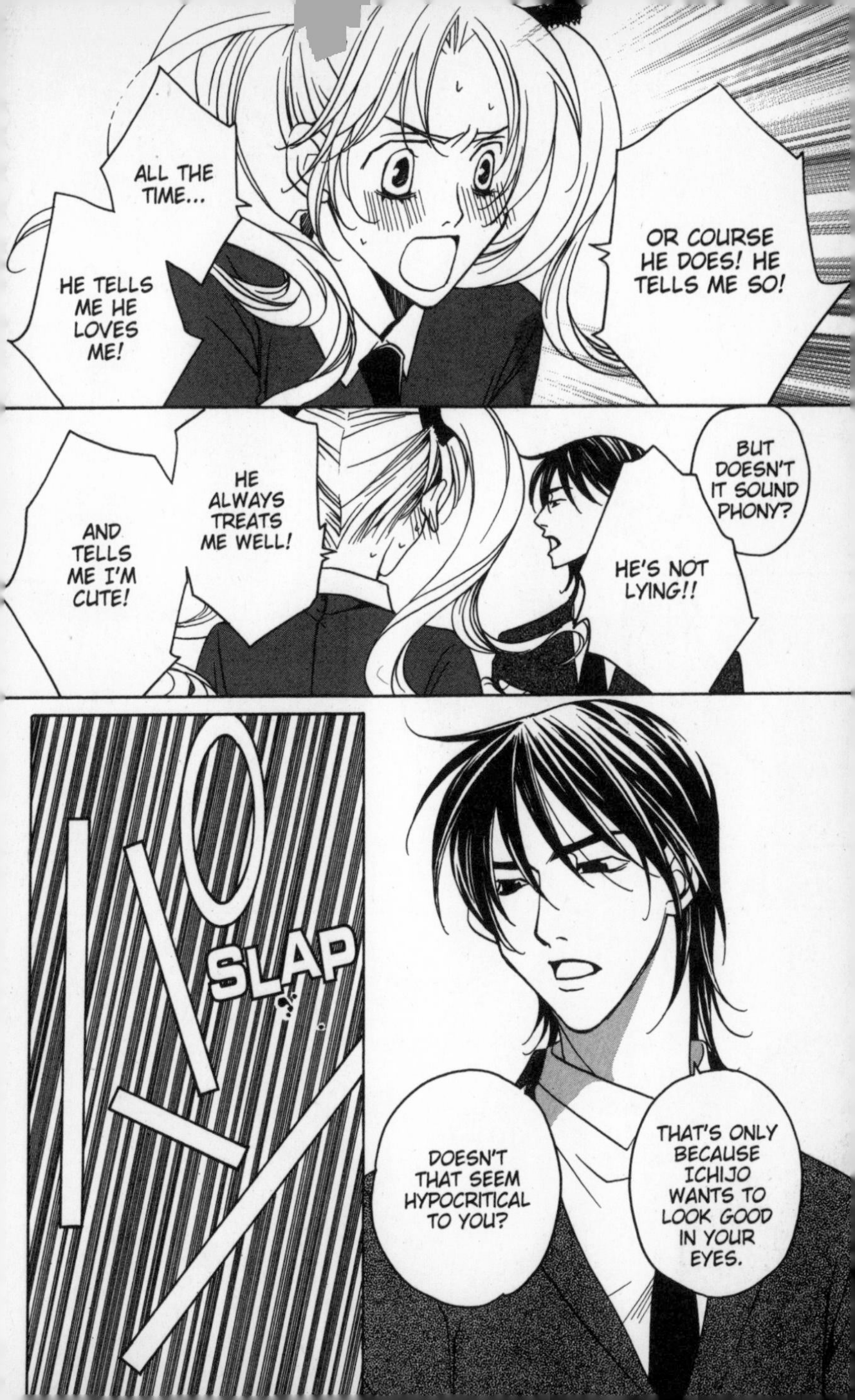
OR COURSE HE DOES! HE TELLS ME SO!
ALL THE TIME...
HE TELLS ME HE LOVES ME!
BUT DOESN'T IT SOUND PHONY?
HE'S NOT LYING!!
HE ALWAYS TREATS ME WELL!
AND TELLS ME I'M CUTE!
THAT'S ONLY BECAUSE ICHIJO WANTS TO LOOK GOOD IN YOUR EYES.
DOESN'T THAT SEEM HYPOCRITICAL TO YOU?
SLAP

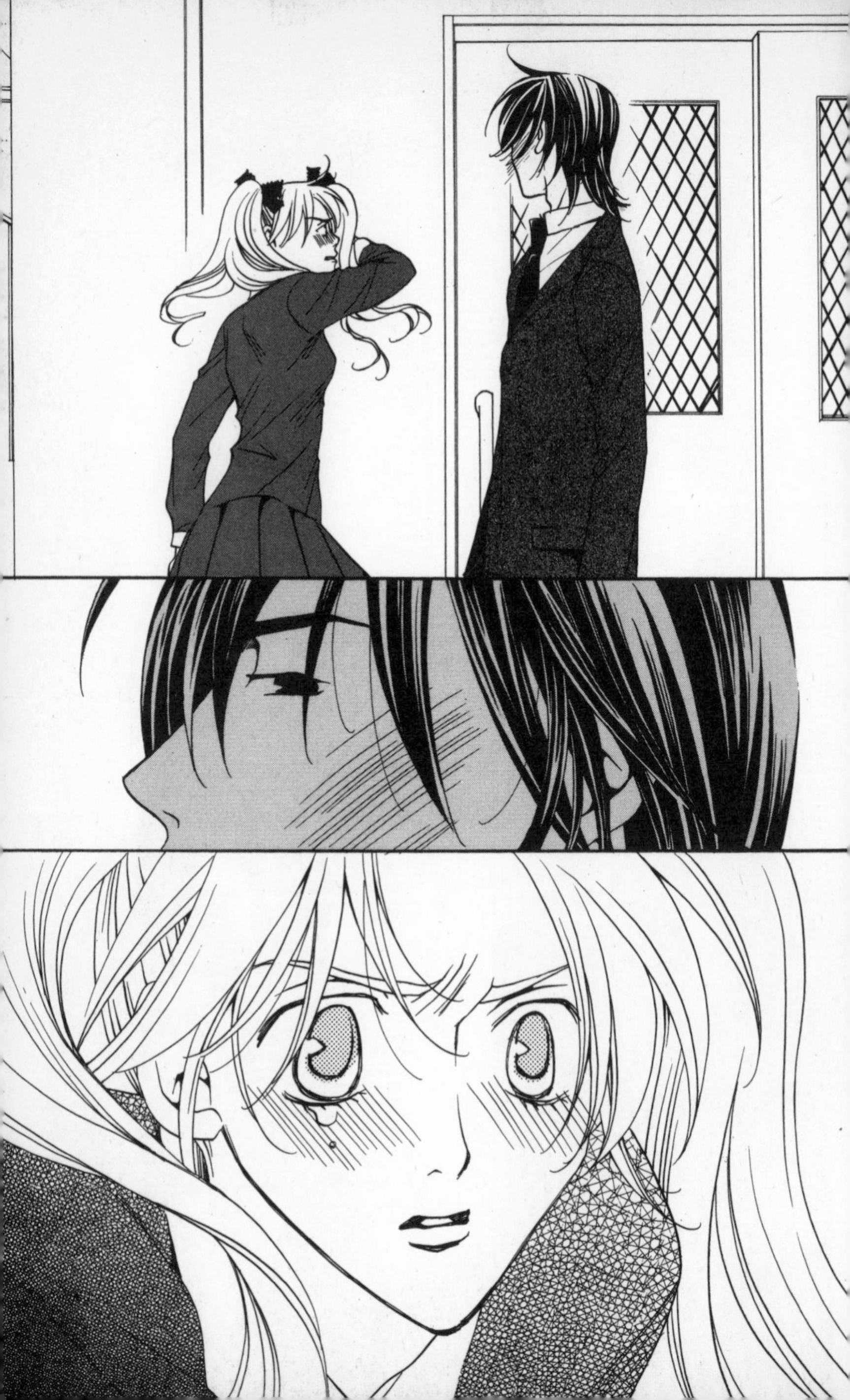

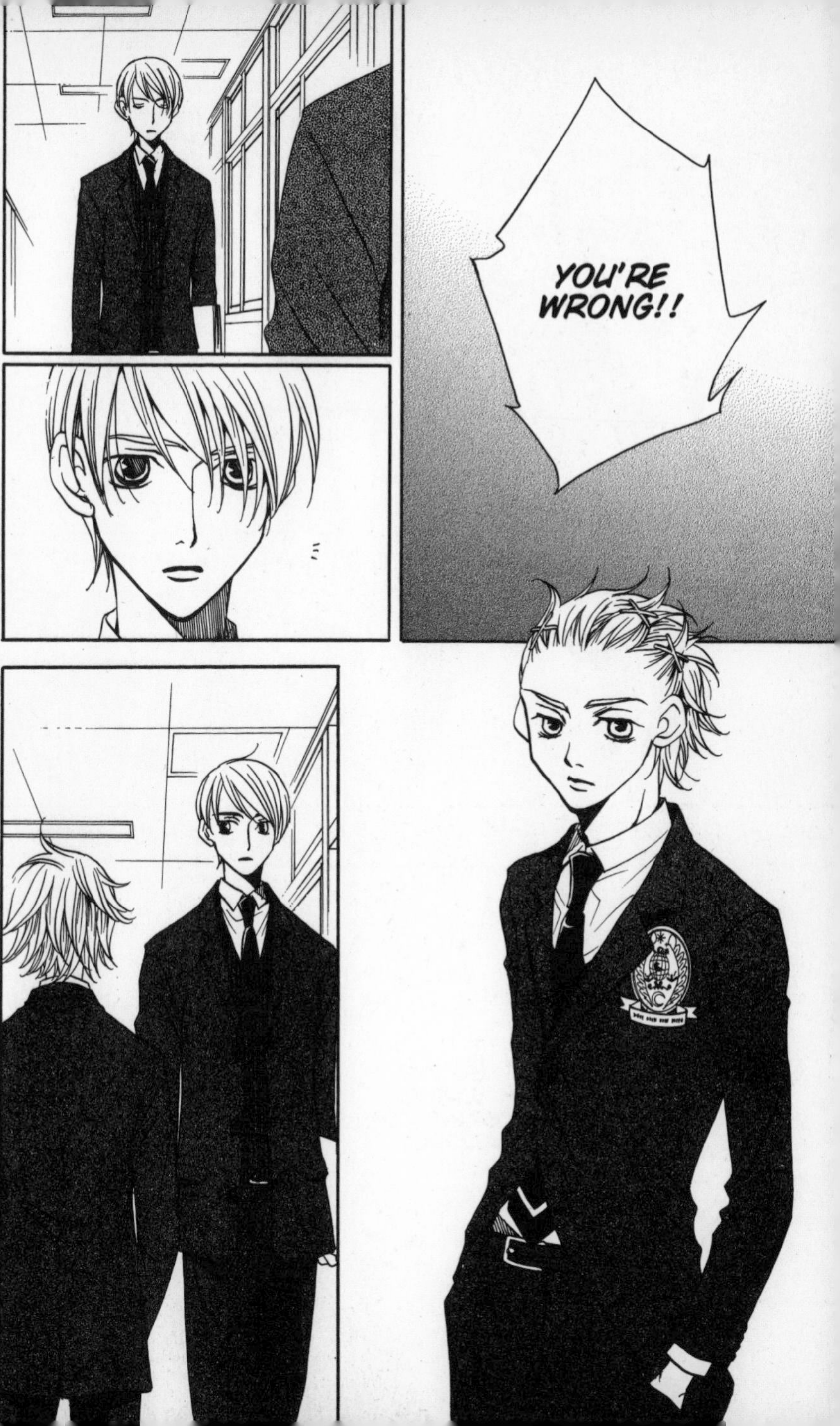
YOU'RE WRONG!!

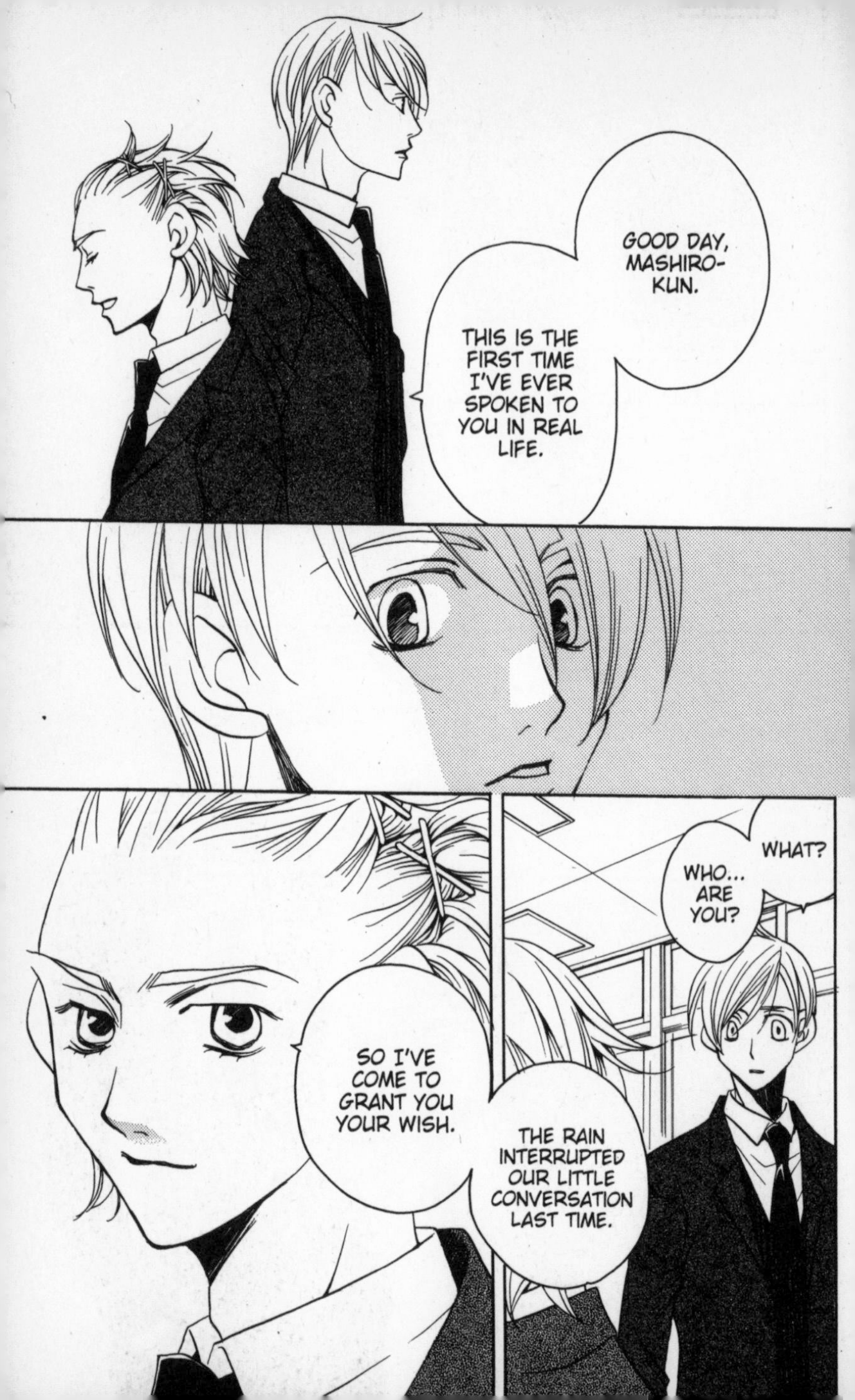
GOOD DAY, MASHIRO-KUN.
THIS IS THE FIRST TIME I'VE EVER SPOKEN TO YOU IN REAL LIFE.
WHAT?
WHO... ARE YOU?
THE RAIN INTERRUPTED OUR LITTLE CONVERSATION LAST TIME.
SO I'VE COME TO GRANT YOU YOUR WISH.

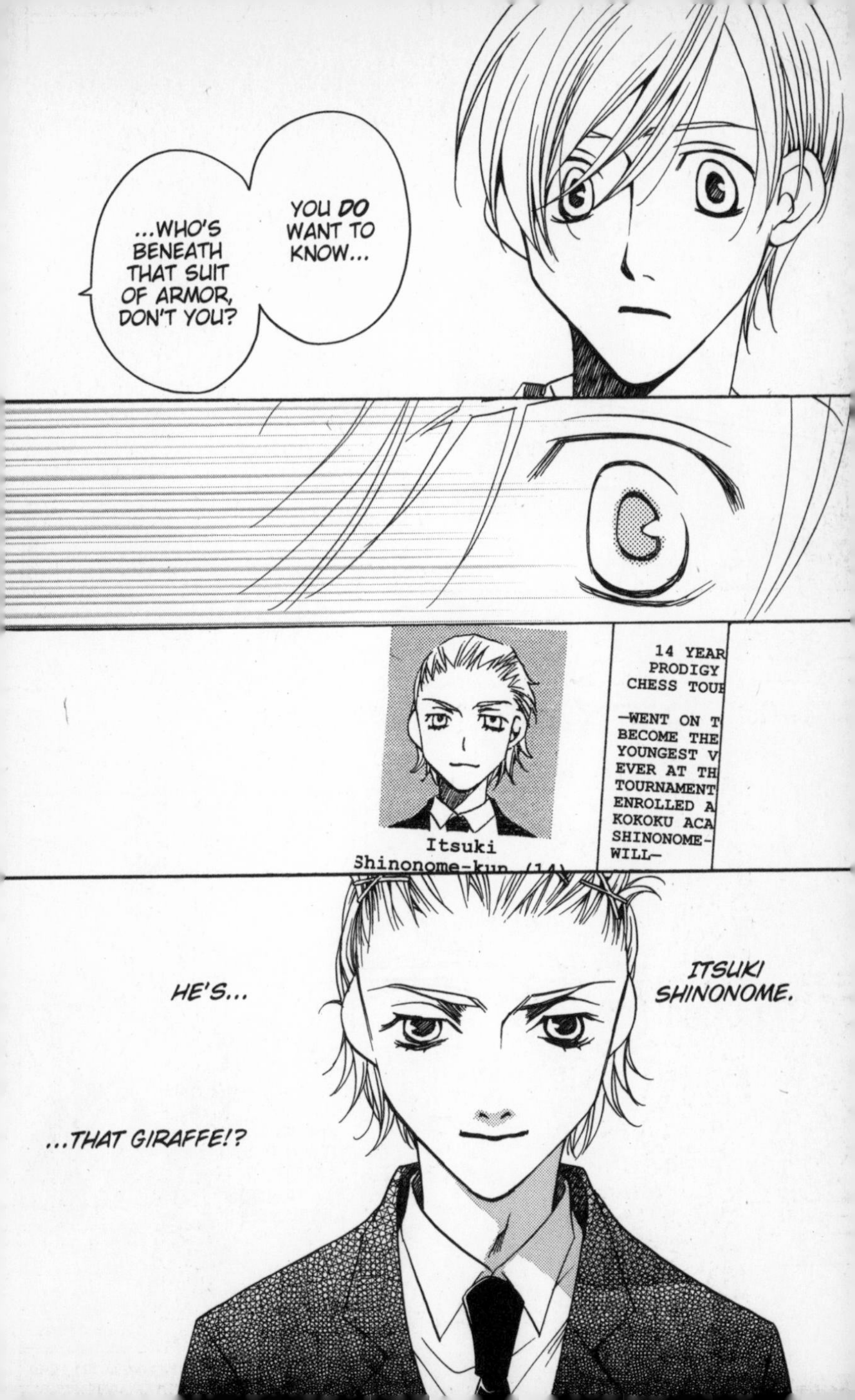
YOU DO WANT TO KNOW...
...WHO'S BENEATH THAT SUIT OF ARMOR, DON'T YOU?
14 YEAR
PRODIGY
CHESS TOU
—WENT ON T
BECOME THE
YOUNGEST V
EVER AT TH
TOURNAMENT
ENROLLED A
KOKOKU ACA
SHINONOME-
WILL—
Itsuki Shinonome-kun (14)
ITSUKI SHINONOME.
HE'S...
...THAT GIRAFFE!?

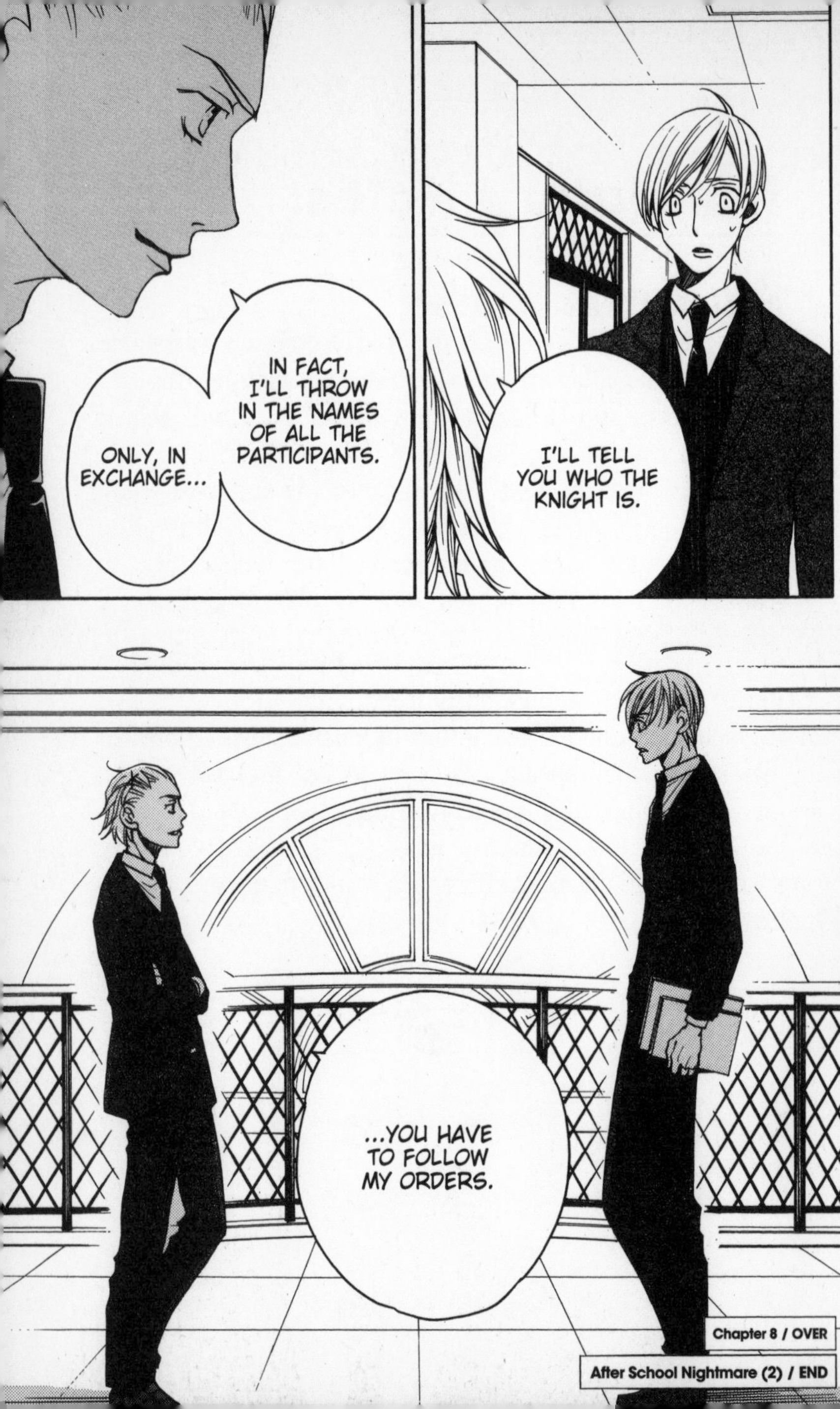
I'LL TELL YOU WHO THE KNIGHT IS.
IN FACT, I'LL THROW IN THE NAMES OF ALL THE PARTICIPANTS.
ONLY, IN EXCHANGE...
...YOU HAVE TO FOLLOW MY ORDERS.
Chapter 8 / OVER
After School Nightmare (2) / END

Translator's Notes:

Pg. 14 - Red Demon who Cried
A popular children's story about a Red Demon who wanted to befriend some villagers but was rejected because they thought he was scary and dangerous. His friend, the Blue Demon devises a plan to help him out by pretending to attack the villagers so that the Red Demon can come and save them, winning their trust and frienship. In the end, though the Red Demon gets the friends he had wanted, he cries because he realizes the Blue Demon will never be able to come back because of what he did.

Pg. 16 - Beautification Committee
In Japanese schools, the group of people responsible for maintaining the appearance of the school grounds can be made up of students as well. From picking up litter to tending the flowers, these students work on a purely voluntary agenda though the extra effort does win them points with the teachers.

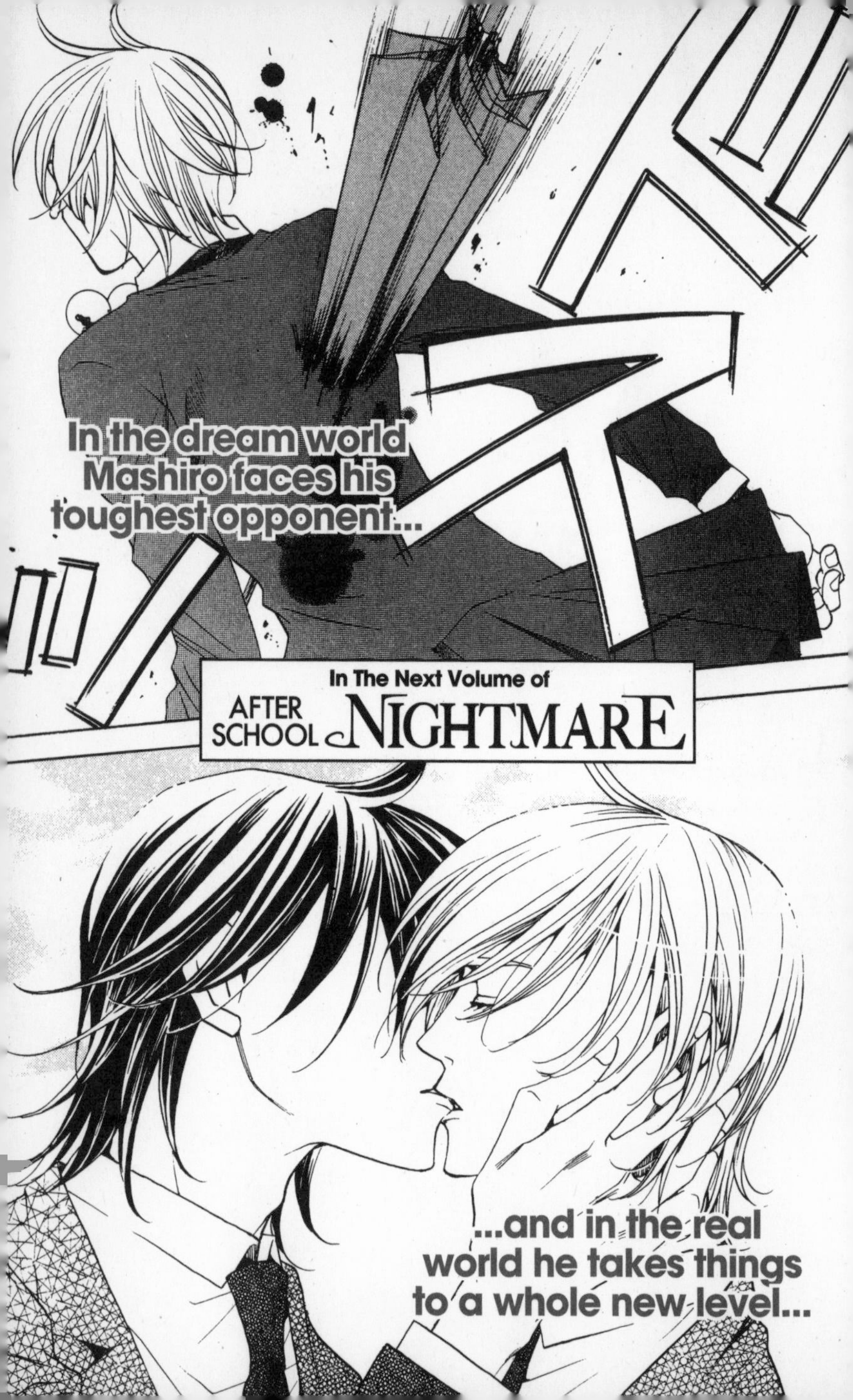
In the dream world Mashiro faces his toughest opponent...
In The Next Volume of
AFTER SCHOOL NIGHTMARE
...and in the real world he takes things to a whole new level...